TOM PAINTS THE FENCE

Tom Paints the Fence

Re-negotiating Urban Design

Bernd Kniess
Christopher Dell
Dominique Peck

SPECTOR BOOKS

Contents

There are people inside the house, outside on the lawn, in front of the house, on the scaffolding, inside the roof, on the street, in the trees. They are researching, building, living, practicing, drawing, talking, listening, dancing, discussing, tightening screws, provisionally arranging objects, cooperating, destroying. There is a program: maximum mixed-use development.

Julia Lerch Zajączkowska

Preface As if wanting to hide, the compact functional building crouches in the shade of tall trees. Its weather-worn puce paint allows the abandoned L-shaped building to inconspicuously sink into the environment's earthy and green color palette, a garden that has been left to itself. As the faded wooden fence and a little gate add to the enchanted impression of the ensemble, the house has a place that is no place: it is extraterritorial.

After years of vacancy, the property is to be revitalized and given its final use at the Internationale Bauausstellung (IBA, or International Building Exhibition) from 2008 to 2013. The revitalization was led by the Urban Design (UD) teaching and research program at the HafenCity University (HCU) in cooperation with a theater institution, the Kampnagel Internationale Kulturfabrik.[1] It is called the University of Neighborhoods (UoN).

This book, *Tom Paints the Fence*, seeks to portray the UoN's inception, development, and implementation, as well as the ongoing reverse construction processes leading to the final demolition in its various facets. The basis for this—along with prolific experiences and memories—is materializing the actions of those who participated in the project. The book aims to unlock these materializations, which were found in a relatively unorganized archive of various provenances, and make them accessible. The archive's material is very heterogeneous, almost unfathomable in its analog and electronic manifestations. It ranges from project folders, usually kept in chronological order for each actor, to architectural drawings, construction logs, project documentation, and student projects ordered

---

1   Theater and production venue for contemporary performance arts in Hamburg-Winterhude.

by semester, lecture, and article, right up to objects, mementos or furniture that had become part of the UD studio at its current location, the HCU.

The weakness of the UoN's archive is also its strength. Particularly the diverse nature of its legacy reflects the richness of the events that occurred on and around the property over the course of five years. Thus we considered it sensible to pursue the project's heterogeneity on our own, instead of viewing it in a subdividing and linear way. In doing so, we regarded the project as a series of cases in which heterogeneous episodes of topics, actors, actions, things, and discourses converge in certain locations. We used a method we call "project archaeology" to make these places accessible. It's based on heterogeneity, employing a research strategy that explores, examines, and unravels different cases for fundamental principles from various perspectives and using various methods of observation. To use the same analogy: this book provides elements for urban research by opening up excavation sites, territories, vector fields, and archive layers of a project in the city, while aiming to make the project's richness visible in terms of *city* as a produced totality. Unlocking as wide a field of experience as possible allows us to employ different interpretative approaches, and the readers to actively gain their own access to the material. Thus, the UoN's history can be updated and rendered fruitful for the present.

This book is therefore not an introduction nor aimed towards a certain scholastic canon, but a commitment to the ideal of methodic plurality. In this sense, all the following cases mentioned, interpreted, and dealt with in a specific way are always to be seen as examples of bigger clusters of themes. On their small scale, they can always be related to the scale of *city*. The cases are examples of a series of similar situations that readers are also experiencing, each in their own way, in their urban environment. The cases are also examples of an understanding and reflective way of dealing with *city*, which is supposed to offer keys to understanding related phenomena or questions. Cases or materials of various scales or representations appear more than once for a reason. Sometimes a map can therefore be a structure within a diagrammatic context, available information on a specific referent, and sometimes an indexical sign within a larger-scale overview.

If that brings visibility and its methods into the conversation, we must also mention the university regimen concerning visibility. Of course, it's inherent in university projects that they keep much of their operation from the public, especially when the projects' requirements well exceed the limits of the academic sphere. This is because it's the protected space of the university or lab that provides the foundation for facilitating research projects. Should we change the role of the university correspondents now, we will later have to make visible what we consider important in the light of public visibility.

It goes without saying that, because of the material's structure and abundance, there is not just one perspective that can create a narrative for the UoN. Instead, this book seeks to reorganize archived things in a way that they continue the *city's* narrative, which is embedded in the project itself. It remains fundamental that the book's authors constitute a "We," consisting not only of the named publishers but also, in accordance with the project's uniqueness, of a network of diverse and deeply connected collaborations, interactions, and exchange relationships between various actors. They can't all be named here, but they equally represent the "We" of a co-authorship that emerged in the diagram of UD as a form of reference. Whenever the text mentions a "We," this co-authorship is always included as a reference.

Without anticipating the book's content, you could say that the usual progress of planning disciplines in a linear order of steps won't work at the UoN—the interests of the participating actors are just too diverse. This served as the exceptional situation and challenge of the project. Without actively being able to even attempt to oversee the situation when we began, we nonetheless seized the chance of being in charge of the project. Why? Because we saw it as an opportunity to deal practically with the concept of *city* within the context of the newly established Urban Design master's program. Why, you may ask, should you grapple with *city* practically and in the course of your Urban Design studies? Is practicing in a studio not enough?

We realized that once a broad consensus exists among planning disciplines, that once city is no longer supposed to be understood as the object, we had to take a different route to understand *city* as a process. We wanted to get out into the city, into the field, to find out what else *city* can be. Referring to the dictum of French philosopher Henri Lefebvre, who argued that *city* is (socially) produced, we have reckoned with the fact that we with our actions are inevitably part of this never-ending process that (re)produces *city* on a daily basis. We are all constantly partaking in its creation. However, that's more involvement than architects or urbanists would care for when it comes to maintaining their believed superiority in terms of designing a *space* or *city*. The fact that you can't shape a city solely by arranging functions or correctly using certain techniques indicates that we have reached the limits of designability in terms of architecture and *city*.

If you can't rely on the conventional use of the planning disciplines' tried and tested methods, you end up facing fundamental questions again. Who affects the *city* process in what way, and what actions constitute this? How effective are spatial actions, and what kind of materializations result from them? Asking those kinds of questions means appreciating *city* as an assemblage of agency that's permanently being shaped and designed. This, however, shifts the concept of design itself: it's no longer the domain of experts, but is now something that emerges from actions of the *dispositif* [2] *city*. The question is: how does this *dispositif* come to have this function? Following that is the demand for new methods of reading and displaying *city*, which can raise awareness about urban situations and relations in regards to potentialities. And so it may seem like serendipity that the work of UD, from the moment it was

2   We understand *dispositif* (*apparatus*) as Foucault did, as a "thoroughly heterogeneous ensemble consisting of discourses, institutions, architectural forms, regulatory decisions, laws, administrative measures, scientific statements, philosophical, moral and philanthropic propositions–in short, the said as much as the unsaid. Such are the elements of the apparatus. The apparatus itself is the system of relations that can be established between these elements. Secondly, … the nature of the connection that can exist between these heterogeneous elements. … In short, between these elements, whether discursive or non-discursive, there is a sort of interplay of shifts of position and modifications of function which can also vary very widely. Thirdly … a sort of … formation which has as its major function at a given historical moment that of responding to an *urgent need*. The apparatus thus has a dominant strategic function." Michel Foucault, "The Confession of the Flesh," in Colin Gordon, *Power/Knowledge: Selected Interviews & Other Writings 1972–1977* (New York: Pantheon Books, 1980), 194–95.

created, was formed from the exceptional situation described above. It was the UoN project that allowed us to develop and test out methods and practices on a "real" project.

Tom paints the fence.
At first, the book's title, *Tom Paints the Fence*, thematizes only one certain action: the type of action performed by a protagonist on an object. The title interrelates the form of action between what is acting and what is being *treated,* to show that there is a need for purposeful change. The action—the act of painting—should be opposed to a certain material property of the object, namely the fact that paint ages. Everyone knows you paint your fence to protect it from the weather. Let's say the fence is made of wood. The slats are placed in horizontal, vertical, and diagonal structures. According to its purpose—encasing or excluding something—the fence on site is assembled into an overall shape that relates to something in its environment. Up to this point, the relationship between acting and what is being treated is completely clear. But the fence acts, too: it encloses and excludes, it ages, becomes brittle, becomes moldy, falls apart, obstructs, distracts, looks ugly or delicate. Plus, the state of the painted fence has an effect beyond that: it offers representative character. This brings a certain interest into play, not necessarily the same as the interest in performing an action.

"Tom" refers to the title character in Mark Twain's well-known novel, *The Adventures of Tom Sawyer*. The title hints at the episode in which Tom is bullied by the neighborhood kids because he has to paint the fence as punishment. Tom's smart negotiations and consistent painting give the act of painting an unforeseen appeal. Clearly affected, the neighborhood kids want to take up the brush themselves. The fact that the title also refers to this type of social interaction led us to use it for our book. We believe that the title announces a political understanding of *city*, which binds it to constant negotiations and a certain attitude. The project's problem is the project. "Projects viewed as singular ventures combine diverse knowledge effectively; apparently, however, they also tend to forget quick-ly."[3] Throughout the first exploration of the archive and the decision about the book title, we determined the formats of the project's archaeology.

Round Table Redesigns

In the Round Table Redesigns, we play with the "afterward-ness" of the UoN's final project report. The report was intended to clarify the rudimentary aspects of teaching, research, and practice that have been part of the UoN's experimental setup, as well as the relation between participating disciplines in their various constructions—multi-, inter-, trans- (i.e. pro-) and anti-disciplinary—and, finally, discuss the possibilities that these disciplines create.

The countless documentations of all imaginable projects that were worked on at the UoN are proof of how the title "University of Neighborhoods" has been operationalized. There is no denying the fact that, in spite of the given diversity of interests and competences among people in charge of the project—this includes everyone from the project board to people who man-aged operations only for a few hours—they always interacted with other actors according to the respective project content. The format of the Round Table Redesigns embodies an alternative within planning. By utilizing such "afterwardness," this method moves away from underlying consultations and thus removes the motive's obvious as well as implicit aspects from the situation. The documentation of the final session of *Potenzialitäten des Urbanen* (Potentialities of the Urban), a 2012/13 lecture series, became *Understanding UoN: Methods, Tools & Theory* (MTT). The discussion of the documentation of the tree house work-shop turned into *What Is Urban Design to Do in the Age of Uncer-tainty?* Excerpts from the edited documentations can be found in the respective parts in the book, where they were explained by the moderators and co-producers while respective printouts were stuck to the wall. The different scales of the images fits the already-described fact that placing it on the wall enables

---

3   Gernot Grabher, "Temporary Architectures of Learning: Knowledge Governance in Project Ecol-ogies," *Organization Studies* 25, no. 9 (2004), 1491–1514.

both an overview if you're looking at it from farther away and a richness of detail once you walk closer to the image.

Elements

Repeatedly dealing with architectural elements serves as the main focus of this book. In addition to the fence, we work with six other elements. These elements are divided into material elements such as bed, window, stove, and roof and meta-elements such as plan and game. Surely, such an examination of architectural elements is nothing new. In other words, the question of elements is always the focus when redefining the space of teaching, researching, and practical work in architecture, and relating them to sociopolitical issues. In ancient times, Vitruvius had not explicitly discussed those elements at first. In his treatise *Ten Books on Architecture,* he instead regarded those elements as part of a comprehensive order of architecture, the character of which he described in six basic categories: order (*ordination*), arrangement (*disposition*), eurythmy (*eurythmia*), symmetry (*symmetria*), propriety (*décor*), and economy (*distribution*).[4]

The Renaissance would discover Vitruvius again, albeit with a new reading. Leon Battista Alberti, for instance, wanted to precisely define the contextual architectural composition.[5] Because now, designing architects had—unlike in ancient times—abandoned carrying out mechanical and practical skills (*fabrica*) in favor of planning skills. Now, ideas and their justifications mattered. Thus, the six elements the neighborhood, the ground (the construction site), the layout (floor plan), the wall, the ceiling, and the opening served as an instruction manual for architectural design. As the neighborhood and ground elements were guided by the planned urban and spatial order and the derived layout design, they eventually gave an order to those elements that are explicitly about building—wall, ceiling, and the opening connecting the inside and the outside.

---

4   Vitruvius, *Ten Books on Architecture*, trans. Morris Hicky Morgan (Cambridge, MA: Harvard University Press, 1914), 13.

5   Leon Battista Alberti, *Zehn Bücher* über *die Baukunst*, vol. 1 and 2 (Darmstadt: Wissenschaft-liche Buchgesellschaft, 2005).

In the nineteenth century, Gottfried Semper transformed the elements' principles in terms of functional theory.[6] Following a central topos of architecture history—the primitive hut— Semper defined the stove as a synonym for the fireplace, as "the first and most important, the moral, element of architecture."[7] Semper carefully assigned the protective structural elements roof, enclosure, and earth fill to the stove. Whereas the focus here lay on the socializing effect of the central element that's protected by the others, Le Corbusier's five elements— pilotis, free plan of the floor, free plan of the façade, horizontal window, and roof garden—basically aimed for a fundamentally new aesthetic around the beginning of the twentieth century.[8]

In the 1960s, Robert Venturi was interested in "a more or less ambiguous combination [in the form of a moment in time] of old meaning, called up by associations, with a new meaning created by the modified or new function, structural or programmatic, and the new context." Venturi thus built the foundation on the level of elements, for an interest that had been lost during the modern era, in the existing city with its outmoded aspects and their possible transformation.[9] However, in the context of the recent *Venice Biennale 2014: Elements of Architecture* curated by Rem Koolhaas / OMA, we experience an arrangement of micro-narratives of fifteen elements that have been produced in unwavering pragmatism. The floor, the wall, the ceiling, the roof, the door, the window, the façade, the balcony, the corridor, the fireplace, the toilet, the stair, the escalator, the elevator, and the ramp help us to understand and surmise what it means to have elements of once primitive forms of the habitat recruited and reprogramed by the evolving needs of comfort and security in the Digital Age. Koolhaas reminds us that we have not even started dealing with the ever-growing vastness of this potential dark side.[10]

6   Gottfried Semper, *Die vier Elemente der Baukunst* (Braunschweig: Vieweg, 1851).
7   Semper, 55.
8   Le Corbusier, *Kommende Baukunst*, ed. Hans Hildebrandt (Stuttgart/Berlin/Leipzig: Deutsche Verlags-Anstalt, 1926).
9   Robert Venturi, *Complexity and Contradiction in Architecture* (New York: Museum of Modern Art, 1977), 38.
10   Rem Koolhaas, *Elements of Architecture: Central Pavilion* (2014), 193.

If we look at the elements in the book at hand again, we're doing so in the light of a specific empirical circumstance whose range of experience stems from our own practice. We refer to the fact that working on the UoN project is shaped by an exceptional situation on various levels: on the one hand, there is the IBA held on the Elbe islands in Hamburg from 2007 to 2013. On the other hand, there is a newly founded university for Built Environment and Metropolitan Development, whose various academic departments are still scattered among several locations in Hamburg. Then there is the cooperation of these two institutional actors on the UoN project, which activates a further location. And lastly, the protagonists of a newly founded master's program in urban design appear, who challenge disciplinary limits in view of their subject. The situation itself is thus supported by extraordinarily effective historical and political categories (urban development, architecture, housing, etc.) which, once they are detached from their underlying argumentations, often lead (or led) a separate life of their own; this aspect alone allowed for a reinterpretation of elements in the sense of the motive in *Tom Paints the Fence.*

The list of seven elements not only points to the fact that it's about elements in a structural-constructive sense. Instead, the list is about relevant elements of project work at the UoN. There is the stove, which is also central to our observation of its socializing effect. The structural elements window and roof have had a lasting influence on the project's relational structure due to their handling alone. The same goes for the fence, which metaphorically illustrates the drawing and exceeding of boundaries, as well as the organization of the organization. Finally, the bed represents the missing antithesis to the community-gathering stove, and is considered to be a metaphor for the individual's area of retreat within the community. While looking at the concept of living, it became the key element of theoretical examination and experimental practice to us. The plan as the product of urbanists and architects is the representation of their practice and ideology, which is being questioned again in regards to its meaning and agency. The notion of play, in which all aspects of our work converge, might hint at the methods with their different modes of coming into play, of how rules are applied during play (including the breaking of and perhaps the resulting need to re-establish rules), and of how individual steps are documented, in order to track and understand the course of play.

All papers gather evidential and also contemplative aspects in regards to the element as a starting point for an abstract practice that attends to alternating implications of concept and matter. They should be seen as an attempt to get the UoN project's final report (which inevitably reduced the project's initial contingency) to deal with both levels of this "matter vs. concept" issue as well as its interrelation in projects that are not yet realized. The style of the evidentiary aspects thus varies, as these contemplations can be traced to the facts stated here, while it also represents the many languages in the project's archive. The problematization of future potentialities has always implied the problematization of their present experience. For us, the practice of problematization cannot function solely on the basis of texts. In addition, a series of visual materials should enable the reader to form his or her understanding of the project.

Outlook: A metaphor for the *city's* history

Within its five years of existence, the UoN project served as the basis for the concurrently founded UD interdisciplinary study program, in the form of an experimental lab for researching the reciprocal influences of teaching, research, and practice. The experimental lab does not imply that the UoN, as part of the IBA Hamburg, was subject to any rules of conventional planning. Quite the contrary: its construction was shaped by negotiating, merging various actors, and connecting diverse control mechanisms, many of which were hard to decipher. In view of this conflict situation, we took a process-oriented approach of, as we called it, enabling architecture. This certainly refers to Cedric Price's *Fun Palace* and its philosophy of enabling.[11] To this end, we understand the UoN as an enduring experimental setup for enabling temporary uses, whose compacting and overlapping processes were challenged by us

---

11   Royston Landau, "A Philosophy of Enabling: The Work of Cedric Price," *AA Files* 8 (January 1985): 3–7, www.jstor.org/stable/29543432 (last accessed October 31, 2019).

as well and were explored up to the point of self-induced states of shock.[12] Participating actors had to take a position on the situations they had created and practiced an appreciative and constructive approach to contingency.

Therefore, *Tom Paints the Fence* stands as a metaphor for the history of *city*, which we re-assemble here using the example of the University of Neighborhoods and its various facets. The book's focus was on handling the existing, both materially and situationally, in its ongoing analysis, negotiations as part of appropriation processes, practical transformation, and the permanent exploration of the resulting potentialities. We consider this to be work on processes in (urban) research, planning, and design which aims to shape the course of action so openly that new influences, realizations, possibilities, and errors will always be considered. The operational framework is no longer drafted in order to reach a set target and necessary planning steps. Instead, it now deliberately exposes itself to the uncertainty of continuous development and the use of countless participating actors. We have to negotiate how to transfer these uses into open structures and how we can derive forms from this, regardless of their duration. Finally, everything amounts to a form of organization that didn't attempt to eliminate the operational framework of indeterminacy, insecurities, and disarray, but rather created *dispositifs* that made it possible to work constructively and inter-subjectively with contingency.

Bernd Kniess, Christopher Dell, and Dominque Peck

12   Gernot Grabher and Joachim Thiel, *Self-Induced Shocks: Mega-Projects and Urban Development* (Berlin: Jovis Verlag, 2015).

INTRODUCTION

**Bernd Kniess
Christopher Dell**

What *city*?

We speak of the urban as having a political quality.[1] In doing so, while taking our point of departure from the theories of French philosopher Claude Lefort,[2] we differentiate between the political and politics. Whereas politics represent the institutional distribution and execution of power and respective forms, the concept of "the political" means giving instructions, i.e. a *mise-en-forme*. Discussing the political thus addresses and highlights the form-making of human coexistence and the produced nature of political form. Lefort's axiology lies the foundation for our conceptualizing of *city*. Instead of reducing *city* to a given social form, we instead investigate the conditions and ways of its making. In other words: what our research emphasizes is the derivation of the generative and contingent principles that support an urban form's existence or coming into existence and that co-determine socio-spatial configurations.

It is precisely these principles that make up the political. Along these lines, *city* is defined both as a sufficient and necessary requirement of the political. Sufficient, because it is the place where conflicts have found their expression, as we know from Henri Lefebvre.[3] And necessary—in Hannah Arendt's opinion—as it only takes shape as a condition of the political. According to Arendt, public space only becomes political once it is secured in a city, which is bound to a tangible place.[4] However, these arguments presume that—apart from the political, which cannot be the subject of this essay—one examines what *city* is and what the concept should mean.

It comes easy to us in our everyday lives to talk about city or town ("I'm going downtown," "I come from ...," "City should ...," "Forms of urban living," etc.). However, in recent disciplinary discourse, it has become obvious that this speaking of and about city is increasingly revealing a crisis. This crisis is tied to the blurred lines between city as an object and *city* as a concept. There is a lack of conceptual clarity that will not only follow us throughout this book, but that is also an inevitable characteristic of the urban. Here, everyday experiences of the city obscure the city as a *city*. For a while, this didn't bother us. However, in recent years, we have started to suspect, in view of rather important demographic, economic, and migratory processes, that we know little about what we produce every day: the *city*. Talking and thinking about it comes to a halt once it collides with the concrete urban experience. Plus, in order for that to even happen (city as *city* becoming the topic), at least one disruption of familiar procedures is necessary.

1   City/Urban—you could speak of a parallel to the discourse on the difference between politics and the political. (Cf. Thomas Bedorf and Kurt Röttgers, ed., *Das Politische und die Politik* (Frankfurt am Main: Suhrkamp, 2010). However, we don't remain dogmatic in differentiating in terms of *city*: we continue to use the word "city," and by that we mean its urban aspect.

2   Cf. Claude Lefort, "Permanence du théologico-politique?," in idem, *Essais sur le politique* (Paris: Seuil, 1986), 281.

3   Henri Lefebvre, *Metaphilosophie* (Frankfurt am Main: Suhrkamp, 1975 (1965)), 186.

4   Hannah Arendt, *Was ist Politik?* (Munich: Piper Taschenbuch, 2005), 46.

Debating *city* and its knowledge

It is clear by now that it is no longer only specialist planners and actors in political administrations who manage urban development. Foremost instead are people who are affected, knowing that there are others who articulate their issues and their notion of *city*, who organize themselves and actually play a decisive role in designing urban politics. Projects that are conducted among segments of the public mobilize in a different way than, for instance, groups based on socio-demographic characteristics or class relationships, in terms of judging the way the(ir) "good city" is conveyed. In doing so, they take the daily press, planning committees, referenda, and many other forms of allegedly "democratic opinion-forming" and turn them into spaces for representing their wishes. This relates to the belief that by talking, one can find out what is given as a city, and what can be done to develop a good city (or to inhibit a bad one), in order to finally implement what has jointly been learned (more or less with compromises and concessions in terms of circumstances) in the form of (urban) planning.

Undoubtedly, these spaces of representation and the ways in which the word "city" is used have the potential to ignite debates. However, what a debate cannot achieve is to exist on its own—if anything, what we observe today is that debates on the city rather tend to lack public attention or fade into obscurity. Therefore, it does not seem easy to keep up controversial discussions about *city*.

This is not only due to the fact that interest is disappearing, that the space of public debate isn't offering much, that it is too abstract, or the like. Rather, something else comes to the fore, something that is apparent throughout so-called participation processes again and again: even before negotiating the question "What do we want to do in order to find a good project for a good city?" individual sectors of society seem to have determined for themselves what a good project and a good city are. It isn't automatically made clear whether the "we" asking the question is the same as the "we" that has to take action.

The negotiation itself appears exclusive, because each opinion is put on display via public media platforms and advertised more or less professionally using appropriate marketing strategies. Terms such as "best practice" or presuppositions that aim for an "image" or the "code" of a district or of the whole city quickly take up space. The social movements that have recently become increasingly powerful and professionalized may serve as an example of this development; they represent the entire political spectrum with slogans such as "Right to the city" and "Hamburg for good integration," which they use to demonstrate their claim to power and authority. The scale of the project ignites their political demands, which are subsequently manifested not on the scale of the nation-state, but on the scale of the neighborhood, of the district, and the city.

Certainly, whenever an urban structure as a material function is placed in relation to its agency, it sets off the political agency of subjects in order to generate new political forms. The negotiations, however, about what a city should be about die down rather quickly or do not get started at all. Why is this? They are conducted according to the form of the respective example. What remain, once the discussion is over, are more or less bad options for action in a particular community or the option of continuing in the direction that has already been followed, in order for this to be realized by the institutions of urban politics. The question of what to do in order to achieve a good city is replaced by the question of what remains to be done. The act of approving or criticizing how one shapes the changing way of dealing with *city*—as it is found—is only replaced with the attitude of *laissez faire* or even *laissez passer*.

Between the time when excitement is generated by "new ideas for the city" and the time when this excitement subsides, there is a post-political state of lacking alternatives,[5] where talking and thinking about *city* even seems to impede these negotiations. Even if the given situation when using the word "city" obstructs the way to understanding *city* rather than paving it, this may nonetheless have a positive quality: because when all this talking seems pointless, the thinking process begins and we are able to realize that it is also the way we negotiate *city* that prevents us from bringing about good change.

Agency of the political
As is becoming more and more apparent, an important part of *how* we deal with the negotiations on the urban is not just talking about them, but also the planning disciplines' spaces of representation and the way in which those representations are interpreted and opera-tionalized, which then contribute to the above-diagnosed impasse or crisis. It all boils down to us having to look not only through but also at the lens through which we see *city*—even more: perhaps the lens is opaque and we need a new and different one in order to be able to see the *city's* truth.

It is all too easy to forget that a city is not an area that makes itself spontaneously and passively available to our curiosity. Thus, we're not claiming to get rid of an inattention in regard to the city (as we have seen, this does not exist, but is rather the opposite), but to create new perspectives that define the parameters for making it possible to understand *city*. It's about tapping into a field of knowl-edge that adds theoretical energies to the way we look at the city's everyday life, where one can talk about the representation of *city* as well as its actors and the things it assembles, and how this representation becomes negotiable.

The perspective mentioned above touches on issues of the political in a way that changes our view of our own agency as a form of existence, what it is capable of, and how the political agency is related to questions of scale of dispositions. The fact that we ask ourselves these questions regarding our own performative potential

5   Colin Crouch, *Postdemokratie* (Frankfurt am Main: Suhrkamp, 2008).

enters other basic levels in regard to the state of our world, similar to that of *city*. After all, as Hartmut Böhme observed, things cannot occur other than "as relations of our activities of a cognitive or practical form."[6]

The image of the city

Let us return to the aspect of how the difference between city, the thing, and *city*, the concept, is becoming blurred: the fact that our concept of *city* seems weak isn't only due to us talking about it, but also to the relationship that this talking maintains to the concrete experience that we have with *city*. Recognizing that our specific experience with *city* no longer corresponds to the notion that we have of it can be the first step toward starting to break up the fixated network of associations and connections into which the use of the word city has long been embedded. For our work, this means that negotiating *city* is by no means idle talk; it is part of the political transformation of what we understand of it. Nevertheless, we are convinced that the change depends on our attempts to combine explicit *city* experiences with a new conception of the *city*, without finishing the latter by doing so, but rather opening it up. *Tom Paints the Fence* deals with such an attempt.

Spatial triad: Why spatial practice is essential

An essential aspect for experiencing *city* is the question of perception, to be seen as something consisting of different levels. Their types can be conceptualized in reference to the triad that Henri Lefebvre brought into the discourse on the urban: spatial practice, representational space, and representations of space. The fact that Lefebvre's triadic categories—intended analytically, but not ontologically—are today mostly reduced to dichotomies such as spatial representation vs. representational spaces, planner vs. occupier, design vs. use, and so on, is a characteristic of the contemporary spatial discourse.

The model of action, however, that is the motor for building these categories is simply assumed, not examined in its structure. This outmaneuvers the question of the third category, namely that of spatial practice. As a result, it is essential for our work to consider representational spaces, design, and use, as conveyed by spatial practice. This includes investigating representational spaces in terms of their mediality and materiality. The partial observations at hand focus at the same time on built structure, architectural analysis and behavior, usage, history, and context. They attempt to comprehend how practices and objects are related to discourses, to understand how materiality ultimately takes place,[7] and to find extended options in the constant process of reassembling.

---

6   Hartmut Böhme, *Fetischismus und Kultur* (Hamburg: Rowohlt Taschenbuch, 2007), 14.
7   Cf. Alexa Färber, "Greifbarkeit der Stadt. Überlegungen zu einer stadt- und wissens-anthropologischen Erforschung stadträumlicher Aneignungspraktiken," *dérive. Zeitschrift für Stadtforschung* 40 (2010): 102.

Introduction

Far from being grounded in arbitrariness, our project points to the political dimension that we associate with Deleuze's understanding of diagrammatic reasoning, a process that does not attempt to represent an objective world but to create prototypes of a new reality.[8] In sum, urban research as it is presented here attempts to enter spatial production itself, right at the interface between the translation of social practices into spatial structures and the regulation of the social. What this book aims for is to get involved in order to show, and to show in order to get involved.

Basic indicators for defining space

At this point, we'll take another, closer look at two relevant concepts of space that can be associated with Lefebvre's approach. Let's start with the concept of relative space. Where it stems from a Euclidean notion of space, the concept adds a timeline to absolute space. The term "relative space" here refers to the changeability of spatial perception; space is considered relative to the person experiencing the space subjectively. In contrast to *relative* space, which is based on the physical hypothesis of a motion from point A to point B, the conception of *relational* space focuses on a positional time-space relationship; objects exist only insofar as they exist in relation to other objects.

Both concepts are used in this book: on the one hand, we focus on the logic of observation, of subjective perception of space, while on the other hand, this subjectivity is valorized by contrasting it with its relationality. This is the foundation of our work. From this is derived the advocacy of the analytical deconstruction of urban situations. This method is the only valid way for us to understand parts and arrangements of elements, categories, principles, and the resulting impact that constitute such situations.

What relates this conception to Lefebvre's triadic scheme is to understand and display urban situations in an entity as performatively produced—in all their diversity, variety, heterogeneity, and complexity—to record and represent the way they are organized. That is the requirement for applying the analysis to any possible transformation, namely a conceptual reorganizing or a (re)design of a built situation. We are interested in designing structures of enabling instead of the original and teleological closed form. By this, we mean engaging in a diagrammatic endeavor that provides a whole catalogue of possible forms.

In organizational studies, such a procedure would be called improvisational organization. Why improvisational? It is because the understanding of space proposed above operates not against, but

8   Gilles Deleuze, "Écrivain non: un nouveau cartographe," *Critique* 343 (1975): 1223: "… un diagramme ne fonctionne jamais pour représenter un monde objective; au contraire il organise un nouveau type de réalité. Le diagramme n'est pas une science, il est toujours affaire politique. Il n'est pas un sujet d'histoire, ni surplombe l'histoire. Il fait de l'histoire en défaisant les réalités et les significations précédentes, constituant autant de points d'émergence ou de créationnisme, de conjoncts inattendues, de continuums improbables. On ne renonce à rien quand on abandonne les raisons. Une nouvelle pensée, positive et positiviste, le diagrammatisme, la cartographie."

with contingency. Accepting contingency as the urban form's onto-logical constituent, our method negates any deterministic or closed form. In regard to our research, that means: the conception of spatial improvisation helps to reveal space as whatever we do with and to it, while we initiate and maintain practical research and design. The question of "What is space?" is modulated into "How is space being produced?," provoking the next questions: "What accounts for its produced state?" "What actions taken by human and nonhuman actors play into it?" "What socio-material structures necessitate it or develop with it?" "What practices produce and utilize which presuppositions about space?"

The proposition that space should be seen as being co-produced in contingency every day is not only the source of new urban political questions such as, "How can we move from reaction to interaction in view of how unplannable the urban is? How can we grasp urban areas of life not deformatively, but instead performatively?" The understanding of action itself changes as well. As Bruno Latour notes, "If action is limited *a priori* to what 'intentional,' 'meaningful' humans do, it is hard to see how a hammer, a basket, a door closer, a cat, a rug, a mug, a list, or a tag could act. They might exist in the domain of 'material,' 'causal' relations, but not in the 'reflexive,' 'symbolic' domain of social relations."[9] When space is being consti-tuted in terms of practices, the focus of attention shifts to the kind of action that includes indeterminacy: improvisation. Far from being a makeshift solution of any kind, improvisation appears as a principle of spatial potential, of creating and orienting oneself within the ever-changing forms of urban existence.

Drawing on indeterminacy

Let's recapitulate: In the course of describing spatial and urban production, not only the impact of social action emerges, but also its complexity in a barely limitable heterogeneity. Thus, one funda-mental characteristic of the produced *city* comes to light that we will deal with from now on: a high level of contingency and indeter-minacy. Urban situations could have come about differently, and their constitutive as well as constituted character is far from being reducible to objective monocausality.

But what does this mean for design? Again, we intend neither to dispel indeterminacy as an urban feature and transform it into habitual certainty, nor to quickly eliminate it or accept it as an unfor-tunate condition. Rather, design work to us means processing inde-terminacy constructively with the goal of understanding resources embedded in indeterminacy and making them available for a design process. But what does that mean?

If we use the title Urban Design in the German-speaking world, we virtually use a trick to exploit the vague translation that is created through its use. After all, we are not only referring to the German meaning of *Städtebau* that limits its focus to the design aspects of

9   Bruno Latour, *Reassembling the Social: An Introduction to Actor-Network-Theory* (Oxford: Oxford University Press, 2005), 71.

Introduction

urban planning with urban morphological analysis and urban design. Rather, the aim is to understand the diversity of disciplinary knowledge as well as the methods for producing knowledge, in order to relate them differently to the design process—a relation that seeks to illuminate the potentialities of both. Examining a *city* under these premises cannot be separated from a certain circuity and tardiness, which goes without saying: playing extensively with single components is part of the interdisciplinary practice, in the same way that it serves the shared conceptual practice.

A method that approaches *city* in this way can no longer be linear, but circular. The classic Task that purposefully searched for its answers and solutions, turned into the Take,[10] which now iteratively circles the problem until it reveals its origin, while constantly producing new findings, questions and possible solutions. Everything remains a question of form, but that of open form.

If we understand urban space as something performatively produced, we do not consider it to be something passive and informal in its socio-material state formed or defined by acting subjects, but instead to be structural form, which also defines the actors in their agency and thus participates in the (trans)formation of use as well. And that is exactly why architects or planners are not obsolete. Surely, they are finally released from their self-declared demiurgic role as diagnosticians and healers of society, which they have never been able to fulfill anyway.

What is more important, however, is realizing that the design of things cannot be separated from the social production of space. The result is an understanding of design that makes it possible to structure a henceforth open form in a certain way; to create as many new interfaces and support structures as possible, whose continuous use we cannot yet even envision, but whose creation, however, we can certainly initiate. The design of a possible future as an artistic or technical solution and form is replaced by a complex, iterative process of examining and interrelating actors, circumstances, practices, motives, and discourses; in the form of diagrammatically "*re*-presenting things" (Latour) and the never-ending process of uncovering possibilities for re-, dis- and/or general associating within a collective.

This also includes a didactic challenge for the approach in an interdisciplinary study program of Urban Design (UD). Here, students are trained to be aware of and practice processing the materially and socially heterogenous practices from which *city* emerges. In this context, political and aesthetic questions are confronted by the epistemological. When talking about the logic of space-producing action, we not only assume that practices—like dwelling—are productive, but also that these practices have epistemological value. This idea is paramount in analyzing and producing connections and new

10   The Take is a structuring form of circling the research object in its sub-areas and approaching it with the knowledge of various disciplines and methods. It allows for a varied approach as an iteration of and experimental setup for preliminary research questions, which can be developed continually by regulating the different parameters Tools, Methods, and Circumstances.

interfaces. It is precisely with this perspective that the focus of the epistemological interest expands from the ontological *what* (knowing that) around the performative *how* (knowing how); it is no longer simply a matter of "what is being mapped," but instead of "how it is possible to map anything from such a territory."[11]

Researching and dealing with *city* as the subject therefore does not mean relying solely on numbers and texts, but also getting involved with the productivity of trained practices in the range of various manifestations in order to increase one's knowledge. This raises the question of how to arrange and organize these practices in a respectful manner and in such a way that they become accessible to the collective knowledge.

City as a studio

According to the common stereotype, architects and planners are always locked inside their offices, bent over drawings, pondering drafts and models or explaining and presenting them. Another reality shows them in dense rows, sitting in front of their computers. Another shows them in the role of construction planners. More recent images are commissioned by real estate developers and are professionally and elaborately produced. Architects stereotypically assume the role of creative artists who explain the world or reinvent it, to instantly stack virtual cubes on top of each other within the real urban space. Brave new urban world. UD has little to do with this image. Students and teachers take their content from a situational analysis and the participatory examination of constellations of people, things, and discourses that produce *city*. Having advanced to a living model, the urban situations consisting of the built environment, urban practices, and discourses provide the cityscape to be analyzed, of which the researcher is a part. In accordance with Ian Hacking's motto "We represent in order to intervene, and we intervene in the light of representations,"[12] the *city* itself serves as a studio.

The lens through which we look at *city* in its state of having been produced is shaped by examining and designing new notations and divisions. What we intend is to make readable the scripts that have been manifested into the built environment by the activities of the users. In this way, we aim to find new interfaces for possible modes of design and make them available. Certainly, we draw upon historical references in this work. On the one hand, we found relevant links within the broad range of empirical urbanism, the ethnographic city description, the morphological and situational analysis, and its visual presentation methods. We identified references in the spectrum of educational models for interdisciplinary work, study, and research on the other. Rereading *city* turns these references into a mostly untapped resource; in the same way, our approach relies on the *dérive* and *détournement* of the Situationists.

11   Bruno Latour, *Reassembling the Social: An Introduction to Actor-Network-Theory* (Oxford: Oxford University Press, 2005), 174.
12   Ian Hacking, *Representing and Intervening* (Cambridge: Cambridge University Press, 1983), 31.

Introduction

Dérive stands for an unprejudiced devotion to the *city*, and *détournement* for the shifting, distorting, re- and misinterpreting of the ordinary. The serial, catalog-like structure and the exposing of urban moments that we undertake might be seen as reminiscent of the cut-up techniques of situationist city cartographies, particularly of Debord, Jorn, or Constant. The question of perceiving *city*, developing and revealing inner connections and the techniques of mental or cognitive mapping, trace back to Kevin Lynch. The Chicago School represents the still unmet requirement to finally merge both its perspectives on *city*: the description of socio-spatial structures and processes by Ernest Burgess, who wanted to deduce generalizable regularities from them, and Robert Ezra Park's fascination with the diversity of urban lifestyles and respective locations, which he translated into his ethnographic studies. Black Mountain College represents John Dewey's educational concept and the interdisciplinary methods that were practiced at the UoN.

Further, our lens on the urban is based upon and in contrast to the study *Learning from Las Vegas*. Based on, because UD tries to develop new forms of expression in the same way it understands *city* as an ensemble of activities. The contrast, however, stems from a particular position: whereas Venturi et al. address the "ugly and ordinary"[13] not entirely without irony, the catalog-like archaeology of UD points at the attempt to maintain an evaluation. In order to make them readable, UD's position is to accept urban situations in their conditions and having-become. Codes, categories, and typologies serve analytical purposes and theoretical conceptualization, while a superficial language of conventional architectural style is omitted. It is not far-fetched to allude this concept to Edmund Husserl's *epoche*:[14] We think of a specific form of mediation of observational action. This form aims at suspending judgment in a way (even if it's never fully possible) that one can switch from claiming to displaying, and from problem-solving to problematizing.

Replacing Claiming with Displaying

Whether what is is showing itself or something else, depends on the way we position ourselves to and process what is.[15] *Tom Paints the Fence* is not intended to be a finished documentation of a project; it doesn't represent in that sense. Nevertheless, we do work with representations. The key is to switch from the mode of illustration to that of organization: a scenography is enacted, a process in the past is taken up in its elements, structures and movements, reorganized from a present-day perspective and thus opened toward the reflection of what is in the past. (Reflecting on what happened is not the narration of something that is believed to have happened).

---

13   Robert Venturi, Denise Scott Brown, and Steven Izenour, *Learning from Las Vegas, Revised Edition: The Forgotten Symbolism of Architectural Form* (Cambridge, MA: MIT Press, 1977).

14   Edmund Husserl, *Ideen zu einer reinen Phänomenologie und phänomenologischen Philosophie* (Den Haag: Martinus Nijhoff, 1950), §30–31, pp. 62–69.

15   Lambert Wiesing, *Sehen lassen. Die Praxis des Zeigens* (Frankfurt am Main: Suhrkamp Taschenbuch Wissenschaft, 2013), 14.

The same applies to the way this book was made: instead of being the product of one author, we've dealt with the collective interplay of various actors and a series of compartmentalized improvisations, with the co-production at the heart of it. This all implies that, should we want to open up the form, we must abstract from the narrowing of such aesthetics in architectural composition that forces the pre-made and always the same programs and sets of fixed forms as design parameters. This has nothing to do with negation, nor is there a need for arguing something that is always new. Instead, the aim is to expand the options of agency by the specific conception of space as being genuinely improvised.

Freed from the conventional design strategy, there is a clear view of what architecture does, of how *city* is made performatively and how space is produced—everything that is generally overlooked in design processes that always desire something new. Wherever parking lots, kiosks, ground floors, intersections, bus stops, or quarters are focused on as hubs of activity, architecture interlocks with social, cultural, economic, and ecological engineering, and turns a kitchen into a hotel, a park bench into a venue for negotiations, and a single-family home into a genealogy of home repairs.

Displaying revisited

One might claim that this book does not represent, but present. Let us mention three aspects here in more detail to elaborate upon what is meant by this claim.

The first essential aspect of the work of visualization consists of a transposition process that is already used by a new generation of researching architects for their work, such as Atelier Bow-Wow, Eyal Weizman with Forensic Architecture, OMA/AMO, and others. Tools for visualization that were traditionally reserved for architectural and urban design, the planning and ultimately the production of the prospective architectural object, are now retrospectively transferred to the analysis of existing buildings and urban situations. This way, information is made accessible by processing it—a method that was previously reserved for archaeology and which is aimed at making transformation visible. For example, the procedure of drawing on photographs allows significant things to be rendered visible that would otherwise remain hidden in the totality of the photographic image. Using isometric drawings allows for intuitively understanding spatial structures and respective formal and compositional characteristics in their specific relational context quickly and without complication. Three-dimensional CAD planning tools and rendering software help to spatially reconstruct occurrences that were only recorded on film.

A second aspect regarding visualization methods is the diagrammatic linkage of graphic and verbal media, with which it is possible to describe (urban) spatial situations in their specific context. On the one hand, such a formal structure defines specific sets of parameters of the building structure, use, and location; on the other hand, it also draws upon various modes of visualization: the drawing, the plan, the image, the text, etc.

Introduction

Finally, the third aspect emerges from the catalog-like arrangement of series and lists which renders differences and analogies visible.

While people have always attempted to gain an overview of the city or the world by means of maps and later panoramas from a bird's-eye perspective and from central vantage points, we have attempted to show that a representation of the totality of the city is hardly possible. The aspects, projects, and cases presented here thus stand for distancing from the scale of the absolute, with the intention of writing reports, lists, maps, and diagrams and using them to shift toward describing what is relational. Intervening in the practice of researching is about redrawing connections of the urban, which no overall picture could anticipate. As we deal with a return of city here, it requires us to understand *city* as a relational network of socio-material constellations in which the principle of the urban is embedded. So, *city* was never gone. Only now—in the context of the perspectives and readings—it is coming into effect in a new epistemological, aesthetic, and political way.

Diagrammatic tableau. Wall. Production of knowledge.
In this context, the wall as an architectural fundamental is given special attention. In our research and visualization work, it appears as epistemological space, because materials of all kinds can be attached to it and—for the time being—arranged in no hierarchal order. This way, one can "come into play"[16] with it, that is, to performatively go through the heterogeneity of research materials on a certain topic, field, or concern and reenact it while displaying or observing it. What the wall enables is a specific topological synchronicity of the non-simultaneous. It allows various documents in their diverse materiality to be placed next to each other equitably, giving an overview and thus creating an epistemological space that builds up the tension between different versions of real space and its visualization. The goal is to investigate the mode of difference and of similarity of the examined elements without preferring either dimension. Thus, the wall presents a diagrammatic tableau that allows for new relations and referential connections between documents and elements of documents to be discovered; in so doing, it reveals more about the documents themselves.

This process is less about localizing many documents from one point of view, but rather about pursuing several modes of noting reality and eventually presenting them, in order to find out what vectors and motifs they entail, what practices they contain, what potentialities they can facilitate, and what new arrangements they could set off. Thus, gathering documents on the wall not only serves the task of rearranging and showing spatial practices; it also enacts a practice of gathering and arranging which signifies and manifests a certain point of time in the research.

Yet the drawback of this wall-hanging is surely that it creates a disorder, a flood of complexity, and doesn't really help in finishing

16   For a detailed explanation of "coming into play" as a research method, see
www.pm.ud.hcu-hamburg.de/

the work. The benefit is exactly this disadvantage: by using it as learning surface that re-enacts non-coherence and multiplicity,[17] it succeeds in preventing a quick closing of processes and dismantling of closed teleologies. Instead, it promotes an open-form structuring of singularities that can then be reassembled. Getting closer to the wall, letting the eyes wander over its surface, hanging and taking down materials, and even walking past it every day: these all express ways of understanding in relational terms the epistemological space of a certain constellation of documents. Referring to French philosopher Michel Foucault, one could also call it tableau logic of nonhierarchical collections and archives.

Tom Paints the Fence is another result of these kinds of visuospatial forms of reasoning,[18] which is closely linked to the action of hanging, observing, and constantly reassembling in different sessions. Its heterogeneous, openly arranging and fragmentary character suggests this assumption by serving a quality that not only keeps us from reducing complexity too rashly, but also constantly reminds us that we ourselves produce space with our actions, despite the fact that or maybe precisely because our practices and assumptions about space that are embedded in these practices differ. The act of hanging materials on the wall has the discursive effect of introducing a third party during the session that participants negotiate about. Instead of remaining in the self-referential circle of exchanging terms, the discussion always offers a material counterpart that it uses to work off its tasks and to relate to itself. The wall acts as *res publica en miniature.* It insists upon and shows us in two ways what concerns us. On the one hand, as a sort of newspaper on the wall, it makes what concerns us public to the *sensus communis*, the discussion group. That's the *publica's* part. On the other hand, in its materiality, it is the *res* that constantly resets the negotiation to the concrete question: "What is it all about?"

Measuring the learning success of the wall is initially aimed at finding out something about the differences in knowledge materials and practices in order to be able to develop other ways of working together. Just as we are guided by the realization that there are no permanent solutions that could be implemented without an alternative, so do we need all the more new modes of negotiating a provisional composition of *city*. This is where the question of indeterminacy as an epistemological issue, as discussed above, returns. To make indeterminacy constructively accessible requires designing difference—including the knowledge of different disciplines. Only in this way can indeterminacy be understood as a challenge and the connectivity of knowledge be kept in view. Applied as a diagrammatic set of heterogeneous knowledge materials, the method of wall-hanging produces new arrangements. This, however, requires

17 John Law, "Pinboards and Books: Juxtaposing, Learning and Materiality," version of 28 April 2006, 18. Available at: www.heterogeneities.net/publications/Law2006PinboardsAndBooks.pdf

18 Kay Owens, "Visuospatial Reasoning in Twentieth-Century Psychology-Based Studies," in *Visuospatial Reasoning*, Mathematics Education Library 111 (2015).

Introduction

abandoning the old dichotomy of agency vs. structure against. Instead, one should point out that action can very well produce structure and vice versa.

The procedure, however, turns out to be quite laborious. In order to re-gather the heterogenous and incoherent material in different ways in order to create new forms of knowledge, one needs more than just stamina; one needs a technological form of practicing. That is the structuring form of what we call the Take. It should be mentioned that we intend a construction in which design does not play a role—the case is rather the opposite. The key is to make an epistemological shift: we do not reduce the careful and insistent assembling and (re-)assembling of heterogenous bodies and formats of knowledge to a means to make "the design," but rather raise it to the level of a design process in its own right.

The wall-hanging and respective sessions are thus in no way trivial, but instead are part of the art of making, for which UD serves as an institutional framework. It doesn't promise an easy-to-handle knowledge container, but supposes an improvisatory practice that knows that learning is always provisional—it is always subject to change, and it is always specific and local.[19] This explains *why* we pay specific attention to the material arrangements and specific contextual constellations of the urban. Finally, it is about the efficacy of actions and things in regard to producing space and distributing knowledge. Whether it is a street corner, a kiosk, an exchange of activity where tomato seedlings are swapped for dishes, a planning adjustment, or a roof that's been torn open—all of these participate in the process of urban research and production, and they are all attested independent and epistemic meaning.

Relationality and diagrammatic reasoning

In light of understanding built structures as script—that is, as a recording medium and an interface of social action—our focus lies on the mediality of urban situations in its social contingency, which reveals different types of purposes, structures, and forms. The prerequisite to this procedure is the overcoming of both a sociological view that does not have the tools to analyze the normativity of the built environment in combination with an analysis of the latter's constituent (architectural) parameters, and an architectural perspective that, assuming that spatial conditions configure social conditions, supports a spatial determinism. As stated above, what we are interested in is penetrating the multiple interconnection of social and material configurations in their reciprocity or relationality and making them readable.[20]

It's not just the space that is relational; the associations between practical and material structures are as well. Only conceptual and representational unlocking of these relationships in their relationality offers a design-related view of the embedded potential of new

19   John Law, Pinboards and Books: Juxtaposing, Learning and Materiality, 21.
20   See, for example, Victor Buchli, *An Anthropology of Architecture* (London and New York: Bloomsbury Academic, 2013).

(re)configurations of *city* in the future. This is what we call diagrammatic reasoning. In concrete terms, this means that any analytical focal point or deep drilling we undertake may be read as either an intersection on a timeline of urban transformation or as the product of that transformation.

Diagrammatic reasoning seeks to combine conceptual thinking with a method of arranging knowledge. It enables the production of different forms of representation and relates them in such a way that they are able to keep research and design processes open while structuring them. Whether it is an array of drawings, images, texts or their organizing structure in charts, catalogs, and lists, diagrams make a divergent field of forms of re-presentations available. Moreover, it is crucial that the representational character of its components changes into the non-representational aspect of a structure and thus informs on actions and procedures. There are descriptions emerging between the components and the whole, as well as between individual parts, that are changeable and contain within themselves the option of constantly reassembling. On the one hand, complex circumstances, lines of argumentation, and thought processes can be displayed; on the other hand, their vectors point projectively in directions that are yet to be discovered in order to access possible fields of action.

Enabling forms of knowledge

Let's return to the beginning: UD was confronted with the question of how knowledge of *city* can be shaped so that those actors who apply the knowledge are enabled and empowered to produce their own as well as new open forms or spaces. This is what we call enabling forms of knowledge. They introduce forms that are not looking for solutions to given or identified problems, but are focused on designing arrangements that let questions emerge. This does not mean questions or facts taken from a ready-made pool, but rather questions of relevance, in which the *res* regains its *publica*. This helps in understanding how types of enabling knowledge refer to the open form. We ask how a phenomenal urban reality is created and, moreover, how knowledge about *city* is produced and presented and how it becomes an object of political negotiation. The fact that representations are used is indisputable. What is questionable, however, is exactly how this is done and in what social contexts this representational action is embedded.

Assembling the urban

So, to sum up: Overall, the materials gathered in this book testify to the production of an epistemological space that in the first place interprets singularities in view of their diversity. Furthermore, it constantly makes us aware of our own presuppositions, and finally, it ties our learning process to an experience that we ourselves must enact and develop further. Processed through this triad, gathered knowledge material proves to become epistemologically productive, especially once it is separated from final descriptions

Introduction

and categorizations. Taking into account the action-related nature of the built environment also means understanding the material constellations of a *city* as social facts, and *space* as (socially) produced.

This changes the sociological double-barreled question that was once introduced into the discourse by Émile Durkheim.[21] On the one hand, it accounts for the debate of whether there is a certain type of social phenomenon that justifies distinguishing in principle from other, non-social phenomena. On the other hand, the question is whether social phenomena are to be "seen as things" and attributed the same degree of reality as objects that we can touch.

Contrary to the notion of an inherent logic of the social that organizes in self-sustaining systems, we try to track what kind of constellations come together when an urban network is assembled: What does a certain urban situation consist of at a certain point of time? What requirements are embedded in it, and how are they produced in detail?

The approach to understanding materiality as arrangements, and thus as an assemblage of things and humans, that can be reassembled in a new way takes a threefold turn in doing so. To begin with, it seeks to put aside the kind of idealism that defines the object's synthesis in the consciousness of a pre-formed subject, or reduces it to a linguistic field. In second place, it implements the disengagement with a conception that unitizes any kind of material diversity within an object. Without abandoning the relationality of the manifold, the coherences rather experience opening and pluralization. Such openings require the third aspect, the inclusion of the temporality of the arrangements as an open, performative process.

The question of how these three aspects can be combined and turned into action leads directly to the next question: How does one act improvisationally, i. e. open and structured and at the same time with an arrangement, a gathering, network, an *assemblage*, or an *agencement*? What is meant by this? And how can it be represented in a way that creates new, multiple courses of action, without falling back upon only "alleged" proposals for action?[22]

Following the extension of instruments originally limited to the area of local sites of knowledge production to the analysis of urban situations, UD wants to discuss a concept of the urban that understands it as a relational process that is (socially) produced and that gathers heterogeneous human and nonhuman actors. Against this background, UD is looking for a reading strategy that seeks to get under the skin of the *city*. As we have seen, this includes the practices of deceleration and small-scale pacing. It compels us to meticulously reread, show many small aspects, associate, deduce, and take the given of *city* seriously in order to harvest constructive agencies from it.

21   Émile Durkheim, *Regeln der soziologischen Methode* (Neuwied and Berlin: Suhrkamp Taschenbuch Wissenschaft, 1961).

22   Neil Brenner, David J. Madden, and David Wachsmuth, "Assemblage urbanism and the challenges of critical urban theory," *City* vol. 15 no. 2 (2011): 225–40.

Book as procedure

Eventually, the book itself remains the attempt to characterize a procedure that is by no means reduced to the method as form, merely applied to content. Rather, the procedure of translating research into a book claims to be content at the same time. According to this method, the form of translating contains its meaning, which is in turn implemented through the diagrammatic approach. As indicated earlier, this presupposes not only producing and analyzing texts, images, drawings and diagrams, but also relating them to each other. Although it denies all-too-simple assumptions about a given city, such an analysis is not (de)construc-tivism that detaches itself from the given. On the other hand, it presents a procedure that binds the construction to the analytical-structural decomposition and fragmentation of the given.

Thus the given is not ontologized—i.e. naturalized—as a deter-mined and finalistic fact, but understood as being produced in contingency. What follows is a strategy of rendering visible, pointing out, and associating that always asks for implicit presuppositions, evasive maneuvers in what is read. What does the procedure want to say? What does it aim at? Does it pursue a thesis, a theory, or does it remain in reading as a mode of practice that leads me myself to a constant confrontation with the conditions as they are becoming?

The latter can certainly serve as a target of our reading. What was the prerequisite to the UoN project—namely, to be the remnant subject to a final dismantling—is also true here: what the procedure processes, dismantles, and examines for its fundamentals in analytical dissection is directed to a questioning and expanding of its ingrained modes of production or forms of representation as a whole. The fact that we also put forms of communication as modes of collective understanding to the test sheds light on why we do not formulate a message in the sense of packaging information and neutrally transmitting it to a recipient, and why we abandon any simplified understanding of communication as a transparent means of transport. Welcome, dear reader. The stage is yours.

Introduction

Round Table Redesign: Understanding UoN

Ingrid Breckner
Christopher Dell
Alexa Färber
Bernd Kniess
Ben Pohl
Moderation and preparation:
Dominique Peck
Dorothea Wirwall
Robert Stürzl
Julia Strohwald

Ingrid Breckner was Professor of Urban and Regional Sociology at HCU Hamburg from 1995 to 2021. She contributed to projects in teaching and research at the UoN.
Christopher Dell was Professor of Urban Forms of Knowledge, Organizational Theory, and Relational Practice at HCU Hamburg from 2008 to 2010 and from 2016 to 2019. He co-conceptualized the UoN project and contributed to projects in teaching and research.
Alexa Färber was Professor of Urban Anthropology and Ethnography at HCU Hamburg from 2010 to 2018. She contributed to projects in teaching and research at the UoN.
Bernd Kniess has been Professor of Urban Design at HCU Hamburg since 2008. He was responsible for the UoN project.
Ben Pohl studied in the master's program Urban Design. He was a research assistant at the Teaching and Research Program Urban Design until 2015. He was among the first people to move into the UoN as a research station.

Dominique Peck studied in the master's program Urban Design, to a large extent at the UoN. He has been an academic assistant at the Teaching and Research Program Urban Design since 2015.
Dorothea Wirwall, Robert Stürzl, Julia Strohwald supported the project Tom Paints the Fence as student assistants.
For more information on the contributors, please see the chapter Three Questions to the Contributors on page 415.

The roundtable format

Dominique Peck:
When we started working on *Tom Paints the Fence*, we were looking for situations within the project that could help us disclose practical forms of the UoN's knowledge-producing processes, in order to reflect on them. Many of these situations took place in the form of dialogues, roundtables, or other forms of discursive exchange and were embedded in various teaching formats. During this exchange, the gathering of several approaches, and different ones in particular, bears testimony to a basic understanding that neither does just one kind of city exist, nor is no other kind possible. Dealing with *city* as something that exists cannot be about simple empiricism; rather, findings have to be considered in regard to possible designed futures. This also means that you reflect on the position that you work from or use as an argument.

Each position tries to face the problem of its own conditions of possibility, and every time that happens, the people who are speaking are confronted with the challenge of identifying shortages and pitfalls and laying them bare for themselves and others.

Understanding UoN

One of the two episodes that were chosen for *Tom Paints the Fence* is the seminar titled "Potentialitäten des Urbanen" (Potentialities of Urban Form), under the responsibility of Alexa Färber, Bernd Kniess, and Kathrin Wildner, which took place at the UoN during the summer semester of 2013, at the same time as the Hotel?Wilhelmsburg student project. As this format had been designed to be an interdisciplinary dialogue between sociocultural and artistic approaches and those regarding spatial planning, it offered insights into the respective speakers' work. The goal was to reflect with students and teachers on questions regarding urban resources. The guests were Martin Nachbar, Erol Yildiz, Sabine Bitter, Helmut Weber,

Jeanne van Heeswijk, and Stephan Lanz. The roundtable—in the form of a circle of chairs with teachers and students participating—concluded the seminar. At first, the guests' individual positions regarding earlier sessions on differences and regularities were debated, before making connections to the UoN's project. Likewise, students revisited individual aspects of the discussion in seminar papers; for instance, they asked how the UoN project combines university and neighborhoods, how and why it is a place of critical spatial practice, and what concept of design is being worked with. If there was a thrust to be taken from the papers, it was probably students trying to understand *city* through networks, to which they attributed specific agency in the form of potentiality.

In the present *Round Table Redesign: Understanding UoN*, we swap the conceptual frame of the seminar "Potentialitäten des Urbanen" and a report taken from the research of students' papers around the UoN. They were chosen based on the methods applied, as taught in the seminar "Methods, Tools & Theory" (MTT). Theses for discussion were gathered in the *Round Table Redesign* in order to structure the conversation. The main approach is to address UD-specific aspects within the modus operandi of Urban Design research and design projects and Urban Design thesis projects. Examples include the Situationist method of *dérive*—committing oneself to the spatial field—and the operationalization of methods within a methodological pluralism.

Let's begin: Dorothea, can you start by showing us the student works?

Dorothea Wirwall:
We based the *Round Table Redesign: Understanding UoN* on eleven books and brochures—Urban Design thesis projects, Urban Design projects and papers from the methodology seminar "Urban Territories." In order to grasp the structural approach of the papers and to interrelate them, we created a graphic notation for each one and marked them with content-related codes. We chose three of those works based on their significantly different approach to form the basis for this conversation today.

The first one, *Alle(s) unter einem Dach*—meaning everyone (and everything) under one roof—is by Lene Benz. She is interested in family businesses, mainly those shaped by migrants in Wilhelmsburg. She worked with the basics of grounded theory. In the course of her research, she realized: "If I really want to find out more about how these businesses operate, I need to get access to them"—the principle of "getting involved." At first, she went from door to door, asking, "Excuse me. Are you a family business?" During the second step, she was able to connect with two entrepreneurs she knew from previous projects. This way, she exceeded in establishing very personal contact with the families, which led to her understanding of detailed family and business structures.

Jenny Ohlenschlager based her Urban Design thesis project on custodians, applying Henri Lefebvre's theory of the production of space. She took the question "How do custodians produce space?" and used individual case studies to develop patterns or structures of practices, actors, and places. She generated the case study's data through participatory observations, interviews, and graphic analyses of the locations and spaces. Overall, this multi-method design led to job profile descriptions beyond classic notions or scopes of services from regulations.

Franziska Meichel-böck's thesis *Nicht Stadt, Land, Hafen* —meaning "not city, countryside, or harbor"—is influenced by the perspective of her discipline, landscape architecture, which seeks to approximate an urban space's ambivalence between industrial use and scenic influence. She understands the various layers that she extrapolates from observations into drafts and maps and transfers the material as components into palimpsest-like displays. Her work shows how *city* in its use can be recorded by observation and mapped. She uses known tools and methods from landscape architecture, and together with the descriptions of spaces she develops new ways of interpreting sites. In addition to that, she analyzes urban development policies regarding the harbor, which is close to her study area: Which regulations are relevant? How do businesses develop? The result of this work is an assembly of simultaneous processes in urban development in the Grasbrook study area, which could serve as the basis for a leap forward.

[see p. 66 – Materials]

Alexa Färber: Thank you very much for your remarks. Could you explain to us what you are addressing with "a leap forward"?

Dorothea Wirwall: Instead of saying that Franziska had transformed her view of space into a design in the classical sense, I used "a leap forward" to mean that she placed approaches to a possible future as an interpretation of the present at the end of her work.

Dominique Peck: Thank you for the introduction, Dorothea. With this material at hand, we'll move on to the round of talks. The first thesis I want to start with is:

UD has stepped up with the UoN to overcome *Städtebau*.

I add the question of what "overcoming" means, which aspects of urban development have to be overcome, and how this opinion has been transferred into the Urban Design teaching and research program.

Bernd Kniess: Well, the term "overcoming" refers on the one hand to what is handed down and passed on; and on the other hand, it relates its Middle High German meaning of "agreeing upon," which allows an accord to be reached with that which already exists, to the meaning of "coming over," thus subsuming the process of becoming something and getting somewhere. I like that about the term, and it anticipates a significant aspect of urban design. The claim of overcoming goes back to the HCU 2007 Structure and Development Plan (hereinafter known as STEP), which we have "overcome" in the meantime. I repeatedly checked how it was worded: "*Städtebau* (urban design) connects the artistic competences of an architecture-informed practice of *Städtebau* with a technical, infrastructural and process-driven practice of urban planning." As the term "*Städtebau*" is used twice here, we saw a dilemma in the different semantic content, which we tried to diminish by using the English expression *Urban Design* (UD) for a broader understanding of urban development. The goal of UD was in any case to characterize the interface in order to move toward an independent vocational field. In STEP, it was agreed to implement a new program between the programs of study of Architecture and Urban Planning.

This served as my brief to conceptualize the program of study. What became important to me as a starting point was the new HCU's self-image and its inter- and transdisciplinary standards. A contestation of urban form can only work in an interdisciplinary constellation. It cannot work any longer from a purely disciplinary perspective, which positions urban design as the core competence. What we need instead is a combination of creative and urban research-related competence; in other words, an extended understanding of design that is based on research. That was the starting point.

Christopher Dell: You went through a change as an architect as well—you worked on certain projects and gained experience. After all, your own interest has strongly developed, coming from the object scale of architecture and working your way toward the scale of the city. What I'm trying to say is: you didn't come from the field of urban planning. You're in line with a number of protagonists who more or less intensively went down a similar path: Robert Venturi and Denise Scott Brown, but also Rem Koolhaas, who said architecture and urban design needed research, and that this research was already part of the design. They thus expanded what architecture and urban design should and can be.

I suppose it was an important factor for you to say, "Here at the HCU, I have a good chance to develop a machine that can take this form of urban research to a new level." It's seldom the case that various disciplines are brought together in one place.

Ingrid Breckner: What interests me about this thesis is the discourse once again—I experienced this very strongly in Vienna—about the possible retrieval of *Städtebau*, which always becomes a residual category in architecture. You do it, and it's part of the deal. But if you ask yourself who is doing it, how are they doing it, with what concept and based on what knowledge and experience, then you generally get vague answers. And whether or not *Städtebau* seems fully tangible, our age virtually cries out for re-institutionalizing it. This questions the role of *Städtebau*: is it supposed to optimize built objects, or is it qualitatively relevant to the respective city? Depending on the position, various fields of research emerge: if built objects are supposed to be contextualized better, it's probably about materiality, scales, and corresponding different shapes. If *Städtebau* is thought to contribute to creating urban space, conceptions of *city* become relevant, including history and specific differences. Of course, this requires a wide variety of skills from various disciplines, in order to say, "My building is a piece of *city*!" and not simply, "My building is better or nicer than other buildings, because I have embedded it in urban planning."

Bernd Kniess: This is of course an extension that's happening here—not to understand city merely as something built. This extension also raises the question of what else *city* is, and how this *what else* can be unlocked in an understanding of urban design.

Ingrid Breckner: Exactly.

Bernd Kniess: But most of the time, you still find the known starting point in architecture as well as *Städtebau*, in understanding city merely as built environment.

Ingrid Breckner: Yes, physically and aesthetically.

Alexa Färber: Bernd, do you have the impression that buildings, the way Ingrid described them as the one alternative, are actually being changed or designed and play a role in UD, or is it about "city-city"?

Bernd Kniess: For now, it really is about "city-city," about its structure. We understand the form as something self-contained and don't truly consider it suited for understanding cities in the way we understand them. In order to explore *city* in its diversity and heterogeneity, I have to overcome this closed form that is architects doing *Städtebau* without any further capacity for researching what *city* is and does. This means I have to open up this form, and I have to try and make information available that is enclosed in the city in a way that I gain insight from it in terms of the city's presence and history as well as its possible future. In doing so, I need to refrain from wanting to display the "whole" truth, which of course doesn't exist in such a way.

However, gathered information should help me understand this object of personal interest, of how it came into being. This prompts the questions of prerequisites: how do things come into being? Taking this phenomenon that draws our attention, we seek to describe it in its present being, to trace its becoming in the past, perhaps the conditions of production under which it came into existence, the forces that affected and still affect it. With this knowledge, we try to reverse the timeline in order to make possible futures imaginable. But this doesn't happen through the representation of a form or an object as a product of the classical architectural design process. Instead, we are looking for structures that will eventually enable us to design the urban form.

Christopher Dell: Alexa's question is important. When you focus on urban production and action, it's easy to say, "You're taking a praxeological approach, and you're losing sight of the city's materiality as a result." When it comes to urban design, it's quite the opposite. The material requirements for the production of the city are just as important as the empirical data, what Bernd calls "information." However, we no longer consider the material passive—as something that's waiting and depending on you to give it a form. The question is reversed once you say, "Form comes from movement; it's the material that's affecting us." Material is never passive, but rather part of the researcher's coming into play. That's why UD's methods are so unusual; they expect you to get involved and to cast yourself into the urban situation in order to enhance the affecting qualities of materials in their circumstance of production in the first place. This is necessary in order for you to build structures that in turn enable other circumstances of production instead of remaining closed off. In other words, that which has long been practiced in the field of humanities—participatory observation—is now coming more into view in creative disciplines as well: gathering "information" on what you actually can and want to "design." Yet, this is not meant as a 1:1 correspondence of disciplines. Instead, it implies that processing this information—because it is processed in the disciplines of design —works differently than in the humanities.

Alexa Färber: But I meant my question a little differently. Dorothea used an allegory when presenting the students' works: the "leap forward." Is there a design? No, there isn't. I'm also always interested in the everyday life of making science; or of making theory, of university. Therefore: are two years enough to come to a proposition or design when in reality, research and dealing with *city* have priority? I'm looking at it from the outside and feel like it has become a principle to say, "No, design comes at the end." But it never happens, because at that point, the two years of theory have already come to an end. The possibility of designing existed only in the projects that students worked on over several classes. So, what can be achieved in two years of UD, and would design be possible as well if the program of study went on for longer?

Alexa Färber: And by "situation" you mean whatever is "out there"?

Dealing with the given situation is constituent for further proceedings at the UoN

Ingrid Breckner: I think what Christopher said was important. There is something new happening in *Städtebau*, namely movement. This dynamic thinking of urban development as something that is not fixed, but that has become or is becoming, something that can and must be developed further: this processing is new for me. I find the program of study so interesting because it doesn't start with static constructs that are placed somewhere and that then, when added up—as when playing with building blocks—create a city. Addressing urban development with a dynamic understanding urgently requires dealing with the space and time of its respective interweaving. Thus, the second thesis should be: "UD understands that the situation *has become* constituent for further proceedings." Otherwise, we end up with something static again.

Bernd Kniess: Correct. We don't see *city* as a purely architectural situation that you look at from a bird's-eye view, like a plan. Instead, we see it as something that can only be understood through movement. And that includes the understanding of the production of space. In architecture, the often-used spatial concept is still that of a container, the building that facilitates something—living, working, recreation—but it simply has to be given in order to make anything possible at all. That is the original task of architecture: providing space. In turn, understanding space as produced means that it doesn't just exist, but is rather the result of actions taken by actors and the surrounding objects in locations within a vector field of interests, motives, and discourse. This brings us to the question of spatial action in which human, as well as non-human, actors are involved. And yes, this undoubtedly predetermines a different framing; space, and thus *city*, can no longer be understood to be a static object.

Christopher Dell: I really like this transformation of *having become* into *becoming*. That has something to do with the concept of the *given*; I think it has a political connotation. On the one hand, the emphasis on the *given* here is aimed against the notion of tabula rasa, against an attitude: "That didn't work. Let's get rid of that. Try again." But on the other hand, the given is not used in an ontological sense; one would say you were dealing with something "this way and not another." In this context, what matters is distancing oneself from the common understanding of design, that is to say, problem solving and / or inventing. By referring to the given, we want to get beyond problem-solving and discover questions that are embedded in urban situations. Back to a situation that can't be treated as the exterior, but instead as a specific situation that we choose, that we commit to, where we intervene in order to represent. So what we take as a given is precisely not the problem (however it's described), but rather the situation. The fact that we do research like that requires us to take the circumstances of the situation as something relevant, rather than say, "We have to get rid of that and make it new." And at the same time, we don't consider the circumstances of a situation as determined in a finalistic sense. Instead, we see them as actualizations of potentialities that can be actualized and assembled in new ways. The latter is what can be seen as the design extension of participatory observation. Thus, I regard researching the *city* through the lens of *what has become* and *is becoming* as very appropriate, because it addresses both layers.

Ingrid Breckner:
I think this holds another important epistemological perspective. I don't know if *Städtebau* has an epistemological perspective. As far as I understand, and have understood it so far, *Städtebau* has the perspective of optimizing the architectural design. In a scientific sense, however, referring to Ludwik Fleck,[1] epistemological means constantly being clear of what the facts are that we are dealing with, and to understand those facts as an outcome of specific styles of thinking (*Denkstile*) in scientific communities (*Denkkollektive*). Facts that were relevant during a certain time in history are changing. There is a difference when dealing with medical facts in 1935, or 1970, or 2015. Accordingly, in architecture, one always has to repeatedly search for what a city is. What do theory and research in UD need in order to boost the epistemologically necessary search for respective and relevant facts? With reference to the third thesis about UD, I take the view that the element of design is an important one: it shows us that

analytical perceptions of designed objects make it possible to check whether and how earlier assumed scientific facts have been adapted for the object and the surrounding city, and what meaning they have. I'd like to focus on conceptual approaches to arriving at an even more distinctive meaning than in the student work presented at the beginning of this conversation, even if they're not finished architectural or urban designs that one could start building straight away. Readings alone are not interpretations that allow conclusions to be drawn for the respective disciplinary action. The implementation of interventions within urban spaces is important as an orientation for students and to prevent them from panicking: if asked what to do, they have to be able to suggest more than merely analyzing or moderating.

Projects at the UoN are pro-discipline

Ben Pohl: Of course, there are many different disciplines that come together in UD, and it's also clear that someone with a professional architectural background handles architectural or urban design in a completely different way than someone working in sociology would. However, that is also an opportunity. Typical urban development may be a discipline in its own right, but as Ingrid already mentioned at the beginning, it's also in a difficult situation because it's not accurately defined. I've wondered whether urban design, the way it's being practiced here, is a new discipline or simply and deliberately not new at all.

1   Ludwik Fleck, *Entstehung und Entwicklung einer wissenschaftlichen Tatsache. Einführung in die Lehre vom Denkstil und Denkkollektiv* (Frankfurt am Main: Suhrkamp, 1980).

Christopher Dell: If that were the case, then we'd definitely have to follow Ingrid's suggestion to stand up for another epistemology, because what we don't need at this stage is amateurism. Thus, we should firmly state that disciplines are connected and that a diagram of disciplines emerges from practice. One could say that there are certain lenses that are being developed here and that allow us to look at things differently. Plus, some of these lenses or optics are design units yet again, because they make it possible to see this or that, so that we can do one thing or the other with them.

Alexa Färber: I was thinking about how to relate thesis one to three with regard to what you said about "facts," Ingrid. Basically—and this leads to actor-network theory (ANT)—one wouldn't refer to Latour and say "matters of fact," but instead talk about "matters of concern." The way the UD works is not to take situations as facts that are self-contained and fixed, but as rather processual while assembling relevant situations in the form of matters of concern, thus placing the fragile aspects of these situations in the foreground.

Christopher Dell: Of course, it is closely linked to what is called "motive" here. You commit to a situation in order to understand its requirements. In the understanding of knowledge, the comprehension of the committed subject transforms, as the subject is no longer a container into which knowledge is poured, nor the receiver. There has to be perception-action and epistemic action, a commitment that you have to articulate for yourself as a reflective action in order to then develop the matter of concern out of the situation.

At the UoN, science and design are reassembled

Bernd Kniess: One comment on the question of "discipline, yes or no:" are we overcoming the discipline, too, or are we creating a new one? I personally am quite comfortable in this halfway situation. I don't think we have the need or the urge to define or claim that we are a new discipline. The case is quite the opposite. To specify it using the UoN as an example: if we come to realize that *city* is a process and the urban can't be linked to a certain moment, the question is, "What are the consequences for the design, what is the origin of form, and what are the conditions of the design process?"

Ben, maybe you can add something from your experience. If we create a situation at the UoN, we definitely understand this designing of the situation as such, and not at all as non-designing. With the proposition of a process, we may have overcome design on the object level, but at the moment we may have also overstepped it to such an extent that we have also lost it in its classical form.

After all, we still only rarely succeed in UD projects when trying to achieve form and structure equally, in other words to gain form, which is already contained in the analysis' structure. This means that we exercise the practice of design on several different levels and rather on a small scale—the UoN is evidence of that—and we also succeed in designing form. But perhaps this really is a procedure that requires practice.

Ben Pohl: Within the context of the UoN were attempts on many levels to consciously shape situations and processes. Not only were internal and institutional processes of the project thus changed; we also tried to connect the project to everyday life in Wilhelmsburg. That was of course a longer and more careful way of figuring out possibilities. Lene Benz, for example, describes this in her work as "getting involved." This kind of involvement constantly shifts the relationship between researcher and research, and designer and design; after a certain point it's no longer clear who or what is actually involving whom, is researching or shaping the situation. We've experienced this at the UoN again and again, and it's not an easy process of negotiation. If you want to stay capable of acting, then design can perhaps be understood as part of the creative process of various actors. And, as you say, this new method has to be practiced and rehearsed, and that can only work if you do it together. Disciplinary tools were to some extent altered when they were used. If, for example, you need an analytic drawing, or you build up trust by interviewing someone and listening to them professionally, you realize that it wouldn't make any sense to keep the disciplines of research and design separated; different abilities apply to different situations. Rather, one has to find out what means can be used creatively by someone coming from a research discipline, and where they might have a creative background; can they realize in a certain situation that it would be good to know more about current processes and how to apply their resources in research as well?

Ingrid Breckner: But I think that you have to explain which one is the creative aspect and which one is the researching one. The research committee at the HCU repeatedly claims that the architectural design was already research; however, they don't tell you how high the proportion of research is.

Bernd Kniess: That's the classic problem.

Ingrid Breckner: Right. That's why I think you have to state clearly that this is design, because … At the UoN, you can talk about design elements, because you cooked and ate there, right up to dealing with hotel business, where a certain form came into existence; I think this ensemble of different creative elements opens up the mind for now. As soon as you arrived there, those elements created "aha moments"—surprises—and raised questions like, "What's happening now?" It is not tasks A through C that have to be worked on and handed in.

Nothing is ever finished; instead, you enter a process and experience how that process is constantly changing and presenting new challenges. You have to take a stand regarding the question, "Is this a pile of trash, or is it something that helps people to think differently about living in confined spaces?" The perception provoked by the beds in tubes is necessary for the conceived and designed understanding of space and time to become tangible.

Alexa Färber: Does that mean that design is reflection? In other words, is it reflecting and bringing the transformation to mind that I am kicking off with research? Because that would also be a little similar to what I do as an ethnographer. After all, I'm not thinking, "There is a situation and I'm looking at it." This field doesn't exist, but I create it by having a motive for research. I like this term, because it suits ethnography. Would design, then, already be a reflection of the transformation that arises through the process of research?

Bernd Kniess: Design has always been based on the process of researching—from the very beginning. First, I have a motive for why I am reflecting on relating to something, and from that moment onward in which there is room for involvement, I obviously design the steps that are necessary for me to stay involved.

Alexa Färber: Great! That's what I do as an ethnographer as well! I just want to know if there is anything that you do differently as an architect.

Bernd Kniess: On the one hand, we use a different language. Our form of expression is strongly based on images, which in turn affects our texts. On the other hand, we always keep an eye on the practical designing, even while researching. Research and design overlap in various ways. This means that, when examining different disciplines, their methods and tools, we try to expand the possible ways of representing what we are looking at. That's what we mean by the term "diagrammatic reasoning." We understand it as a language that emerges from things, their meanings and representations: between textual descriptions and representations that we borrow from architecture and planning—maps, plans, drawings (two- and three-dimensional), charts, lists, diagrams, photography, et cetera—but essentially by putting various forms of representation into a certain order, while their temporal progress doesn't lead to a conclusive unambiguity.

Alexa Färber: But that wouldn't lead, for example, to the conclusions that Ingrid wanted.

Ben Pohl: Yes, it would. That was the case, particularly at the UoN: for instance, we didn't take a purely ethnographic approach and find that situations are only shaped by researching and writing, publishing a book about it, and then discussing it with others. This interdisciplinary approach, with an architect, for example, adds the ability to interpret certain questions in architectural terms. This was how we built a kitchen, which is something rather unusual for ethnographers—intervening structurally to design situations. The questions and experimental settings were, so to speak, adapted through materials again and again. That happened at the UoN, and without architects it wouldn't have been possible to make those

physical changes, and thus influence the field of research again.

Bernd Kniess: And vice versa.

Christopher Dell: That was the reason for collaborating with the Kulturfabrik Kampnagel.[2] We wanted to design situations using various materials, people, structural changes, and so on, and wanted to take urban situations seriously as a performative matter. That comes first—taking it seriously in that specific way. Second, we realized that those who handle the performative aspect professionally are the performance artists; they are constantly involved with it, even if they might not necessarily

2   Theater and production venue for contemporary performance arts in Hamburg-Winterhude.

reflect on their actions in an academic sense. We, however, who try to reflect on actions in regard to the urban, don't consider ourselves performance artists. So we brought the two together.

Thus, you end up saying, "Once I am in the field as an observer, I am a performer." What needs to happen for me to take that role seriously? After all, I have to shape this performance somehow, and if I do, I can't get an objective result. You could say this process is being developed to an extreme within the specific motive-driven overlap of research and design. This way, new ways of representation arise as well, which Bernd talked about. A kind of form-giving diagrammatic reasoning: not one that represents things 1:1, but that produces a heterogeneous representation of information so that it can be reassembled in new ways. That really shows research as a way of making things. At the same time, I agree with Ingrid that you have to clarify what the differences are and what properties result from them.

Ben Pohl: You can probably see the tightrope that we crossed there when comparing it to projects like 72 Hours of Urban Action. I don't want to bash it, but that's just the opposite of what we're doing, displaying quick answers in physical forms; young architects with power tools who create an intervention in the urban space within 72 hours. This may look similar to the UoN, but the work at the UoN is permanently connected to adjusting the questions, or at least that's the ambition. Whether this is successful in every project is another question. But it's the attempt that is rather disregarded in projects that are based on action.

Alexa Färber: Surely, time plays an important role.

Bernd Kniess: I doubt that you can figure out a question in that format.

Alexa Färber: Everyone might end up having some sort of question, though.

Ingrid Breckner: Processuality is difficult to plan because of unexpected events that intervene; it happens, but it comes about randomly before it shapes anything. I think that at the UoN, processuality is always kept in mind.

Alexa Färber: Exactly, because there is continuity.

Ingrid Breckner: This kind of continuity has to be carefully orchestrated so that participating students can still see how their actions create something; they have to feel like they're part of an orchestra and sense how their playing helps to create an entity.

Alexa Färber: The example of an orchestra is a good one. It requires continuity as well. That's why I talked about time earlier. There are several classes of students, or teachers, who stay for not even a semester, or for 72 hours, and then they're gone. Continuity is an important factor when it comes to enabling processes of design.

I have another thought regarding this question of disciplines: UD is "pro-discipline." I think we can describe it the way you did earlier, Bernd: it's in-between, yes, and it makes it possible to address disciplinary matters and turn them into issues. The reason for this is, of course, the fact that not only are different disciplines involved in the process of teaching, but also that individual W disciplinary competencies are brought to the table. And questions like "Where am I even going with this? What does it connect to?" are things (of importance), because in the UD setting they become problems that can be addressed.

Ingrid Breckner: Compared to that, urban planning is less orchestrated; it's more a combination of existing disciplinary strategies and instruments following a specific aim; the things that are being connected are rather random, something you can see in the research papers, which turn out well up until the end. With more help or less help, there is an actual entity being created, which then represents a profile of competency. However, this doesn't happen with everyone: they see two individual entities in front of them and are only able to move them here or there; connecting and constantly recreating something with those entities often falls by the wayside.

Alexa Färber: And here we have the possibility of declaring exactly that as our main topic.

Ingrid Breckner: May I add two sentences about UD's pro-disciplinary character? To me, UD is something of a scientific praxeology—in other words, a scientific space for experimenting, where the focus lies on active learning, namely active researching and designing. After all, science always has its difficulties when it comes to taking action. Many scientists claim they don't take action but instead only analyze things. I find it appealing that UD is systematically and programmatically acting while emphasizing the interaction between thinking, researching, and creating. I suppose students that have studied different subjects are interested in that, too. They notice that they may have learned about methods and theories, but they realize in UD how to connect what they have learned and can thus improve themselves professionally.

Referring again to the topic of time: I do think that with the experience at hand you can think of a possible division for a two-year cycle, in which every element of the study process has to be experienced at least once. Afterwards, you might have to think about how different backgrounds, experiences, and levels of knowledge can be considered in a way that specific requirements can be used more productively. Sometimes that's quite difficult, not least given the teaching capacities.

UoN is an attempt to design a joint symbolic space for negotiations

Christopher Dell: The *Lehrhappening* (didactic happening) was a similar way of introducing the UoN as an event format, where one can actually have the experiences they have to have. Ingrid, the way you described it was fantastic. I would say that the concept of taking action is slowly being expanded here, that it's no longer about subjects that can be reduced to a rationalist determinism, subjects that think in an externalized space of reason and then act in the world, but that there are an awful lot of unintentional parts in the acting out of the world, the production of space. After all, according to Latour, things take actions as well; a concept that is crowded with indetermination. However, the task would be to emphasize the indeterminacy rather than canceling it out. Then again, that's a design and knowledge task.

Ben Pohl: Are you relating that to UD or the UoN? Because I think the UoN was a special case.

Ingrid Breckner: There were both. Alexa said that it was a long process with several classes. My question now is: How do you manage to use this experience and come up with a format to connect the two elements better and make them come alive over the course of two years?

Bernd Kniess: That's true—the approach was to connect theory, research, and practice. I find it interesting that you put the term praxeology into play; after all, it carried great weight within Applied Theatre Studies in Giessen, Germany, which resulted—as we know—in a new form of theater. Just think about the performance group Rimini Protokoll and their notion of experts of the everyday.

Ingrid Breckner: Absolutely right. I'm thinking of pedagogical attempts at "activity-oriented learning," as it's practiced at the Laborschule Bielefeld, for example.

Christopher Dell: … or Black Mountain College.

Ingrid Breckner: That was a completely different type of school: from architecture to teaching formats, to the activities of the students and teachers.

Bernd Kniess: What was interesting about Giessen as well as at Black Mountain College was the stage as central moment of practice: the rehearsal stage. The stroke of luck for UD was the UoN's rehearsal stage.

Christopher Dell: Even though we've only claimed that for now.

Bernd Kniess: I think it's interesting in regard to the connection. Ingrid called that scientific praxeology.

Alexa Färber: Okay, scientific praxeology seems to be something other than what I'd thought. I'd thought of the analysis of science as practice, and not of the performance of science as practice.

Christopher Dell: Maybe we have to expand the term "performance" in the sense of improvisation, where creating and reflecting become one. That means there is a certain mode in which one does something, while also analyzing and depicting that mode. However, this analyzing and depicting is strongly influenced by the type of action, an iterative process that we named Take. To stick with the example of Rimini Protokoll: they no longer perform a stage play, but create a performative diagram, in which *city* and whatever has always been going on within it become visible as arrangement and dispositive. On the other hand, the theater directors' methods become the work's central moment. We had Kampnagel on our project for this purpose—to reflect on these aspects and to then incorporate them into our work.

Dominique Peck: At this point, I would like to fit in another thesis, namely the question of a researcher's position regarding the field:

The embedded researcher does not refer to the conditions of production, but instead is part of them

This provokes the question of whether or not I am still able to distance myself from the object in front me.

Ben Pohl: The embedded researcher was a working concept for us. It describes a contract researcher in particular, who, for example, visits schools or a team of doctors and tries to use action research to understand the processes that he was involved in and to bring about changes if necessary. When living at the UoN, we applied this approach to ourselves and—with this shift in perspective—had to realize first that we are inevitably embedded in certain urban structures and can't escape these structures at all. The task is therefore no longer an external order or perspective, but rather a task of the self, one that is internal. So we can't conduct research *about* these urban processes, but only to the extent in which we ourselves are involved. There is nothing left for us to cut open and look into, to see what's inside; we have to take action ourselves, from the inside out. That's closely tied to the question of what makes it legitimate for me to research certain things. Hans [a fellow student] and I have tried to answer that in our work, from the process of living and our everyday life. From this, we developed our thesis question, which we didn't research on our own, auto-ethnographically, but which we also applied to the whole area surrounding the Elbe islands. In our case, it was about cooking and eating, which we related to exploratively in different restaurant locations.

Alexa Färber: I've never understood the difference between what you call "embedded research" and participative observation or field research.

Ben Pohl: We'd have to discuss that. The way I understood participatory observation is that it doesn't start with itself, but rather consciously enters the field in order to find out something about others. Perhaps the difference that we see is that these are things that we are interested in or moved by. They relate to our personal lives, and that's something we have to research for our own actions and sense of agency.

Alexa Färber: That's what it says in the books and brochures? You described what you're interested in and what's important to you personally? Or did you leave that out? I don't think you can visit some random island without any personal motivation, only to carry out a task. It was the same for Bronisław Malinowski, the "father" of participatory observation as a method of anthropological field research, around 1910, when he recorded his motivation in a diary that according to him was never to be published. Of course, motivation could be: I earn a lot of money, a reputation, or something. In Ingrid's seminar on research concepts, we always made clear—be it throughout the process—what the personal interest in knowledge is, in order to be able to distance ourselves from exactly that later on and to say, "I'll translate this into a scientific epistemological interest here, because I have embedded it in this or that literature and compared it to these research findings." I want to challenge you a little bit, because it didn't really become clear to me why you would need a detour via a commissioned embedded researcher in order to say that you want to carry out contemporary field research which always reflects your own role and is no longer excluded from ethnography.

Ben Pohl: Maybe it should be linked back to the rest of the process once again. As I've said, the UoN's projects haven't been limited to ethnographic methods. This continued with the hotel project and our experience, contacts, and the trust that were built up—all of this had an influence on the designing of new situations. Not only did we work for a scientific production and write a book; we also worked for an evolving field of practice, a place I lived in for over two years, that was part of my life. Oftentimes it wasn't really clear what part was professional and what was private. Both merged into one another.

Alexa Färber: I think the difference is that you were in the center of another teaching practice, but also the IBA, and therefore gathered other things around you that went beyond this research. That may simply be different with individual field research.

Bernd Kniess: Isn't that an indicator of a different understanding of work? Working as a researcher in the field, and with quite a bit of personal interest in working on a project?

Ingrid Breckner: Observation includes the researching aspect, and the participatory aspect points to "being in the field." What you did was much more—at times, you focused only on participating, and then you went out again to reflect on it. After all, the ideal goal of participatory observation is for you to disclose your personal interest. But here there's an especially radical idea of self-thematization in being a subject who is also doing the research, in that you expose yourself even more to the situation whose design you are influencing. The question is, how realistic and perhaps risky is it if the researcher is excluded and the embedded becomes too strong?

Ben Pohl: You might have to differentiate between two things. We used the catchword "prototypical procedure" in our work to reflect on what we actually did, while we used the title "Entwurf eines utopischen Forschungsdesigns" (Draft of a Utopian Research Design) to make the case for having a locally embedded researcher. That's because we thought that in the small living and working economies in Wilhelmsburg—or in urban life in general—we needed a level of explication, of becoming conscious. In doing so, we aimed to get a better understanding of how this practice works, how *city* is produced, if we to wish to design it. There is a "locally embedded" bakery, restaurant proprietor, and car mechanic, but where is the locally embedded researcher? Perhaps I can interview the baker and the others, involve them and draw from their everyday expert knowledge, but they don't all necessarily have time to think about the urban production around them. To what extent are these actors able to theorize their own actions or make them explicit in order to make them negotiable? That's the point where you can look at it differently again; the thesis would be that research should generally be embedded deeper in everyday life.

Alexa Färber: But that's why you're participating instead of just conducting interviews. Because you know that you get an important version of reality by reflectively talking about it, one in which people explain themselves, though the practice is something different but equally as important.

Christopher Dell: Well, you might also say that the design element here is more important than one thinks. Because this book by Ben and Hans does look special. It's quite distinctive, not a conventional report. And that was surely a strategy, telling participants in your research that they are part of the book. You gain something by doing that, you look inside and you find people who do the same as you, and you can make new connections. The book also expects you to really make connections. Perhaps someone meets someone else, who then again might meet someone else. Perhaps there will be a ping-pong match and someone finds a job while playing. It's not the same as becoming a boxer in order to reveal to an academic audience the secrets of boxers in a neighborhood.

Bernd Kniess: That's what I meant by "changing the working concept," which also includes resolving the separation of being a private citizen and being a researcher. You entered a project and stopped separating privacy from work; it became one, something you often see in work procedures that are increasingly characterized in projects of limited duration.

Alexa Färber: Absolutely. That's my thesis of the "ethnographic entrepreneurial self."[3] I think that both sides, one being what ethnography requires and the other what the entrepreneurial self requires, are very close—for instance, the way work and leisure merge

---

3   Alexa Färber, "Das unternehmerische Ethnografische Selbst. Aspekte der Intensivierung der Arbeit im ethnologisch-ethnografischen Feldforschungsparadigma," in *Horizonte ethnografischen Wissens. Eine Bestandsaufnahme*, ed. Ina Dietzsch, Wolfgang Kaschuba, and Leonore Scholze-Irrlitz (Cologne, 2009), 178–202.

into one another—which was another reason why Malinowski was both motivated and "annoyed." Since the invention of stationary field research of limited duration, the temporary working relationship between researchers and "informants"—I'm sure the same applies to the UoN—has played a part in this ambivalent intensification. Social relations that were no longer considered merely functional, but were instead based on a personal and oftentimes amicable proximity. Similar to the entrepreneurial self, the requirements imposed on social relations in the time-limited frame of an ethnographic research project are opaque or just genuinely multilayered.

I've just had another thought, regarding the example with the boxer: perhaps Loïc Wacquant, to whom you're referring, Christopher, didn't give the book back to the research field or say it would be something magnificent for those he'd learned to box with. I don't know for certain, but I believe he was able to find other ways of making his scientific knowledge available to the field.

Christopher Dell: One hundred percent. It isn't the book's goal to reveal its own structure of knowledge, though. *Body & Soul* is surely one of the best sociologically sound studies that exists.[4] It gives us concise descriptions of a Chicago district in the post-Ford and post-Keynesian era. We find excellent descriptions of boxing and its secrets, which Wacquant gets from eavesdropping during his daily training sessions at the gym. What you don't find, however, is how the study functions as a diagram or mechanical procedure, or how this diagram is connected to the *city*. Without explicitly referring to *Body & Soul*, Wacquant later describes this functioning in the book *Towards a Social Praxeology*. In UD's projects, we also aim to bring these two planes together in order to bring the design of research into the field as a relevant aspect.

Alexa Färber: But that way you're reducing scientific products to the book. After all, the book is not the only product.

Ingrid Breckner: Addressing the subject of things given and things given in return. It's about making things explicit.

Alexa Färber: Yes, but you could also hold a lecture.

4   Loïc Wacquant, *Body & Soul: Notebooks of an Apprentice Boxer* (Oxford: Oxford University Press, 2006).

Christopher Dell: I didn't say I was reducing anything. I was interested in working out differences in the medial processing of research and the reflection on media in the knowledge production process.

Alexa Färber: And I doubt that there is a fundamental difference. What makes a difference, however, is the meaning of the book in regard to giving something back to the field.

Ingrid Breckner: Another point is what happens regarding the process as a strategy and practice of giving and giving back, and to label that accordingly.

Ben Pohl: That was a quintessential point, because we did start out like, "Hello. We're writing a book about the restaurant business in Wilhelmsburg," while knowing that we were making a promise and that we really had to deliver on it. We couldn't have left and never come back again. Our appearance made us authentic, which in turn opened every door to us and created a situation in which everyone was ready to participate in the work. And of course we later discussed what kind of book we were actually making and whether we needed a special book for restaurant proprietors, because they might not understand certain things. Then we said to ourselves, "No, technically everything that is important is now in the book, and it's a good thing that parts of the book are overwhelming, because we don't even know what people are interested in. Everyone has different levels on which the work can be understood. Whether these are realizations that we've expressed in little codes, or people just looking at the photographs, or reading themselves into the other connections. Later, we also invited the proprietors to the book release at the UoN. Unfortunately, only three showed up, but that's exactly the point: they don't have the time; they can't leave their businesses. Afterwards, we went to see each one of them, to talk to them again, and hand them the books.

Alexa Färber: Have you found out what they are doing with the books now?

Ben Pohl: No.

Christopher Dell:
Maybe you can relax that a little by saying it doesn't need to differentiate too much—that instead there is a different framing; it's the lens that we use to look at the whole thing, because it's part of UD and it's about questions regarding urban research and not sociology. But of course, Loïc Wacquant could have done his studies within the framework of the UoN, and I am convinced that it would look completely different because the structures work differently.

Ingrid Breckner:
About these processes, I want to know what sticks with people who fill research with their content. I think that's something we can find out. We chose a specific research format during a project on regional food supply in which we invited agricultural producers from northern Germany to the university and asked them to bring some of their food products. We used the food and made a buffet. Many producers came because we took them seriously as subjects of research. They said, "Finally, someone has come to us without wanting to interview and research us or visit the market with us, and instead given us a stage at the university to tell people about our products and about what we do and so on!" Suddenly, they were very open and talkative. It was the first time where they could present themselves, as actors in a field as well.

Bernd Kniess: Where embeddedness is also open to actors, if they would like to participate. That seemed to work well with the tomato-swapping activity in the beginning. It wasn't a situation of asking people to answer your questions, but one where exchanges took place. Then they wanted to know what it is that we're doing with the exchanged goods, what value it has for us.

Christopher Dell: That would bring us to *Tom Paints the Fence*. Because it is the same topic—questioning this value. I realized something else: as you said before, for the first time the task was—to put it in curricular terms— not just to give yourself tasks, but others as well, which would then set the situation in motion. After all, that's precisely your example. Tasks being set in both directions.

Ingrid Breckner:
Especially since they are constantly being reduced, in fact, by the share in which UD competence plays an important part.

Bernd Kniess: Yes, or is expanding, as the discussion about whether to amend the HOAI and add stages 0 and 10 shows. Those are exactly the kinds of stages that we deal with here, too. Stages from which the other nine transform into something completely new. That's what is interesting about it.

Dominique Peck:
I wanted to address that once again, with the following thesis:

The costs of performance cannot be calculated according to the HOAI[5]

We already talked about the ethnographic entrepreneurial self. Of course, this program of study should, as you read to us in the beginning, train people who will then find work somewhere or create their own job position that isn't structured for now according to the *Honorarordnung für Architekten und Ingenieure* (Schedule of Services and Fees for Architects and Engineers) and its nine stages.

Alexa Färber: Who decides on the HOAI?

Ingrid Breckner: The Chambers of Architecture. I liked the idea of addressing the subject of regulation with the HOAI. You would have to argue what kind of regulations exist and in what way they limit or facilitate what UD does. What would have to be changed in order not to fall into quixotry with what you're doing and to avoid sending students there who would then tell us we're all very nice and exciting, but it wasn't more than two years of entertainment.

5   Official Scale of Fees for Services by Architects and Engineers.

Bernd Kniess: The experiences are very diverse. There are people who find their way in completely new fields, by all means in leading positions as well, be it as consultants, planners, or researchers. There are others who find their place in the discipline from which they came from. They work in offices or in administration, which of course would have been possible for them to do with "just" a consecutive program of study. However, after studying UD, they gain a perspective on their own discipline and look beyond it. Six months ago I met Lisa, who at first graduated in landscape architecture and who with newly gained self-confidence told me about her new job at a landscape architecture firm, where she was able to use everything she learned from us. She, the great skeptic throughout her studies, suddenly appeared so poised, because she used what she'd learned from UD and it had started to make sense to her.

Ingrid Breckner: I think it's important to discuss such experiences. Recently, sixty alumni met in Urban Planning and told incredibly fascinating stories about their fields of work. I found it interesting to see how narrow certain fields still are. It was good to make yourself more aware of different approaches and ways, and to see how you could better orchestrate things to make it fit even more.

Bernd Kniess: We only did or tried that once with a UD salon. The issue is that we don't have as many graduates as you do yet. Four or five showed up and talked about what they are doing now, followed by a discussion. I don't think you should only do that among students; you should include colleagues as well.

Christopher Dell: In this context, curriculum research would be the opportunity—also in regard to the concept of form—to address the fact that the urban design profession is not a finished form, something can simply be entered, and to explain that this is where one learns how to create this form. However, in order for this to work, it would have to really be incorporated into the curriculum in a reflective and critical manner.

Round Table Redesign: Understanding UoN

MATERIALS

ALLE(S) UNTER EINEM DACH
Everyone (and Everything) under One Roof

Lene Benz
Urban Design Thesis Project, 2013
Examiners: Prof. Bernd Kniess (Urban Design),
Prof. Kathrin Wildner (Urban Ethnology)

SITUATION 1

In her master's thesis, Lene Benz deals with family businesses
located in the Hamburg district of Wilhelmsburg. She begins with
the assertion that in family businesses, the fine line between
working and living has been dissolving and the "dissolution of the
boundaries of work" as described by sociologists Karin Gottschall
and G. Günter Voss could be applied to the model of family businesses (p. 10). In order to carry out her research, she uses
methods of qualitative fieldwork. She aimed to use methods of data
acquisition and evaluation in accordance with grounded theory,
though she admits to not having consistently followed this
approach.

[Legend]

Front Matter/Bridges/ Back Matter		Sections	
Photos		3D-Model	
Texts		Links	
Footnotes		Scan	
Quotes		Table	
Illustrations		Report	
Plans		Family Tree	
Palimpsest—Collage		Ground Plan	
Diagrams		Axonometry	
Network Diagrams		Index	
Process Diagrams		Isometric Drawing	
Statistical Diagrams		Structure Diagram	
Screen Shots		Encoding	
Mapping		Lyrics	

[Overview]

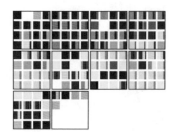

[Situtation 1: pp. 1—16]

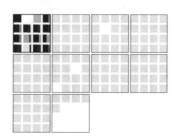

ALLE(S) UNTER EINEM DACH

FAMILIENBETRIEBE IN WILHELMSBURG

...er Thess
... Design / HCU
... Benz
...kultur: 30216/09
... 2013

INHALT

1. EINLEITUNG

2. DARLEGUNG DES FORSCHUNGSGEGENSTANDS

Grounded Theory

ZUWANDERUNG AUF DIE ELBINSEL – EIN GESCHICHTLICHER RÜCKBLICK

Geschichte zum Thema

AN INDIVIDUAL MOTIVE

She describes two motives for choosing her thesis topic in Urban Design. First, her interest in the examination of working models, or the relationship between working and living, was already manifested in her previous study of sociology (bachelor's thesis: *The Entreployee and Their Networks*, 2008). Second, the topic is socially relevant to her from previous field visits and medial presence: "When Mom-and-pop Shops Turn into Kebab Shops" (cf. Smechowski 2011; 4). With access to the field made possible by previous research stays in Wilhelmsburg, she hoped to get settled in the field and to establish contacts that would be valuable to her research.

SITUATION 2

For Lene Benz, the subject of family businesses required not only the development of theoretical knowledge about small-scale ethnic economies and the role of the family in them, but also close and trusting contact within the field.
By working out the history of immigration in Wilhelmsburg, the families' origins, and current statistical data on demographics, she establishes a link to the location and the topic's relevance. In doing so, she again addresses the relationship between living and working in individual eras and waves of immigration.
Academically, she draws in particular upon Felicitas Hillmann (*Urbane Marginalität*), Erol Yildiz (*Urban Recycling*, 2009), and Mark Terkessidis (*Interkultur*).

[Situtation 2: pp. 1–24]

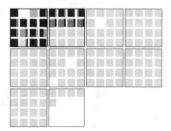

Lene Benz: Everyone (and Everything) under One Roof

STATISTISCHE ERFASSUNG ETHNISCHER ÖKONOMIEN IN HAMBURG

DIE ROLLE DER FAMILIEN IN UNTERSCHIEDLICHEN KONTEXTEN

> „So furchtbar und abscheulich nun
> die Auflösung der alten Fami-
> lienwesen innerhalb des kapi-
> talistischen Systems erscheint,
> so schafft nichtsdestoweniger
> die große Industrie mit der
> entscheidenden Rolle, die
> den Frauen, jungen Personen
> und Kindern beiderlei Ge-
> schlechts in gesellschaftlich
> organisierten Produktions-
> prozessen jenseits der Sphäre
> des Hauswesens zuweist, die
> neue ökonomische Grundla-
> ge für eine höhere Form der
> Familie und des Verhältnisses
> beider Geschlechter."

Karl Marx

Hannah Arendt 2011

SITUATION 3

As a third theoretical basis, Lene Benz develops an understanding
of the function and role of families in family businesses.
Throughout this process, the role of the network becomes apparent
and individual family structures are presented, such as those of
the ancient world and the modern age, as well as the "whole house"
family structure of the eighteenth century (p. 27). She attempts
to use the latter model to answer the question posed in her
research. "Sociologist Trutz von Trotha explains that in the
so-called 'whole house' of the pre- and early modern world, the
house, the farm, the succession of generations, the permanence of
the paternal name, securing the source of livelihood and the protection of the family and relatives were at the heart of a family
(von Trotha 2008: 1; 25). Derived from this is the origin of the
household, which has shaped later economic systems." (p. 25).
In order to define the term "ethnic economy" for this work, Lene
Benz uses academic texts from previous research by Schuleri-Hartje
et al. 2005, who observe the term from three perspectives: the
niche model, the culture model, and the response model. Apart from
this, she also uses her own material. By applying empirical and
theoretical content to the definition of the term, she manages to
give her readers an understanding of the term in relation to her
research. She is able to compare information collected empirically
to the theory and thus distill the image.

[Situtation 3: pp. 25—64]

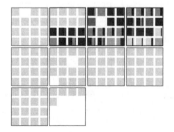

Lene Benz: Everyone (and Everything) under One Roof

Terkessidis 2010

Haußermann + Siebel 2004
Familie und Stadt

6. DIE ETHNISCHE ÖKONOMIEN AM BEISPIEL DER FAMILIENBETRIEBE IN WILHELMSBURG

Schuleri-Hartje

ethnische Ökonomien

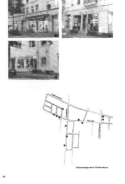

SITUATION 4

Only after establishing a better theoretical understanding of
ethnic economies, the associated role of the family, and initial
access to the field, does she formulate her research question.
"In the process, the principle of openness developed by Uwe Flick
is to be applied (Flick 2006: 477; 56). To Flick, openness means
to be guided by the questions and hypotheses, but not to cling to
them." (p. 56).

RESEARCH QUESTION

In what ways do working and living influence each other in family
businesses?
Questions for analysis (p. 56):
• What conception of public and private can be discerned in the
  families?
• How is that which is private (living) practiced in the public
  sphere (work)?
• How is living accommodated at work in family businesses?

What role do networks play in family businesses?
Questions for analysis (p. 56):
• What types of networks are there?
• How and why are they developed?
• How far do they extend?

The questions are based on the following assumptions (p. 56):
• The family business is divided into pockets of "private" and
  "public."
• As independent organizational forms, family and work organize
  each other. (Family structures have to adapt to the business and
  are thus also rationalized.)
• The business is the family's home. It serves as a meeting place
  and central point for family, friends, and others.

[Situtation 4: pp. 49—80]

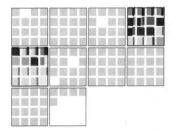

Lene Benz: Everyone (and Everything) under One Roof

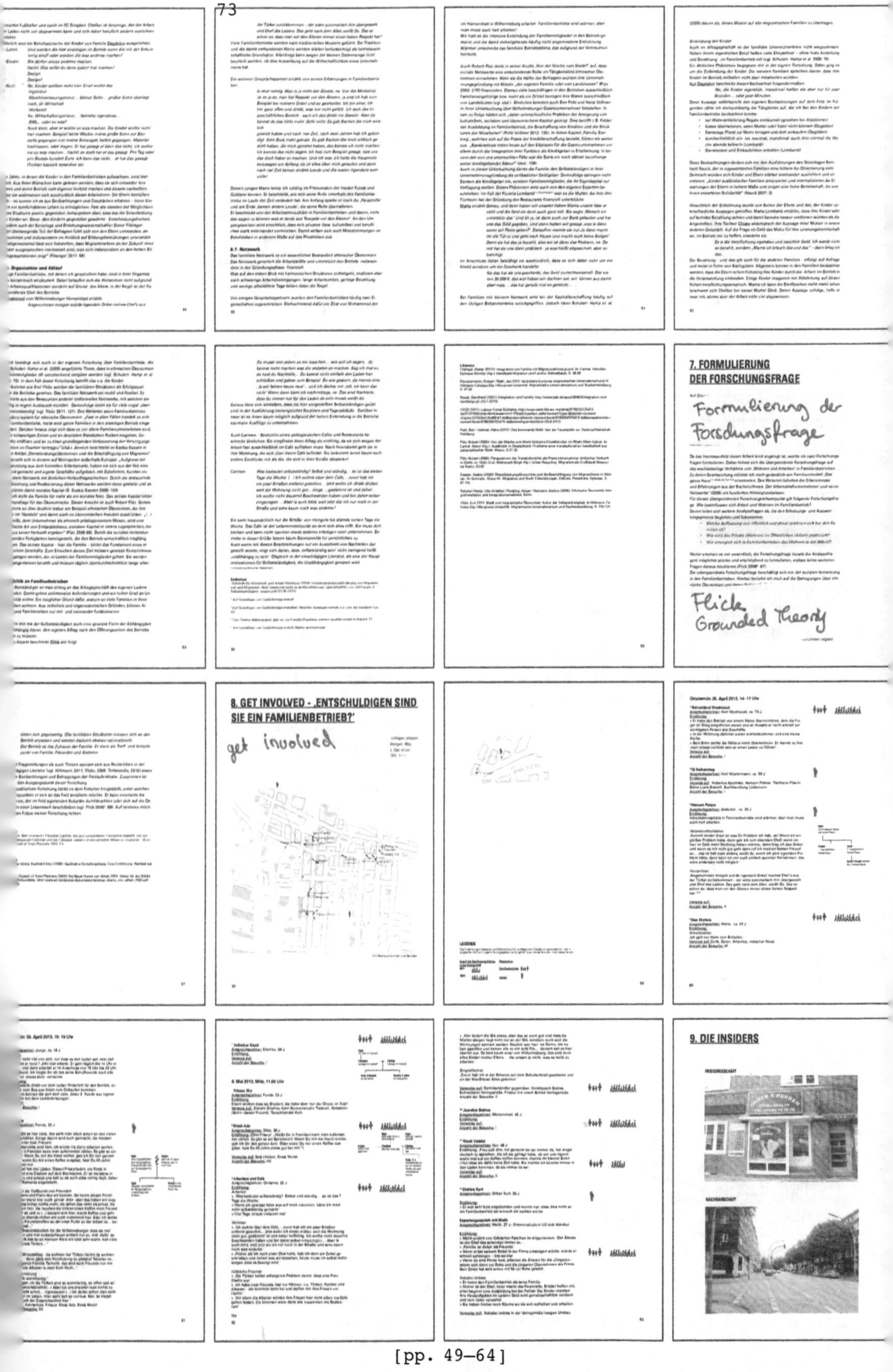

7. FORMULIERUNG DER FORSCHUNGSFRAGE

Formulierung der Forschungsfrage

Flick
Grounded Theory

8. GET INVOLVED - ‚ENTSCHULDIGEN SIND SIE EIN FAMILIENBETRIEB?'

get involved

9. DIE INSIDERS

GETTING INVOLVED CATALOG

In order to gain initial access to the field, Lene Benz approached
it generally and with a coarse search grid. By combing through
individual retail businesses and restaurants, she hoped to gain a
varied insight and overview of small-scale economies in the area
of research and to make initial contact with potential research
subjects. This moment of "entering the field" is what Benz calls
"getting involved." She would start a conversation with the simple
question, "Excuse me. Are you a family business?" By referring
respondents to other businesses or actors, she gained access to
information that she needed in order to get acquainted with and
select family businesses for her case studies. The search grid was
then refined before businesses were selected and examined for those
case studies. Furthermore, she was able to draw upon existing contacts in the district, which she used as insiders for her research
to make contact with other families and to gather initial background information on individual families in the neighborhood.
Lene Benz calls those contacts "gate-openers" (p. 6).

SITUATION 5

As part of her qualitative research, Benz describes the living
environments of three families and their businesses in Wilhelmsburg. In order to trace the families' networks that are relevant to
research, a trusting relationship with the families is required.
She reflects on her options for access and success in the field and
notes that it was easier to engage in a conversation with the women
in the families than with the men (p. 7). In order to build trust
with her counterparts, she prefers heart-to-heart talks to a
guided interview. The daily routines of the actors in the family
businesses are closely tied to their opening hours. Therefore, it
was important to Lene Benz that she know the rhythm of the business
and family and adapt to it in order to successfully conduct conversations and interviews, as well as to accompany the families in
their everyday life.
This is followed by a description of the family's location, premises, and practices. Through open conversations with different
family members, Benz is able to convey the area of tension between
privacy and public family life and to trace the family's networks

[Situtation 5: pp. 65—149]

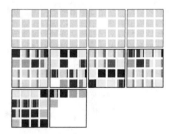

Lene Benz: Everyone (and Everything) under One Roof

N- ARBEITSORTE

...ides Kontakte zum
...d

Güldane Yildiz (22 J.)

Funda Sevci (21 J.)

GESCHICHTE DES LADENS

...E FAMILIENBETRIEBE

...sestudy 1

FAMILIENBETRIEB ATASÖNMEZ

WOHN- ARBEITSORTE

FAMILIE ATASÖNMEZ

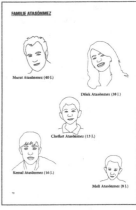

Murat Atasönmez (40 J.)

Dilek Atasönmez (38 J.)

Cherket Atasönmez (13 J.)

Kemal Atasönmez (16 J.)

Meli Atasönmez (8 J.)

...EIBUNG UND ERÖRTERUNG

Familiennetzwerke
Stammbaum

MERK

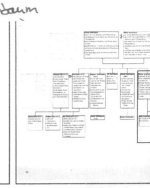

internally, locally, and throughout Europe. She uses collages, renderings of temporal structures on site, and the coding of interview quotes to do this.

By using the genealogy of the three families and their business networks, she is able to demonstrate the interweaving of family and company networks, which are also reflected in the physical acquisition of the shops, the associated apartments, and the family practices.

Consider: The act of living occurs in public. The reason for this is an interweaving of living and working in the business and the adjoining spaces. From this realization, Lene Benz calls for a different understanding of privacy and its necessities as a logical consequence. This became particularly clear to her through close observations that illustrate the need for synchronized family and business activities. "A demarcation between private and public spheres becomes redundant as the families, due to their lifestyle, spend the majority of their days in their business. Due to long opening hours, the place of residence is relocated to the business." (p. 143)

Lene Benz finds that oftentimes, the familial and social environment of the family businesses she studied follow similar lifestyles. They form a web of small-scale ethnic economies and family businesses that extends beyond the street, city-wide and internationally.

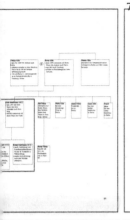

BESCHREIBUNG LADEN

FAMILIÄRES BETRIEBSNETZWERK

Betriebsnetzwerk Familie

VERORTETES BETRIEBSNETZWERK

HAMBURG

BERLIN

ALLES UNTER EINEM DACH

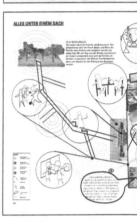

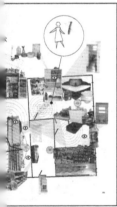

ZIRKULATIONEN

AUSSEN   INNEN   WOHNUNG

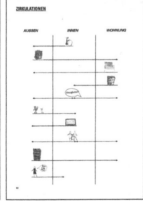

FLUKTUATION IM BETRIEB

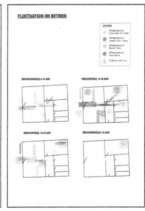

GESCHICHTEN DER STRASSE

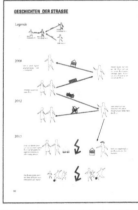

Casestudy 2

FAMILIENBETRIEB DAGDALEN

WOHN- ARBEITSORTE

FAMILIE DAGDALEN

Birol Dagdalen (45 J.)

Nur Dagdalen (40 J.)

Ibo Dagdalen (12 J.)

Altan Dagdalen (16 J.)

Eivan Dagdalen (10 J.)

[pp. 81—96]

BESCHREIBUNG UND ERÖRTERUNG

FAMILIÄRES NETZWERK

BESCHREIBUNG LADEN

FAMILIÄRES BETRIEBSNETZWERK

ALLES UNTER EINEM DACH

[pp. 97–112]

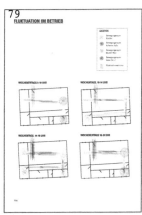
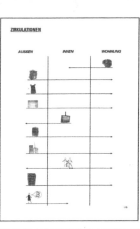
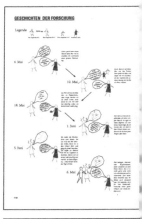

FLUKTUATION IM BETRIEB

ZIRKULATIONEN

AUSSEN INNEN WOHNUNG

GESCHICHTEN DER FORSCHUNG

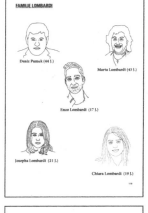

case study 3

WOHN-ARBEITSORTE

FAMILIE LOMBARDI

Deniz Pumuk (44 J.)

Marta Lombardi (43 J.)

Enzo Lombardi (17 J.)

Josepha Lombardi (21 J.)

Chiara Lombardi (19 J.)

BESCHREIBUNG UND ERÖRTERUNG

FAMILIÄRES NETZWERK

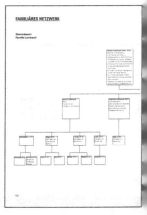

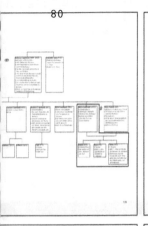

FAMILIÄRES BETRIEBSNETZWERK

Einbindung in den familieneigenen Betrieb

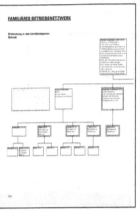

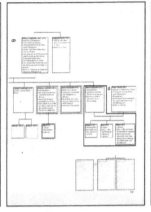

BESCHREIBUNG LADEN

VERORTETES FAMILIENNETZWERK

HAMBURG

ALLES UNTER EINEM DACH

CHIARA'S MENTAL MAP

FLUKTUATION IM BETRIEB

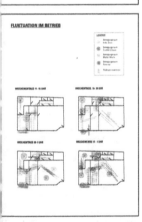

11. ORTE DER FAMILIEN

WOHN- UND ARBEITSORTE

HERKUNFTSORTE

HAMBURG-WILHELMSBURG

europäisches
Netzwerk der
Familien

ITALIEN

12. REFLEKTION

Reflektion als
Fazit

Die Heimatsehnsucht als notwendiges Mittel

Abbildung von Heimaturlaube

13. LITERATUR

ZOOM-INS

Lene Benz begins her work by examining family-run ethnic small-
scale economies. On a theoretical and partly empirical basis, she
develops a basic understanding of these kinds of economies, the
role of the family in different eras (especially in family businesses), and the history of the district examined. In doing so, she
is guided by research from her original discipline, sociology.
What is remarkable about her work is her understanding of
accessing the field and her own role in it as a researcher (1).
Thus, she considers participatory observation and her field stay to
be a process of interaction, as Rolf Lindner describes it in *Die
Angst des Forschers vor dem Feld*: every human and social-scientific
study is a specific form of social interaction. This is especially
true of field research (Lindner 1981: 51). By, as she puts it, "getting involved," Lene Benz tries to bring herself into the conversation in order to obtain referrals to other family businesses.
She presents this process of getting involved in the form of mapping and protocol to make access to the field comprehensible (2).
Moreover, she is able to fall back on previously established contacts and insiders (3). Through inclusion and commitment to the
field and the individual requirements posed by the actors, she is
able to gain adequate insight into the family life of her case
studies, while also being able to produce a complex, multifaceted,
and descriptive image of the families' living environments. Examples of this are the family trees and family business networks,
which include information on each family member going back three
generations (4).
Beyond the family trees and business networks, she notices these
structures in the families' environments. She is able to reveal
entire networks of family businesses and small-scale economies:
within the same street, the city, and even the world (5). This
gives an indication that migration is not a process that is eventually completed. The connections people have to places in various
countries may change over time, but they are still passed on to
subsequent generations.
The question can be raised as to what importance these international networks and this model of work will have in the future, and
how they can be used as a resource in questions of migratory movements in urban areas.

Lene Benz: Everyone (and Everything) under One Roof

. DARLEGUNG DES ORSCHUNGSGEGENSTANDS

s ist der Forschungsgegenstand?[1]
jenstand der Forschung ist der Familienbetrieb. Dabei steht wechselseitige Verhältnis von ‚Wohnen und Arbeiten', vie die Einbindung des familiären Netzwerks in den Betrie- im Fokus der Untersuchung. Mit ‚Familienbetriebe' sind roökonomien gemeint, welche höchstens fünf bis sieben arbeiter beschäftigen und mindestens zur Hälfte aus Fami- angehörigen bestehen. Aufgrund des Untersuchungsortes t ein weiterer Forschungsschwerpunkt auf Familienbetrie- , die als ethnische Ökonomien (-> ethnische Ökonomien) bezeichnet den können.

ist das Forschungsfeld?
qualitative Feldforschung fand im Reiherstiegviertel in ıelmsburg und auf der Veddel – zwei Stadtteilen auf der ıburger Elbinsel – statt. Diese Orte waren mir bereits aus usgegangenen Forschungsprojekten in Urban Design annt und somit konnte ich auf bereits etablierte Kontakte schen den KommilitonInnen und den Akteuren des Un- uchungsfeldes zurückgreifen. Die Kontakte fungierten im men der Forschung als sogenannte ´Gate-opener´ und chterten mir den Einstieg in das Feld. Dabei erwies es sich als große Hilfe, das Vertrauen der Familien zu gewinnen, auf diese Weise einen adäquaten Einblick in deren Ar- s- und Privatleben erhalten zu können. Aufgrund der His- (-> geschichtlicher Rückblick) und Sozialstruktur Wilhelmsburgs und Veddel (-> Statistische Erfassung) weisen viele der Familienbetriebe n migrantischen Hintergrund auf, was als ein weiterer Un- chungsparameter in die Forschung einfloss.

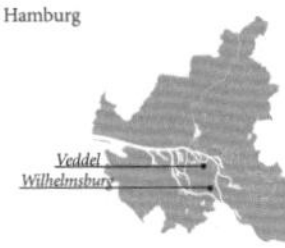
Hamburg
Veddel
Wilhelmsburg

n und wie lange fand die Forschung statt?
rsten Recherchen zu der vorliegenden Arbeit begannen lärz 2013. Der Zeitraum des Aufenthalts im Feld belief sich ie darauffolgenden Monate April bis Juni 2013. Seit Juni ıde ich mich in der Phase der Auswertung und Analyse, n August dieses Jahres abgeschlossen wurde. Der Visua- ungsprozess vollzog sich kontinuierlich parallel zur Erhe- und Auswertung.

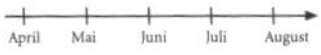
April
Mai
Juni
Juli
August

Was ist das Erkenntnisinteresse?
Ethnische Ökonomien haben mittlerweile in vielen Städten und Metropolen eine bedeutende Rolle eingenommen (vgl. Hillmann 2011). Dennoch ist die Thematik ethnische Ökonomien, insbesondere mit dem Fokus auf Familienbetriebe, noch relativ unerforscht. Die dazu verfügbaren Forschungsarbeiten und Literatur sind im Laufe der letzten zehn bis fünfzehn Jahre entstanden (vgl. Hillmann 2011; Yildiz, Mattausch 2009; Floeting et al. 2005; Pütz 2004). Damit reiht sich diese Arbeit in ein relativ junges Forschungsfeld ein, in dem gezwungenermaßen manche ‚Wissenslücken' offen bleiben. Gleichwohl konnten Überlegungen aus vorherigen Forschungsarbeiten aufgegriffen und in diesem Kontext geprüft werden. Kleinere, untergeordnete Forschungsfelder – wie hier der Familienbetrieb – konnten somit deskriptiv und explorativ erörtert werden. Ausführliche Angaben statistischer Daten folgen unter Punkt drei dieses Kapitels (-> Statistische Erfassung).

Wie groß ist die die Stichprobe? Wer sind die Akteure?
Während des gesamten Forschungsaufenthalts wurden 13 Betriebe aufgesucht und befragt. Dabei handelte es sich nicht ausschließlich um Familienbetriebe, da ich mich dem Feld zunächst allgemein angenähert habe(-> Get Involved). Im weiteren Verlauf konzentrierte ich mich auf die Erforschung von drei Familienbetrieben. Einer davon hat sich mittlerweile in zwei Betriebe unterteilt (-> Familie Atasönmez.).
Die befragten Familien entstammen der zweiten bzw. dritten Generation ehemaliger Gastarbeiter aus der Türkei und Italien. Sie sind entweder in Wilhelmsburg geboren oder in jungen Jahren zugezogen. Familie Dagdalen, Familie Atasönmez und Familie Lombardi haben je drei Kinder im Alter zwischen acht und 21 Jahre. Mir fiel es leichter, einen Zugang zu Frauen, als zu Männern zu gewinnen, sodass die meisten Gespräche mit den Müttern und teilweise mit den Kindern der Familien geführt wurden. Gespräche mit den Vätern kamen nicht zustande.

In welches Forschungsfeld ordnet sich die Arbeit ein?
Die Arbeit knüpft an den aktuellen Forschungsdiskurs zu ethnischen Ökonomien an. Dabei habe ich mich entschieden, mich primär auf die Literatur von Felicitas Hillmann (Urbane Marginalität, 2011) und Erol Yildiz (Urban Recycling, 2009) zu stützen. Das Buch ‚Interkultur' von Mark Terkessidis (2010) stellte eine weitere adäquate Quelle dar. Darin befasst sich Terkessidis im Zuge einer zeitbezogenen Auseinandersetzung mit dem aktuellen Diskurs von Integration und Migration. Darüber hinaus lieferte die Masterthesis ‚Das kommende Mahl' von

Interkultur
Marginale Urbanität
DAS KOMMENDE MAHL

Pohl und Hans Vollmer – aufgrund eines vergleichbaren :hungssettings und -interesses – Anregungen und Ideen en eigenen Forschungsprozess.

:he Forschungspraktiken wurden angewendet?
Forschungsfeld näherte ich mich unter Anwendung schiedlicher Methoden. Eine Methode war die Praktik 'erweisens(-> Get Involved), mit der ich mir zu Beginn das For- ıgsfeld erschloss. Die zentrale Erhebungs- und Auswer- smethode stellte die Grounded Theory (vgl. z.B. Strauss Oertzen 2006) dar. Sie wurde nicht konsequent, aber in :zen angewendet. Im Vordergrund der Forschungsphase das Kodierparadigma, in welchem Datensammlung und /se ineinander verschränkt werden. So konnten bspw. en direkt überprüft und auf neue interessante Aspekte ıh reagiert werden. Nach Jürgen Oertzen bildet dieser ıng einen triadischen Prozess zwischen Datenerhebung, ren und dem Schreiben von Memos (vgl. Oertzen 2006). 'und der kleinen Stichprobe konnte in dieser Forschung Theorie entwickelt werden. Dennoch sollen gewinnbrin- e Hypothesen und Erkenntnisse auf dem Forschungsfeld scher Ökonomien - mit dem Fokus auf Familienbetriebe eriert werden. Demnach erörtert die vorliegende Arbeit ıit empirischen Methoden, explorativ erhobene Material, er deskriptiven Beschreibung.

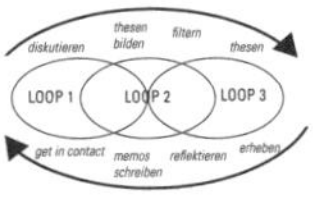
diskutieren
thesen bilden
filtern
thesen
LOOP 1
LOOP 2
LOOP 3
get in contact
memos schreiben
reflektieren
erheben

'äch vs. Interview
rste wichtige Erfahrung machte ich bei der Zeitplanung es? Forschungsfeld/es, da ich mich den Menschen und Tempi, Routinen und Tagesabläufen anpassen musste. n ersten Erfahrungen dieser Untersuchung zählte, mich 'orschunsfeld sowie den Menschen und deren Tempo, ıen und Tagesabläufen anzupassen. Auf die Frage, wann Betrieb zum Interview vorbeikommen könne, wurde sätzlich geantwortet: „Immer, ich bin immer hier." Dies tete, dass die Interviews im Feld während der Arbeit ıden mussten; in Anwesenheit von Kunden, Lieferanten, den, Bekannten und der Familie. In der Folge entwickel- :h daraus offene Interviews bzw. Gespräche, sodass auf enbasierte Interviews größtenteils verzichtet wurde. Das ew steht in wissenschaftlichen Arbeiten für eine signifi- Gesprächsform mit festgesetztem Regelwerk (vgl. Flick/ 2006[4]). Diese konnten in dieser strengen Form in der jenden Arbeit nicht eingesetzt werden. Um eine gemein- und offene Gesprächsebene entstehen lassen zu kön- vurden die Gesprächssituationen individuell gestaltet. 'enen Interviews bzw. Gespräche dauerten unterschied-

lich lange. Es wurden darin verschiedene Bereiche thematisiert, wie z.B. die Tagesabläufe und Verantwortlichkeitsbereiche der Familienmitglieder im Betrieb mit Ausnahme von den Gesprächen in der letzten Erhebungswoche, in denen Thesen überprüft und standardisierte Fragen gestellt wurden, sodass sich diese als Interviews bezeichnen lassen können.

Collage
Die Collage diente mir als Arbeitswerkzeug, um einen Überblick über die erhobenen Daten und Erkenntnisse zu erlangen. Durch das Verorten im Grundriss begann ich das Datenmaterial zu gliedern. Die Collage bildet u.a. Handlungsstrategien der Familien sowie Gegenstände und Mobiliar der Betriebe ab. Dafür verwendete ich unterschiedliche Materialien wie Fotografien, Beschreibungen, O-Töne der Familien, Notizen, Zeichnungen etc.[2]

Endnoten
[1] Diese und folgende Fragestellungen beziehen sich auf Andreas Böhm (Theoretisches Codieren. Textanalyse in der Grounded Theory, 2007)

[2] Neben den eben genannten Methoden wendete ich zusätzlich die Kartierung, Fotografie und teilnehmende Beobachtung als Untersuchungsmethoden an. Auf diese werde ich in der MTT7 -Abgabe ausführlicher eingehen.

Literatur
Böhm, Andreas (2007): Theoretisches Codieren. Textanalyse in der Grounded Theory, ORT, S. 483

Flick, Uwe/ König, Burkhard (Hg.) (2006): Qualitative Sozialforschung. Eine Einführung. Reinbek bei Hamburg.

Oertzen, Jürgen (2006): Grounded Theory, in: Behnke et al (Hg.), Methoden der Politikwissenschaft. Neuere qualitative und quantitative Analyseverfahren, Baden-Baden, S. 145-154

Strauss, Anselm L. (1994): Grundlagen qualitativer Sozialforschung. Datenanalyse und Theoriebildung in der empirischen soziologischen Forschung, München

8. GET INVOLVED - ‚ENTSCHULDIGEN SIND SIE EIN FAMILIENBETRIEB?'

„Wir fangen etwas an; wir schlagen unseren Faden in ein Netz der Beziehungen. Was daraus wird, wissen wir nie. Das ist ein Wagnis." (Arendt / Gaus 1964: 31 f.)

Ein Netz aus Familien und Betriebe

LEGENDE

Die Erzählungen basieren größtenteils auf Grundlage von Gedächtnisprotokollen, die in doppelten Anführungstriche angegeben sind, gehen aus transkribierten Interviews hervor.

Anteil der Familienangehörige in der Belegschaft
50%
100%

Personalien
Familienbetriebe
Insider

58

Ortstermin: 25. April 2013, 14- 17 Uhr

¹ Schneiderei Wodniczak
Ansprechpartner: Herr Wodniczak, ca. 70 J.
Erzählung:
> Er hatte den Betrieb von einem Mann übernommen, dem die Finger im Krieg eingefroren waren und so musste er recht schnell zur wichtigsten Person des Geschäfts.
> In der Wohnung dahinter waren Ankleidezimmer und eine kleine Küche.
> Sein Sohn wollte die Näherei nicht übernehmen. Er meinte zu ihm ‚man müsse verrückt sein so einen Laden zu führen'.
Verweis auf: -
Anzahl der Besuche: I

² IG Reiherstieg
Ansprechpartner: Herr Wüstermann, ca. 50 J
Erzählung: -
Verweis auf: Hubertus Apotheke, Hamam Palace, Tischlerei Pöschl, Salon Lucia Scarelli, Buchhandlung Lüdemann
Anzahl der Besuche: I

³ Hamam Palace
Ansprechpartner: Abdullah, ca. 30 J.
Erzählung:
Arbeitsatmosphäre sind Familienbetriebe sind wärmer, aber man muss auch hart arbeiten.

Verantwortlichkeiten
‚Kommt immer drauf an was für Problem ich hab, ne! Wenn ich ein großes Problem habe, dann geh ich zum obersten Chef; wenn ich hier im Café mehr Werbung haben möchte, dann frag ich den Onkel; und wenn es mir nicht gut geht dann ruf ich meinen besten Freund an.... das ist halt auch anders, weißt du, wenn ich jetzt irgendein Problem hätte, dann kann ich mir auch einfach spontan freinehmen- das wäre anderswo nicht möglich.'

Hierarchien
‚Angenommen morgen würde irgendein Onkel meines Chef's aus der Türkei zurückkommen – der wäre automatisch ihm übergestellt und Chef des Ladens. Das geht nach dem Alter, weißt Du. Das ist schon so, dass man vor den Älteren immer einen hohen Respekt hat.'**

Verweis auf: -
Anzahl der Besuche: II

⁴ Don Matteo
Ansprechpartner: Marta, ca. 40 J.
Erzählung:
Arbeitszeiten
‚Ich geh nur Heim zum Schlafen.'
Verweis auf: Zonk, Baron, Atlantico, indischer Kiosk
Anzahl der Besuche: IIII

Vater
Chef Goktwaren Bektas
und Hamam Palace

Bruder
1. Geschäftsführer
HamamPalace

Sohn
2. Geschäftsführer
HamamPalace

bester Freund Abdullah
Ber HamamPalace

Ortstermin: 30. April 2013, 15- 19 Uhr

⁵ Bäckerei
Ansprechpartner: Junge, ca. 16 J.
Erzählung:
Er erzählte nicht viel von sich, nur dass es den Laden seit zwei Jahren gibt und er rund 1 Jahr hier arbeite. Er geht täglich bis 14 Uhr in die Schule und dann arbeitet er im Anschluss von 15 Uhr bis 20 Uhr in der Bäckerei. Ich fragte ihn ob das seine Schulfreunde auch alle täten was er - etwas stolz- verneinte.
Beobachtung:
> Bushaltestelle direkt vor dem Laden förderlich für den Betrieb, da viele Leute vom Bus aus direkt zum Einkaufen kommen.
> Außerdem kennen die sich dort viele. Jeder 2. Kunde war irgendwie bekannt mit dem Verkäuferjungen.
Verweis auf: -
Anzahl der Besuche: I

⁶ Friseur Ilka
Ansprechpartner: Funda, 23 J.
Erzählung:
> Frauen gibt es hier viele, das sieht man allein schon an den vielen Friseurgeschäften. Einige davon sind auch gemischt, die meisten nur für Männer bzw. Frauen).
> ‚Familienbetriebe sind hart, ich würde nie darin arbeiten wollen.'
> Weißt Du in Familien kann man aufeinander zählen. Es gibt so ein Sprichwort: Wenn Du mir die Hand reichst, geb ich Dir den ganzen Arm. Oder wenn Du mir eine Kaffee ausgibst, hast Du 40 Jahre etwas gut bei mir.
> Unser Chef hat drei Läden: Diesen Friseurladen, ein Kiosk in Harburg und eine Eisdiele auf dem Steindamm. Er ist meistens in seinem Büro und schaut uns halt so ob alles richtig läuft, daher sind hier 4 Kameras angebracht.

Arbeitsplatz als Treffpunkt von Freunden
> ‚Jeder Hans und Franz den wir kennen, der kennt diesen Privatraum. Früher stand hier auch ‚privat' dran -aber das haben wir weggemacht, das bringt nichts mehr, die einen sehen das nicht als privat, die kommen hier rein, die rauchen die trinken einen Kaffee mein Freund kommt mal ab und zu (...) bedient sich hier halt, macht Kaffee und geht zur Arbeit so abends chillen wir auch manchmal hier. Also ich denke schon, dass Freundetreffen so der erste Punkt an der Arbeit ist,... bei uns zumindest..."
> „Es ist selbstverständlich für die Wilhelmsburger, dass sie mal reinkommen und mal vorbeischauen einfach nur so, mal ‚Hallo' sagen. Ich merk das so an meinem Kreis wir sind sehr warm, halt viele Südländer viele Türken,..."

Kulti Multi
> „WilhelmStraussWeg - da wohnen viele Türken (lacht) da wohnen nur Türken... dann gibts den Korallusring da gibtsnur Italiener ne,... das ist die ganze Familie Tschulla- das sind auch Freunde von mir und ganz viele Albaner is zwar Kulti Multi..."

Kulturzuschreibung
> „Es ist halt warmherzig."
> „Viele sagen ‚oh die Türken sind so warmherzig, so offen und so'. Das ist selbstverständlich (...) Aber bei uns erwartet man nichts zurück, also nicht sofort,... irgendwann (...) ich denke schon man sieht sich zweimal im Leben, man sieht halt so voraus. Klar, so klappt dann halt auch der Zusammenhalt hier."
Verweis auf: Fahrschule, Friseur, Kiosk Ada, Kiosk Murat
Anzahl der Besuche: IIII

Vater
stiller Geschäftsführer
einer Reinigungsfirma.
(Überschrieb den Sohn
aus Steuergründen der
Fema)

Mutter
putzt seit 29 Jahren
teilweise auch für
ihren Sohn

Sohn
offizieller Geschäftsführer Reinigungsfirma
(Ausbildung zum
Erzieher)

Tochter Funda
(Auszubildende
Friseur Ilka)

60

s Weiteren standen mir zwei ‚Insider' zur Seite. Im Rückblick betrachtet spielen ‚Insider' der Erforschung von Familienbetriebe eine wesentliche Rolle. Das Netz der Familienbe-ebe ist so dicht geknüpft, dass es ‚Insider' braucht, die mit den Familien und deren Ge-ichten vertraut und dennoch distanziert davon sind, da sie keine Angehörige sind. Die In-erinnen Funda und Güldane halfen mir dabei, in kurzer Zeit Einblicke in das Arbeits- und milienleben der Familienbetriebe zu gewinnen, indem sie einerseits Kontakte herstellten 1 andererseits Hintergrundgeschichten über die Familien lieferten.

„Das ist halt auch so bei uns dass der Laden nicht nur ein Geschäft ist sondern halt auch ein Raum. Ein Eigen-tum auch,... und dem alles gemacht wird. In mach alles hier. Ich bekomm hier mehr Besuch als Zuhause. Wir schließen meistens den Laden ab, räumen auf und machen sauber und dann setzten wir uns noch nach hinten und chillen 2-3 Stunden. Vorne machen wir aber dunkel, dass uns hinten keiner sieht."

„Viele machen das immer so, sagen wir mal sie haben 6 Wochen Urlaub, dann gehen sie 2 Wochen Strandurlaub und den Rest gehen sie in die Heimat der Familie."

„Also in Familienbetrieben muss man sich aufeinander verlassen können... also es kommt auch auf den Menschen an, aber wenn ich und mein Bruder ein Betrieb aufmachen, muss ich mich auf ihn verlassen können und er sich auf mich anders geht das gar nicht. Es ist was anders wenn du was anders geht von deiner eigenen Schwester und deinem eigenen Bruder. Das ist schon hart - passiert aber oft weil, umso mehr Geld dazwischenkommt, umso mehr Probleme."

dane Yildim (22 J.)

ort:	Wilhelmsburg, Reiherstiegviertel
:	Mohammed (56J.), Autoingenieur Fatma (50J.), Hausfrau und Mutter
wister:	Cem (25J.), Bankkaufmann
:	ausgebildete Friseurin
it:	muss fast täglich im Laden stehen, da sie die einzige Ausgebildete Fachkraft ist. Daher hat sie meistens nur am Sonntag frei, den sie gern mit Freunden und ihrer Bestern Freundin Funda verbringt

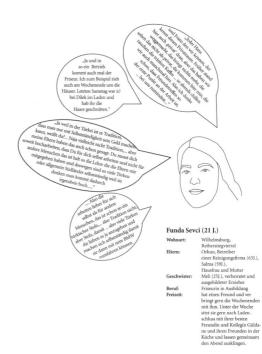

„Ja und in so ein Betrieb kommt auch mal der Friseur. Ich zum Beispiel zieh auch am Wochenende um die Häuser. Letzten Samstag war ic! bei Dilek im Laden und hab ihr die Haare geschnitten."

„Ja weil in der Türkei ist es Tradition, dass man nur mit Selbstständigkeit sein Geld machen kann, weißt du?... Naja vielleicht nicht Tradition,... aber meine Eltern haben das auch schon gesagt: Du musst dich soweit hocharbeiten, dass Du für dich selbst arbeiten und nicht für andere Mensch... weil so ist halt es die die Lehre die die Türken mir mitgegeben haben und deswegen sind so viele Türken oder allgemein Südländer selbstständig weil sie denken man kommt dadurch irgendwie hoch..."

„... Also die arbeiten lieber für sich selbst als für andere Menschen, das ist schon so ein türkisches Stolz... also Tradition nicht, aber vielleicht z. B.,... also viele Türken die lieber, als jemand der außtgeben und natürlich damit machen sich selbstständig damit sie dann mit dem BMW rumfahren können."

„Ich kenn diesen Privatraum, der und Frau Irmen, der weggemacht das heißt sie hat hier auch privat die Bücksitzs auch sehen sie nicht als Privat haben wir machen die trinken auffe... wir auch manchmal hier, so schon, dass Freundestreffen so rein, de: erste Funda an der Arbeit ist, - bei uns zusammne."

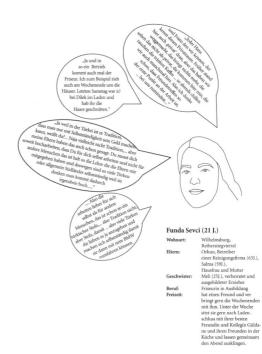

Funda Sevci (21 J.)

Wohnort:	Wilhelmsburg, Reiherstiegviertel
Eltern:	Orkun, Betreiber einer Reinigungsfirma (63J.), Salma (59J.), Hausfrau und Mutter
Geschwister:	Meli (25J.), verheiratet und ausgebildeter Erzieher
Beruf:	Friseurin in Ausbildung
Freizeit:	hat einen Freund und ver bringt gern die Wochenenden mit ihm. Unter der Woche sitzt sie gern nach Laden-schluss mit ihrer besten Freundin und Kollegin Gülda-ne und ihren Freunden in der Küche und lassen gemeinsam den Abend ausklingen.

MILIÄRES NETZWERK

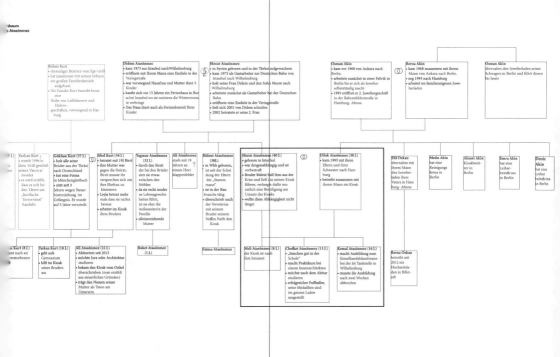

[pp. 66–67, 80–81]

FAMILIÄRES BETRIEBSNETZWERK

Übersicht aller Familienbetriebe
Familie Atasönmez

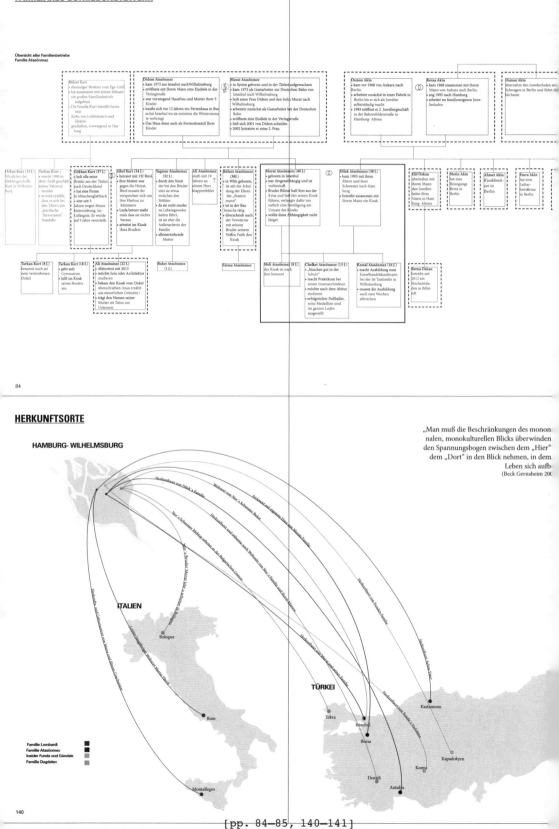

Bülent Kurt
- ehemaliger Besitzer von Ege-Grill hat zusammen mit seinen Söhnen ein großen Grill-Familienbetrieb aufgebaut.
- Die Familie Kurt betreibt heute eine Reihe von Leihhäusern und Elektrogeschäften, vorwiegend in Harburg

Didem Atasönmez
- kam 1973 aus Istanbul nach Wilhelmsburg
- eröffnete mit ihrem Mann eine Eisdiele in der Veringstraße
- war vorwiegend Hausfrau und Mutter ihrer 5 Kinder
- kaufte sich vor 13 Jahren ein Ferienhaus in Bur... wo sie meistens die Wintermonate verbringt
- Das Haus dient auch als Feriendomizil Ihrer Kinder

Mesut Atasönmez
- in Syrien geboren und in der Türkei aufgewachsen
- kam 1973 als Gastarbeiter zur Deutschen Bahn von Istanbul nach Wilhelmsburg
- holt seine Frau Didem und den Sohn Murat nach Wilhelmsburg
- arbeitete zunächst als Gastarbeiter bei der Deutschen Bahn
- eröffnete eine Eisdiele in der Veringstraße
- ließ sich 2001 von Didem scheiden
- 2002 heiratete er seine 2. Frau

Osman Akin
- kam vor 1968 von Ankara nach Berlin.
- arbeitete zunächst in einer Fabrik in Berlin bis er sich als Juwelier selbstständig macht
- 1993 eröffnet er 2. Juweliergeschäft in der Bahrenfelderstraße in Hamburg- Altona

Berna Akin
- kam 1968 zusammen mit ihrem Mann von Ankara nach Berlin.
- zog 1993 nach Hamburg
- arbeitet im familieneigenen Juwelierladen

Osman Akin
- übernahm den Juwelierladen sei... Schwagers in Berlin und führt d... bis ins heute

Orkan Kurt (35 J.)
Filialleiter des Elektrogeschäfts Kurt in Wilhelmsburg

Tarkan Kurt †
- wurde 1996 in dem Grill-geschäft seines Vaters ermordet
- es wird erzählt, dass es sich bei den Tätern um „kurdische Terroristen" handele

Gökhan Kurt (37 J.)
- holt alle seine Brüder aus der Türkei nach Deutschland
- hat eine Firma in Mönchengladbach
- sitzt seit 3 Jahren wegen Steuerhinterziehung im Gefängnis. Er wurde auf 5 Jahre verurteilt.

Sibel Kurt (34 J.)
- heiratet mit 19 J Birol ihre Mutter war gegen die Heirat, Birol musste ihr versprechen sich um ihre Ehefrau zu kümmern
- Leyla betont mehr mals dass sie nichts bereue
- arbeitet im Kiosk ihres Bruders

Yagmur Atasönmez (32 J.)
- durch den Streit der bei den Brüder sitzt sie etwas zwischen den Stühlen
- da sie recht moderne Lebensgewohnheiten führt, ist sie eher die Außenseiterin der Familie
- alleinerziehende Mutter

Ali Atasönmez starb mit 19 Jahren an einem Herzklappenfehler

Bülent Atasönmez (38 J.)
- in Wbb geboren,
- war drogenabhängig und ist seit der Scheidung der Eltern der „Stamm mann"
- ist in der Bau branche tätig
- überschrieb nach der Verwirnis mit seinem Bruder seinem Neffen Fatih den Kiosk

Murat Atasönmez (40 J.)
- geboren in Istanbul
- war drogenabhängig und ist...
- Bruder Bülent half ihm aus der Krise und ließ ihn seinen Kiosk führen, verlangte dafür mo natlich eine Beteiligung am Umsatz des Kiosks
- wollte diese Abhängigkeit nicht länger

Dilek Atasönmez (38 J.)
- kam 1993 mit ihren Eltern und ihrer Schwester nach Hamburg
- betreibt zusammen mit ihrem Mann ein Kiosk

Elif Özkan übernahm mit ihrem Mann den Juwelier-laden ihres Vaters in Hamburg- Altona

Metin Akin hat eine Reinigungsfirma in Berlin

Ahmet Akin Kioskbesitzer in Berlin

Emra Akin hat eine Leiharbeitsfirma in Berlin

Tarkan Kurt (8 J.) benannt nach seinem verstorbenen Onkel

Tarkan Kurt (18 J.) hilft im Kiosk seines Bruders aus

Ali Atasönmez (22 J.)
- Abiturient seit 2013
- möchte Jura oder Architektur studieren
- bekam den Kiosk vom Onkel überschrieben (man erzählt aus steuerlichen Gründen)
- trägt den Namen seiner Mutter als Tatoo am Unterarm

Büket Atasönmez (1 J.)

Fatma Atasönmez

Meli Atasönmez (8 J.) der Kiosk ist nach ihm benannt

Chefket Atasönmez (13 J.)
- „bisschen gut in der Schule"
- macht Praktikum bei einem Innenarchitekten
- möchte nach dem Abitur studieren
- erfolgreicher Fußballer, seine Medaillen sind im ganzen Laden ausgestellt

Kemal Atasönmez (16 J.)
- macht Ausbildung zum Einzelhandelskaufmann bei der le Tankstelle in Wilhelmsburg
- musste die Ausbildung nach zwei Wochen abbrechen

Berna Özkan betreibt seit 2012 ein Hochzeitsladen in Billstedt

HERKUNFTSORTE

HAMBURG- WILHELMSBURG

„Man muß die Beschränkungen des monon... nalen, monokulturellen Blicks überwinden den Spannungsbogen zwischen dem „Hier"... dem „Dort" in den Blick nehmen, in dem... Leben sich aufb... (Beck Gernsheim 200...)

ITALIEN
Bologna
Rom
Montalegro

TÜRKEI
Tekra
Istanbul
Bursa
Denizli
Antalya
Konya
Kapadokyen
Kastamonu

Familie Lombardi
Familie Atasönmez
Insider Funda und Gündale
Familie Dagdelen

3. LITERATUR

ndt, Hannah / Gaus, Günter (1964): Was bleibt? Es ist die Muttersprache. In: Gaus, Günter: Zur Person. Portraits in Fra-
and Antwort. Band I. München, S. 19-32

ndt, Hannah (2011): Vita Activa oder Vom tätigen Leben, München

k, Ulrich; Beck- Gernsheim Elisabeth (1990): Das ganz normale Chaos der Liebe, Frankfurt am Main.

k-Gernsheim, Elisabeth (2004): Wir und die Anderen: Kopftuch, Zwangsheirat und andere Mißverständnisse, Frankfurt
Main

t, Lene (2008): Der Arbeitskraftunternehmer und seine Netzwerke, Konstanz

n, Andreas (2010): Theoretisches Codieren. Textanalyse in der Grounded Theory. In: Reader, Urban Territories I, Ham-
s. S. 392-398

kner, Ingrid (2007): Minderheiten in der Stadtentwicklung. In: Buckow, Wolf-Dietrich / Nikodem, Claudia / Schulze, Erika
fiz, Erol (Hg.): Was heißt hier Parallelgesellschaften?, Wiesbaden, S. 83-92

khaus Verlag (Hg.) (1991[19]): Brockhaus Enzyklopädie in 24 Bänden: Bd. 16, Mannheim, S.140

khaus Verlag (Hg.) (1992[19]): Brockhaus Enzyklopädie in 24 Bänden: Bd. 17, Mannheim, S. 300

, Angela (2008): Fremdarbeiter, Gastarbeiter, Einwanderer – Migration in Geschichte und Gegenwart. In: Geschichts-
statt Wilhelmsburg Honigfabrik e.V., Museum Elbinsel Wilhelmsburg e.V. (Hg): Wilhelmsburg - Hamburgs große Elb-
, Hamburg, S. 97-113

ilpasch, Ralf (2005): Grundwissen Soziologie, Stuttgart.

pean Council of Town Planners (2003): Die Neue Charta von Athen 2003. Vision für die Städte des 21. Jahrhunderts,
/www.srl.de/dateien/dokumente/de/neue_charta_von_athen_2003.pdf (20.8.2013)

Uwe/ König, Burkhard (Hg.) (2006): Qualitative Sozialforschung. Eine Einführung. Reinbek bei Hamburg.

ing, Norbert (2011): Wohnen und Sozialraum. In: Fischer, Veronika / Springer Monika (Hg.): Handbuch Migration und
lie, Schwalbach, S. 48-68

, Max (1965): Überfremdung. In: Gesammelte Werke Bd.V, Frankfurt am Main, S. 374

ing, Max (2011): Wohnen und Sozialraum. In: Fischer, Veronika / Springer Monika (Hg.): Handbuch Migration und
lie, Schwalbach, S. 127-140

schall, Karin / Voß, G. Günther (Hg.) (2003): Entgrenzung von Arbeit und Leben. Zum Wandel der Beziehungen von Er-
stätigkeit und Privatsphäre im Alltag, München und Mehring

Irene (2005): Familienkultur im Wandel – Perspektiven einer europäischen Ethnologie, http://www.eundc.de/
0006.pdf (02.08.2013)

nk, Johannes (2009): Familie: Konzeption und Realität, http://www.bpb.de/izpb/8017/familie-konzeption-und-realitaet
013)

ann, Felicitas (Hg.) (2011): Marginale Urbanität. Migrantische Unternehmertum und Stadtentwicklung, Bielefeld

(International Organisation for Migration) (2008): World Migration 2008. Managing Labour Mobility in the Evolving
al Economy, Geneva

ermann, Robert / Rath, Jan (2011): Veränderte Konturen migrantischen Unternehmertums in Hillmann, Felicitas
Marginale Urbanität. Migrantische Unternehmertum und Stadtentwicklung, Bielefeld, S. 87-88

ert, Margret (2008): Eine Insel wird zum Industriegebiet – Portrait des Reiherstiegviertel. In: Geschichtswerkstatt Wil-
burg Honigfabrik e.V., Museum Elbinsel Wilhelmsburg e.V. (Hg): Wilhelmsburg - Hamburgs große Elbinsel, Ham-
S. 40-59

Karl / Engels, Friedrich (1968): Das Kapital, Bd. I. In: Marx Engels Werke, Bd. 23, Berlin/DDR, S. 514

Nauck, Bernhard (2007): Integration und Familie, http://www.bpb.de/apuz/30453/integration-und-familie?p=all (23.7.2013)

OECD (2011): Labour Force Statistics, http://www.oecd-ilibrary.org/sites/9789264125476-de/07/01/04/index.
html;jsessionid=61bqkh3qss4am.delta?contentType=&itemId=/content/chapter/9789264125469-61-de&containerItemId=/
content/book/9789264125476-de&accessItemIds=/content/book/9789264125476-de&mimeType=text/html (25.8.2013)

Oertzen, Jürgen (2006): Grounded Theory, in: Behnke, Joachim / Gschwend, Thomas / Schindler, Delia / Schnapp, Kai-Uwe
(Hg.), Methoden der Politikwissenschaft. Neuere qualitative und quantitative Analyseverfahren, Baden-Baden, S. 145-154

Oswald, Ingrid (2007): Migrationssoziologie, Konstanz

Pohl, Ben / Vollmer, Hans (2012): Das kommende Mahl. Von der Feuerstelle zur Tischnachbarschaft, Hamburg

Pongratz, Hans J. / Voß, G. Günter (Hg.) (2004): Typisch Arbeitskraftunternehmer? Befunde der empirischen Arbeitsfor-
schung, Berlin

Pries, Ludger (2011): Familiäre Migration in Zeiten der Globalisierung. In: Fischer, Veronika / Springer Monika (Hg.): Handbuch Migration und Familie, Schwalbach, S. 23-35

Pütz, Robert (2000): Von der Nische zum Markt türkische Einzelhändler im Rhein-Main-Gebiet. In: Escher, Anton (Hg.): Ausländer in Deutschland. Probleme einer transkulturellen Gesellschaft aus geographischer Sicht. Mainz, S.27-39

Pütz, Robert (2009): Perspektiven der Transkulturalität als Praxis Unternehmer türkischer Herkunft in Berlin. In: Yildiz Erol,
Mattausch Birgit (Hg.): Urban Recycling. Migration als Großstadt-Ressource, Berlin, S. 63-82

Reinstorf, Ernst (1955): Geschichte der Elbinsel Wilhelmsburg - von Urbeginn bis zur Jetztzeit, Wilhelmsburg

Sassen, Saskia (2000): Dienstleistungsökonomien und die Beschäftigung von MigrantInnen in Städten. In: Schmals , Klaus
M.: Migration und Stadt: Entwicklungen, Defizite, Potentiale, Opladen, S. 87-115

Schubert, Klaus / Martina Klein (2011): Europäische Wirtschaftsgemeinschaft, www.bpb.de/nachschlagen/lexika/politiklexi-
kon/17463/europaeische-wirtschaftsgemeinschaft-ewg (14.07.2013)

Schuleri-Hartje, Ulla-Kristina / Floeting, Holger / Reimann, Bettina (2005): Ethnische Ökonomie: Integrationsfaktor und Inte-
grationsmaßstab, Berlin

Seifert, Wolfgang (2011): Ökonomische Situation. In: Fischer, Veronika; Springer Monika (Hg.): Handbuch Migration und
Familie, Schwalbach, S. 111-127

Smechowski, Emilia (2011): Existenzgründung bei Migranten - Wenn Tante Emma zu Onkel Ali wird, http://www.taz.
de/!77624/ (04.04.2013)

Strauss, Anselm L. (1994): Grundlagen qualitativer Sozialforschung. Datenanalyse und Theoriebildung in der empirischen
soziologischen Forschung, München

Terkessidis, Mark (2010): Interkultur, Berlin

von Trotha, Trutz (2008): Eltern-Kind-Beziehung: Frankreich und Deutschland, http://www.berlin-institut.org/online-hand-
buchdemografie/bevoelkerungsdynamik/faktoren/eltern-kind-beziehung.html (02.08.2013)

Weber, Max (1972): Wirtschaft und Gesellschaft. Grundriss der verstehenden Soziologie, Tübingen

Weber-Kellermann, Ingeborg (1992): Der Oikos, das ganze Haus. In: Deutscher Werkbund Baden Württemberg: Oikos. Von
der Feuerstelle zur Mikrowelle, Gießen, S. 29-31

Yildiz, Erol (2011): Stadt und migrantische Ökonomien: Kultur der Selbstständigkeit. In: Hillmann, Felicitas (Hg.): Marginale
Urbanität. Migrantische Unternehmertum und Stadtentwicklung, Bielefeld, S. 119-131

Bildnachweis

S. 1-5, 15, 16-17: Geschichtswerkstatt Wilhelmsburg Honigfabrik e.V., Museum Elbinsel Wilhelmsburg e.V. (Hg): Wilhelmsburg - Hamburgs große Elbinsel, Hamburg, S. 46- 103

S. 6- 13, 19: Reinstorf, E. (1955): Geschichte der Elbinsel Wilhelmsburg - von Urbeginn bis zur Jetztzeit Wilhelmsburg, S. 335
-377

NICHT STADT — LAND — HAFEN
Not City — Countryside — Harbor

Franziska Meichelböck
Urban Design Thesis Project, 2013
Examiners: Prof. Bernd Kniess (Urban Design),
Martin Kohler (Urban Planning)
Available via: Library HafenCity University Hamburg,
Dienstapparat (reserved material) 22, Mas 090(13)

SITUATION 1: SETTING THE SCENE

A photo essay addresses the difference between the image that many
may have in mind when thinking about the Hamburg harbor and the
reality of what that location actually looks like. The author
translates this distinction in the photos into a concept of a
"hyphenated landscape"—for example, a harbor-landscape, logis-
tics-landscape, or city-landscape—through which trans-territorial
relationships of human and nonhuman actors are brought into focus
and the supposedly natural spatial categories and their potentialities become blurred. "Shouldn't we find a way of dealing with *city*
and *countryside* by returning to what exists and incorporating it
into the new?" she asks (p. 25).
In the second part of her work, titled "Research Design," the
author highlights the continuous production of space with reference to Henri Lefebvre. As her research subject, she takes the
changing patterns of everyday use of the urban. These patterns are
mapped as traces and are then superimposed before finally making
city readable as a palimpsest, as the result of a very lengthy and
slow formation of layers, which one should be familiar with before
intervening in it (Corboz 2001, p. 164; p. 25).
In the chapter titled "City-landscape," the author visits similar
approaches as taken by Kevin Lynch, Thomas Sieverts, and Christopher Alexander, for example, and uses them to bring her motive into
focus, namely to "make performative urban appropriation readable"
(p. 33) in order to enable a transformative means of interacting
with the urban.

[Overview]   [Situtation 1: pp. 1—48]

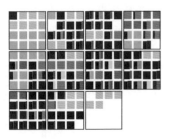 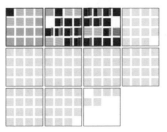

licht

**Stadt
Land
Hafen**

Impressum

**Nicht Stadt
Nicht Land
Nicht Hafen**

Inhalt

Photoessay →

image of the harbor

[pp. 1–16]

fACTual image of
the harbour

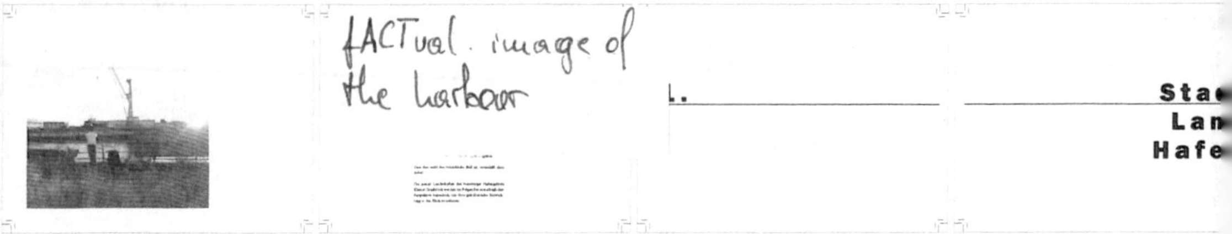

Sta
Lan
Hafe

Motive / Research Interest

how does transform-
ation take place?
how can this trans-
formation be made
visible / available?

Palimpsest
Mille Feville   traces
Assemblage
problematizing the
research situation as
landscape
(in dept to the
author's discipline)

Address the built
environment through
its use
→ relations?

Stadt
-Landschaft
Hyphen

Aufnahme
Kleiner
Grasbrook

SITUATION 2: UNDERSTANDING TRANSFORMATION

Chapter 3 of the paper deals with "recording the subject of
research," in other words, what the location is actually like.
Following the theoretical, conceptual basis of the palimpsest, the
author gathers individual aspects of where the place is situated
in the world on various levels. Where data can be tallied and precisely located, maps are used, while hand-drawn sketches are shown
wherever continuous progressions or fuzzy boundaries are involved.
Overall, the data was collected through site visits and research
in archives. This chapter borrows many of the familiar approaches
discussed in chapter 2: in this way, a map is produced that closely
resembles a Nolli map, alongside photographs of boundaries and
barriers or landmarks as in Lynch, or drive-by photographs taken
of people walking around; Robert Venturi, Denise Scott Brown,
and Steven Izenour, inspired by Ed Ruscha, demonstrated something
similar in *Learning from Las Vegas*. It seems obvious: activities
leave traces that can, in turn, be read by others.
These individual aspects are assembled here in a list and on
a map. Typical spaces in the research area come to light and are
displayed in the form of aerial photography, hand-drawn maps,
and isometries.

[Situtation 2: pp. 33—96]

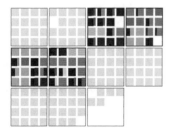

Franziska Meichelböck: Not City — Countryside — Harbor

spatial arrangements
are described as the
inadvertant outcome
of roles, concepts, vistas
of business, logistics
tourism

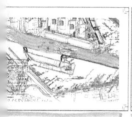

arders

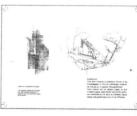

sentation signs
landmarks

94

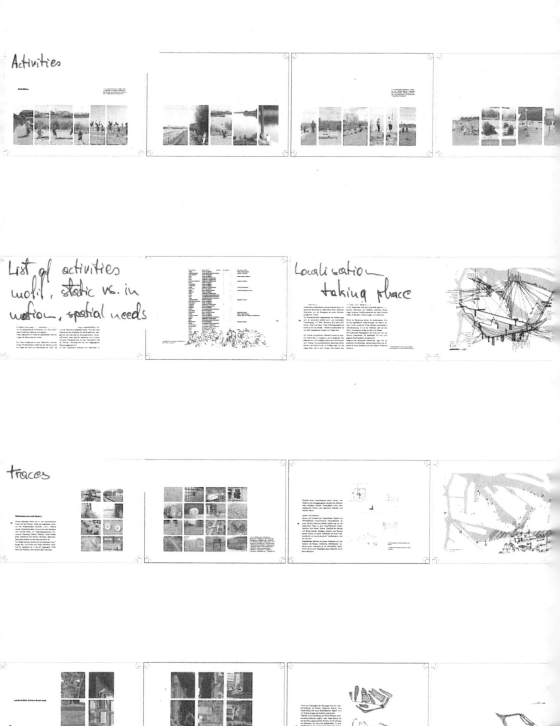

Activities

List of activities
mobil, static vs. in
motion, spatial needs

Localisation
taking place

traces

[pp. 65—80]

patterns

4. _____ **Hafengrundlage**
"base layer"

loading / mobilising
urban development
processes

business
mapping

inventory
type of use

understanding urban
transformation
through assembling
historic episodes

SITUATION 3: MAKING TRANSFORMATION AVAILABLE

"Harbor Basis" is the title of Chapter 4: an attempt to address the
complex situation of the harbor as a focus of current and future
urban development policies. A list card (p. 93) displays a com-
plexly organized commercial area that has developed as an active
form for the handling of goods. The development of individual
aspects of the active form of the Hamburg harbor in the Kleiner
Grasbrook district is explored on this basis. This chapter works
similarly to an essay, describing various things, events, and
situations as aspects of urban development. This is how the author
writes about the introduction of standards in the area of cargo
shipping, changes to regulations affecting logistics companies,
and the increasing prominence of stages for musicals in Hamburg.

[Situtation 3: 81–128]

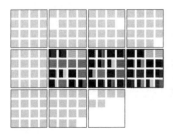

Franziska Meichelböck: Not City — Countryside — Harbor

97

SITUATION 4: ASSEMBLING PROJECTIVE READINGS

The fifth chapter attempts to translate the aspects of "knowing
how" shown in previous chapters—i.e. the question of whether and
how developed capacities of being active can be designed—into a
consistent form. Again, the representations show similarities to
familiar concepts such as Frank Lloyd Wright's Broadacre City and
Thomas Sievert's Zwischenstadt (intermediate city).
Under heading 5.1, "Intermediate Landscapes," the author suggests
overriding the potentialities of the assigned spatial categories
through actions.
5.2 "Routing" is a landscape-planning intervention. As envisaged
in point 5.1, the routing itself should provide alternative possibilities of use. The author adds initial suggestions in the form
of photographs overwritten with short explanations. As a sign
of discovery, types of use are transcribed.
5.3 "Signs of Discovery" describes patterns of use that have been
further developed into the future via site-specific qualities.
5.4 Shows two places whose particular transformative power is
emphasized here by the author. In doing so, the focus is again on
the potentialities of functions in their context.
5.5 "Spatial Phenomena" demonstrates how places can become central
through their use and how a possible future development can be
achieved. In order to do this, the individual aspects of urban
development and the completed connections between those aspects
are translated into diagrams.
Throughout the chapter, references are made to content from previous chapters. In this way, the translation efforts taken by the
author can be traced. The two concluding titles, 6.1 "Leap Between
the Elbe River" and 6.2 "Dealing with Traces and Layers," shed
light on how urban development could take a different approach to
the city as it now exists.

[Situtation 4: 113—167]

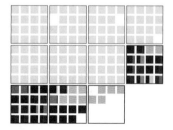

Franziska Meichelböck: Not City — Countryside — Harbor

recently
harbour as symbolic
value in urban
development
processes

5. **Lesarten
Zwischen-
landschaften**

projective readings
of transitional
landscapes

urban interventions

knowing how to
understand urban
situations

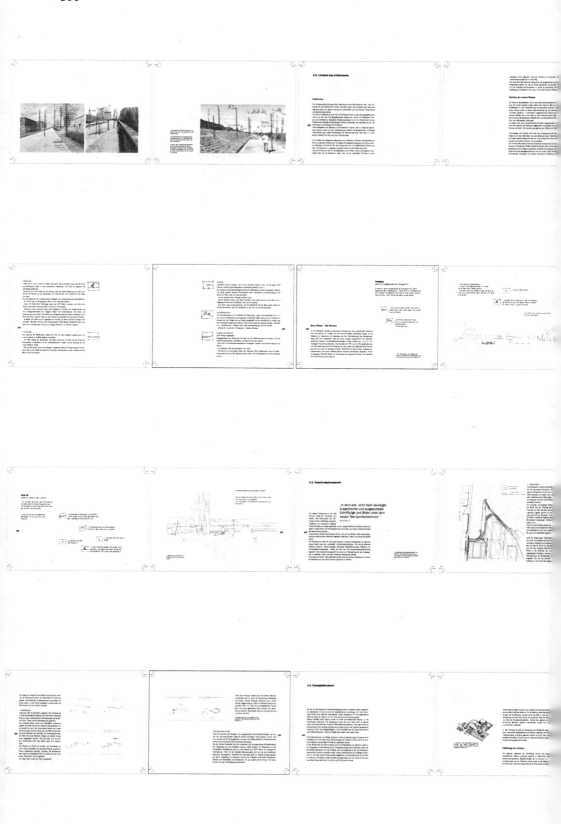

Quellenverzeichnis

Nachrichten

Veröffentlichungen im Internet

Literatur und gedruckte Quellen

Bildnachweis

ZOOM-INS

In her master's thesis, Franziska Meichelböck attempts to develop
an interpretation of urban landscapes that opens up new perspectives in the discourse on the development of these landscapes. The
author, who comes from the field of landscape architecture,
achieves this by considering her area of study a landscape that has
not yet been defined. She assumes that one is able to read *city* and
countryside like a palimpsest (1) and makes reference to André
Corboz, a former professor of history and urban development at the
ETH Zürich (p. 25).
The methods she most often uses to explore her area of inquiry are
mapping and sketching. Consequently, she uses these means of representation not only to reproduce what is supposedly seen, but
also as an analytical tool to develop methods of interpretation
(2).
Through frequent participatory observations, she is able to create
a detailed documentation of activities in the area of study. For
her, these activities and their remaining traces serve as a key to
reading the intermediate landscape of Kleiner Grasbrook (5).
Through various recordings of the activities, spatial conditions,
and background knowledge of planning, as well as the history of the
Hamburg harbor, she identifies individual landscape patterns in
their respective research area (4). She introduces the concept of
an intermediate landscape and projects new images and potentials
regarding the Kleiner Grasbrook, which open up the discourse on
the area and bring forth a new perspective.

Franziska Meichelböck: Not City — Countryside — Harbor

> Gebrauch und Planung. Was steht dazwi-
schen? Stadt? Land? Hafen?

> Die Stadt als Vermittler. Normen, Richtlini-
en und Werte beschreiben eine Verhaltens-
form. Das 'Tatsächliche' lässt sich in der
Stadt ablesen.

9 Detaillierte Ausführung des
methodologischen Aufbaus der Arbeit in
MTT7- Methods von Franziska Meichelböck

10 Materialität ereignet sich in Praktiken,
die Akteure und Aktanten in Beziehung
setzen. Dadurch sind unterschiedliche
Elemente oder Entinitäten (Einheit, Dasein)
temporär verbunden, werden durch spezifi-
sche Praktiken und Dingeffekte stabilisiert
oder unumgänglich (Vgl. Färber 2010: 102)

29

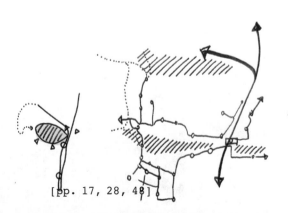

49

> Die 'zentrale' Inseln Kleiner Grasbook
wird nur von Verkehrsinfrastruktur tangiert

▷ 'Eingang' zur Inseln

> Verbindungen des ÖPNV zu und auf dem
Kleinen Grasbrook

⊶ Buslinie und Haltestelle
▬ S-Bahntrasse und Haltestelle
⋯⋯ Fährlinie

[pp. 17, 28, 48]

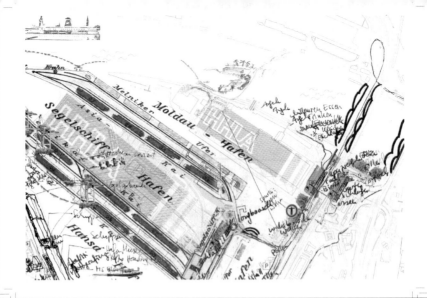

Aktivitäten

> (v.l.) Argentinienbrücke / Berliner Ufer / Klütjenfelder Hauptdeich (Veddelkauf) / Berliner Ufer/ Am Holtlhusenkai / Berliner Ufer / Fußgängerbrücke Spreehafen

Bezeichnung	Anlass/Motiv	Statisch	Bewegung	Räumliches MUSS
Angeln	Hobby nachgehen	x		Wasser, Wasserzugang
Ausblick genießen	Zeitvergehen lassen/Individuell	x	x	Ausblick, Weitblick
Auto reparieren	Hobby nachgehen	x		
Baden	Hobby nachgehen		x	Wasserzugang, begehbar
Essen	Treffpunkt/Gemeinschaft	x		
Feiern	Treffpunkt/Gemeinschaft	x		
Feuerwerk anschauen	Treffpunkt/Gemeinschaft	x		Ausblick, Weitblick
Filmen	Hobby nachgehen	x	x	
Fotografieren	Hobby nachgehen	x	x	
Geocatching	Hobby nachgehen		x	
Grillen	Treffpunkt/Gemeinschaft	x		Gerade Ebene/Fläche
Hula-Hupp	Hobby nachgehen	x		
Joggen	Sport/Training machen		x	Zusammenhängende Strecke
Jonglieren	Hobby nachgehen	x		
Kiffen	Treffpunkt/Gemeinschaft	x		
Lernen	Zeitvergehen lassen/Individuell		x	
Lesen	Zeitvergehen lassen/Individuell		x	
Liegen	Zeitvergehen lassen/Individuell		x	
Longboard fahren	Hobby nachgehen		x	Asphaltierte Ebene
Mini-Motorrad fahren	Hobby nachgehen		x	
Musik spielen	Hobby nachgehen	x		
Picknicken	Treffpunkt/Gemeinschaft	x		
Radfahren	Sport/Training machen		x	
Radfahren	Hobby nachgehen		x	
Roller fahren	Hobby nachgehen		x	
Relaxen	Zeitvergehen lassen/Individuell		x	
Rollerblades	Sport/Training machen		x	Asphaltierte Ebene
Rudern	Hobby nachgehen		x	Wasser, Wasserzugang
Schiffe beobachten	Hobby nachgehen	x		Visuelle Nähe zum Wasser, Schiffterminal
Schlafen	Zeitvergehen lassen/Individuell	x		
Singen	Treffpunkt/Gemeinschaft	x		
Sitzen	Zeitvergehen lassen/Individuell	x		
Skateboarden	Hobby nachgehen		x	Asphaltierte Ebene
Sonnen	Zeitvergehen lassen/Individuell	x		
Spazierengehen	Treffpunkt/Gemeinschaft	x		
Spazierengehen	Zeitvergehen lassen/Individuell		x	
Spielen	Treffpunkt/Gemeinschaft		x	
Surfen	Sport/Training machen		x	Wasser
Tanzen	Treffpunkt/Gemeinschaft	x	x	
Trinken	Treffpunkt/Gemeinschaft	x	x	
Unterhalten	Treffpunkt/Gemeinschaft	x	x	
Walk			x	
War				

> Aufzählung der bekannten Aktivitäten auf dem Kleinen Grasbrook.

[pp. 52 / 65 / 70]

> Containerlandschaft // Container/ Stapeln/ Hafen-Kräne/ Fähren/ Hafenbecken/ LKW/ Warten

> Lagerhallen // gleichmäßige Verteilung/Logistiklandschaft/ Lagerhallen/ Gewerbegebiet/ LKWs/

82

> Kulturlandschaft // Touristenbusse/ Parkplatz/ Schilder/ Schiffe/ Kasse/ Shop/ Museum/ Event/ Besucher/ Öffnungszeiten

> Produktionslandschaft// Schutt/ Kräne/ Bauarbeiter/ Rohbau/ Containerbüros/ Dixiklos/ Bauzaun/

> Grünflächen/Park // Gras/ Wiese/ Wasserzugang/ Bäume/ Ufer/ Weiden/ Deich/ Schafe/ Picknicken/ Freizeit/ Sport/

> Stillstand // Ruhe/ Viel Nichts/ Leere/ ohne Benutzung/ Absperrung/ Vandalismus/ Verfall/

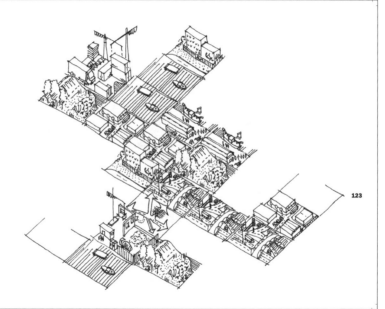

123

129

[pp. 81, 122, 129]

Afrikahöft
»Der Park im Gewerbegebiet«

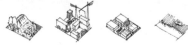

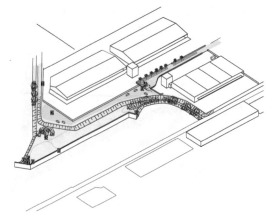

1 Spazierengehen
2 Feiern
3 Grillen
4 Relaxen
5 Schiffe beobachten
6 Angeln
7 Picknicken
8 Filmen/Fotografieren
9 Parken

> Isometrie des Afrikahöfts sowie der Sackgasse der Indiastraße. Angrenzend hier das Gewerbegebiet (Logistik und Lagerei) sowie der Rest des Süd-West Terminals (Sugartminal)

Literatur und gedruckte Quellen

> **Alexander, Christopher (1995):** Eine Muster-Sprache, Löcker Verlag, Wien
> **Augé, Marc (1996):** Orte und nicht-Orte. Vorüberlegung zu einer Ethnografie der Einsamkeit, Fischer Verlag, Frankfurt/Main
> **Baccini, Peter und Oswald, Franz (Hg) (1998):** Netzstadt – Transdisziplinäre Methoden zum Umbau urbaner Systeme, Hochschulverlag ETH Zürich;
> **Berger, Alan und Waldheim, Charles (2011):** Logistiklandschaften, in Arch + 205, S. 76- 83, zuerst schienen unter dem Titel logistic landscape in Landscape Journal, Nr. 27, 2008, S. 219ff copyright: Broard of Regents of University of Wisconsin System
> **Bornholdt, Hanna (2008):** Kanäle, Straßen, Eisenbahnen – Die Entwicklung der Verkehrsinfrastruktur in Wilhelmsburg, in Wilhelmsburg, Hamburgs große Elbinsel, Geschichtswerkstatt Wilhelmsburg Honigfabrik e.V., Museum Elbinsel Wilhelmsburg (Hg.), Medien-Verlag Schubert, Hamburg, S. 27- 39
> **Braun Harry und Rahn, Klaus (2008):** Der Hamburger Hafen - Eine Zeitreise in Bildern, Dorothee Engel (Hg.) Sutton Verlag, Erfurt
> **Brinckerhoff Jackson, John (1984):** Landschaften. Ein Resümee. In Landschaftstheorien. Franzen B., Krebs S. (Hg.) (2005), König Verlag, Köln, S. 29- 44
> **Corboz, André (2001):** Die Kunst, Stadt und Land zum Sprechen zu bringen, Birkhäuser Verlag, Basel/Berlin/Boston, 2001 (Bauwelt Fundamente Nr. 123)
> **Dell, Christopher (2010):** Taktiken strategische machen, in Generalist, Magazin für Architektur, Darmstadt, Juli, S. 68-73
> **Dell, Christopher und Kniess, Bernd (Hg) (2010):** Von Recht auf Stadt, UD Metalab - Studio für angewandte Theorie, HafenCity Universität Hamburg, Professur Urban Design
> **Driesen, Oliver (2010):** Die Welt im Fluss – Hamburgs Hafen, die HHLA und die Globalisierung, Hoffmann und Campe Verlag, Hamburg
> **Ellermeyer, Jürgen und Postel, Rainer (Hg.) (1986):** Stadt und Hafen, Hamburger Beiträge zur Geschichte von Handel und Schiffahrt, Hans Chrittians Verlag, Hamburg
> **Engel, Sandra und Tode Sven (2007):** Hafen – Stadt – Hamburg, Verlag Hanseatischer Merkur, Hamburg
> **Engel, Sandra (2007):** Einleitung in Engel, Sandra und Tode Sven, Hafen – Stadt – Hamburg, Verlag Hanseatischer Merkur, Hamburg
> **Färber, Alexa (2010):** Greifbarkeit der Stadt: Überlegungen zu einer stadt- und wissensanthropologischen Erforschung stadträumlicher Aneignungspraktiken, in Dérive Nr. 40/41, Understanding Stadtforschung, Wien, S. 100-105
> **Kähler, Gert und Schürmann, Sandra (2010):** Spuren der Geschichte - Hamburg, sein Hafen und die HafenCity, HafenCity Hamburg GmbH (Hg.), Arbeitshefte zur HafenCity, Nr. 5
> **Klauser, Wilhelm (2011):** Landschaften der Risikogesellschaft, in Arch+ Nr. 205, Berlin, S. 86-89
> **Lange, Ralf und Rademacher, Henning (1999):** Hafenführer Hamburg, Zeise Verlag, Hamburg
> **Lefèbvre, Henri (1972):** Die Revolution der Städte. Reprise der dt. Ausg. München, Frankfurt a. M.
> **Lynch, Kevin (1960):** Das Bild der Stadt, (Image of the City), Cambridge/Mass. 2. Aufl., 6., unveränd. Nachdr. (2010), Birkhäuser Verlag, Basel (Bauwelt-Fundamente Nr. 16)

> **Markert, Magret (2008):** Der Sprung über die Elbe – Wilhelmsburgs Weg in die Mitte der Stadt, in Wilhelmsburg, Hamburgs große Elbinsel, Geschichtswerkstatt Wilhelmsburg Honigfabrik e.V., Museum Elbinsel Wilhelmsburg (Hg.), Medien-Verlag Schubert, Hamburg, S. 191- 205
> **Markert, Magret (2008):** Eine Insel wird zum Industriegebiet- Portrait des Reiherstiegviertel, in Wilhelmsburg, Hamburgs große Elbinsel, Geschichtswerkstatt Wilhelmsburg Honigfabrik e.V., Museum Elbinsel Wilhelmsburg (Hg.), Medien-Verlag Schubert, Hamburg, S. 41- 58
> **Meyer, Kurt (2007):** Von der Stadt zur urbanen Gesellschaft, Jakob Burckhardt und Henri Lefebvre, Wilhelm Fink Verlag, München.
> **Müller, Christa (2011):** Urban Gardening, Über die Rückkehr der Gärten in die Stadt, Oekom Verlag, München
> **Prominski, Martin (2004):** Landschaft entwerfen: Zur Theorie aktueller Landschaftsarchitektur, Dietrich Reimer Verlag, Berlin
> **Schöbel, Sören (2008):** Landschaftsurbanismus, in Multiple City. Stadtkonzepte 1908/2008. Hg. Wolfrum S, Nerdinger W, Schaubeck S. Jovis, Berlin, S. 14-18.
> **Schöbel, Sören (2010):** Stadtgrün 2025, Entwicklung von urbanen und suburbanen Lebenswelten in Stadt und Grün / Das Gartenamt, Ausgabe 2010/6, S. 53-55
> **Seifert, Jörg (2011):** Stadtbild, Wahrnehmung, Design - Kevin Lynch revisited, Conrads U., Neitzke P. (Hg.), Birkhäuser Verlag, Basel und Bauverlag BV, Gütersloh, Berlin, (Bauwelt Fundamente Nr. 148)
> **Simmel, Georg (1903):** Die Grosstädte und ihr Geistesleben. In: Die Grosstadt, Jahrb. D. Gebe-Stiftung, Hg. Th. Petermann, Bd. 9, Dresden, S. 185-206
> **Sieverts, Thomas (1997):** Zwischenstadt- Zwischen Ort und Welt, Raum und Zeit, Stadt und Land, Braunschweig; Wiesbaden: Vieweg Verlag; Auflage: 3., verb. und um ein Nachw. erg. Aufl. (1999) (Bauwelt Fundamente Nr. 118)
> **Sitte, Camillo (1909):** Großstadtgrün, als Anhang: in der Städtebau nach seinen künstlerischen Grundsätzen, 4. Aufl. (2002), Birkhäuser Verlag, Basel, Boston, S. 187-211
> **Uhlmann, Gordon (2008):** Die Veddel – Stadtentwicklung im Fluss - Von der Weideinsel zum Wohnquartier zwischen Hafen und Industrie, in Wilhelmsburg, Hamburgs große Elbinsel, Geschichtswerkstatt Wilhelmsburg Honigfabrik e.V., Museum Elbinsel Wilhelmsburg (Hg.), Medien-Verlag Schubert, Hamburg, S. 59- 80

[pp. 146, 164—165]

HAUSMEISTER_INNEN
Caretakers

Jenny Ohlenschlager
Urban Design Thesis Project, 2014
Examiners: Prof. Michael Koch (Urban Planning: City Planning and
District Planning), Prof. Alexa Färber (Urban Anthropology and
Ethnography)
Available via: Library HafenCity University Hamburg, Dienst-
apparat (reserved material) 22, Mas 118(14)

SITUATION 1

Jenny Ohlenschlager's master's thesis deals with the significance
and role of caretakers as space-producing actors in the social
network of a *city*. Her research poses the question of what it means
to accompany the transformation process of a building as an acting
caretaker in everyday life, not only as a person acting individually but in the assumption of responsibility and stabilization
in the process of everyday spatial production (p. 9).
On the basis of relevant theories such as Henri Lefebvre's production of space, Michel de Certeau's practice of everyday life
and his understanding of utilizing strategies and tactics, and
Max Weber's theory of social action, as well as Bruno Latour's
actor-network theory, she develops a mixed-method approach to
even dwell on unforeseen and surprising aspects of the production
of space.

[Overview]   [Situtation 1: pp. 1—19]

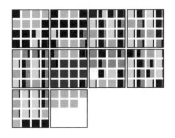
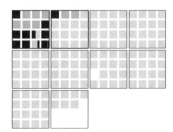

HAUSMEIS TER_INNEN INH

AUGUST 2014 / HCU HAMBURG / MASTERSTUDIENGANG URBAN DESIGN
MASTERTHESIS
JENNY OHLENSCHLAGER / 3034129
BETREUUNG / PROF. DR. MICHAEL KOCH / PROF. DR. ALEXA FÄRBER

GRUNDLI EGENDES

I GRUNDLEGENDES
1. DAS INTERESSE

2. DIE FORSCHUNGSFRAGE

3. DIE METHODIK

Handwritten notes:
Methode & Theorie Mix
- ANT
- Grounded Theory
- Produktion des Raumes
- Soziales Handels (Weber)

3.1 Die Kunst des Handelns von Michel De Certeau

3.2 Die Grounded Theory der Chicagoer Schule

HAUSMEISTER_INNEN

RAUMPRODUKTION

Der Ort: Wilhelmsburg das Feld

3.5 Die Theorie der Produktion des Raums nach Henri Lefebvre

DER SOZIALE RAUM IST AUS-
GANGSPUNKT UND RESULTAT DER
RÄUMLICHEN PRAXIS.

SITUATION 2

She introduces the topic in the second chapter with quotes of
interviewees representing subjective impressions and images of
the role of caretakers before tracing the profession's historical
development from being a product of early capitalist patriarchal
life in the era of industrialization to being defined nowadays as
part of operative facility management. With regard to a caretaker's range of actions and responsibilities, she asserts that this
profession cannot merely be described by a profession's specific
working profile, but must be seen as an individual vocation.
The main part of her research is presented in the third chapter.
Inspired by actor-network theory, she looks at the production of
space in eight case studies. The presentation is based on the triadic structure of the complex causal relations of the actors themselves, the places of activity in their functional assignments,
and the underlying institutional work orders (cf. p. 32).
Jenny Ohlenschlager's densely described situational analysis is
based on participatory observation and attendance of and interviews with her actors in the specific cases. Diagrammatic reasoning
supports the production of insights in what she calls "actor-
space-structure," displaying the relation of the most important
actors and actants in their movements and actions on site, supple-
mented by images of the places of activity. She closes the chapter
with "Controversy," in which she addresses the issue of the mode
of representation being reduced to a certain time span and makes
clear that defined indeterminacies (p. 80) indeed came to light
which could not be pursued further in this thesis project.

[Situtation 2: pp. 17—80]

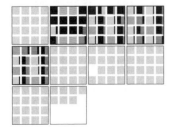

Jenny Ohlenschlager: Caretakers

[pp. 17–32]

7 Casestudies

Kräftegefüge
Ort – Akteur – Arbeits-
system

1. Casestudy

2. Casestudy

[pp. 33–48]

116

6. Casestudy

7. Casestudy

[pp. 65–80]

SITUATION 3

This chapter is dedicated to coding the produced material with the
leading question of what exactly caretakers do and how their various activities can be characterized without losing the specific
aspects of each sampling (p. 84).
Four categories emerged in the coding process: "being," "looking,"
"making," and "saying" (ibid.). These four categories indicate a
process of interdependent activities which she then describes in
relation to the actor group "caretakers" and translates into
activity-based processes.
She concludes the chapter with an examination of "everyday" social
actions, taking up Max Weber's four motives of the acting subject.
In doing so, she seeks to merge the power structures in which caretakers find themselves, the needs of the buildings' occupants which
they are supposed to meet, and the activity-based processes that
could be identified by observing their actions. She then graphi-
cally illustrates this self-developed concept of social actions
taken by caretakers (p. 109). Concerning the motive of the acting
subject, she differentiates between rational by purpose, rational
by value, emotional, and traditional; the triad of actor, place,
and system is based on the causal network of subjective meaning.

[Situtation 3: pp. 81—112]

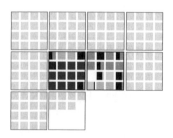

Jenny Ohlenschlager: Caretakers

ANALYS SIERTES TÄTIGK EITEN

Kodierung der Tätigkeiten alles Hausmeister_innen

GUCKEN MACHEN SAGEN

[pp. 81–96]

Tätigkeitsprozesse
erkennen und
aufzeigen.

Soziales Handeln
Max Weber

Zusammentragen der
Analyse + Theorie

Soziales Handeln
Hausmeister-Innen

SITUATION 4

In this chapter, the caretaker's produced spaces are reassembled
in accordance with Lefebvre, with a focus on their specific spatial
practice, pointing out its exemplary character of analysis using
text and diagrammatic representations.

The final chapter summarizes the role of caretakers in transforming
spaces. Ohlenschlager describes the caretakers as acting subjects
who take on an important, mediating role between the actors of
property owner and user, and who apply their own motives and evalu-
ations to determine which demands made by the other actors are to
be followed and which are not. In the area of tension between the
demands and needs of the different actors and their specific interests, caretakers often serve as a mediating link. In the field
between efficiency-increasing measures as a demand made by the
owners and the everyday social needs of the users, Jenny Ohlenschlager discovers a follow-up question: What does profitability
mean? Who determines the definition of capital and values that have
influence on the profitability of a building? Moreover, there is no
building that is not based on its social production. Who decides in
which building the "social" should not play a role while profitability is given priority? What knowledge is this decision based
on? Isn't it the caretakers, mediators between actors and actants,
who would have to gain this specific knowledge through their practice and then make those decisions themselves? (p. 144)

[Situtation 4: pp. 113–151]

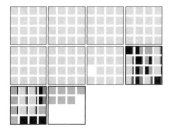

Jenny Ohlenschlager: Caretakers

Produzierte Räume der Hausmeister-innen

① Raum der Begegnung

② Raum der Ordnung

③ Raum der Dokumentation

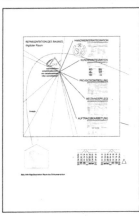

④ Raum der Aushandlung

⑤ Raum der Reparatur

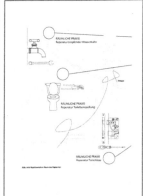

ZOOM-INS

Jenny Ohlenschlager has placed the actor "caretaker" at the center
of her work. The author dares to take a leap from her original discipline (landscape conservation and design) to researching a group
of actors along the criteria of the social sciences: she draws upon
various methods of qualitative social research and sets her findings in relation to theories of the acting subject and the production of space (1), which made this thesis project in its comprehensive complexity possible, but which could also be criticized.
Her structured work allowed her to combine the methods conclusively, even if not all of the theories and methods were consistently developed and implemented.
Ohlenschlager manages to accompany eight caretakers in their
everyday life and to produce a dense description of the actor on
site through participatory observations and interviews. She uses
the actor-network theory as a perspective from which to establish
a causal network from empirical material (2). Throughout the process, she codes her empirical data to filter out the caretakers'
activities and to draft processes of activity (3). Lefebvre's
theory prompts her to interpret and collate their specific produc-
tions of space. She uses this theory practically as a method in
order to label specific space-producing activities of the caretakers (4).

Michel de Certeau: Raum wird durch soziale Praktiken produziert.

HAUSMEISTER_INNEN

These: Hausmeister_Innen stellen eine schwer wegzudenkende Rolle im Akteursgefüge eines Gebäudes dar.

ANT: „Der einzige brauchbare Slogan lautet: den Akteuren folgen." (Latour 2007: 386)

Grounded Theory: Dokumentenanalyse / Interviews / teilnehmende Beobachtung / Kurzgespräche

FORSCHUNGSFRAGE: Was bedeutet es, als Akteur_In Hausmeister_In im Alltag den Transformationsprozess eines Gebäudes zu begleiten? Welche Rolle spielt dabei das handelnde Individuum Hausmeister_in? Wie übernehmen Hausmeister_Innen heutzutage Raumverantwortung und stabilisieren und produzieren sie Raum?

Grounded Theory: Kodierung der Tätigkeiten der Hausmeister_Innen

Max Weber: handelndes Subjekt (Hausmeister_In)
subjektiver Sinn seines Handelns bezogen auf ein von Akteur_Innen artitkuliertes, gemeinsames, das Gebäude betreffendes Bedürfnisses

Henri Lefebvre: Raum ist ein soziales Produkt.

RAUMPRODUKTION

bb. 001: Prozessgrafik

I GRUNDLEGENDES / 3. DIE METHODIK

11

3.1 Die Kunst des Handelns von Michel De Certeau

Um menschliche Verhaltensweisen zu verstehen, unterscheidet der französische Soziologe und Kulturphilosoph unterschiedliche Modalitäten des Handelns und die Formalitäten der Praktiken. Er unterscheidet zwei wesentliche Typen des Handelns. Die Strategie und die Taktik. Strategien produzieren, rastern auf und zwingen Räume auf. Strategien haben etwas Eigenes, setzen einen Ort voraus und werden durch Macht organisiert. Als Auswirkungen von Strategien, nennt er den durch das Eigene gewonnen Sieg des Ortes über die Zeit, die Beherrschung von Orten durch das vorauseilen der Zeit von panoptischen Praktiken sowie eine Macht, die sich spezifisches Wissen, Orte zu eigen machen. Strategien produzieren Räume, die im besten Fall mit den abstrakten Vorstellungen von mächtigen und willensstarken Subjekten übereinstimmen.

Taktiken hingegen sind durch das Fehlen von dem Eigenen bezeichnet. Sie gebrauchen, manipulieren und funktionieren Räume um. Ohne Macht dringen sie in die Ordnung eines fremden Ortes ein. Taktiken sind grenzüberschreitend und unterwerfen sich dennoch der Ordnung des Ortes. Sie sind untrennbar von dem Moment in dem er stattfinden, ihren zeitlichen und gesellschaftlichen Kontext. „Die Taktiken setzen auf einem geschickten Gebrauch der Zeit, der Gelegenheiten, die sie bietet, und auch der Spiele, die sie in die Grundlagen einer Macht einbringt." (de Certeau 1988: 92)

Michel de Certeau sieht die Kunst des Handelns in dem Gebrauch, dem Benutzen von Produkten, die einem aufgezwungen werden. Das Taktieren ist ein Umgang mit Orten und Macht. Für de Certeau gilt es den Schwächsten zu stärken.

(vgl. de Certeau 1988)

3.2 Die Grounded Theory der Chicagoer Schule

Die Grounded Theory ist eine in den 1960er Jahren, von den beiden amerikanischen Soziologen Barney Glaser und Anselm L. Strauss entwickelter methodischer Ansatz der qualitativen Sozialforschung, Daten verankerte Theorien aufzustellen. Galt es zu ihrer Zeit als nicht angemessen neue Theorien aufzustellen, sondern die großen Vorfahren zu verifizieren, waren sie anderer Meinung. Für sie gab es nicht genug Theorien, um die Gesellschaft und „das Soziale" zu erklären. Nur müssten diese in der Empirie entstehen. Vereinfacht lässt sie sich der Prozess der Theoriebildung nach der Grounded Theory wie folgt darstellen. „nachdenken, ins Feld gehen, beobachten, interviewen, Notizen machen, analysieren." (Glaser/Strauss 1994: 42) Dieser Prozess wird wiederholt, bis die Theorie im Feld durch die Forschung gesättigt ist. Es besteht eine Gleichzeitigkeit von Datengewinnung und Theoriebildung. Die Analyse beinhaltet in der Regel das Kodieren, Kontrastieren und Kategorisieren des erhobenen Materials. Während dieses Prozesses spielt ebenso das Kontextwissen sowie die theoretische Sensitivität des Forschenden eine Rolle. Der wesentliche Aspekt der Grounded Theory, für die Erforschung von Hausmeister_Innen, lag im offenen Kodieren ihrer Tätigkeiten.

3.5 Die Theorie der Produktion des Raums nach Henri Lefebvres

„Der (soziale) Raum ist ein (soziales) Produkt" (Lefebvre 1974). Henri Lefebvre Theorie zur Produktion des Raumes, ist eine räumliche Theorie, gesellschaftlicher Praxis, die vom Subjekt und ihren räumlichen Beziehungen ausgeht. Über die räumliche Praxis der Hausmeister_Innen wird folglich dessen Raumproduktion deutlich. Hierfür muss man jedoch die drei miteinander verwobenen Produktionsprozesse genauer betrachten. Die Gleichzeitigkeit, der konzipierten, wahrgenommenen und gelebten, und doch voneinander getrennten, drei Produktionsmomente sind wesentlich für Lefebvres Theorie.

„1. Die materielle Produktion, die eine räumliche Praxis und damit auch den wahrnehmbaren Aspekt des Raumes (espace percu) produziert.

2. Die Wissensproduktion, die eine Repräsentation des Raumes und somit einen konzipierten Raum (espace concu) produziert.

3. Die Bedeutungsproduktion, die mit Räumen der Repräsentation verbunden ist und einen erlebten oder gelebten Raum (espace vecu) produziert." (Schmidt 2010: 208)

DER SOZIALE RAUM IST AUSGANGSPUNKT UND RESULTAT DER RÄUMLICHEN PRAXIS.

Die sinnlich erfahrene Materialität vom wahrgenommenen Raum — Der gedanklich konzipierte, geplante Raum

RÄUMLICHE PRAXIS — REPRÄSENTATION DES RAUMES

Produziert den wahrgenommenen physischen Raum, Setzt ihn und setzt ihn voraus. Materieller Aspekt der sozialen Praxis — Vorstellungen vom Raum, Raum des Wissens und der Logik

Der gelebte Raum der gesellschaftlichen Praxis

RAUM DER REPRÄSENTATION

Repräsentiert soziale Beziehungen und Alltagspraxis. Wird im Gebrauch verändert und ist Resultat sowie Ausgangspunkt der räumlichen Praxis.

I GRUNDLEGENDES / 3. METHODIK

Abb. 002: Die doppelte Triade der Raumproduktion

15

[pp. 11–12, 14–15]

2. GEBÄUDE UND IHRE HAUSMEISTER_INNEN

Die im weiteren Verlauf vorgestellte Gruppe acht verschiedener Hausmeister_Innen, zeigt in der Summe ihrer Differenzen ein breites Handlungsspektrum, aus an dem sich Bedeutung der Hausmeister_In-Rolle für den von ihnen bewirtschafteten Raum aufzeigen lässt. Jedes Sample besitzt auf Grund seiner Unterschiedlichkeit eine Berechtigung und Relevanz. Anhand jedes ausgewählten Samples ließen sich verschiedene Aspekte zeigen, die aus unterschiedlichen Forschungsperspektiven relevant scheinen. Im Rahmen dieser Arbeit werden die Samples entlang eines Fragekomplexes behandelt, der die Praktiken und das Handeln der Akteure fokussiert. Die Darstellung erhebt daher keinen Anspruch auf Vollständigkeit oder Repräsentativität des Hausmeister_Innen-Daseins. Im Gegenteil. Die Samplings sind keine durch Induktion gewonnene Typologie, geschweige denn ein geschlossener Katalog. Die Versammlung ist vielmehr ein an Raum, Zeit und forschende Subjektivität gebundene Momentaufnahme. Ein Potpourri gelebter Praxis des heutigen Hausmeister_Innen-Daseins.

Abb.008: Verortung Hausmeister_Innen

2.1 Die Grundschule und ihr Hausmeister

Karsten Seefeld (-50) ist in seinem Leben schon vielen verschiedenen Tätigkeiten in der gesamten Bundesrepublik nachgegangen. Er hat eine Biographie mit vielen Brüchen. Er war kurzfristig sogar obdachlos. Aber ihm ist wichtig, dass er nie ohne Arbeit war. Seit 2007 ist er der Hausmeister der Grundschule Rotenhäuser Damm. Angestellt ist er von dem Unternehmen Gebäudemanagement Hamburg GmbH GMH. Als 100 %tige Tochter der Schulservice Hamburg Gesellschaft für Facility Management mbH ist es ein Unternehmen der Hansestadt Hamburg und für den Bau, die Sanierung und die Bewirtschaftung der Schulbauten im Hamburger Süden zuständig. „Wir fühlen uns in jeder Phase für die Immobilien unserer Auftraggeber und für die Menschen, die sie nutzen, im hohen Maße verantwortlich." (GMH Hamburg: 2014) Dass er für die GMH arbeitet, merkt er eigentlich nur an seiner Emailadresse und Arbeitskleidung. Jacke, Hose und Sicherheitsschuhe. Sein Arbeitgeber hat ohne dass sich seine Tätigkeit verändert hat in den letzten Jahren oft gewechselt. An den gestickten Logos der Arbeitskleidung lässt sich die Geschichte der zuständigen Instanzen - Behörde für Sport und Bildung BSB, Gesellschaft für Wohnen und Bauen GWG, Schulservice Hamburg und jetzt GMH - ablesen. Er steht in regelmäßigem Kontakt zu seinem Serviceleiter und der Verwaltungsebene. Vor allem durch die administrative Arbeit. Zur Unterstützung im Alltag hat Karsten Seefeld den Betriebsarbeiter Henrik Klemm, den er sich jedoch mit weiteren Schulen im Stadtteil teilt. Ohne ihn würde der Hausmeister oft, zum Beispiel beim Tragen von schweren Gegenständen, aufgeschmissen sein. Manchmal braucht man auch einfach jemanden um an zwei

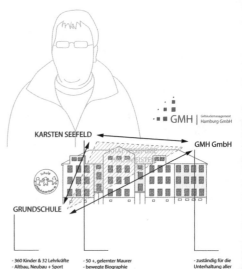

KARSTEN SEEFELD

GMH GmbH

GRUNDSCHULE

- 360 Kinder & 32 Lehrkräfte
- Altbau, Neubau + Sport und Bewegungszentrum SBZ
- Außengelände mit Spielgeräten
- Hort mit Ganztagsbetreuung
- SBZ Nutzung bis spät in den Abend
- umliegend Wohnsiedlung, Park und weitere soziale Einrichtungen

- 50 +, gelernter Maurer
- bewegte Biographie
- Tätigkeiten an der Grundschule: 1€ Jobber, Ehrenamt, Schulbewacher dann Hausmeister
- wohnt in Werkdienstwohnung
- Engagement über das Maß hinaus wird von allen geschätzt

- zuständig für die Unterhaltung aller Schulen im Hamburger Süden
- Vorgesetzer: Serviceleiter Herr Koch
- engster Kollege: Betriebsarbeiter Henrik Klemm
- GMH gibt Richttätigkeitenlinie und zur Verfügung stehende Handwerkerfirmen vor
- übernehmen Vertrags- und Rechnungswesen

Abb. 009: Kräftegefüge / Karsten Seefeld

3. TÄTIGKEITSPROSSSE

Die vier Kategorien weisen auf einen Prozess sich bedingender Tätigkeiten hin. Ausgangspunkt eines jeden Tätigkeitsprozesses ist ein das Gebäude betreffendes Bedürfnis einer der Akteur_Innen beziehungsweise ein gemeinsames Interesse Mehrerer. Während das Sein eine gewisse Grundbegleitung darstellt, folgt dem Gucken stets das Machen oder das Sagen. Gegebenenfalls folgt dem Gucken jedoch auch Nichts. Ebenso besteht eine gewisse Gleichzeitigkeit innerhalb einer Tätigkeit. So ist das Sein oft Voraussetzung für alle weiteren Kategorien. Und auch das Machen oder das Sagen können gleichzeitig Tätigkeiten des Guckens darstellen.

Während dieser Tätigkeitsprozesse eignen sich die Hausmeister_Innen ein spezifisches Wissen über das Gebäude und dessen Nutzer_Innen an. Dieses Wissen entsteht durch und mit dem dichten Netzwerk von Akteur_Innen und Aktanten mit all ihren Entitäten, welches die Hausmeister_Innen während jeder einzelnen Tätigkeit um ein Gebäude assoziieren.

Auch wenn selten ein Bedürfnis, auf das es zu reagieren gilt, dem anderen in Gänze gleicht, ähneln sich die Prozesse sowie die Konstellation der involvierten Akteur_Innen und Aktanten. Durch die ständige Wiederholung sich ähnelnder Prozesse, entwickeln die Hausmeister_Innen ein praktisches Bewusstsein für ihr tun.

Da an die Hausmeister_Innen eigentlich immer mehrere, verschiedene Bedürfnisse gleichzeitig herangetragen werden, müssen die daraus zahlreich entstehenden Tätigkeitsprozesse parallel bearbeitet werden. Diese Parallelität beeinflusst die Entscheidung über Prioritäten und die daraus resultierende Tätigkeit, die folgt. Die Zusammensetzung der Tätigkeitsprozesse ist für

die Hausmeister_Innen jeden Tag neu. Die einzelnen Tätigkeiten und Tätigkeitsprozesse sind jedoch repetitiv.

Abb. 031: Stereotypen der Tätigkeitsprozesse

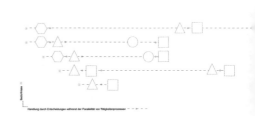

Abb. 032: Parallelität von Tätigkeitsprozessen

[pp. 36—37, 106—107]

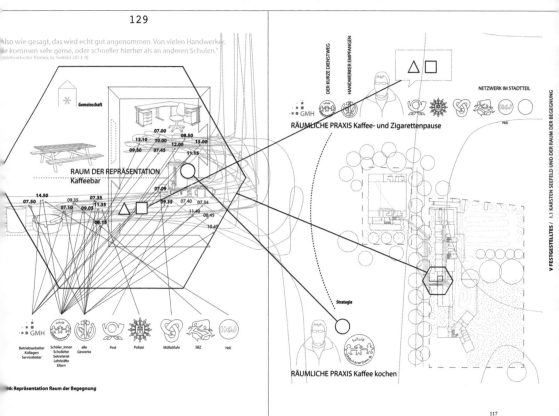

"Also wie gesagt, das wird echt gut angenommen. Von vielen Handwerker. ...e kommen sehr gerne, oder schneller hierher als an anderen Schulen."

Gemeinschaft

RAUM DER REPRÄSENTATION
Kaffeebar

Betriebsarbeiter
Kollegen
Servicleiter

Schüler_Innen
Schulleiter
Sekretariat
Lehrkräfte
Eltern

alle
Gewerke

Post

Polizei

Müllabfuhr

SBZ

HdJ

...86: Repräsentation Raum der Begegnung

DER KURZE DIENSTWEG
HANDWERKER EMPFANGEN

NETZWERK IM STADTTEIL

RÄUMLICHE PRAXIS Kaffee- und Zigarettenpause

Strategie

RÄUMLICHE PRAXIS Kaffee kochen

V FESTGESTELLTES / 1.1 KARSTEN SEEFELD UND DER RAUM DER BEGEGNUNG

117

QUELLEN
Literatur

...verein Reiherstieg eG (2013): Wohnzufriedenheitsanalyse 2013, Hamburg: Bauverein Reiherstieg eG.

...ckhardt, Lucius (2005): Politische Entscheidungen in der Bauleitplanung, in: Fetzer, Jacob/Schmitz, Martin: Lucius ...khardt. Wer plant die Planung? Architektur, Politik Mensch., Berlin: Martin Schmitz Verlag, S. 45-58.

...Certeau, Michel (1988): Kunst des Handelns, Berlin: Merve Verlag.

..., Christopher (2011): Replaycity: Improvisation als urbane Praxis, Jovis Verlag, Berlin

...erabend, Paul (1982): Wider dem Methodenzwang, Frankfurt: Suhrkamp Verlag.

...e und Hansestadt Hamburg (2003): Stadterneuerung Wilhelmsburg S3 Kirchdorf Süd: Abschlussbericht., Hamburg: ...örde für Bau und Verkehr Hamburg.

...er, Barney / Strauss, Anselm L. (2008): Grounded Theory: Strategien qualitativer Forschung, Bern

...our, Bruno (2007): Eine neue Soziologie: Wie kann man die Aufgabe wiederaufnehmen, den Spuren der Assoziationen ...olgen?, Frankfurt: Suhrkamp Verlag.

...lner, Rolf (1981): Die Angst des Forschers vor dem Feld, in: Bausinger Hermann / Sauermann Dietmar(Hrsg.): Zeit- ...ft für Volkskunde 77, Verlag W. Kohlhammer: Stuttgart, S. 52-66.

...bvre, Henri (1974): Die Produktion des Raums, in: Dünne, Jörg/ Günzel, Stephan (Hrsg.) (2006) Raumtheorie: Grund- ...ntexte aus Philosophie und Kulturwissenschaften, Frankfurt am Main: Suhrkamp Verlag.

...er, Peter (1996): Hausmeister in Wien: Aufstieg und Niedergang einer Respektsperson, in: Wiener Geschichtsblätter ...eft 4/1996, Wien: Verein für Geschichte der Stadt Wien.

...Sozialökonomische Forschungsstelle (Hrsg.) (1999): Beschäftigungsinitiativen im Bereich sozialer Dienste: Das ...besorgerwesen in Wien, Wien: SFS.

...midt, Christian (2010): Stadt, Raum und Gesellschaft: Henri Lefebvre und die Theorie der Produktion des Raumes, ...gart: Franz Steiner Verlag.

...er, Max (1987): Wirtschaft und Gesellschaft: Grundriss der verstehenden Soziologie, Tübingen: J.C.B. Mohr

...eva, Albena (2012): Mapping Controversies in Architecture, Farnham: Ashgate Publishing Limited

...aur, Bruno / Yaneva, Albena (2008): Die Analyse der Architektur nach der Actor-Network-Theorie (ANT)., in: Swiss ...ral Office of Culture (Hg.): Explorations in Architecture: Teaching, Design, Research, Basel: Verlag Birkhäuser, S. 80–89.

...n, Hans-Peter (Hrsg.) (2013): Facility Management. Erfolg in der Immobilienbewirtschaftung., Berlin: Springer- ...

...iche, Ulrich (2005): Facility Management . Grundbegriffe, Bonn: GEFMA e.V.

...öper, Ute (Hrsg.) (2010): Aussicht auf Veränderung. Kunst-Parcours quer durch Hamburg entlang der S-Bahn Linie 3, ...tverlag der Akademie einer anderen Stadt: Hamburg.

VII ANGEHÄNGTES / ABBILDUNGSVERZEICHNIS / 2. QUELLEN

149

[pp. 116–117, 149]

PLAN

Foundations of the Critique
of Planning Economies
in an Improvisational Perspective

Christopher Dell

On a hot day in July, in room 3.111.1 of the HafenCity University of Hamburg—the Urban Design research group had been browsing through various analog archive folders as part of its work on documenting their teaching and research project, the University of Neighborhoods (UoN)—when suddenly someone cried out, "This plan is nothing but a red herring!"

Who's afraid of never having been being modern? A very brief history of urban planning

The future is a wonderful invention, but had people not pervaded it with their goals, there would not have been the chance to delve into the future with full verve; people would see nothing but fog and face the dark hole of time. However, as soon as one projects goals onto the future, pitfalls arise, because anybody or anything may sneak past the goals, undermine or misinterpret them, or eventually face constellations in which someone or something may circumvent the goal elegantly.

The question of how to reach the future by setting goals is as old as the future itself. In order to solve this issue, once upon a time the general idea of *plan* made its grand debut in semantic history. I am thinking of the notion of *plan* as it was brought into French common language sometime during the eighteenth century. Borrowed from the French word *plan*—the floor area of a building and its layout—people in the second half of the century began to understand the word "plan" as some sort of basic idea, draft, undertaking, or intention. The origin of the notion's rise from a technical term in architecture to a general idea was derived from conflating it

with a degeneration of the French verb *planter*, which roughly translates to erect, construct, to place, and to put something in the ground with one part still sticking out, and from the Latin word *plantare*, meaning to plant.

The fact that this semantic development had taken place in France isn't surprising, as the country had already set the stage for and given a big hand to René Descartes in the 17th century's heyday of absolutism. Interpreting space as a rational construct, gracefully stripping it from its symbolic characteristics, the pioneer of modern rationality invented the spatial concept we know today as Cartesian space. In Descartes' eyes, space was nothing more than a *res extensa*. Reduced to an extended thing, space was deprived of all qualities other than being measurable in terms of length, width, height, and depth. As a result, arithmetic and geometrical proportions no longer operate as qualities of space-in-itself. Geometry converts into a form of thought, the latter now termed human consciousness, which is projected onto things by the said form. Shifting the pivotal point from the cosmic world to the human mind marked the beginning of modern rationality, which was to allow the human cogito to separate the world according to imagined methods. This doctrine paved the way for Kant's later explanation of space as "nothing but an inner mode of representation."[1]

Descartes, who was generally known as a notorious skeptic, wasn't lacking concrete proof regarding his spatial theory. Impressions of urban

---

1   Immanuel Kant, Paul Guyer, Allen W. Wood, and Immanuel Kant, *Critique of Pure Reason* (Cambridge and New York: Cambridge University Press, 1998), 430.

planning that he made during the Thirty Years' War around 1619, when he visited the area around Ulm and also Frankfurt am Main, found their way into the famous 1637 publication *Discourse on the Method*. In this work, he discusses German urbanism: "Again, these old cities ... are usually less well laid out than the orderly towns that planners lay out as they wish on level ground." In light of how houses are placed next to each other in a supposedly irrational Germany, Descartes adds that "they had been placed where they are rather by chance than by the will of thinking men."[2]

In view of cultural history, it may be not far-fetched to claim that what followed the Cartesian furor was a downright explosion of the planning spirit. Not only did it benefit the modern era with rationally arranged parks, castles, or city enlargements. Also other disciplines, such as economics, for example, did not want to wait at the back of the queue and directed their paradigms according to society's new miracle remedy named *plan*. It should therefore come as a no surprise that Karl Marx named one of his most influential works "Floor Plans": *Grundrisse: Fundamentals of Political Economy Criticism (Rough Draft)*. In this text, Marx, for example, discusses cooperative production as the "economy of time, along with the planned distribution of labor time among the various branches of production." Planful distribution "remains the first economic law on the basis of communal production."[3] And in his *Economic and Philosophic Manuscript of 1844*, Marx concludes: "The plans and projects of the employers of capitals regulate and direct the most important operators of labor, and profit is the end proposed by all those plans and projects."[4] Let us state the following. Looking at the observations above, one can from the 18th century onward speak of two types of plans. First, the plan as an epistemological tool. Saying "I have a plan" means that I know what I have to do if I want to achieve something specific and also how I would have to do it. And second, the word "plan" as referring to a material drawing medium, for instance, an architectural drawing.

The story is well-known. After the Cartesian conception of space had achieved its historical triumph, it eventually gave rise to modernist city planning. Emerging as a scientific discipline by the end of the 19th century, planning interpreted the city as a rational or rationalizable object. The city should be manageable in both formal and functional terms. Such an approach made sense, as the invention of urban development as a discipline was mainly due to the fact that, in the course of the explosion of cities caused by industrialization, a disturbing flip side of progress became apparent—the swift quantitative and qualitative dynamics of what *city* is. The Middle Ages and Baroque period could still conceptualize cities as teleological creations without needing to ground this assumption in modern rational thought. Cities could be tackled through elaborate (due to being relatively minimal) planned urban

2   René Descartes, *Von der Methode* (Hamburg: Meiner, [1637] 1960), 9.

3   Karl Marx and Martin Nicolaus, *Grundrisse: Foundations of the Critique of Political Economy (Rough Draft)* (London: Penguin Books, 1993), 173.

4   Karl Marx and Martin Milligan, *Economic and Philosophic Manuscripts of 1844* (Amherst, NY: Prometheus Books, 1988), 40.

enlargements. Entirely new city projects such as Versailles and Caserta
were countryside rationalisms, and
Mannheim and Karlsruhe rather small.
In contrast to the territorial projection
of the supposed homogeneous, the
urban fabric of the 19th century
emerged as a heterogeneous form. It
utterly cried out its ontological status
as a battleground for the conflicting
interest groups that the young modern
democracies had brought to center
stage—the bourgeoisie and proletar-
iat. What came to light in the ever-growing cities were the inequal conditions of real life, which seemed to
deeply betray the French and American Revolutions' famous postulates of
equality. This situation, which Engels
so vividly described in his book *The
Condition of the Working Class in England*, served as and continuously remained a topos of modern urban
planning. It finally led to the apotheo-
sis that was put forward by the French
architect Le Corbusier during the first
half of the twentieth century, discred-
iting metropoles as barren entities. Le
Corbusier was especially concerned
about the chaos of cities, which
seemed violating and proof of their
degeneracy. Le Corbusier considered
"... corridor streets, full of noise and
dust and deprived from light," as a
major problem to be tackled. As is
known, the alternative proposed by
the radical modernist was to rebuild
the city in a functionalistic fashion.
Yet, according to Le Corbusier's diagnostics, city authorities and investors
alike had anything but a plan. Where
their endeavor to plan in its proper
meaning could have resulted in engagement in "a formidable battle," the
city's authorities seemed in fact to be
engaging in the battle "without knowing the objectives."[5]

Notoriously, this thing called *city*
didn't really want to follow the functionalist call to order and remained
rather contingent. Even after getting
caught in the cybernetic clutches of
retrocausality, of calculable and con-
trollable processes in the midst of the
20th century, *city* still would insist on
its fugitive ontology. After the impressive failure of rational functional and
structuralist paradigms alike, postmodern planning since the 1970s instantly turned to the simulacrum and
fled from the thing that was *city*. The
idea of calling postmodernism a critique of the modern era later turned
out to be sheer euphemism. Although
postmodernism acknowledged the
city's ambiguity and indeterminacy,
it ignored the consequence of questioning the city's ontological and
fundamental determination. Rather, it
distanced itself from *city* as an object,
engaging in formalisms, culturaliza-
tion, or event culture in order to find
refuge. Where it did not realign its self-
relation toward *city*, postmodern planning, offended by the fight (lost by
others) against indeterminacy made
the gross error of withdrawing from
city's reality entirely. In line with the
posit of the "end of history," postmo-
dernity then shrank down to a short
tale, or better yet, no story at all, and
thereby lost its most important source
of knowledge, namely indeterminacy.
Paradoxically, while neglecting political agency, postmodern planning was
all the more fatally effective in shaping
precisely the reality that it did not

5   Le Corbusier, "A Contemporary City" (1929),
cited in: Gary Bridge and Sophie Watson, eds.,
The Blackwell City Reader (Blackwell Publishers, 2000), 345.

believe in. Nowhere is this better exemplified than in contemporary urban
architecture. Take, for example, the
synergy of idling formalisms of Pots-
damer Platz in Berlin or a *Parc de la
Villette* in Paris with the tendency to
homogenize a financially driven New
Urbanism; a form that can best be observed at the HafenCity in Hamburg.

Today we know that modernism
and its tale of the end of the figurative
as well as postmodernism and its account for the end of the plan were historic projects that we have left behind.
Was it wrong to treat *city* as an object?
No. Without rationalizing it, the process of order of modern societies and
thus in their metropoles would not
have been possible. As with the current crisis of urban planning, however,
this utilitarian relation to rationalization doesn't give rise to substantial
identifications[6] anymore—if it ever did.
It rather leads to an overdrive. Rational
concerns often seem to only be arrangeable esoterically in an attempt
to formally integrate the heterogeneity
of present-day forms of life and its
multiple contradictions in terms of
urban planning: functional efficiency
in the office district, functional relaxa-
tion in a loft townhouse or suburban
home, functional collective ecstasy in
public places. This functional (be it
modern or postmodern) attitude towards *city* alone may generate stability
in terms of construction and economic profits for the building and
housing industry; however, it won't do
the same for urban users. The real-es-
tate industry, so it often seems, functions only with medial claims and bor-
rowing from premodern mysticism.

Urban planning, which has less and
less real chance of intervening in a
city, increasingly ends up in an eventization that resembles the imitation of
pre-Enlightenment rites. There is no
better proof of this event culture than
signature architecture, the perfect
example of which—the Guggenheim
Museum Bilbao—has entered architectural nomenclature as the "Bilbao
effect." It's magic!

The situation impressively demonstrates what Bruno Latour sought to
describe with his thesis that actually,
despite our own self-understanding,
we have never been modern. Latour's
thesis draws our attention to the fact
that while formalization processes
based on rationalization may be able
to order the world, they nonetheless
lack the binding forces to constitute or
keep collectives together and, as part
of this, to stabilize individuals. In light
of this, it seems rather astonishing
that urban or spatial planning is still
understood as a rationalist approach
to the formulation of decision premises for future spatially relevant actions.[7] The guiding line for planning is
still based on a simple premise: when
strategies are articulated and approved of, they will eventually be implemented in the future in an unprob-
lematic way. If this were true, spatial
planning would be strategic per se. In
reality, however, one is witnessing a
permanent crisis in spatial planning—
and actually ever since the idea of
rationalist planning came about.[8]

6   Hartmut Böhme, *Fetischismus und Kultur*
       (Reinbek bei Hamburg: Rowohlt Taschenbuch
       Verlag, 2006), 22.

7   Torsten Wiechmann, *Planung und Adaption*
       (Dortmund: Rohn Verlag, 2008), 3.
8   Wiechmann, *Planung und Adaption*, 3; cf. also
       Hans Heinrich Blotevogel, "Rationality and
       Discourse in (Post)Modern Spatial Planning,"
       in *The Revival of Strategic Spatial Planning*,
       ed. William Salet and Andreas Faludi
       (Amsterdam: Royal Netherlands Academy of
       Arts and Sciences, 2000).

Plans are and have been able to connect the heterogeneous entities "future" and "goal." But they bought this ability with the price of esoteric belief: to make this connection transparently functional works only under *tabula rasa* conditions, i.e. when one excludes the existence, change, and context of urban situations. In this sense, planning has never "really" been modern. Today we are forced to confront ourselves with this fact. The *tabula rasa* approach is becoming less and less effective, or even counterproductive. Consequently, "planning" has to explore ways of dealing with the existing. But what happens to this existence while planning? How does this work?

Who's afraid of the red herring? A building application in progress

At this point, we should return to the research group and to the plan they called a "red herring," and zoom in on it. There is no doubt that the UoN project had a goal that was to guide it through the future: over the course of five years, it was to and aimed to implement the experimenting and testing of contemporary forms of education at an interface of culture, knowledge, and urban development.[9] The starting point for this endeavor was the building of the former public health office, a one-story building from 1952 with a gabled roof and approximately 550 square meters of floor space, which had spent a quiet life as a hidden ruin for years in the Hamburg district of Wilhelmsburg. The original owner, the Free and Hanseatic City of Hamburg,

granted the HCU use of the house and property for a limited period of time. The contract included the complete demolition of the building and the return of the land to the city by December 31, 2013. The building had a tiered and L-shaped building cubature. The central front building once covered the main entrance and connected two narrower sections of the building: one wing with office and examination rooms along a central corridor in a north-south direction and—perpendicular to that—a second wing to the southeast. In addition to the entrance area, the event hall, and examination and office spaces, several sanitary rooms with various layouts were found in the building, including individual and public restrooms, one for the disabled, and a small shower room. In order to be able to tackle the interim and remaining use of the building as a university facility, we had to file an application for the change of use. The plan of this change is the central motif of the following discussion.

In the archive folder for the UoN's building applications, the research group stumbled across the initial application process of the project in the 2009–2010 log. Here, they discovered various plans among which they were able to quickly identify the relevant ones that had come back from authorities stamped and signed. The application process was set in motion by the first written correspondence on March 8, 2009 and with the description of the planned construction. As a planning application, attached to the decision were specifications of elevation, the site plan and construction. When the group of researchers took a closer look at the documents, they noticed a questionable detail: despite being an

9   Teaching and Research Program Urban Design at the HCU Hamburg, ed., *Broschüre Universität der Nachbarschaften* 04.10 (Hamburg, 2010), 7.

appeal for a change of use, the application document was titled "Application for a building permit according to authorization procedure §61 Hamburgische Bauordnung HBauO (Federal Building Code of Hamburg)." The planned construction is described as a conversion and change of use of the former public health office Rotenhäuser Damm 30, 21107 Hamburg. Why the combination of change of use and building application? To find answers, the researchers looked through the UoN's event calendar and found the project's opening event on June 12, 2009. The application from March 2009 therefore served first and foremost to prepare the event in June 2009 in terms of building regulations. For one, the focus was on generating a change of use and applying for it in order to legally legitimize us, a university, being in the building—after all, the latter had been operating as a public health office until then. The building's historically determined condition in terms of function was also the reason why the initial correspondence with the district office referred to and assumed a change of use. Surely, it was clear to everyone involved that at some point, something would at the same time have to happen or be changed in terms of construction. Thus, as the researchers supposed, the appeal for a change of use was tied to a building application.

Who worked on the application? While checking the curriculum calendar, the researchers found that it had been submitted by Group 6 (Architecture): "Preparation of the Building Application." The group, including students Sarah Timmermann, Kathrin Rupp, Bianca Eschrich, and Sandra Latussek, prepared—in coordination with Bernd Kniess, Ben Becker, and the Wilhelmsburg building regulation agency—the document during winter break 2008/09. Moreover, the group linked the application to a performance for the authorities: on March 19, 2009, the students presented it along with a speech to Mr. Kühn, the official in charge at the building regulation agency, and to Carola Schuhmann at the tax office (department for building and property management). By means of a performance that included a PowerPoint presentation, the group discussed the framework conditions regarding building regulations, as well as the curricular process that the UoN had gone through up to that point for the pending application. The performance was successful, as it seems. Ben Becker's construction log reads: "flexible public official."[10] The fact that the application's procedure was part of a curriculum was given evidence by the way the presentation also self-reflectively thematized the group's approach: it meticulously described visiting the building department, reviewing the application documents to simplify the procedure, the renewed consultation appointment at the building department with Mr. Kühn, talking to everyone involved after filling out the application and compiling the building documents, getting the contractor and architect's (Bernd Kniess) signature, and finally the submission with the concomitant presentation. From a technical point of view, the latter was about common topics: First, to illustrate a simplified approval procedure that could be

10   Teaching and Research Program Urban Design HCU Hamburg, ed., Arbeitsbericht Universität der Nachbarschaften (UdN) 2008/09, UoN Project Archive, 37.

implemented for buildings of classes 1 and 2, but no special buildings [§ 2 HBauO].[11] Second, students show that the development plan or construction stage plan reveals the property as "area of special use" and "housing."[12] The description gave form to the following argumentation: As the filed use "educational facility as well as accommodation for a supervisor"[13] met the declared land use, there was no need to deviate from plan B; a mere change of use would suffice. Due to the fact that the subject of the proceeding was ultimately an existing building, the need to provide proof of stability, technical building services, fire safety, and clearance areas no longer existed. Furthermore, the building was neither a meeting place (it held up to 200 people), nor a special structure (the rooms held up to 100 people).

So far, so good. But the research group is interested in how the topics regarding plan and design were handled in the context of teaching and research as well. What kind of design was included in this floor plan? Nothing. One could only find mundane changes that were not worthy of being labeled as true architectural design. However, since the researchers were told so, they were very conscious of the fact that this plan had served as the central pillar of the UoN and its procedure. So the researchers attempted a different reading. In the course of investigating the plan for a while, the researchers were able to notice, for instance, a change at the end of the L section which may trace back to initial sketches by the students. Here, a caretaker's apartment had been drawn in, which, as the researchers know, was later to become a studio. But why a janitor's apartment? After all, students are supposed to work here. The researchers checked the application once again and noticed an appendix: "An apartment for a supervisor or caretaker is assigned to the actual purpose of the building (university educational institution — editor's note), is however subordinate to it in terms of floor size and cubic capacity."[14] Apparently, at the time when the application was submitted, the contention over the safety issue had already found its way into the plan. The researchers quickly diagnosed that the apartment from the first application did not really resemble what was eventually built. Here we can already identify a crucial point of the plan's representational strategy: discovering what is usually a mistake in architectural design—the non-resemblance of the plan to a project—is under particular criteria the essential manner for inscribing a later development into the body of the plan *as a potentiality*. This holds true not only for the apartment tract, but also for a

11   The building classes (BC) are categorized according to the building's style, height, and surface area. Principally, the higher the BC, the higher the respective requirements in terms of fire safety. Building class 1 a) detached buildings of up to 7 m height and no more than two utilization units of no more than 400 m², b) detached buildings used for agriculture and forestry. Building class 2: buildings of up to 7 m and no more than two utilization units of no more than 400 m². The admissibility is checked according to BauGB [§ 14, 29-37, 172 BauGB], adhering to regulations regarding distance space [§ 6 HBauO], applied divergences of the building code [§ 69 HBauO] as well as adhering to the Federal Nature Conservation Act Hamburg [§ 9 HmbNaturschutzgesetz] §68 registered inspector.

12   Teaching and Research Program Urban Design of the HCU Hamburg. ed., Arbeitsbericht Universität der Nachbarschaften, 35.

13   Ibid.

14   Teaching and Research Program Urban Design of the HCU Hamburg, Bauantrag, UoN Project Archive, March 19, 2009, 5.

whole array of critical points in the building. Two more spacious seminar rooms were already laid out as well. The researchers also found suggestions in terms of emptying the event hall as well as the demolition of walls. However, this first planning stage didn't include the future kitchen foyer yet. The foyer served as the basis for the changes, though it had not yet been noted in the plan, i.e. the meeting room was still the closed space of the kitchen. Nonetheless, the plan included extending the foyer and demolishing the closets—which were never knocked down. A vestibule was also planned, but never built; the proposal didn't even consider the L section. Only the kitchen, boiler room, and theater room (in which a wall had been torn down), as well as the storage room, were shown.

Because the first application dealt with minimal alterations, the researchers realized that the plan did *not* contain—apart from the apartment—a projection or a design in its proper sense. The title "red herring" is therefore justified by the fact that one could barely see anything designed in the plan. As a medium for development, this plan was practically useless, so why all this work? At this point—the reader may forgive that the author does this in an anticipation of what the researchers will find out later in the course of their endeavor—I would already like to zoom in on the investigated procedure's punchline, the shift in mediality. What I wish to stress here is that the plan becomes readable as a design only from a different perspective, namely once the word "medium" is detached from the closed form of the idea and object. Instead, the new reading of the medium plan shifts the focus toward the actions of mediation. In this view, the plan modulates into a material sign that doesn't transport a given idea or determined content, but rather constitutes, shifts, discloses, and derails or enables a process, activities, and methods of use. One has to understand the word "change of use" here in its entirety: it is about the transformation of uses. Not in order to end up with a constructible form, but with the possibility of structural change itself. The proof of that? The UoN would, for example, not have been able to build up the social relationships that were (for economic reasons alone) necessary to bring and keep the project in motion by using the traditional teleological design guidelines or a design's pressure and constraint. The construction site would have been empty and no student would have been interested, let alone those who supported the project from the outside. After all, the benefit of participants was to turn the medium building and its medium plan into an active motive/motif generator: that is, to find and create a giant practice room in which the questions that one would like to ask would appear, that would help to find out what to do and what is at hand. Something like this can only be achieved by refraining from both: freezing the procedure in a plan and a predefined problem, and reducing it to a finalistic implementation or realization. A project like the UoN couldn't have been generated from a finalistic plan, because it needed participating actors. As the project had to be capable of constructively integrating interferences caused by actors, the purport couldn't exist before a plan.

Reverse functionalism[15]

However, when we state that traditional plans allow too little liberty, we are by no means engaging in today's inflationary euphemization of the irrepresentable, the mute, the invisible, the irrational, the unthinkable, and so on. By this is meant that in our context it would, for instance, have been foolish to refrain from using techniques that traditional planning provides, especially when considering the methods of analysis and representation that modern functionalism achieved. What we aim for, however, is *reformulating* functionalism. This is accomplished by switching from the projected function to processing the existing use. In representational terms, this connotes to extending the ontology of the image or plan as objects to an ontology of operations. The switch shifts the focus from the object a representation depicts to the relationships the representation creates in relation to the actions it affects or may affect. Besides the conventional relationship of resemblance between original and copy, between what was (image) or will be (plan) at a certain site and what we see on the image or plan we have before our eyes, in our case light is shed on an additional important strategical relationship: the play of topological operations that produce what we call *dwelling*. Such a relationship does not abandon resemblance, but alters it. As we will illustrate in the course of this essay, such an alteration can take on many forms. With respect to design—which is genuinely

directed toward the work of representation—the switch from the purely representational to the play between resemblance and its alteration is connected to a turn from design to redesign. One should already point out that its operational method depends on a new model of action. Far from a concept of action that reduces the latter to a rationalistic object or subject, redesign and its representations assume a constructive embrace of the action's contingency. That is what we call "technological improvisation."[16] Technologically improvising here means setting the plot as the medium and thus rewriting the plan into an open score. Only when a plan is no longer a mere supply vehicle does it become an actor that enables the structuring of further operations. And that is exactly how specific plans like the one the research team discovered here are constructed.

One might claim that while redefining the plan, the researchers were more likely to be dealing with a non-plan. However, this non-plan was by no means without an objective. It *did* aim at something, namely the change of use. It was designed to allow for the university to combine two heterogeneous logics: on the one hand, the active form's logic of the reuse the building, and on the other, the discursive form's logic of the building code.

The deeper the researchers delve into the plan under the lens of its operational context, the more the aspects described above become apparent. For instance, as reconstruction measures were only necessary for emptying the event hall, the application said: "In the context of reconstruction,

15   See also Christopher Dell, "Reverse Functionalism," in Tomás Valena, Tom Avermaete, and Georg Vrachliotis, eds., *Structuralism Reloaded* (Stuttgart: Axel Menges, 2011).

16   Christopher Dell, *The Improvisation of Space* (Berlin: Jovis, 2019).

only non-bearing walls are to be removed, which won't affect the building's stability."[17] The researchers were only able to define a single designed setting in the plan; namely, the apartment. It offered a "naive" new wall, which stemmed from the question regarding the length of the escape route, and which is also addressed in the cover letter. The application read: "Escape routes are to be facilitated via four ground-level accesses (maximal length 23 m) and windows in each room. The existing fire sections will remain unchanged."[18] The research group considered the wall "naive," as it made the back part (the apartment) accessible from the outside through a hallway and an existing door, while separating it from actual university use. In the later implementation, builders solved this differently.

The researchers then went on to look for activities that link to the application's approval. They found what they were looking for in the construction log. On May 20, 2009, things really kicked off, and lively activities are noted until June 11, 2009. While everything was leading up to the opening event, a virtuoso curricular blast of operations unfolded: green-waste removal, building inspection with an asbestos sanitizer, disposal of mineral wool, clearing out, connecting construction site power, asbestos removal, more green-waste activities, working in the building, windows ("after removing the boards in front of windows, any glass residue is removed. Afterwards, PE sheets are applied to the window frames for waterproofing. For safety reasons, wooden boards (e.g. shuttering boards) are mounted to the

existing window frames"),[19] walls were knocked down, sanitary installations repaired, a temporary water supply installed, kitchen furniture and a terrace set up, the process was coordinated with the district police officer, Mr. Dehning. The students eventually presented the project to the Reiherstieg redevelopment advisory council in order to raise funds for a neighborhood festival.

We don't wish to underestimate the range of knowledgeability in terms of installation or performance art among the researchers, but we can bet that they were quite astonished when they identified an absurd game as the most interesting activity in the planning research perspective. The moment they believed they had discovered the thread behind the red herring, they once again found themselves on the verge of despair—the research group had to recognize a "tomato bingo" as a central aspect of the report! The game was part of the workshop "Arbeiten, Wohnen, Leben" (Working, Residing, Living) with Ton Matton. It was supposed to prepare the UoN for its first use, the neighborhood party and the summer school. The report says:

> Tuesday was the crucial and extremely productive day of the workshop. One round of 'tomato bingo,' developed by Ton, where he acted as host and croupier, was intended to lighten up the mood; a relaxed start to the simultaneous discussion about the goals of the workshop and the UoN in Wilhelmsburg in general. Ton describes his idea of a meaningful completion of the workshop:

17   Ibid.
18   Ibid.

19   Teaching and Research Program Urban Design of the HCU Hamburg, ed., Arbeitsbericht Universität der Nachbarschaften, 52.

contrary to what one might take from the task, it shouldn't be about the planning and construction of a 'fancy' piece of kitchen furniture.[20] Rather, he advocated questioning the whole approach thus far in the development of the 'culture kitchen' project and thus the UoN's approach in developing rapport in the district and setting new impulses here. The kitchen furniture's design and look was not a criterion for the success or failure of the kitchen project. The 'beautiful'[21] title University of Neighborhoods encompassed the project's great charm and decisive quality. Apparently, the project lacked the right medium to enter a (literally) real 'exchange'[22] with the neighborhood. This was, however, crucial for the success of all programmatic projects, which were not prescribed as 'from above,'[23] but instead as something that was developed with and from the local population. What the project and the difficult establishing of contact with the neighbors needed was a medium of exchange. Simply claiming participation was not enough; one had to playfully offer something in return. Incidentally, tomato bingo had provided a useful starting point: tomatoes. In the weeks leading up to the workshop, Ton had been driving around with two hundred homegrown tomato plants in his car. These plants—individually repotted—had now proven to be an ideal medium of exchange and communication. For the rest of the day, students were busy repotting the tomato plants, and then using them as a means of exchange to organize the equipment needed for cooking (plates, cutlery, etc.) around the neighborhood. Using wooden boards found in the attic of the former health department, the students built a shelf to store the great amount of plates, mugs, cans, etc. Apart from organizing the necessary equipment, the campaign naturally fulfilled other purposes as well: it was an unconventional form of advertisement for the neighborhood festival and a guarantee for real participation of the population, as the neighborhood—due to its active participation—could now better identify with what was taking place.[24]

Ton Matton's workshop already contained all elements of what the research group now called "enabling planning": creating new uses and relations within existing constellations and situations. The non-plan of the application for a change of use provided the conceptual and legal structure for a possible transformation of the building to new uses—in other words, uses that cannot be planned beforehand. While the UoN was composed neither of social actions of rational subjects, nor of the supply of communication, but rather of a relational practice of diagrammatically connecting actors, plans were given the task of setting the score of the relational game.

Surely, readers will ask themselves how the UoN managed to stay on track in the midst of all this madness of activity and openness. Apart from the fact that this kind of open course increases the chances of attracting negative attention as a troublemaker

20   Ibid., 55.
21   Ibid.
22   Ibid.
23   Ibid.

24   Ibid.

in the faculty of the actual, i.e. disciplinarily and institutionally secured HCU, which it is a part of, after all. The many mediation discussions certainly helped. However, there was also someone needed to offer support whenever results had to be delayed. This "protective hand" was Michael Koch. His backup allowed the achievement of a technological level with non-plans and improvisations, although it was never finished, a definite ending was never reached.

Red herring revisited

The next planning document that the researchers found in the archive folders at this point was dated exactly one year later: a change request to the building application (which in the meantime was filed under the reference number M/BP/00827/2009/WB) from March 12, 2010. What shifts were made in the 2010 plan that still followed the same argumentation but offered new content? The researchers immediately noticed planning adjustments, meaning a change of an already approved building project. This plan entailed everything that was later to take place and justified *a posteriori*, what had taken place after all in the first flush of practical building excitement. Thus, the wall of the stage area, among others, was removed before the opening, but was only drawn in the adjustments plan.

Did the plan include everything? Once again, not really. Upon closer examination, for instance, the researchers ultimately found the vision to change the closets, something that never happened. But what *was* in the plan already? For example, the kitchen foyer (with a large door facing the

park), the plenum, the roof opening, the apartment (almost the same way it was built later), as well as the sanitary block as it was implemented in the end. But the researchers also stumbled across ambiguities: The kitchen was faked, because the foyer wasn't supposed to be used as a kitchen, despite having been one temporarily. Apparently, the kitchen was moved throughout the process and situated in different locations. In the original plan it was still in the meeting room; from there it wandered to the one next to the boiler room, and then into the foyer as a provisional kitchen, where a wall had been knocked down at some point. In the larger L section, the adjustment plans now also noted demolished walls that were to enlarge the rooms. Thus, the storage room advanced to becoming the stage, and it always stayed that way. The demolition of the living spaces, however, had not yet been applied for. The part that was to be torn down according to the application for a change of use was left in place and pragmatically used as sanitary blocks and bathrooms. This meant that the bathroom and toilet were not, as originally planned, placed where the kitchen was supposed to go. Moreover, the change request presented a service entrance room as well, where the boiler was later installed. Finally, the event room, which was already drawn in the first plan; here, the walls were not even included in the planned change anymore.

The researchers summarized: The first plan was the result of the first semester to make the opening possible in order to move into the building as a university. The second plan emerged from the summer semester, the studio "UdN Bauhütte, Planung und Ausführung" (UoN builder's hut, planning, and implementation) an elective subject. The researchers recalled that it was a group in the co-op next to the office in the university building on Averhoffstrasse. It was there that, after months of work, the adjustment plan was created.

Is it design? Is it a plan?

Altogether, the researchers remained a little confused about still not having an answer as to what planning and design was meant here. Only one aspect seemed safe to them: the results of the student works were, at least in comparison to the common design performance in architecture studies, rather meager. The first plan, drawn by students based on the first semester's plan, didn't show anything but what had already existed, plus two or three gray margins and a vestibule as new construction. Surely, the purpose of the plan was to present the existing situation in order to apply for a change of use. But nothing was designed here at all. What followed was another change of perspective. Now the researchers focused their attention on tasks at hand, which proved to be more complex than initially thought. The tasks worked in both ways simultaneously. On the one hand, in order to start at all—even if it was only about minor construction work that was declared as university operations—one needed permission for university usage, which required an application for a change of use, one that was based merely on the already existing building. Whoever presented what already existed and drew a plan for it quickly ran the risk of delivering a fixed form and thereby concluding the process. In order to not prevent but rather enable usages that could not be planned yet, one had to refrain from presenting what was already there in final form. The plan's analyses had to relate to a particular perspective that focused on possible fields of action and respective connections. The approach to not only generate a change of use, but to also designate it as building application and attach a construction specification proved to be essential. Connecting the change of use with a reconstruction this way became the central part and point of the plan. We should note the core of the process: it consisted of offering a minimal structure that allowed for maximal openings in the existing building. As a few gray drawings, a vestibule, and walls were relating a reconstruction measure to a change of use, the building project was able to be advanced and opened in a very specific way. One thing is clear: the box was supposed to be reconstructed, but nobody knew how yet. Right from the start, the state of knowledge was that the plan applied for something that was not there yet.

The researchers, however, insisted: "This may all be true, but what is different about this method? Traditionally, it is part of the basic principle of design to project something that is not there yet. How does the UoN's procedure still differ from that?" There is only one explanation: The plan diverged from the usual plan in that it asked for something that didn't even exist as an idea yet. The researchers seemed to have disregarded the fact that these actions taken into account by the "improvisational perspective"[25] of the plan were those of a transformation, of the reworking and revision

25   Christopher Dell, *Epistemologie der Stadt* (Bielefeld: Transcript, 2016).

of existing information and its medial translation. This plan—and this applies to all of the UoN's plans—aimed at relating to various characteristics of the elements that it dealt with and at establishing new connections. It did not freeze or render the design, but instead evoked processual events that were set and held in motion by means of relational tensions or critical relationships, acts of reception, or the open interconnection of what was collected within them. A demolition, for instance, was part of the UoN's technological improvisation, and the gradual disappearing of walls was itself an event. Tearing down the outer wall of the kitchen created new means of access, and the kitchen became part of the park opposite. As a series of different architectonic and improvisational works, the UoN's project revealed structures that would have been overlooked in the conventional design routine.

In light of this, the researchers decided to rename the plan "non-plan." They saw it as a plan that followed no plan (as a teleologically projected idea). Had the researchers believed in informal urbanism, they could have comforted themselves by assigning an "informal dimension" to it. They could have also suspected, in terms of "progressive" teaching, that the participants of the UoN were feeling constrained by fixed plans that they always had to experiment with at random. Surprisingly, the non-plan revealed itself by no means as a matter of informality. Quite the opposite: precisely by the *mise-en-forme* of the UoN's rapport to normativity, i.e. the need for a change of use in line with strictly formal building code, the plan found its structure. The request for legal

authorization to even enter the building served as the hinge that guided and embedded the plan structurally, anchored without denying the form, but opened it. Perhaps one should rather have called it an "open plan." What we find here is a third rapport inscribed in the plan: additional to the mimetic relationship of the representation to its referent and the operational relationship between the resemblance and non-resemblance there emerges the important relationship of the plan to a politics of seeing and interpreting, that is the social form of visuality-giving.

Is it knowledge?

The researchers didn't loosen the reins. They remained enamored of the plan's requirements and dug their way to the next dimension: academic performance. After all, the UoN served as curriculum and was thus embedded accordingly. Therefore, it gave weight to the argument that students usually managed to design an entire museum, a football stadium, or an opera house in one semester. In their semester here, however, they didn't achieve anything apart from something that had already existed, simple walls and an even simpler vestibule. The researchers were losing heart. How could they have measured the learning effect? Again they found themselves forced to change their perspective. Only from a genealogical point of view did the learning effect become apparent, namely when looking back to the UoN's primary condition: a competition, prior to the UoN, called Experiment auf der Insel (Island Experiment). Back then, when the competition was held, all participants except for one team preferred the *tabula rasa* method. This meant that they all followed the "problem" they identified with the "solution." All their plans envisioned the immediate demolition of the existing building and erecting a designed house instead. As pointed out earlier, this kind of planning could only be of marginal importance in teaching contemporary architecture and urban design. The central task and challenge was not to design something new, but to face and to understand what existed already. While only one group pursued this idea in the competition, it at the same time—without hesitation and still caught up in traditional design ideas—proposed big gestures: for example, ripping open the roof. In the end, none of the groups followed up on the question that the competition was based on. None of them questioned the prerequisites and conditions or even asked what—considering the situation—could or was supposed to take place here. This task corresponded to the traces of program that were left behind by what once was a public health office. But knowing that this former office, as it had been found in its used structure as an existing building, was going to shape the coming program drastically slowed down the planning process. A deliberate, respectful, and careful way of reading the built structure in its "script-ness" was required. Far from just applying a given method, the project had to invent its own procedure of reading in terms of two logics: the logic of practices embedded in the material structure of the building as well as the logic of enabling practices that were still to be actualized.

Of course, the UoN was confronted by and confronted itself with the former use. This can partly be seen in the first plan, by the small-scale changing of rooms, for example, that suggested and originated in the practice of a public health office. However, one aspect was obvious: after the transformation of use, the building would no longer be a public health office. Therefore, unveiling the scripts was interesting in only a specific manner. By this is meant that reading them as scripts would require a thoroughness that would allow one to understand the building's former use in its full depth. What revealed itself as being fundamentally inscribed in the building and what was now rising to an epistemological level was the single workers' "dwelling." We think, for example, of the assembly hall's basal disposition, which in its first use was a living room with a terrace in front of it, one that in turn had no relevance for the health office and was overgrown. The building's history held different overlapping uses that were partly hidden or that had disappeared. In this sense, what we call the building's scripts did not offer singularity, but multiplicity, in which various practices were inscribed. By no means were they to be reduced to simple categories such as living room, dining room, kitchen, or the like. This points to the specific social form of visuality-giving, i.e. the procedure of script-reading as we understand it. As the UoN's experimental setup showed, it was precisely the deep involvement with and the exposure of the building's architectural structure that made its enabling character visible. To read the building's potentialities through a script lens and expand it with minimal shifts was the core of how it would open up to new uses. Thus, one had to deduce from the non-plan a deconstruction of any script analysis' teleology: the scripts were interesting in their use, but only when this use was considered in accordance with a use related to future potentiality. That is what in an improvisational perspective is termed a point of interconnection. To identify points of interconnection in relation to the building's architectural topology and to look for options to rewire them is at the heart of such a reading process. The use of a door, for instance, wasn't outlined here as a fixed, finalized form, but as a structure that could be opened up for the potential space of new ways of use. This clarifies how the question of improvisation came to the fore in the reversal from (planned) function to (found or enabled) use. In this context, the script performance doesn't mean a given text in the sense of traditional theater, where actors repeatedly perform the same texts written by one author, but the structural framing and pattern for reappropriation and improvisation, which becomes possible only through knowledge of the structure. Understood in this way, the script introduces a notation that depends on the activation of new uses, and enables them at the same time. Again, this intended shift from form to structure does not mean abandoning the former, but rather that the form rises to a meta-form, i.e. from a shape to a conceptual and score-like frame.[26] The script's form of knowledge marks this as the moment when the notation is linked to a faculty: One has to be capable of reading the script in a certain

way in order to initiate and maintain new uses. At this hinge, historical reading becomes intertwined with architectural work. There is one very simple example that provides insight into the main aspects: at the UoN, for instance, after the walls were removed, it turned out that they were not part of the supporting structure. They turned out to be a structure that had been installed later and that could therefore be removed again. The result of the removal was an event room that traced back to the use of the unmarried people's accommodation while having new usages assigned—for example, a seminar room. This was simple, but in no way trivial. After all, it was about clear placement, which obviously drew from previous scripts. The special function as social meeting point was the event room's topological correlation within the structure of the building, as can be seen by the accentuated corner situation, the large windows, the opening towards the terrace, and the second entrance or exit. In this context, placement meant giving the meaning contained in its script back to the space in order to regain a starting point for future development.

Curriculum diagramming: A critical ontology of space

This development was in no way linear, but unfolded from different priorities within the whole and broadly set up curricular process of practical and concrete urban and district analysis, which entwined the UoN project from the first semester on. The fact that on the same day that Group 6 (Architecture) "Preparation of the Building Application" presented its plan, Group 1 (Architecture) "UoN Germ Cell" did a

26   Christopher Dell, *Die Stadt als offene Partitur. Diagramm, Plan, Notation, Prozess, Improvisation, Repräsentation, Citoyenneté, Performanz in Musik, Kunst, Design, Stadtentwicklung* (Zurich: Lars Müller Publishers, 2016).

presentation as well, was a separate occurrence. Group 1 recommended the planning implementation of a minimal space program and a number of diverse planning varieties that significantly differed from the original application for a change of use (see the chapter on "Roof"). All in all, analyses carried out during the teaching program led to connections, here called program proposals. In other words, attempts to discover and connect adequate usages for the building in its urban context. In spatial-practical terms, this process began in the event hall and spread from there. The uses were distributed throughout the building. Practices sought places: for example, the location of the caretaker's apartment. This change, the second of its kind, had at least already been part of the change of use. Its emphasized meaning was similar to that of the accentuated corner space at the top in the plan. And further: although the structure of what was later to be the residential wing was relatively uniform, students found and defined a space within the curricular process, which they doubled by removing the wall for whatever reason. However, one thing is certain: the reasons for this removal cannot be deduced from the plan due to the structure being identical. One could have gone to the other side of the hall as well. In this wing, we also see an equivalence of scripts that didn't hint at any specific use apart from the historical one—probably the living situation in the unmarried people's accommodation. It was exactly this equivalence that qualified the spatial structure for an expansion, i.e. achieving larger units by removing a wall, which later took place on the opposite side of the building's

connecting part. The sanitary rooms and the bathroom already offered suggestions of future residential use, which in turn included the enlargement of the rooms. Beginning in the event room, the use spread in the other direction, the shorter part of the L section, into the associated seminar rooms and via the accentuated hallway. They were opened far enough for a polyvalent, multi-functional unit to emerge from it, which allowed for a working, exhibition, and meeting spot. Within the complex of seminar rooms, a regional area was developed which connected to the hallway in order to transition into the foyer at one end and include the apartment on the other.

Finally, the researchers arrived at the question of the central interface of the building: How is the relay of uses distributed? What should the entrance situation be like? How does one arrive? How is one welcomed? How can an "identity" of the UoN be embedded here, as self-understanding and -relation in such a new way that it emancipates itself from the existing script of "public architecture"? The call for self-reflexivity and -relation reveals itself as the decisive factor: it explains that here, the concept or postulate of an identity of space—a *genius loci* as it were—always means positioning instead of the deduction of an alleged original idea.

The research came to the conclusion that the example of the non-plan showed why the procedure of using analyses of the existing building as a means to uncover structurally relevant starting points for future enablement could be difficult to identify. Surely this method required a much longer time frame than, for example, the *tabula rasa*-oriented draft, which could be used to randomly plan within a space that is considered a neutral container.

Overall, the researchers now understood the UoN's open (non-)plan as a representational process in the form of a critical ontology: the method respected the given as such and at the same time still treated it as something not yet developed in its potentiality. Developing the given's potentiality as a possible space required the double movement of respect, caution, and recognition on the one hand and milling, dismantling, deep drilling, using, intervening, and creating on the other. An illustration of this was the act of opening the roof, something that the team came up with only much later— one and a half years after the project began. Due to the lengthy process of reading the building, however, the roof opening was connected to a completely different foundation within the built structure.

Eventually, the change request attached to the building application incorporated diverse practices and analyses. How crucial the (building and cultural) practice's role was, became visible in hindsight considering the kitchen's double door, which was still closed in the planning adjustment, as well as the windows next to it, which were not pointed out in the plan. Only during the building measures, in the act of making itself, did it become clear that the opening of the event room and kitchen were considered equal and were formed as French doors. In this respect, although the interferences that the UoN carried out were extensive, they didn't lead to any further planning adjustments based on the French doors. Here, the

practice on, and effects of, materials didn't appear as irrational moments that had to be tamed by a plan. On the contrary: the plan was unlocked in a way that practice and things were able to unfold their efficacy in a structural and open manner. And in this case, the word "improvisational" genuinely applied. Seen in this light, the countless notations, scribblings, hand drawings, photographs, stories, protocols, instructions, and even plans created in the process were by no means passive mediators of information. Rather, they came to function as diagrammatic material, as open scores that significantly set in motion, coordinated, and at the same time kept open the action context of actors and things. This allowed the UoN—unlike approaches of playing structure vs. agency or informality vs normativity off against each other—to incorporate social expectations and normativity into the open plan. It is along these lines that the plan represents diagrammatically, independent of being figurative or non-figurative—that is, if one recognizes in it a specific architectural structure, a person, an action, a discursive proposition or not. The plan is a diagrammatic operation, because its image is its topology. It is defined by all the relations we described above, the actions taken, modifications and mistakes made, the interconnections identified, the rewirings opened or actualized, and so on. The visual regime of the plan is that of the *mis-en-scène* of the plan's contingent rapport between the doable and the not doable, between determinacy and indeterminacy, a rapport that plays at the same time on their analogies and non-similarities. In this way, the diagrammatic procedure may be understood as the paradoxical rewiring of heterogeneous logics: between the operations carried out with and within the building, the operations undertaken by the making, reading, and use of representations, the mode of circulation of visuality-giving and the discursive and epistemological critique that embarks on the significations hidden by or embedded in the former's operations and forms. As illustrated by the Take, iterative time-based translation, transposition, and modulation are what the procedural unfolding of the diagrammatic space is all about. That is its recursive state. The visible allows itself to be put on display in moments of signifying tropes and operative agencies, while the discursive signification and the coming into functioning of the project deploys a visuality that in some moments may be blinding—sensitively invoking the red herring's smoke screen.

The open plan *did* something: it persuaded the building department, authorized students and teachers to take action, obligated them to think further, and prohibited the finalization of the process. The liberties that the UoN took, based on the approval of the building application's change request, give an insight into what was definite. Unlike the planning method of the traditional design, the UoN's planning mode never resulted in anything completely new. Anything that was new in the plan of a "planning in the existing" emerged from the analysis of, and practice on, what existed. The latter, however, needed an opening in the plan's form itself: as a meta-form, it had to provide structural openings for practical reconstruction, namely in a way that reinterpretations and shifts could still be added to the draft. Not only was one able to create openings in the scripts available, but to also develop them within the plan.

Temporary conclusions

While the understanding of a plan as the orientation of a finalistic action applied only to a limited extent here, it nevertheless remained valid. But instead of a single target, the researchers were dealing with a range of multiple targets. It is precisely in that act of constant rewriting of itself that the improvisation becomes technological and a substantial part of the planning process. As the drawn plans regarding the building application and the legal transformation of the building's use impressively demonstrate—contrary to the idea of informal building strategies—the UoN does *not* renounce knowledge in the form of representation. In fact, the researchers even found the most common and conventional architectonic means of representation, floor plans, and building applications. What was different from the conventional planning was the representations' mode of reading and showing the built and to be built, namely a diagrammatic one, while their practice was improvisational.

The researchers then came to the temporary conclusion that there was something special about planning with the existing. To say that this kind of planning works diagrammatically again points out the heterogeneity between the building's physical logic and the logic of its use. Especially the seemingly unlikely coming into functioning of this heterogeneity was an aspect that the whole work of the UoN was focused on. As a result of that, the building could not be reduced to compositional nor to semantic inter-pretations. At the same time, one would be wrong to assume that plan-ning with an existing building provides a design analysis that automatically accounts for conclusions regarding a form to be designed. If the design pro-cess takes the reading of the built as a script as its starting point, fragmen-tary elements of built situations in turn become active materialities that affect rather than passively fill a form. In light of this, it was about working out how phenomena are embedded in their respective actions as well as their organizational principles and thus dis-covering new diagrammatic framings, i.e. creating meta-forms and score-like notations for design processes.

One very effective framing method or meta-form turned out to be the teaching format of the Take. It con-sisted of developing structural princi-ples and rules that crystallized from the serial repetition of research and spatial reading exercises, and inter-vened in these principles and rules if necessary. For example, anyone who genealogically examines the UoN building's scripts in their structure will continually come across certain prin-ciples of structural reconstruction. This kind of research strategy oper-ates in reverse to functionalism and formalism, which take the environ-ment for granted, claiming that archi-tecture matches its function or form, thus presuming the homogeneity be-tween physique and function or form. As pointed out earlier, in our case it is about thematizing the heterogeneity and asymmetry between them in order to eventually and experimentally extract the potential of what is now called "planning in the existing," without being reduced to naive

empiricism. Just as such criticism of functionalism, formalism, or even structuralism, and their assumption regarding a homogeneous connection between form or structure and use, undermines and transcends the com-mon understanding of function and category, it equally raises the question of a new definition of design. Archi-tecture, i.e. built structure, always comprises different information about actions. At this point, the researchers referred to Bruno Latour's dictum that today, it is precisely the knowledge that lies within indeterminacy that is at stake: "to learn how to feed off uncertainties, instead of deciding in advance what the furniture of the world should look like."[27]

Material and cultural activities are mixed into a paradoxical form of oper-ation that we call improvising organi-zation. It is a form of organization that is based on the knowledge of how to permanently rewire information and activities (here of research and teach-ing, learning and building).[28] The dis-proportional growth of this field within the UoN has to be discursively consid-ered in relation to the increased atten-tion given since the 1990s to the con-cepts of the performativity of the city and the production of space. At the same time, however, intersecting areas appeared between the social and eco-nomic fields, which also played a part in the rough creation of a master's program in Urban Design at the HCU. With this in mind, the UoN's framing was understood as a prototype, turn-ing the building and associated activi-ties into an experimental area for how

27   Bruno Latour, *Reassembling the Social: An Introduction to Actor-Network Theory* (Oxford: Oxford University Press, 2005), 115.

28   Christopher Dell, *Die improvisierende Organisa-tion* (Bielefeld: Transcript, 2012).

specific spaces are produced and how this method can be shown in the context of a teaching and research project. Urban questions were interrelated with the curriculum's various module forms in the same way as with those relating to building. Programming and structural practice merged into each other; the neighborhood's structures, relations and functions slowly but steadily trickled into the UoN; while in the end—with the *Hotel?Wilhelmsburg*—these functions proliferated throughout the building. The UoN used the variety of presentation techniques to demonstrate how recipients as well as students and teachers could be set in discursive and physical movement through a self-construction. The relational interconnection, rewiring, overlapping, connection, and penetration of various contexts, activities, and materials served not least to generally question conditions and possibilities of planning. The areas of interior and exterior (discussed both socially and in terms of urban development) allowed permeation by the actors of the UoN in the very same way in which they placed their own role between design and political actors, between production and organization. One might describe the building based on Susan M. Pearce's[29] terminus "object in action" as "building in action": one that can carry, accept, and always transform meanings. This describes the dynamic that became building practice as was carried out by the UoN. In the end, this kind of practice, which included the transformation of how it could be developed through arranging actors, things, and framings, through spatial re-contextualizing, shifting of the display, programs and catalogue work, ultimately represented a continuation of the performative structuralist work from the 1960s, as found in Cedric Price, Archigram, Smithsons, or Metabolists. Unlike the latter, the UoN's practice did not assume an externalized space. Instead, it firmly accentuated the research of conditions of spatial improvisation—which neither wants nor is able to externalize nor homogenize space—and the planning-related questions of processuality and contingency associated with it. Far from a libertarian 1960s utopia, the space that the UoN repeatedly recreated was a meta-form shaped by conflicting programs and contractual agreements. As the building application exemplifies, such a meta-form in practice can again deliver motives, occasions, and potentialities for new structural openings of a building's form that enable heterogenous and not-yet-determined modes of use.

Reading the UoN through the lens of its building application plan revealed the project's triple agency: its actions' performative power of singularity, the value of epistemologically framing these actions, and the traces of history they contain as well as, finally, the capacity of wiring and rewiring or letting clash heterogeneous series of actions and their constitutive elements in order to compose new worlds of commonality. In this way, the most fugitive activities—such as tearing down a wall, preparing a place to sleep, cooking a meal, or installing a boiler—reveal themselves as proto discursive, non-propositional, and non-teleological propositions of new architectural and urban design

---

29   Susan M. Pearce, *Museums, Objects, and Collections* (Washington, DC: Smithsonian Books, 1993).

realities. We now see how the UoN glides between two contrary logics. On the one hand, its actions reveal themselves as being true to the project's original postulate of displaying the building process as performance. Under the conceptional umbrella of "dwelling as f*ACT*," a doubling of presence and presentation occurs that claims, "We are here." On the other hand, it is the teaching logic of critique that informs about the impossibility of isolating actions into a sphere of presence. Quite on the contrary, the curriculum forms a diagram that sheds light on how the actions are ingrained in a circulation of discursive and economic imaginary and the interpretation of the latter. Putting forth a local redisposition of agency and operating with singular rearrangements of the circulating actions, the curriculum diagram intentionally played on the ambiguity of significations.

By doubling and contrasting logics, the UoN tells the story of how architecture and urban design is about actions. Most of these actions might—according to today's standards—not look much like the work of architecture and urban design, but they are resolutely material, quantifiable, arrangeable, historicizable. The UoN focused exactly on these different, seemingly ephemeral, activities of dwelling and building to illuminate architecture and urban design not only as objects, but also as procedures. The activities examined here are altogether more mundanely practical and yet, in our eyes, inseparable from design practice, and they are entirely related to the understanding of the design work as such. This essay therefore attempts—as does the whole book at hand—to propose a

methodological path in which the fugitive activities of the UoN are theorized and contextualized in order to position the work as constitutive rather than merely procedural, auxiliary, or incidental. Through laying the emphasis on interpreting a red herring, i.e. a marginal design act of the UoN's genealogy—the representational building application plan—this essay focuses on a shift in urban design theory from mere object specificity to the precarious ontology of improvisational acts, which attempts to refigure the making, positioning, and understanding of the work of urban design as such.

ROOF

Bernd Kniess

"He is making the roof. What kind of roof? A beautiful or an ugly one?
He has no idea. It's just a roof."[1]

The playful shadow of the leafy canopy fills the room. The projection
surface that creates something like that is at the same time translucent in a
way that hardly resists the light, so that one might almost believe one is
standing in a garden. But the view is blocked; the spatial depth is limited to
the moving patterns on a surface and only represents the imagination of a
possible outside. Interior. Not the usual kind of interior; it slightly resembles
a greenhouse. Right at the center, there are kitchen furnishings, assembled
from different pieces of furniture and other materials, each of which has its
own purpose and prior use, and which have now been put together with care
to find their new purpose. The objects placed on and around the furniture
indicate heavy use. Just as the first impression of the exterior of the house
would hardly have led to the assumption that it was a university, one isn't
prepared to enter a space occupied in that way, let alone for the unusual
network of purposes in foyer and kitchen. In its everyday practical chaos, it
still feels familiar. Everything indicates that what has come together here
wasn't intended to be like this—at least not in the professional view of the
architect. The eyes look for explanations, traces that shed light on the
changes that were made in order to reach this state.

The room is framed by two opposite gabled walls, one smoothly plastered and painted, the other with clear signs of use from decades past. With
scratches and holes and the more or less successful attempts to repair them,
tracks of a reddish liquid that had run down the surface and stopped at the
intersection of the brick ceiling on the wall in the upper area, messages
scribbled with different pens and colors on the wall, stickers and notes that
are copied or written on, a postcard. Pots and pans hang from a wooden coat
hanger. A vertical strip of cement finish indicates where the wall that used to
divide the space once stood. The change of material in the floor is proof of
that; the rough ground strip of cement transitions into the old terrazzo floor.

The removed wall, the cut in the roof and ceiling: signs of physical
changes that have created a space within the modest 1950s spatial structure
that promises luxury in its openness. The roof's translucent materiality and
the large window highlight the impression of a threshold space that feels
like it belongs neither to the inside nor to the outside. Greenhouse, entrance
hall, foyer, kitchen, stove: none of these alone, but all together, make the
room. Interestingly enough, the French word *foyer* describes a stove or place
with a lit fire—a household, a home. This seems to be the closest description
of the room: the kitchen foyer, a place where people gather. This text is
about designing the question of how use provides a roof for the project.

---

1   Adolf Loos, *On Architecture*, selected and introduced by Adolf and Daniel Opel, trans.
         Michael Mitchel (Riverside, CA: Ariadne Press, 2002), 73.

Roof(s)

The German word *Dach* describes, in its original Old High German form
dah, something that covers and thus protects, be it a roof, a house, or a
covering, i.e. an article of clothing. In this way, the roof can be something
directly overlying, or something that spans around from close proximity or
at a distance, offering protection. A roof over one's head not only offers
protection from the hostile outside world; it marks a place and offers accommodation, activities, and community. People live and work under one roof—
alone and in companionship. When referring to the protective purpose of a
roof, whether as a shelter, refuge, home or apartment, Germans use the term
Obdach. (The prefix *ob-* means above.) In a symbolic sense, the German
idiom *unter Dach und Fach* (literally, "under the roof and framework" and
equivalent to "wrapped up nicely") as well as a given spatial enclosure
suggest that something is finished and completed, and is thus a safe place.
As diverse as roofs are, they are equally different in terms of their spatial
structure, social, economic, cultural, symbolic, and organizational forms of
construction.

However, let us stick to the roof of a house for now. Standard works of
architectural technology[2] note that the purpose of a roof should be to protect
a building from weathering and thermal loss. If it is equipped with solar
collectors and panels, it can be used to generate heat or power. A roof is
made up of one horizontal surface, inclined on one side, or by two or more
surfaces that are arranged at certain angles to each other. Experts speak of
flat, monopitch, saddle, hipped and half-hipped, tent, or mansard roofs. The
saddle roof is the most common form of construction and one that we associate with houses starting in early childhood. The roof construction stands
for all of the load-bearing components. Its supporting framework can be
implemented as a rafter or purlin roof. In order to precisely describe a roof,
one needs information on the form, slope, ground plan, construction, and
materiality of the supporting framework, its roofing, drainage, and insula-
tion, as well as directions on how to combine its elements. With this knowledge, we can constructively classify the roof as described above: a purlin
roof on reinforcing gable walls connected to large-sized roofing without
battens. The roofing material consists of lighting building elements from
Rodeca GmbH; the product name is PC 2540-6.

In the context of our project, we should not be satisfied to just describe
the roof in its structural form. Other important aspects are the conditions that
framed its construction and, ultimately, the possibilities that arose during its
use. Only in hindsight does it become apparent that at the time of necessary
decision-making, the forces at work had often and to a large extent remained
vague or hidden. Only by thoroughly analyzing data (this is the socio-empir-
ical part of the project's methodology) can the connections become
apparent; how the decision to take on the project, which was initially influenced by spontaneity and affinity, was eventually constructed by facts. In

2   Cf. Ulf Hestermann, Dietrich Neumann, and Ulrich Weinbrenner, *Frick/Knöll Baukonstruk-
      tionslehre* (Wiesbaden: Springer Vieweg, 2006).

other words, the empirical-constructional level in approaching the roof is not enough to determine its purpose for the project; its social and empirical aspects and relations and the embedded symbolic content must be discussed as well. Now, the double twist is that the social conflict situation from which the roof emerges can itself create forms of symbolic roofs. In the symbolic and cultural register, we also encounter the roof, for example, as the definition of organizational structures. Thus, its use in German word formations is common, such as *Dach*-company, -organization, and -associations; similar to English, where *Dach* becomes "umbrella." The preceding *Dach* expresses the idea that it stands for the upper end of an organization, which controls subareas without exercising production or actions, or in order to advocate their legal interests. Such roofs follow hierarchical models of organization and control, each with its own decision-making process and communication structures. Their order generally follows the typical structure of organizations, as described in the form of the "professional pyramid,"[3] which derives the formation of grades from reflections on task differentiation.

We know the corresponding communication model from personnel and organization development. It is recipient- and result-oriented, and its thought and communication structures highlight the endeavor to make information communicable more quickly. Tailored to the individual recipients, those models are supposed to accommodate them with their questions and needs regarding the respective topic, which only means that possible questions are already answered by the message and thus become superfluous. Lucius Burckhardt had pointed out such mechanisms in the field of construction, stating that just as the key fits the lock, so does the solution fit the subject. The benefactor of the solution is the expert. The subject is not traced back to the origin of the problem, but is led directly to a solution that is, of course, constructional.[4] The starting point and focus of communication is and remains solely focused on the goal that is to be accomplished by using strategies and avoiding detours.

The roof as a message

In our project archive, one can find a 70-page brochure,[5] the proposed concept for the "development of a communicative strategy and tactic for mediation" of the Experiment auf der Insel (Island Experiment) project. It dates back to June 2008 and apparently remained unpublished. There is an umbrella message under "Article 3. Strategy," that is supposed to be conveyed to different "dialogue groups":

"The HafenCity University is operating a temporary experimental space on the Elbe island until the final presentation of the IBA in 2013, in which

---

3   Cf. David H. Maister, "Balancing the Professional Services Firm," *Sloan Management Review* (Fall 1982): 15–29.
4   Lucius Burckhardt, *Bauen ein Prozess* (Teufen: Verlag Arthur Niggli, 1972), 14.
5   "Kommunikations-Konzeption – Experiment auf der Insel – zur Profilierung und Bekanntmachung eines temporären HCU-Standortes auf der Elbinsel im Rahmen der IBA Hamburg 2013," UoN Project Archive, 2013.

students and people from near and far constantly transform and design the space and excitedly present a challenging program.

- Visitors are welcome.
- Ideas and participation are welcome.
- Support is welcome."[6]

Several actors are named in this message, as well as places where they should become active. The engaging tone is supposed to kindle an interest in the project and active participation. Undergirding "pillar messages" make use of stereotypes to focus on what potential actors within and outside the university should think about the project—had it been a successful one—and not what they could do to turn it into an actual project in the first place, regardless of what criteria for success should be taken into account for whom. What remains vague is both the idea behind and the aim of the project. The same applies to the experimental space's focus. There is no indication as to what kind of experiments are to be carried out here and what kind of knowledge there is to gain. The communication strategy and mediation tactics do not give any insight into the project itself. In order to gain a deeper understanding, we can only consult both project initiators, the HCU and the IBA Hamburg.

The HafenCity University (HCU)[7] was established in 2006 by the Free and Hanseatic City of Hamburg. It was primarily higher-education policies and location-related goals that led to the founding of the new University of the Built Environment and Metropolitan Development, which was supposed to restructure the programs of architecture, engineering, and urban planning in Hamburg. Four departments from three different schools were initially to remain at their old locations and be brought together under the virtual roof of the new university with the goal of its materializing in the eponymous district.

The HCU considers itself a "laboratory for building and urban development, offering space for a broad examination of metropolitan issues in the future—a space of science, building, and urban culture, and of the debate on architecture and metropolitan development."[8] Furthermore, it seeks to face challenges of the metropolitan environment with the scientific model of transdisciplinary methods, "which develops out of urban lifeworlds and seeks sustainable solutions for current structural-spatial, ecological, social, cultural, and economic challenges."[9]

The IBA[10] joined the project and set itself the ambitious goal of using its running time from 2006 to 2013 to seek "answers to the most urgent questions of the 'modern city'; their guiding themes are city and climate change,

---

6   "Kommunikations-Konzeption," 41.
7   Cf. "HCU HafenCity Universität Hamburg," HCU HafenCity University Hamburg, accessed May 24, 2018, www.hcu-hamburg.de.
8   "Die Zukunft entsteht in den Metropolen," HCU HafenCity University Hamburg, accessed May 24, 2018, www.hcu-hamburg.de/fileadmin/documents/Universitaet/Imagebroschuere_deutsch_Juli_2015.pdf.
9   "Die Zukunft entsteht in den Metropolen."
10   "Zur Internationalen Bauausstellung Hamburg 2006–2013," IBA Hamburg, accessed May 24, 2018, www.iba-hamburg.de.

cosmopolis, and metrozones."[11] The IBA defines building exhibitions overall as "temporary laboratories" and considers them to be "the most influential instruments in urban development,"[12] which should be questioned in this context in the same way as the way experiments are to be carried out here.

In both cases, the term "laboratory" seems to be the metaphor for individual ways of attending to great questions, issues, or contemporary challenges, with the goal of being able to answer or solve them. The aim here is to examine the significance of both laboratory and experiment with regard to the project development of the UoN.

Carte blanche and tabula rasa

Cooperation of the two actors was arranged in 2007. The student competition was held under the title "Island Experiment." The subtitle specifies the enterprise as a "temporary intervention." The tender documents highlight the attractive central location with an adjoining park, in a good middle-class neighborhood, an area for single-family houses, social establishments, and the former flak tower; a 3,290-square-meter property with a lush tree population. Suggestions follow, for instance, when it is a question of the quality of "temporary buildings" that could be placed freely within the "landscape area" or when the advantages of "buildings of practical value" are emphasized, which could "studiously initiate exceptions, grab the observer's attention, convey economically and didactically motivated messages and offer themselves as places for simulating possible new realities (the experiment), of acting, celebrating, communicating, playing, or of civic participation."[13] Developing a spatial program was part of the task. The defined target was to implement the project in spring/summer 2008. The awardees were to be considered after the recommendation of a jury in the further elaboration of service phases four to eight according to HOAI.[14] What is noticeable is that the building on the property had not been mentioned with a word in the competitive tender.

The results demonstrate that the students had understood the instructions in the call for proposals. Of the fourteen works submitted, only one proposal dealt with the existing building. This draft was chosen by the jury in the presentation on December 13, 2007.

A house after all

There is a document with the subject *Border Post IBA – HCU Cooperation Project Next Steps*[15] in our project archive, dated January 24, 2008, in which the IBA's managing director, Uli Hellweg, addressed HCU president Steven

11   "Memorandum zur Zukunft von Internationalen Bauausstellungen," IBA Hamburg, accessed May 24, 2018, www.iba-hamburg.de/fileadmin/Die_IBA-Story/IBAmeetsIBA_Kurzportrait-web.pdf.
12   "Zur Internationalen Bauausstellung Hamburg 2006–2013," IBA Hamburg, accessed May 24, 2018, www.iba-hamburg.de/iba-hamburg-gmbh.html.
13   "Tender text student competition," UoN Project Archive, 2007.
14   Official Scale of Fees for Services by Architects and Engineers. The named services include: (4) Building permission application, (5) Execution drawings, (6) Preparation of contract award, (7) Assisting award process, (8) Project supervision.
15   "Entwurf Nutzungsvereinbarung," UoN Project Archive, 2008.

Spier with a surprising interpretation of the awarded work. According to him, the concept had planned "temporary working spaces for students of the HCU as well as an interim use by the IBA GmbH's Educational Offensive."[16] The spaces were to be available from the end of 2008 to 2013 and allow the HCU to grapple with the IBA's guiding themes, namely in an "artistically orchestrated location on the Elbe island, primarily intended for this purpose."[17] The building of around 500 square meters in size was the former public health office, located "amid the urban Reiherstieg district"[18] on a large tree-covered property. The list of available rooms according to the plan's status is followed by the declaration that the building had been supplied "ready to use (sanitary facilities, provisional heating and electrical installations, telephone connection)"[19] and that the IBA was currently reviewing how the use of individual rooms could be organized. Moreover, a collective meeting was supposed to serve the purpose of realizing "a possible utilization concept at the hands of the HCU and thereby 'define' the existing cooperation between the IBA and the HCU for the duration of the International Building Exhibition."[20]

Performance of actors and the organizational setting

In our search for the motives that eventually led from the Island Experiment to the University of Neighborhoods project, we came upon a short report in the documents that Michael Koch had written much later for a second UoN brochure,[21] in which he referred to the framework conditions at the time. The founding of the HafenCity University as The University for Built Environment and Metropolitan Development in 2006 coincided with the announcement for the IBA 2013, whose focus lay on the Elbe island in terms of urban development policy. Koch described Uli Hellweg's idea of locating the HCU in Wilhelmsburg after all, which he suggested as part of the university's founding process. It was too late, however: the location in HafenCity had already been decided upon and the competition for the new building was already underway. At this point, the university had long been planned as part of the urban development, in the same way that the newly founded university benefited from the space of legitimacy in this new district.[22] Conversely, the IBA needed the HCU in its thematic orientation as space of legitimacy and basically saw it as its more or less natural partner. Without letting decisions about the location mislead him, Hellweg tried to not only get the HCU interested in the topics of the IBA, but also make the exhibition more present on the Elbe island. The property and the vacant

---

16   "Entwurf Nutzungsvereinbarung."
17   "Entwurf Nutzungsvereinbarung."
18   "Entwurf Nutzungsvereinbarung."
19   "Entwurf Nutzungsvereinbarung."
20   "Entwurf Nutzungsvereinbarung."
21   "UdN-Broschüre 2," ed. Urban Design, 2019.
22   Christopher Dell, Bernd Kniess, Dominique Peck, et al., "The Assembly of the University of the Neighbourhoods (UoN): A Documentation of Making New Forms of Agencies Available," in *Housing – A Critical Perspective*, ed. Graham Cairns (Liverpool: Architecture_Media_Politics_Society, 2016).

building, i.e. the former public health office, finally provided an occasion to establish the collaboration in Wilhelmsburg.

Our electronic archive reveals the report of a meeting on April 4, 2008[23] in which representatives of both institutions took part in the HCU's executive boardroom. The IBA representatives gave an account of the further development of the winning project with the participation of the students in cooperation with an architectural firm that was already on board, which served as the basis for calculating a cost estimate. Both partners in the project agreed that the calculated (net) cost of EUR 685,666.80 was too costly in the given framework. The HCU's subsequent counterproposal no longer discussed the building but only the IBA grounds, which were to "serve the purpose of students as working space and laboratory to implement their concepts"[24] while taking into account and incorporating the IBA's ideas for use.[25]

Despite this having been a pragmatic decision, as the available project budget of EUR 540,000 wouldn't have sufficed for financing the construction measures alone, this decision made by the executive board nevertheless led to the proceedings and result of the competition being declared obsolete and the project thus being reset.

The moment when this decision was made in front of the board coincided roughly with my entry into the HCU and hearing about the Island Experiment project for the first time in an e-mail from an extended circle of colleagues. Michael Koch, who, as I later found out, had been an essential part of the project's proceedings up to that point (but had not participated in this significant meeting with the board), conveyed ideas to the president about how the project could be integrated in the 2009 Summer of Architecture, ideas he had taken from a conference at the Hamburg Chamber of Architects. In early June, Martina Nitzl, Koch's research associate, provided me with information on the progress of the project thus far.[26] This was followed by more e-mails and phone calls with various stakeholders, and events started happening very fast. I eventually found out why things were so urgent in a telephone call with the chancellor of the university, who had to make a decision regarding the HCU temporarily taking over the property in order to inform the tax authorities on the very same day.

On June 10, I had an initial meeting about the content with Martina Nitzl, who at the time was busy with a project proposal for further fundraising. Less than a week later, there was a briefing in front of the presiding committee regarding framework conditions for the possible takeover of the project; this was continued in early July with representatives of the IBA, the International Garden Show (IGS), and the HCU. The agenda of this meeting mentioned handing over the project to a core team of Professors Koch, Dell, and Kniess, the conclusion and documentation of the competition phase, and the *Project Proposal National Urban Development Policy* which was

23   "Gesprächsprotokoll HCU-IBA," UoN Project Archive, 2008.
24   "Gesprächsprotokoll HCU-IBA."
25   "Gesprächsprotokoll HCU-IBA."
26   "Realisationskonzept IBA," UoN Project Archive, 2008.

submitted on June 30, 2008. They discussed changes to the quality agreement with the IBA and a future structure for the project. Questions regarding the project's advisory board, the sponsorship, public relations, sponsoring, fundraising, demolition, and asbestos removal were also discussed.[27] The project proposal presented already suggested a significant realignment. When talking about the existing structure, it was now about the "resource" that was supposed to be "continuously transformed," with students and all departments at the HCU involved in the "interdisciplinary development and building process." Along with the temporary preparation, the building's content-related orientation was also to be developed throughout ongoing studies. The objectives of the project, such as the development and communication of new perspectives on *city*, the inclusion of everyday realities in design and transformation processes that were to be made tangible, the goal of getting students and citizens interested in the development of the Elbe island, as well as the integration of local employment agencies and educational institutions in the processes, all conveyed an expanded understanding of building culture as part of everyday urban reality.

Unaware of the decision made by the board in April, the structural transformation of the existing building was suddenly once again on the agenda. There is an IBA document dated July 30, 2008 on the *Status of IBA Projects for the 2010 Interim Presentation*. It discusses the *Experiment auf der Insel (M3)* and gives insight into the project's structure and participating actors, and also offers an idea of potential organizational settings and procedure. Responsibilities were allocated, planning issues considered, and demonstration targets for the interim presentation in 2010 were set, including their respective forms of presentation. Very practical requirements were listed as well: for instance, the clearance of unexploded ordnance,[28] the establishment of an advisory board, finalizing and signing the quality agreement, the approval by the advisers of the building concept and the submission of the building application under the participation of the redevelopment advisory council and the urban planning committee, and finally the grant of building permission, start of construction, and setting of the IBA landmark. According to the schedule, the reconstruction would be finished in May, and the opening would take place on time in June. The concept for the presentation year was to be finished by September; after that, approval of the advisory board in October and the subsequent start of its implementation, and then the development of the concept by March and its presentation in April. The activities listed here were all responsibilities of the building contractor, which in this case, to state it once again, was the HCU. The overarching theme of the two-page document was metro zones; it shows the color green in the form of a stylized traffic light at the top right corner of the first page.

27   "E-Protokoll IBA-HCU," UoN Project Archive, 2008.
28   "As demolisher, the building contractor is responsible for the property's freedom of unexploded ordnance. Thus, he is liable–before the start of construction in the context of the approval plans–to initiate regular examinations regarding the construction area's exposure to explosives." "Kampfmittelfreiheit: Kurzübersicht zu den Pflichten," Kampfmittelfrei Bauen, accessed May 24, 2018, www.kampfmittelportal.de/bauherrauftraggeber.html.

On August 5, 2008, the land transfer agreement was signed between the chancellor of the HCU and the tax authorities.

From August 8 to 10, 2008, the newly appointed project team of the Teaching and Research Program of Urban Design held a closed meeting to draft the concept of the project's content. The presentation of the resulting concept paper took place on September 1, 2008 in front of the HCU executive board with the expectantly project title: *UoN, University of the Neighborhoods – Enabling Architecture for a Learning City.*[29]

Organizational Roof – contractual agreements

There were various actors indirectly and directly involved in the project just at the HCU; people from the purchasing department, cost center, the department for third-party funding, controlling, the legal office, president, chancellor, vice-president of teaching and research, the deans of different programs of study, professors, students and lecturers from Architecture, Civil Engineering, Urban Planning, Metropolitan Culture and Urban Design bachelor's and master's programs. The diverse networks of relationships were reflected in contracts, minutes of meeting, and memos of conversations, enabling us to anticipate how this form of communication would develop throughout further proceedings when it came to defining competencies and responsibilities, and how the respective maintenance and monitoring would be carried out via available monitoring and quality management mechanisms. Rarely did only one institution participate in proceedings, and both of them were interested in the other party's painstaking observance of their own rules and regulations. Part of the ongoing work was the constant demand for translation, assembling, and (re)connection of actors, regulations, and discourses. It was a matter of redefining the interfaces between actors and their interests time and time again.

An abandoned house

The house lies untouched, while it is itself imbued with a web of discourses. This resulting network of actors and their actions in different places can be understood as the project's display in its causal networks, even if different vectors are far from being clearly defined. The structure is closely interwoven and has gained visibility and effectiveness on levels other than that of structural space. This points to an expanded range of design possibilities, which seems to exceed that of classical or conventional architectural design by far. If we want to know more about this framework, its materialities and energy fields that connect or bind them together and how one might intervene in them, we will also find out what a challenge it is to keep a constant

---

29   After decades of a political stagnation in urban development following the catastrophic flood of 1962 and the subsequent phase when the island was basically left to its own resources, undesirable developments and omissions were now supposed to be reviewed in a tour de force of urban development that also accounted for political opposition. In this context, the project group considers the eponymous "experiment" barely appropriate and equally employable. The suggestion of the project sponsorship's institutional origin, combined with the highlighted interest in the special political and economic situation, predefines the pragmatic references from which the new project name will emerge.

eye on these interrelations, to untangle them again and again, and to understand the conditions under which they had developed, without falling into empiricism that would completely rob them of their indeterminacy.

Open form – from experimental system to *city*

Throughout the next steps, we did not focus our energy on one object (as was the case in the competition), but instead considered the possibility of how the object might develop, in order to figure out how to have designing influence on the processes. We were aware that we thus had to accept indeterminacies of an uncertain future. And this was exactly where the experimental set-up came back into play. François Jacob describes experimental systems as machinery that manufactures the future;[30] small but complete work units in research set up in such a way that they provide as-yet-unknown answers to questions that the experimentalist is also not yet capable of clearly asking.[31] And following Hans-Jörg Rheinberger, we do not understand experimental systems as arrangements for inspection and ideally for giving answers, but rather according to their suitability for the materialization of questions. However, this also means having to face unforeseen actions and the places where these actions' scripts are embedded. In trying to understand the state of what we can know, we set things in motion and receive an order that enables us to participate in what we cannot (yet) know. Bringing this to light requires at least a vague idea of what may surface and a motive to want to find out what is still unknown to us. After all, if I am completely unprepared, I cannot be surprised by the new. I might even overlook it.

In the end, we are left with our interests, as students, teachers, researchers, etc. So what are the motives for dealing with this specific urban situation? What are the questions that we ask of this situation, location, and actors? What are procedures that we derive from this? How do we set ourselves in motion, how do we become active, and how do we eventually translate the rehearsed way of producing space imaginable into future possibilities of its development? How can we think of architecture and *city*, which takes use as its starting point and sets it as a goal? As an open form that provokes possibilities rather than regulating them. Where to start? What actors to follow? It will be those that are remarkable and that affect us, and some other ones. When examining elements and systems more closely, we learn to identify actors from their traces and actions in locations. Things may have come alive having been projected, designed, and construed, but their constant use, i.e. the processes of negotiation and appropriation, constantly influences and changes their form.

The project itself taught us how the absence of motives or questions guiding the process leads to using closed forms of individual steps, which can make previous actions of many (at least for a brief moment) obsolete as

---

30   François Jacob, 1988, p. 12, quoted in Hans-Jörg Rheinberger, *Experimentalsysteme und epistemische Dinge. Eine Geschichte der Proteinsynthese im Reagenzglas* (Göttingen: Wallstein Verlag, 2002), 22.

31   Ibid.

a result of a decision (perhaps the right one at the time) made by one individual. Our motive to develop the project in an open process from what was available resulted in the withdrawing of such kinds of lonely decision again without it ever being up for negotiation. Thus, the motive comes to the fore, the interest in something that makes our interconnections more tangible, in order to open the space up to something that can only ever occur in this framework.

Opening up the form requires committing to the given framework and asking what it is all about. What can we do in a situation that is based on expectations, notions, institutional and individual interests, regulations, contractual commitments, in which the leeway seems predefined? One chance may be to stop doing what is necessary and predefined—something non-contingent—which would mean pursuing the superficial task that was reduced to the first step.

While it was political and representational motives that had led to the plan, it was the same motives that predicted its failure. Why? Because they ignored inevitable events of interaction between human and nonhuman actors and postponed them to a later time, when the spatial setting was created by outsourced processes. This, however, eliminated the chance of becoming familiar with the method or tools, as Rheinberger said in reference to Polanyi, in order to *incorporate* them, while we also *reside* in them.[32] Therefore, we were confronted with the paradox that the necessary requirement for a successful experiment was indeed not doing the supposedly necessary. The real way was to not solve both questions/difficulties separately—to then put up with failure on both ends—but, rather, to see them as one. To trust that the silent knowledge of a researcher gets its external shape and location from a technical apparatus of the experimental system, while casual attention in turn embodies this apparatus with tools in regard to the researcher.[33] Rheinberger calls this dual structure of intervening and reaching out "attention" (*Augenmerk*).

Iterations

Sure, it seems natural before a (new, re- or continued) construction to make clear what needs to be done. This is the typical task for the building contractor as a prerequisite for the next step, the question of how to bring this into shape; the classical role of the architect. With the question of a "temporary intervention with practical value,"[34] it becomes more difficult because it is not clear what is meant by intervention, what utilization means and what its worth is. Therefore, if we focus on the possibility of utilization, we deal with the requirements of a substantial project development as a prerequisite for any spatial implementation. However, such a requirement is

---

32   Karl Polanyi, 1969, p. 148, cited in Hans-Jörg Rheinberger, *Experimentalsysteme und epistemische Dinge. Eine Geschichte der Proteinsynthese im Reagenzglas* (Göttingen: Wallstein Verlag, 2002), 81.
33   Ibid.
34   Cf. "Ausschreibungstext Studentenwettbewerb," UoN Project Archive, 2007.

neither rooted in the classical work of an architect,[35] nor is it part of the architectural training; still, it was a requirement formulated in the competition mentioned here. In general architectural proceedings, the (more or less concrete) task marks the beginning, from which the idea and concept are developed, which are then translated into the design proposal of a spatial arrangement, usually represented by drawings of floors, sections, views, and usually a 3-D image as a rendering. The Island Experiment competition included both requirements: program/project development and design development. The results, however, do not show enough of either aspect for their synthesis to bring a conclusive result. This can also be seen in the fact that all institutional actors continued to work on their strategic interests without seriously considering the competition results and not least therein that neither the competition procedure nor its professional translation into an approach (to cost) via participating architects had generated the desired outcome.

What went wrong? Is it about the procedure in general? Is it about the unfathomable interests of the different actors and their agency? Is it about the professional ability to meet complex situations? Is it about the educational system of Architecture and Urban Planning? Certainly, there is no simple answer, but the given situation seems to offer reason enough to find another way (not merely because the conventional way is blocked).

Take the next take. Mark a predefined target as being of lower priority, take small steps and become absorbed in thoughts, enter into a dialogue with issues, and learn iteratively. Translate placing the experimental set-up at the beginning into an opportunity to allow students from different disciplines such as Architecture, Urban Planning, Urban Design, Metropolitan Culture, and Civil Engineering to have their own theoretical and practical experiences in necessarily interdisciplinary project development and planning and while implementing their work. In doing so, this would also involve practicing what had been lacking in the process so far, the finding of one's own interests in research and design. The experiment that could be the subject here would emerge within the context of a reflexive self-construction, whose use by its builders themselves would offer individual experiences that could always be translated into new spaces of possible development. In this sense, we can actually understand this form of framing as a project roof that provides the occupant with the needed protected space to experiment. A space produced in this way includes the conditions of a set (remaining) life cycle of five years, as well as the resulting aspects of the sustainability and availability of resources. The naive but guiding question that emerges is: What should or can go wrong?

---

35   Cf. HOAI 2013 Appendix 10 (to §34 (4), §35 (7) Basic services of the buildings and interiors service profile, special services, project list).

Forward motion coming from small things—madness takes its course

Allowing that which had formerly been the subject of strategic and contractual, but also design-related and always theoretical, debate to become practical, examining it yourself, inspecting and experiencing it: setting forth to the Elbe island, noticing the neighborhood and the property's enchanted location in the wildly overgrown environment. Making your way through the underbrush, finding the right key on the caretaker's giant key ring, noticing the smell that greets you inside the finally opened up and long-forgotten building. Realizing your own lack of preparation in terms of missing objects (a flashlight), feeling your way along in the makeshift glow of lighters and smartphones. Crunching sounds under your shoes, stumbling over garbage. Of course, there is no infrastructure, no electricity, no water, no heating—you definitely could have known that. On second look, a first assessment of the extent of necessary restoration measures. There is barely a window without damage, sanitary facilities are all destroyed, the dividing walls are partly destroyed. Occupants that were at work here had stopped believing in a proper use. At least that's what you thought at first. You found out much later that it is common practice to prevent a disused building from being used by uninvited users—learning from Hafenstrasse.[36]

You take another look from the outside. Is this still a house or a piece of junk? Is trying to start a self-construction project with students perhaps an undertaking doomed to another failure? Initial doubts and absentmindedly roaming around the neighborhood: Where are you anyway? The gym, house of youth, bunker, a green space behind it, terraced housing opposite that, empty older buildings with annexes, Wilhelmsburg Corner: Bar for Nice People. Who drinks his or her beer here? Who lives here? Who works here? Who meets in the park? The bunker in its grayish black, somber and gloomy, with its attached kiosk exudes real life: the logic of life and the logic of research follow a related game of possibilities.[37] You cannot handle it purposefully and selectively from the start. Either you play or you don't.[38]

Roof over your head

The simple house, a functional building from the 1950s that provided young women in postwar times with a roof over their heads. One former resident who by chance passed by the construction site—she was currently visiting from the United States—later sent us an e-mail with her memories of the five years she had spent there. The three girls shared a room; the only furniture they had were Murphy beds, a table with three chairs, and three small

36   Houses in the Hafenstrasse were supposed to be demolished in accordance with a building assessment that stated the buildings' uninhabitability. By the end of 1981, those houses were "subtly occupied." The property owner had the houses vacated in the spring, but two days later they were "illegally occupied and renovated." "Artificially" making objects of speculation uninhabitable to prevent further use is a widely observed practice.

37   Francois Jacob, 1983, cited in Hans-Jörg Rheinberger, *Experimentalsysteme und epistemische Dinge. Eine Geschichte der Proteinsynthese im Reagenzglas* (Göttingen: Wallstein Verlag, 2002), 26.

38   Ibid.

wardrobes, a sink, and a mirror. There were four or six gas stoves at the center of the kitchen, desks next to the walls that were also used as counter-tops, sinks and in one corner a gas cooker with a tin pot for laundry: a washing machine. There were no fridges. In a small adjoining room, they each had a cupboard they could lock for dishes and groceries. However, the kitchen was used only on weekends. They would welcome guests, play table tennis, and hold Christmas celebrations in the lounge. "Today, this would be called a shared apartment."[39] Roommates would often change, but many friendships were formed nonetheless, lasting until today. Rent was 13 euros per month. After them, the health department moved in. Due to the unsound state of the building—cracks had appeared in the walls—it moved out again. Henceforth, the house stood empty and yet not quite—it found its interim occupants, who provided the house with inglorious fame: the crack house.

Take – an open form of action

Take, as a minimal structure, borrowed from film and music, a sequence of a temporary piece of a recording made step-by-step. Going in circles, playing around with and varying the theme repeatedly—actively practicing it. Itera-tions that pick up the dimension of the Take's exemplifying action. The Take as a method of playfully challenging the vagueness, in order to reveal the implicitly unknown. Cautious first steps and the researcher's fear of the field.[40] Planners are more experienced here than architects; the questionnaire is immediately at hand. The doorbell rings; will somebody open up? Whom and what can you expect, or will the door stay closed? Few answers, eager and tenacious: what do they reveal, and what were the questions again? Neighborhood—and the real questions? How should you record, note, photograph, draw? What are the criteria, the rules for collecting, assembling, evaluating? What insights can be drawn from that? Moving on in the field. Observation of activities, on sports and playgrounds, teenage leisure behavior. Not just human actors anymore, but also things are now being asked. And again, questionnaires, interviews: "What do you prefer?" The production of desires, make-a-wish city. But what exactly are wishes and where do they come from? What do they mean for the individual, for the community, society, city? The city as a place of longing, and wishes cling to it like hopes to promises of happiness.

Realizing that even a simple action is easier to begin a conversation with than by using standardized questionnaires. How do you acquire what kind of material, how do you decide between important and less important, how do you even record and evaluate, gather intelligence, or use field reports, photos, videos? How to extract the intention from a photo, how to use video differently to a staged film? It's not easy to let go of well-estab-lished ways of thinking, behavior and the given form, to open it—unlearning of. Expanding the tools. Drawing in reverse: discovering the range of

39   Excerpt of an e-mail by U. Burmeister to B. Becker on July 20, 2010.
40   Rolf Lindner, "Die Angst des Forschers vor dem Feld," *Zeitschrift für Volkskunde* 77 (1981): 51–66.

possibilities of drawings no longer merely as a tool for expressing the conceptualized space in order to anticipate possible futures, but also a way of using it for analyzing and representing the experienced/produced space. Diagrams, isometrics, perspective representations. Rendering in reverse: the photo and the ability to edit it in order to release the content and make it visible, and to make courses of action representable. Function in reverse: not making arrangements of functions, but the heterogeneity and complexity of everyday use in spatial action, by means of diagrammatically arranging different forms of representation in relational order. Shifting the focus from representations of the conceptualized space to those of the experienced space and to recordings of spatial practice. Learning from Venturi, Scott Brown, Izenour,[41] Wajuro Kon,[42] Atelier Bow-Wow,[43] Forensic Architecture,[44]etc.

Next, an expert panel at UoN and Wilhelmsburg, local actors and creative artists, input, lectures, discussions. Exchange of experience. Bringing together various experts, and the difficulty in communicating, in understanding each other. Remixing the material. Sampling, brainstorming, mind-mapping. Reassembling and displaying what has been worked out on the floor or the wall, getting an overview. Rearranging the performative catalogue. Relational reconnection, incidentally at first; testing and exploring new ties, later on with precision. Making things talk. Focusing on areas of interest. Constantly moving within the field, gaining clarity about what your motive is. Practicing the arrangement and ability of generating catalogues. How exactly does open source work? How do we make our own material available to others to continue working on it? An impromptu approach to an (urban) spatial experimental set-up or strategy. Exemplary development of the priorities. Examining possibilities. Focusing on subprojects within an extended field of topics. How do I follow the motive, and how do I derive a design/research guiding question from it? Initial programming steps—theoretical, abstract, clumsy. Concepts follow; thematic foci are condensed and superimposed on the building as new layers. The different materials are examined for their properties and reassembled—according to what criteria? Memos, codes, and categories are concepts that help to sort the material. Slowly developing ideas and representations of possible steps of transformation. Planning the first stage of development in a progressive structural transformation. How do you program educational formats, and which ones are out there? What role do public relations play? Whom are they addressing? Who is working with the public and how? Who or what is the public, even? Concrete formulation of a request for change of use as the legal basis for even being able to use the building as a university facility. Building work is not building work, but a university course. Construction measures, which are to be worked on here first, require a

41   Steven Izenour, Denise Scott Brown, and Robert Venturi, *Learning from Las Vegas: The Forgotten Symbolism of Architectural Form* (Cambridge, MA: MIT Press, 1977).
42   Wajiro Kon, *Retrospective* (Kyoto: Seigensha Art Publishing, 2011).
43   Atelier Bow-Wow, *Made in Tokyo: Guide Book* (Tokyo: Kajima Institute Publishing, 2001).
44   Forensic Architecture, *Forensis: The Architecture of Public Truth* (Berlin: Sternberg Press, 2014).

placeholder in order to be announced. But how do you draw the plan for a measure that's not even known yet? How do you file a building application of yet unknown measures?

The programmatic roof – from experimental set-up to conversion into recursive action process

At this point it must be highlighted that the program is understood on the basis of its redefinition of writing throughout the 1960s, and the associated shift from pure signification (the meaning) to the signifier (the materiality of the sign). Thus, as in the case of Derrida, to whom Rheinberger refers in the development of experimental systems, the program can appear as a form of writing in which the trace, the structural reference, and interconnection is at the core. From this, Rheinberger derives his notational idea of the conversion and of recursion in notation.[45] In regard to the history of architecture, this can be linked to diagrammatic reasoning and the introduction of the concept of program to architecture in Christopher Alexander's *Notes on the Synthesis of Form*,[46] but also to Cedric Price, whose *Fun Palace*[47] is an examination of a "learning" architecture, which he developed with theater director Joan Littlewood from her idea of the Laboratory of Pleasure and the University of the Streets.[48] This educational program was connected to the creation of a "cybernetic committee," which Gordon Parks and others were part of. Not only do they test a mechanically aligned way of thinking about architecture as programming; they also research the respective notation. *Notes on the Synthesis of Form* and *Fun Palace* are thus fundamental groundwork for the concept of program, which Koolhaas had transferred to an urban scale, thus opening up the concept of function.[49] Three aspects appear essential to us here. First, to understand the notation as an open form with its elements of trace, iteration, and recursion, to keep empiricism from being stuck in the traditional container representations that are assumed to be transparent and neutral. Second, a certain way of treating the program as an open form and improvisational technology. Third, the shift from a teleological form of planning to a performative use.

Programming is to be considered one of the performative actions in order to produce spatial condensation that may also manifest architecturally. The requirements of the university's operations and its administration must always be coordinated in the organizing of a construction site. Teaching formats that operate within the existing curricula of various programs are developed. The currency is comprised of the workloads derived from the

45   Cf. the relation Rheinberger-Derrida: Jacques Derrida, "Performanz – Schrift – Iteration. Wohnen in der Struktur," 164 / 194, and "Metaschaltung / Remix: Improvisierende Stadt-forschung," 202, in Christopher Dell, *Epistemologie der Stadt. Improvisatorische Praxis und gestalterische Diagrammatik im urbanen Kontext* (Bielefeld: Transcript, 2016).
46   Christopher Alexander, *Notes on the Synthesis of Form* (Cambridge, MA: Harvard University Press, 1964).
47   Pier Vittorio Aureli and Stanley Mathews, *Potteries Thinkbelt & Fun Palace: Deux théories de l'évolution selon Cedric Price* (Paris: Edition B2, 2016).
48   Nadine Holdsworth, *Joan Littlewood's Theatre* (Cambridge: Cambridge University Press, 2011), 211.
49   Rem Koolhaas, *Delirious New York* (New York: Moncalli Press, 1994 [1978]), 157.

credit point system defined by the Conference of Ministers of Education and Cultural Affairs: one credit point equals thirty hours. Semester and construction planning become one.

It is spring 2009 and the preparations begin. Various seminars and projects are offered. The declared goal is the formal opening of the University of Neighborhoods project. In addition to lessons, construction site organization and preparations for the opening event, continuous localizing and arranging of meetings with actors from the neighborhood were now among the duties as well. It was a matter of identifying possible collaborators in the fields of education, work, social institutions, art, and culture. Besides, we had already been able to win two partners from our networks. Max Hoffmann GmbH &Co. KG, a construction company based in Hamburg and an essential partner for the supervision of the self-construction site, and Kampnagel, the international center for the finer arts in Hamburg which invited God's Entertainment to collaborate on the opening. They connected with teenagers and neighbors to develop and rehearse the opening performance, *Shivers*.

Builders' hut

Begin. Install the site's electric meter, order construction trailers. Start work in the garden: trim the paths, uncover the overgrown parking lot, make the property accessible. Obtain tools. But how? Administrative routes are slow (see also "The Journey of the Screw"). Quick support from the project partner Max Hoffmann (as well as with the electric meter and the standpipe), from neighbors, and from caretaker Ms. Schlesinger, who opens her garage with tools at the university location at Averhoffstrasse. Declutter the house, get rid of debris. Have asbestos removed from the floors by a specialist company; the house remains hermetically sealed. Further into the garden, prune the trees as instructed by the parks commission. The asbestos removal takes longer, the areas to be renovated become larger, until they equal the entire floor space of the building. According to the previous quotation, the partially commissioned demolition was based on a tenth of that area. The first contract is awarded and the costs are already getting out of hand. The opening date approaches. Finally, progress in the building. Devitrify all of the broken windows and provisionally replace them with plastic sheets. Demolish and dispose of the partially destroyed walls that reveal a space for assembly: the young residents of the women's residence were most likely the last ones to have seen and used it in this state. Provisionally provide water via a hydrant across the street and an adventurous installation of the garden hose right through the trees; repair damaged toilets. A kitchen workshop with Ton Matton and the question of hospitality. Participate in the "tomato activity" and explore the possibilities of swapping and sharing. Build the kitchen furniture and a terrace from found materials.

At the same time, attempt to raise third-party funds. Appointment with the redevelopment advisory council right in the area. A pavilion from the 1960s, used as a senior citizens' meeting place for the Workers' Welfare

Association. Inside, wall paneling made of spruce boards, wooden shelves, crocheted doilies, coffee in colorful plastic thermos and condensed milk in small glass bottles. Ms. Fiedelmeier and Mr. Becker, as scientific staff members with a group of six students of the HCU, introduce the project University of Neighborhoods (UoN): "Item 6: contingent funds."[50] Project title: Neighborhood celebration as part of the UoN's grand opening. Applicant: HafenCity University of Hamburg, project group UoN. Requested funds: 912 euros for cooking utensils, cleaning products, beverages, expense allowances for bands, stage rental, decoration, and advertisement. Decision: the application is accepted (seven votes in favor, one vote against, and two abstentions).[51]

The reopening of the building coincided with the UoN opening and neighborhood celebration in summer 2009 with student projects Kulturküche (Culture Kitchen), Musi(C)ooperation, and Shivers from God's Entertainment und Kampnagel. Students, neighbors, and representatives of institutional actors all talk, eat, and finally meet at the Bar for Nice People. The entire building has been put back to use for the first time; its users playfully explore its possibilities. The situation seems to be a state of exception that yields the unforeseen, especially since each participant eventually finds his or her role, although not right away: Young Wilhelmsburgians catch on quickly; they take charge, and artists lose control.

The performative machine

Three years later, there will have been countless seminars, summer schools, workshops, exams, the related day- and night-long work phases, as well as the liberating celebrations after their presentations. There will have been summer camps; Christmas, summer, and neighborhood parties; conferences, graduate meetings, movie and music nights; dinners and lunches in smaller or bigger groups. It will have been a common place for studying, working, presenting, discussing, exchanging, collecting and arranging, living, cooking, eating, music-making, having fun. Its actors will have guided the project, as they will have been an object of guided IBA tours at the same time. They will have been hosts, guests, and neighbors. Everything will have overlapped in a way that seemed to make the building burst.

Gathering all of this and bringing it to negotiation is what the project reported on. When we broke open the roof, we knew we were breaking down not only the physical form, but also its symbolical and cultural registers. Activities unfolded from the location just as they formed the location the other way around. The diversity of actions brought the University of Neighborhoods to light, not the house that made it possible. Rather, the latter's many forms were articulated inside, its different formats of teaching

---

50   Means from available funds can be used by citizens, organizations, and initiatives for smaller
      projects and campaigns that comply with the targets of the Hamburg program Aktive Stadttei-
      lentwicklung 2005–2008 or the urban restoration. This includes projects that promote self-
      help and autonomy, bolster neighborhood contacts, revive urban district culture, make
      encounters possible, and support civic commitment and engagement.
51   Cf. "Protokoll+Sitzung+25+Beirat+S5.doc," UoN Project Archive, 2008.

and research, events and mediations that interrelated its different rooms in terms of use. For its final act within the IBA's presentation year, everything practiced on site is supposed to find an adequate form of spatial translation once again. And this is nothing different to the performative machine,[52] rehearsed all the years thinking of order as something negotiable, including the fact that actors are subject to changes as participants of a process, and that their skills are reflected in how they behave in relation to the process.[53]

We had tacitly agreed to the claim of the experiment, which was inscribed in the project from the beginning. Based on the science-oriented lab, we wanted to understand its conditions, frameworks, and meanings in order to transfer them to the urban space. Being curious about the "unknown," about ways of approaching it and unlocking potential spaces, guided us in our attempt to answer the question of how to produce knowledge about *city*. Setting up the experiment as a search engine for generating reality is what we were—and still are—interested in.

---

52   Christopher Dell, "Performanz des Raumes," *Arch+* 183 (2007): 134.
53   Cf. Christopher Dell, "Subjekte der Wiederverwertung (Remix)," in Hans-Friedrich Bormann, Gabriele Brandstetter, and Annemarie Matzke, *Improvisieren. Paradoxien des Unvorhersehbaren: Kunst – Medien – Praxis* (Bielefeld: Transcript, 2010), 220.

Nachbarschaften
Abdichtung der Fenster

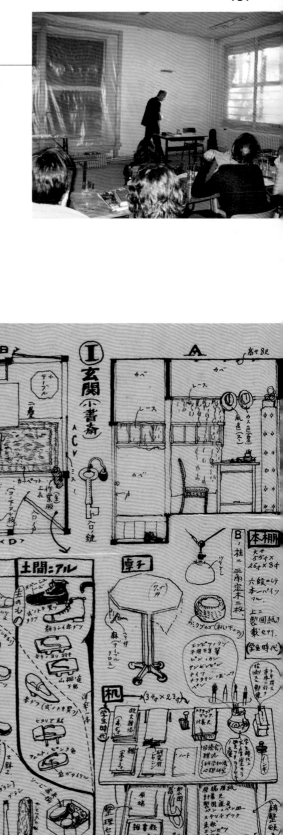

en | + | kleinere Fenster

Schalungsbretter (ausgehend von 5...

Typ	Maße		Bretter	Anzah...
	h	b		
A	166	110	6	1...
B	136	110	5	
C	157	117	6	
D	194	223	8	
E	245	450	10	

| + | kleinere Fenster

Besprechung UdN – Präsidium, 26.08.09
Niels Helle-Meyer, Bernd Kniess, Ellen Fiedelmeier

Ergebnisprotokoll

Ort und Zeit: Lohseplatz 1a, 26.08.09,16.30-18.00 Uhr
Anwesende: Niels Helle-Meyer (NHM), Bernd Kniess (BK), Ellen Fiedelmeier (EF)

Themen:
1. UdN und Arbeitsschutz - Unterstützung durch Kooperationsstelle, mögliche Arbeitsteilung
2. Förderungsvereinbarung Max Hoffmann: Spendenvereinbarung oder Sponsoring?
3. Kriterien "Vorteilhafte Gelegenheit" und weiteres Vorgehen damit
4. Schwierigkeiten in Zahlungsabwicklung mit UdN-Firmen
5. Projektvereinbarung mit "Emelie e.V.": Ausgestaltungsmöglichkeiten
6. Abstimmung Veranstaltungshaftpflicht

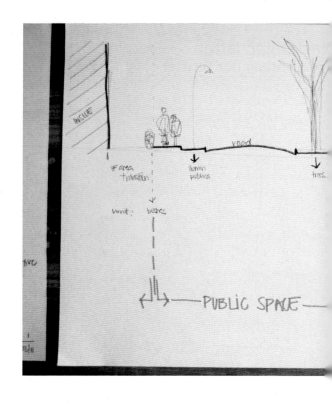

1. UdN und Arbeitsschutz - Unterstützung durch Kooperationsstelle, mögliche Arbeitsteilung

Die Kooperationsstelle hat einen Konzeptentwurf sowie einen Arbeitsteilungsplan vorgelegt. Es zeigt sich, dass der Arbeitsaufwand sehr hoch ist. Es muss eine Lösung geprüft werden, wie gesetzlich erforderliche Leistungen von der HCU und der UdN geleistet werden kann. Grobe Fahrlässigkeit muss ausgeschlossen sein.

Im nächsten Gespräch mit der Kooperationsstelle wird der Arbeitsteilungsplan feinjustiert und auf Angemessenheit wie Machbarkeit geprüft. Gesetzlich nicht erforderliche Leistungen werden zunächst zurückgestellt.

2. Förderungsvereinbarung Max Hoffmann: Spendenvereinbarung oder Sponsoring?

Die Zusammenarbeit mit Max Hoffmann muss klarer werden. Das haben die letzten Koordinationsschwierigkeiten ergeben. Dafür braucht es einen Bauzeitenplan, der den Umfang und die Zeiträume der Arbeiten enthält. Er wird in Vorleistung durch die UdN erstellt. Dieser wird als Basis für die weitere Diskussion mit Herrn Roggenbuck zu Beginn des Wintersemesters 2009/2010 dienen.

3. Kriterien "Vorteilhafte Gelegenheit" und weiteres Vorgehen damit

Erst nach der nächsten Abstimmung mit Herrn Roggenbuck kann damit TOP 3 besprochen werden.

4. Schwierigkeiten in Zahlungsabwicklung mit UdN-Firmen

Bei einer Reihe von Rechnungen der UdN sind Zahlungsverzögerungen durch ungeklärte Schwierigkeiten in der Verwaltung aufgetreten. Kanzler hakt bei AdHOCH nach.

5. Projektvereinbarung mit "Emelie e.V.": Ausgestaltungsmöglichkeiten

Es ist immer noch unklar, welches Vereinsziel "Emelie e.V." hat. Ellen Fiedelmeier klärt. Wenn das geklärt ist, kann eine Projektvereinbarung mit dem Verein, nicht mit Einzelpersonen, angegangen werden. Die vereinbarte Aufwandsentschädigung kann dann

INSIDE

bottom

STREET PROFILE

→ PRIVATE PROPERTY

Fig. 44. — Une salle de l'Hôte
d'un registre manuscrit, in
patriarche de Bourges et
de Bourgogne, à Bruxelle

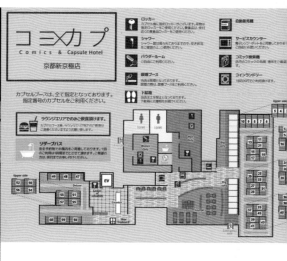

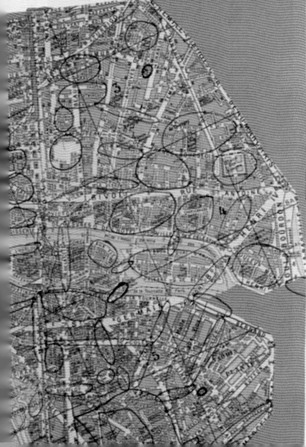

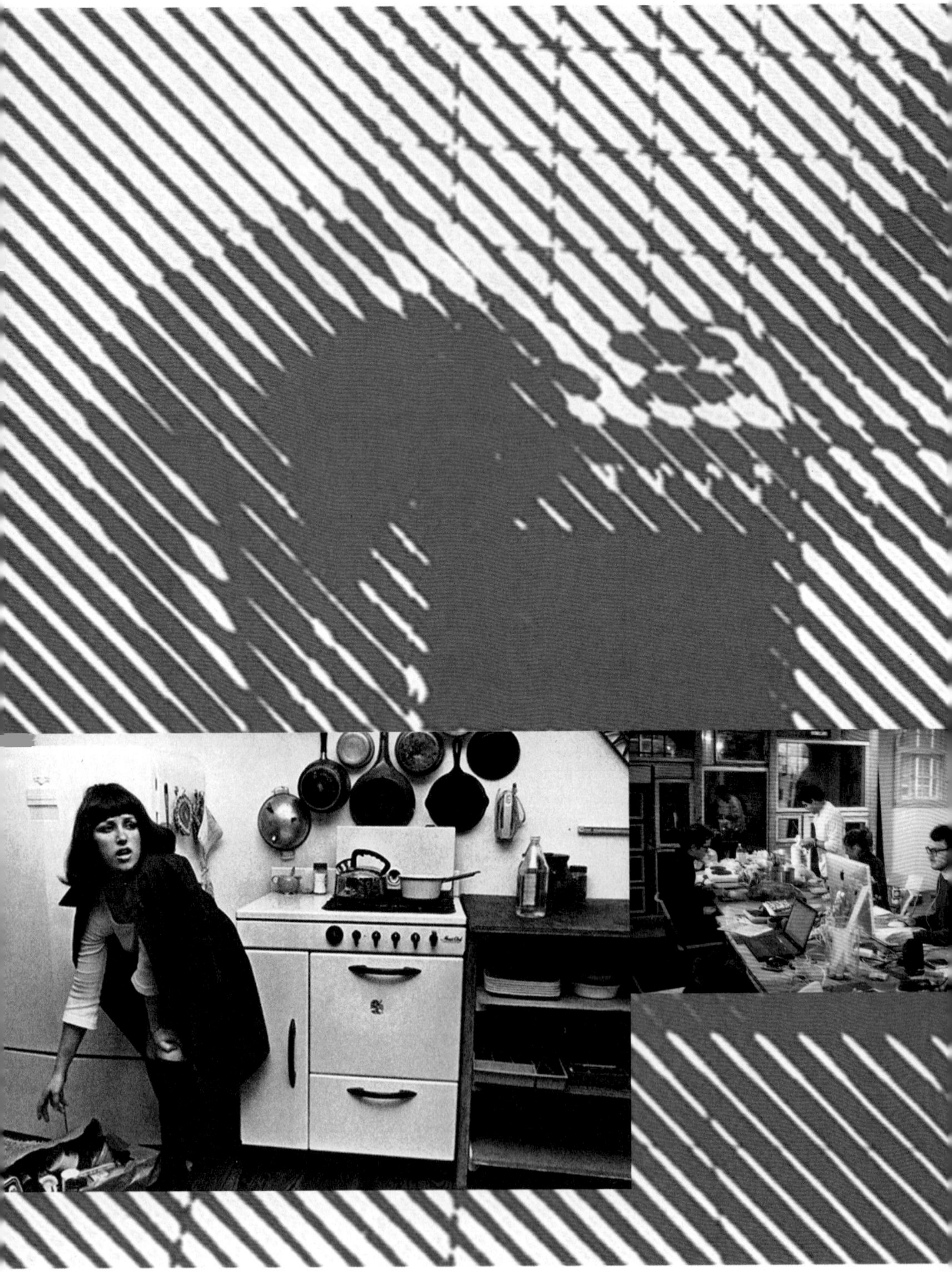

FENCE

DOMINIQUE PECK

Four different fences separate the UoN's site from those adjoining it: facing the Rotenhäuser Damm in the east is a half-height wooden fence with slightly rounded picket tops; facing the Rotenhäuser Wettern,[1] there is wire mesh fencing with two wire cables at the top; facing the Rotenhäuser Feld, a half-height rustic fence (trellis fence); and finally, facing the construction site of the *Sprach- und Bewegungszentrum* (language and sports center), there is a mobile building site fence. The mobile building site fence is 2,000 mm high and 3,000 mm wide, making it approximately twice as high as the other fences. Vehicles can enter and leave the site via a metal gate, which is also mid-height. A gate in the picket fence grants entry to people and anything that will fit through it or that extends just far enough above it to be hoisted over the gate by one or more people. All posts and supports are embedded in the ground.

In this essay, I shall use the object and concept of the *fence* to describe and examine selected situations in terms of a form of practice, along with conditions for it, that enables design. The fence is the theme. It appears as an object on site and in written notations and allows me to delve into layers of architectural anthropological theory and describe a well-known but often insufficiently enabling form of practice: project management.

What does this have to do with *Tom Paints the Fence*? I'll make the connection via the concept of disposition. In the preface to *Extrastatecraft*, architectural theorist Keller Easterling introduces disposition in a few sentences on Mark Twain's abilities, among other things.

> *Mark Twain, once a steamboat captain on the Mississippi, developed techniques for navigating the river. While the passengers saw 'pretty pictures' of landscape scenes, he was extracting information from the changing 'face of the water.' A little ripple, eddy, or 'faint dimple' signaled turbulence or obstacles in a complex and potentially dangerous organization below the surface. These were markers of unfolding potentials or inherent agency in the river—what can only be called disposition.[2]*

My thesis is that Mark Twain had a reason for getting the protagonists of the adventure story *Tom Sawyer* to whitewash the fence that enclosed Aunt Polly's property. I think Twain had an idea of what Victor Buchli, with reference to Michel Foucault, also says about the anthropology of architecture: control always has something to do with spatialization. Where we draw the line that marks the fence,

1   Named after the surface drains that used to drain the surrounding area.
2   Keller Easterling, *Extrastatecraft: The Power of Infrastructure Space* (London: Verso, 2014), 21.

as an object or concept, influences the way we divide the world that unfolds before us, and thus how we realize its disposition.[3]

To me, this means that the aspect laid out in *Tom Sawyer* was also functional in the theme of "enabling architecture for the learning city" in the University of Neighborhoods project. Thus, in discussions for this essay, those responsible for the UoN emphasized that, following this theme, questions of urban design arose among actors. Consequently, it was no longer about urban design "for" and not "with," but "initially by" actors.[4] The project's website and brochures state that it was aimed less at creating an object than at performative and organizational processes that could and should be started, but which could not be predetermined. For such actions, there were no formal rules to abide by per se, but a certain expanding repertoire of opportunities for action and experiences within specific regulations.[5]

In the course of this essay, I shall relate both narratives— the fence-painting episode in *Tom Sawyer* vs. the University of Neighborhoods—to the interest in examining the potential of certain questions; for instance, "How much design can I make possible?" and "Where do I need to locate the agency for that?" What follows are five situations.

FIRST SITUATION: Who is responsible here?

In the run-up to the UoN project, the building had been vacant for more than ten years. The only uses of it that I know of were listed in brief letters from the Hamburg Building and Property Management tax authority (FB-HH-IM) and Police Station 44, Georg-Wilhelm-Straße 77, 21107 Hamburg (PK44). One chain of letters begins with a "notice about adolescent rioters on demolition sites" on October 16, 2008: The police had found four juvenile males at the scene of the incident, taken down their personal details, informed them that they were trespassing, and, if the officer were to actually find damages, that they could be accused of criminal property damage as well. However, the officer could not identify any actual "recent" damage to the already damaged building. According to his description of the situation, though there had been a "No trespassing — District Office Hamburg-Mitte" sign at the intersection of fence and sidewalk, a beaten footpath led through the property from the Rotenhäuser Damm to the park behind it and vice versa. "Unexpectedly," a woman standing by

3   Victor Buchli, "Institutions and Community," in idem, *An Anthropology of Architecture* (New York and London: Bloomsbury, 2013), 89–116.

4   Stefanie Gernert, Ben Pohl, and Dominique Peck, "Fence," UoN Project Archive, May 12, 2015.

5   Christopher Dell and Bernd Kniess, "Ermöglichungsarchitektur …," UdN – Universität der Nachbarschaften, April 16, 2018, udn.hcu-hamburg. de/de/?p=157.

the fence spoke to the officer. She told him about another group of adolescents, female this time, who were then immediately informed by the officer of the fact that they were trespassing and were asked to provide their personal details as well. I can read in the attachments to the document that all adolescents found on site were between twelve and fourteen years old. "No further action was taken." In another short letter, PK 44 informed the District Office Hamburg-Mitte about the incident. The latter forwarded the letter to the tax authority, from where it was sent to the BWF (Hamburg Ministry of Science, Research, and Equality) and finally reached Niels Helle-Meyer (chancellor of the Hafen-City University), with a "request for further action."

We note that there are no spaces that do not belong to anyone. Whom they belong to is not always clear to everyone involved. In the first paragraph of the chapter in which Tom Sawyer whitewashes the fence, Mark Twain describes the situation as being full of life. "Cardiff Hill, beyond the village and above it, was green with vegetation, and it lay just far enough away to seem a Delectable Land, dreamy, reposeful, and inviting."[6] Even before the employees of the UoN entered the fenced-in property and §14 (2) of the Hamburg building code took effect for the UoN project when the construction site became operational,[7] there were people who had been using the dilapidated building as a meeting point for some time. Although certain responsibilities were in place, there was a need for practical short letters—small forms of notation—that had to be followed by UoN employees. The same notations in the UoN's project archive make it possible to recollect this situation.

SECOND SITUATION: How do we keep the project alive?

A few days after the UoN's opening event, Niels Helle-Meyer, Bernd Kniess (project manager at UoN), and Ellen Fiedelmeier (project control at UoN) discussed such aspects of the project as "building security," "event security," "construction site security," and "occupational safety."[8] The chancellor started by explaining that the UoN was now part

---

6   Mark Twain, *The Adventures of Tom Sawyer* (1876), excerpt reprinted in "Whitewashing the Fence," *Lapham's Quarterly* 8, no. 2 (Spring 2015), accessed April 10, 2019, www.laphamsquarterly.org/swindle-fraud/white-washing-fence.

7   The University of Neighborhoods is a construction site. According to §14 (2) of the Hamburg Building Code: "During construction work that may endanger uninvolved persons, the danger zone must be demarcated or marked by warning signs. If necessary, construction sites must be fenced off with a site fence, provided with safeguards against falling objects, and illuminated." *Hamburgische Bauordnung* (HBauO) vom 14. Dezember 2005 (Hamburg Building Code (HBauO) of December 14, 2005), 525, accessed December 12, 2015, www.landesrecht-hamburg.de/jportal/portal/page/bshaprod.psml?showdoccase=1&st=lr&doc.id=jlr-BauOHA2005rahmen&doc.part=X&doc.origin=bs

8   Niels Helle-Meyer, Bernd Kniess, and Ellen Fiedelmeier, "Besprechung UdN und Niels Helle-Meyer (Kanzler). Ergebnisprotokoll," UoN Project Archive, July 1, 2009.

of the HafenCity University (HCU) building stock and thus the running costs of the operation, i.e. water, cleaning as needed, fire safety, occupational safety, and security guards would mainly be taken care of by the HCU (see "Round Table Redesign: What Is Urban Design to Do in the Age of Uncertainty?"). Moreover, the "No trespassing" signs were to be replaced by others that read, "HafenCity University Hamburg, Wilhelmsburg external site, University of Neighborhoods project."[9] Following the experience of the opening weekend, it would be decided that the UoN needed permanent (staffed) building security. The staff of the teaching and research program Urban Design (UD) was located at Averhoffstraße—about fifty minutes away by public transportation—and could not permanently be on site. Next, the contract of the HCU security service was expanded to cover the UoN. Should someone from the vicinity be interested in a "caretaker's apartment,"[10] the HCU could enter into an employment relationship with the potential caretaker. There is a list of selected guard book entries from August 14 to October 12, 2009, only a few weeks after the opening event, in which security guards for the property "HCU – Rotenhäuser Damm" demonstrated what had been happening behind the fence:

19:05 Group of eight juveniles expelled from premises.

> **19:05 Discovery: One kitchen window smashed, rock located in kitchen, window bolted and secured with wooden board.**

05:35 Homeless person expelled from premises.

19:20 Two HCU students pick up orange T4 (VW) and take various technical equipment.

> **03:25 Evidently homeless person tampering with the main entrance. No personal identification at hand. Police notified. Until their arrival, restraining said person required physical strength. Person was known to authorities as drug user. Arrest followed.**

> **02:10 – 02:30 Residents return, admittance + closure.**

01:45 Police due to noise.

> **02:45 Last guests have left.**

> **Citizens' questions answered.**[11]
> *He got out his worldly wealth and examined it—bits of toys, marbles, and trash; enough to buy an exchange of work, maybe, but not half enough to buy*

9   Helle-Meyer, "Besprechung" (see note 8).
10   Helle-Meyer, "Besprechung" (see note 8).
11   WISAG Sicherheitsdienste, "Wachbuch. Objekt: HCU Rotenhäuser Damm," UoN Project Archive, October 13, 2009.

so much as half an hour of pure freedom. So he returned his straitened means to his pocket, and gave up the idea of trying to buy the boys. At this dark and hopeless moment an inspiration burst upon him! Nothing less than a great, magnificent inspiration.[12]

The seemingly high demands on the protection and sustained security of the project required more capacity than the Urban Design program was able to provide. The project board's task following the opening event was therefore the concrete project development depending on external circumstances, such as the recommissioning of a dilapidated building that had been vacant for a decade, and its operation over a set period of time with a predetermined budget in the program of the International Architecture Exhibition (Internationale Bauausstellung, IBA) and the activities of the HCU. Just like Tom Sawyer, the project board had to simultaneously assess the changing state in different locations and refrain from burying their heads in the sand after seeing the budget. In retrospect, the reasoning seems simple: the building is part of the university, which must therefore bear the costs associated with it. However, this argumentation then has to be understood in this way by the university's administration as well. In times when universities can only rarely be what they are capable of being due to policies of austerity, project managers appreciate the costs being temporarily taken care of. Still, throughout further proceedings in the project, the university administration also had to remind everyone involved of cost optimization. According to the project board, the capacities in the teaching and research program did not at all fit the opportunities offered and required by the participation of a university in IBA Hamburg's 2013 program. Throughout the course of the project, the localization of externally bound capacities tied to the UoN was to be a task for the project's management and supervision.

What Tom was doing by reaching into his pocket and examining what he then took out, was what the project board and supervisors of the UoN were doing with work in the UoN's archive. The three letters "UoN" can be found on around seventy file folders that cover half of two exposed concrete walls of the Urban Design studio in the HCU building. This process-born data from seven years of project work makes up the document stock for recollections. Submission plans for building projects, insurance policies, photographs with handwritten annotations, the minutes of meetings, decrees, logs, original and copied contracts with and without traces of highlighters, pencils, ballpoint and marker pens, timetables, magazines, police reports,

12   Twain, *The Adventures of Tom Sawyer* (see note 6).

programs, invitations, and many other kinds of documents comprise the notations on the chaos that the UoN project appeared to be at first sight—a chaos consisting of various project languages that were subject to the conventions and logic of their respective contexts. The collection of documents was compiled over the years by members of the UoN's project team. Staff members committed themselves to the archive time and time again, and developed topologies within the material in order to negotiate the general framework of the project with those involved. Invoking Wittgenstein, we can say that they were able to visualize it because pictorial form is the possibility that things are related to one another.[13]

THIRD SITUATION: Trivial matters vs. alarm

A research assistant on the UoN team is speaking on the phone. A student has called to report on the alarm set off by the Easy Series Burglar Alarm System made by Bosch. The student has succeeded Christopher Dell as director of the Wilhelmsburg Orchestra.[14] He teaches around two hours and forty-five minutes away from his main residence, and spontaneously decided the evening prior to the phone call not to use public transportation to get home, but instead to spend the night at the UoN. After his course, he sets up camp in the attic space above the hallway. But since he does not explicitly point this out to the students in the night camp, those who are last to leave the building activate the UoN's alarm system. As a result, the stairs between the camp and the hallway turn into a kind of fence. "The student is trapped."[15] When he has to use the bathroom, he puts on his pants and shoes, takes a few steps, walks down the stairs, and with his first step into the hallway triggers the alarm system and causes an intervention by the security company in charge. The same moment, an e-mail is sent to the contact address given in the rental and security contract with Bosch, together with an invoice for the required intervention and the associated fee for the security company, addressed to the research assistant, named as the contact person in the contract.

13   Ludwig Wittgenstein, *Tractatus logico-philosophicus: Logisch-philoso-phische Abhandlung*, ed. Kevin C. Klement, Side-by-Side-by-Side Edition, Version 0.58 (May 24, 2020), accessed June 21, 2020, people.umass.edu/klement/tlp/, p. 16, para. 2.151.

14   "The Wilhelmsburg Orchestra, founded in 2010 by Prof. Christopher Dell, is a 'research orchestra.' It is an experimental setup for exploring the logic and rhythms of 'neighborhood'–not only to observe, but also to activate. The orchestra designs its own music, plays, improvises, and accelerates. The practice of music becomes an expression of *city* and what we make of it. Working with minimal musical structures ensures the low-threshold nature of our interaction and, in its superimposition, leads to unimagined complexity." Sebastian Bührig, "Wilhelmsburg Orchester," Buehrig.info, accessed April 24, 2019, *buehrig.info/Wilhelmsburg-Orchester*.

15   Gernert et al., "Fence" (see note 4).

The phone call to the research assistant helps to clarify the facts. She had repeatedly had to deal with false alarms in previous weeks. Mark Twain reinforces his motif by adding secondary scenes and similar narratives to the scene at the fence. "There are wealthy gentlemen in England who drive four-horse passenger-coaches twenty or thirty miles on a daily linc, in the summer, because the privilege costs them considerable money; but if they were offered wages for the scrvice, that would turn it into work and then they would resign."[16] As the end of the UoN project would later show, the central unit in the alarm system had been improperly installed from the start. Whenever it was supposed to report the need for scheduled maintenance, it made an emergency call instead.[17] The member of the UoN team therefore had good reason to invest time in clarifying the facts by following the protagonist (the alarm system) to supposed secondary locations.

FOURTH SITUATION: Picket fence

Following explorations in Wilhelmsburg and an initial exchange on the UoN premises, thirty-three international participants of the "Made In" workshop are standing in front of the "motive wall." Individual aspects of the explorations and exchange are written on index cards and loosely arranged on the wall with masking tape. One arrangement, hung mainly by students of spatial planning and development from the Vienna University of Technology, is listed in the documentation of the workshop as follows: "Impulse production—generating impulses in order to stimulate communication among us and with the residents" / "Contact zone for dialogs—interface" / "Sidewalk as a communication space" / "Participate in ... in this region" / "Learning from shifting contexts" / "Project for all: Tearing down the fence" The question of individual participants' roles and their attitude towards the research field was included in the discussion, as was the question of transparency and openness within the workshop: "Enough with the whispering. Let the lab explode: move boundaries, pierce walls—blow up the UoN!"[18]

The project entitled "Research on Interventionist Action" transposes the front yard seating areas, as they are often found on the Wilhelmsburg island, into the context of the UoN. "The Generation / creation of a situation in the UoN's front garden; By relocating / moving parts of the fence a new interspace is created. The UoN's interior becomes

---

16   Twain, *The Adventures of Tom Sawyer* (see note 6).
17   Gernert et al., "Fence" (see note 4).
18   Tabea Michaelis and Ben Pohl, *Made In. Lokale Praktiken urbaner Produktion – Dokumentation Wilhelmsburglabor 01* (Hamburg and Zurich: Urban Design HCU with Civic City Zurich, 2011).

visible to the outside. The border between inside and outside shifts into the public space." Cf. "The Fence"[19]
The intervention is part of the vernissage. "It is important to make the process transparent through precise documentation. Only then will it become clear how the intervention took place and what happened throughout the course of it: to the fence, to passersby and actionists themselves. What feelings, moods, and reactions are developed? This is what makes a transferability / application in a different scale (micro / macro) or context possible in the first place. This is how it becomes possible to compare the intervention with others."[20]

The suggested necessity of documenting is no accident. It shows that the UoN's settings are always temporary and are transformed according to their use. Another reference to Mark Twain: "If he had been a great and wise philosopher, like the writer of this book, he would now have comprehended that …"[21] The same applies to the positions taken by individual actors or collectives in the project. Here, the fence represents the space between people who are working within the UoN and people who might potentially begin working there. Moving the fence changes the disposition of this situation. The documentation should ensure the possibilities of alternative dispositions even after the conclusion of the workshop.

FIFTH SITUATION: Thievery (threatening the UoN's existence)

Late Saturday night in May 2010, the research assistant who organizes all lectures and events related to building at the University of Neighborhoods is lying in bed, restless. Someone had reported to him and other members of the team that staff members of the security company occasionally leave the UoN's construction site, thus leaving the building unsecured at certain times. After the "work focus on building services," the next three construction phases on the agenda are: foyer, apartment, and sanitary facilities.[22] The UoN employee's restlessness, apart from hearsay about the behavior of the security staff members, is mainly due to the events of one night, about a week prior. Tools had been stolen from a locked container on the fenced-in site; without them, the work to be done was only possible to a limited extent or not at all. The research assistant's unrest compels him to drive from his apartment in Hamburg-Neustadt to the UoN site in Wilhelmsburg to check on the construction site's security himself. What he finds there, or rather doesn't find, is the subject of a series of notes, statements, results of investigations, and forms

---

19   Michaelis and Pohl, *Made In* (see note 18).
20   Michaelis and Pohl, *Made In* (see note 18).
21   Twain, *The Adventures of Tom Sawyer* (see note 6).
22   Bernd Kniess, "Änderungsantrag zum Bauantrag M/BP/00827/2009/WB," UoN Project Archive, March 6, 2010.

for filing charges for burglary, theft, fraud, etc., and a list of damages. The building is apparently lacking materials and resources—just like Tom Sawyer: "He got out his worldly wealth and examined it—bits of toys, marbles, and trash; enough to buy an exchange of work, maybe, but not half enough to buy so much as half an hour of pure freedom."[23]

Around two weeks after the incident, the professor from the Urban Design program and a research assistant responsible for project management meet with two supervisors from the security company in order to review the facts. The supervisors explain that after the incident was reported, the two security guards—who perform guard duty on site daily from 7:00 p.m. to 7:00 a.m.—stated that they would occasionally drive to a nearby McDonald's restaurant in order to use the restroom there, regardless of the fact that a portable toilet is available on the UoN property. According to §10 of the Guard Ordinance (BewachV) of December 7, 1995 and §4 of the Accident Prevention Regulation (UVV) on "Security Services" of the Employers' Liability Insurance Association (BGV C7), the security company is required to regulate the behavior of its guards and security personnel. In the case of the UoN, these instructions define, among other things, relevant terminology such as "important incidents," "weapons," and "key systems" on the first two pages of the guard manual. Further, "eating, drinking, smoking" and "radio, TV and other things," basically everyday aspects for an employee of a security company, are also defined; however, there is nothing about using the bathroom.[24]

The UoN's administration states that in the meantime it has also received statements from neighbors who have noticed the coming and going of the security guards. The security company then asks for a complete list, including prices and equipment numbers, to forward the case to their insurance company for reimbursement. The UoN requests a written statement on the incident from the security company to serve as the basis for discussing further cooperation. The company suggests installing a wireless burglar alarm system for the tool container, which they would pay for themselves. In addition, they assure the UoN's administration that, according to regulations, nobody is allowed to access the property. Entering the premises is only possible when events are held. Should passersby be interested, the security employees will contact the UoN representative on the Urban Design team.[25]

23   Twain, *The Adventures of Tom Sawyer* (see note 6).
24   Ellen Fiedelmeier, "Vermerk. Besprechungen UdN WISAG am 09.06.10, Rotenhäuser Damm 30," UoN Project Archive, June 28, 2010.
25   Fiedelmeier, "Vermerk."

**Viewed side
by side**

In terms of the object and concept of the *fence*, I have enu-
merated five situations that allow a serial observation of
the theme of this essay. It is always about what happens
once someone hops the fence, i.e. participates in the UoN
project or makes participation possible through his or her
activity. Early on in the project, the acquaintance of a student lived in a trailer on the UoN property for a while to
keep an eye on the building. He and his dog did quite a
good job, but the project board found out that he was staying afloat by selling psychedelic substances. The situation
forced the board to find a new solution. Teaching and research operations on site had not yet reached the point
where it was worthwhile to have the employees permanently on site. The only resource that could be brought into
play was the house itself. In a series of workshops, students and teachers alongside building interns and commissioned trade-specific construction companies renovated
the building so that a studio apartment on the Rotenhäuser
Damm could be rented out for residency. UD professors
worked out a program and tendering process and were
able to provide several people with accommodation and
the ability to work on site for three months at a time. Shortly
thereafter, a small group of students took heart and renovated rooms in the no longer dilapidated but nevertheless
eerie, vacant building, moved in for the project, and stayed.
They sublet their rooms or apartments and lived in the UoN
until its demolition. The closer the UoN project came to the
IBA's exhibition year of 2013, the more the project management moved teaching and research events to the Rotenhäuser Damm building. When things got too busy, the security system installed in the beginning only caused
problems and was often tampered with without hesitation
or put out of operation completely.

Meta-dilemma

The UoN project consisted of a series of projects and was
scheduled to continue until the end of 2013. As unique un-
dertakings, projects have always been events and thus always produce provisional results. The risk of failure and
the opportunity to transform existing conditions in projects
create a combined problem or a meta-dilemma, whose
solution is not obvious; instead, actors have to go through
that process, because problems only appear once the implementation has started. By invoking Sharon Zukin,[26] Rem
Koolhaas,[27] or Erika Fischer-Lichte,[28] we can define these
situations as liminal spaces or liminality. They all refer to

26   Sharon Zukin, *Landscapes of Power: From Detroit to Disney World*
      (Berkeley: University of California Press, 1993).
27   Rem Koolhaas and Bruce Mau, "The Generic City," in idem, *S M L XL*, 2nd
      ed. (New York: Monacelli Press, 1997), 1239–64.
28   Erika Fischer-Lichte, *The Transformative Power of Performance: A New Aes-
      thetics*, trans. Saskya Iris Jain (Oxfordshire: Routledge, 2008).

aesthetic experiences that enable performances by using Victor Turner's deconstruction of the material of Arnold van Gennep's major work, *Rites of Passage* from 1909. Van Gennep reveals the flaws and pitfalls of a reduced problematization of social issues, limited only to one rite of passage (marriage, seasons, puberty, etc.), during the process of modernization between the nineteenth and twentieth centuries.

I believe that such a problematization of social issues in transformation within corrupted situations can be helpful to projects like the UoN, as it brings the structure of events into focus. According to van Gennep, the structure of rites is generally categorized into 1. the separation phase (alienation from everyday life, *separation*), 2. the liminal phase (interspace, *margin*), and 3. the incorporation phase (admittance of changed identities into society, *aggregation*), and is only culturally specific and fully differentiated in their content.[29] Turner calls the state in the liminal phase "betwixt and between the positions assigned and arrayed by law, custom, convention and ceremonial."[30] When the collapse of opposites participating in an experiment is translated into a liminal space, they end up in a crisis, from which participants cannot exclusively fall back on proven and recognized behavioral patterns. The liminal phase provides a kind of protective space over the precautionary measures of the event-like nature. The question of how and where the fence is placed enables testing out new, and in my opinion, eclectic patterns of behavior. This theoretical layer is probably nothing new for most readers of this publication. However, I would like to emphasize the aspect of rereading existing material with the intention of revealing its structure. Turner works with van Gennep's archived material—a liminal practice that designs and presents topologies and thus new conclusions in the material. Liminality must be designed. An archive is a good place for that.

Body and material: Aspects of liminality

The experience of liminality is always connected to physicality and emotions. We can find this in the UoN project and in *Tom Sawyer*. The confrontation between the UoN's project board and both leading employees of the security company was dreadful for both parties; accusatory claims were made which could, as both sides threatened, be enforced if needed. The confession by the student in the UoN's attic and by the security employees that the necessity to use the bathroom was going to cost their respective employers money, was uncomfortable and referred to economic conditions that have always played a role between

29   Fischer-Lichte, *The Transformative Power of Performance* (see note 28), 305.
30   Victor Turner, *The Ritual Process: Structure and Anti-Structure* (Ithaca: Cornell University Press, 1966), 95.

the shelter of the experiment and the everyday lives of individual people. The Viennese students in the Made In workshops had to prove to the study and examination department, and the dean of the spatial planning program at Vienna's University of Technology, that they had earned 5 ECTS credits for writing a two-page text with photos of freehand sketches about the process of digging up a picket fence, burying it again one and a half meters further along, and covering the gap in between with leaves. For the same reward, their colleagues calculated integrated regular-frequency timetables for the Vienna suburbs or designed a new city block to replace Vienna's disused North Station. Whether experiencing a crisis in terms of self-perception, perception of one's surroundings and external reality actually leads to a continuous transformation in this sense, is highly doubtful.

Nonetheless, these actors at the UoN had taken part in a project with liminal practices. Fischer-Lichte looks primarily at the example of theater and theater directors, such as Christoph Schlingensief and Frank Castorf in particular. Artistic as well as ritual performances are carefully staged, perhaps created on the basis of script templates and rehearsals; both are able to constitute and entertain reality and partly build upon improvisation. In doing so, it has to be clear that "spectators could also dismiss their transitory destabilization as silly and unfounded when leaving the auditorium and revert to their previous value system. Alternatively, they might remain in a state of destabilization for long after the performance's end and only reorient themselves much later upon reflection."[31] As for the UoN, we can now say that this was a demonstration project that lined up a series of projects and potentialities regarding liminality under the motive of "enabling architecture for the learning city." The conditions of the individual projects as well as the transformation processes tied to them always had to be emphasized, made available, brought into form, and reflected upon.

Project management

Who are the actors that do precisely this at the UoN, and how do they define themselves as speaking, living, and working individuals? This brings me back to Michel Foucault's theory about the spatialization of the operativity of power. When Keller Easterling writes about diagnostics,[32] she reveals all her countless references to Michel Foucault and Bruno Latour; I will mention the latter at the end of this text. Foucault's and Easterling's ideas on the exploration of power and the subject both proceeded analogously—even with a time delay of thirty years. "The exercise of power

31   Fischer-Lichte, *The Transformative Power of Performance* (see note 28), 179.
32   Easterling, *Extrastatecraft* (see note 2), 92.

consists in guiding the possibility of conduct and putting in order the possible outcome. … To govern, in this sense, is to structure the possible field of action of others."[33] This is achieved, among other things, by means of spatial products as parts of dispositives. "The carceral network constituted one of the armatures of the power-knowledge that has made the human sciences historically possible. Knowable man (soul, individuality, consciousness, conduct, whatever it is called) is the object-effect of this analytical investment, of this domination-observation."[34] For Easterling, there are (of course) opportunities in these challenges. "There is often more power in 'knowing how' rather than 'knowing that.' The markers used to navigate a river are indeterminate in order to be practical."[35] The manipulation of complex, never consistently tangible networks via their spatial aspects can be successful because it adopts the principles of intersectionality or transversality. Similarly to Victor Turner, Kimberlé Williams explains that a person may be confronted with various forms of discrimination simultaneously throughout his or her life.[36] The way I read it, all the theorists I've just named suggest that people should be motivated to tackle everything at once. This is about a place in society and the opportunity to define oneself. The conditions of underlying processes that produce the forms—whether regarding architecture or other circumstances—are constantly threatening to fall behind products and permanently lead to a crisis of problematization. It is precisely the situations in which project boards deal with supposedly trivial facts that the existence of the project is potentially threatened. The UoN demonstration project addresses precisely this point within the different circumstances as a formality. What is important in view of their modality is that these notations demonstrate the contingency of negotiation and also addresses the issue of its demonstrability. Whose agenda includes an attempt to re-embed negotiations about securing and structuring of processes in the register of forms?

Let's recollect the relevant aspects from the descriptions: The UoN was the case in which the teaching and research program Urban Design at the public HafenCity University located potentialities of liminality ("Round Table Redesign: Understanding UoN"). After the opening weekend, which was carried out in collaboration with theater directors and thus structurally laid out the experiment for the coming

33   Michel Foucault, "The Subject and Power," *Critical Inquiry* 8, no. 4 (Summer 1982), 777–95.
34   Michel Foucault, *Discipline and Punish: The Birth of the Prison* (New York: Pantheon Books, 1977), 305.
35   Easterling, *Extrastatecraft* (see note 2), 92.
36   Kimberlé Crenshaw, *On Intersectionality: Essential Writings* (New York: New Press, 2018).

years, investigations of the potentialities of liminality along the theme of the project had to be secured. This was always accompanied by frequently organized capacities in the form of projects. Over the years, between the beginning and the end of the UoN, these projects were prepared by different people, but the capacities always played an organizing role at all times and in every project, something that worked well among all participating actors. Sometimes these capacities were carried out in the Urban Design office, at the UoN, in meeting halls of participating or soon to be involved organizations, sometimes on the phone, and in between mostly via e-mail. The goal of these capacities was to come up with a winning strategy that would enable people and organizations to start doing something in their respective circumstances. They were enabling design. This also meant that projects were mostly arranged in several accounting modalities: students received credit points in lectures, research assistants carried out their own projects and got their earnings through papers and lectures in the attention economy of academia, security companies worked as contractors to the HafenCity University and were thus profitable market participants, and everyone had to eat, sleep, and use the bathroom. Everything that happens in life happens in projects. Spatial interventions were carried out with the interest of representing their conditions. There were always inexplicable, unplanned, and precarious situations, whose individual aspects were negotiated in relation to the responsibilities of the gathered actors with the interest of securing the conditions that enable the processes or maintain them structurally. There is generally quite a lot that can be agreed upon in contracts, agreements, and conversations, but something can always happen, especially if that's what the theme of the project is about. There is a threat of never getting past the initial stages or of organizing things by muddling through them. What can organizing actors do?

The experiment binds receptivity to activity. In projects like the UoN, one can't be led merely by reality, but instead, the experience must become the motive.[37] This entails the possibility of an urban design practice that can be brought into play "by" actors. This reference is also included in the fence episode in *Tom Sawyer.* When Jim comes through the gate of the fence with a song on his lips and a bucket in his hand, Tom imagines fetching water. "Bringing water from the town pump had always been hateful work in Tom's eyes, before, but now it did not strike him so. He remembered that there was company at the pump. White, mulatto, and negro boys and girls were always there

37   Christoph Menke, *Die Kraft der Kunst*, (Frankfurt am Main: Suhrkamp, 2013), 83.

waiting their turns, resting, trading playthings, quarrelling, fighting, skylarking."[38]

At first, Jim refuses to trade jobs and wants to move on.

"Can't, Mars Tom. Ole missis, she tole me I got to go an' git dis water an' not stop foolin' roun' wid anybody. She say she spec' Mars Tom gwine to ax me to whitewash, an' so she tole me go 'long an' 'tend to my own business– she 'lowed she'd 'tend to de whitewashin'."[39]

Only when Tom starts removing the bandage from a fresh wound on one of his toes does Jim spend time with Tom instead of fetching water. The trading of jobs, however, doesn't take place. Jim now has to just hurry up to meet the expectations of "ole missis" and fulfill his own responsibilities. Tom has to come up with something more interesting.

Only when the *Big Missouri* steamboat, personified by Ben Rogers, passes by the fence does Tom realize that he needs to approach the game from a different stance.

"'Like it? Well, I don't see why I oughtn't to like it. Does a boy get a chance to whitewash a fence every day?'

"That put the thing in a new light. Ben stopped nibbling his apple. Tom swept his brush daintily back and forth— stepped back to note the effect—added a touch here and there—criticized the effect again—Ben watching every move and getting more and more interested, more and more absorbed. Presently he said:

'Say, Tom, let me whitewash a little.'" [40]

Tom summarizes: Ben would, just like himself at the beginning of the day, quickly lose interest in painting the fence. He can't hand it over yet. After all, it is also important to him that the work be done with a certain amount of craftsmanship and care.[41]

"'Ben, I'd like to, honest injun; but Aunt Polly—well, Jim wanted to do it, but she wouldn't let him; Sid wanted to do it, and she wouldn't let Sid. Now don't you see how I'm fixed? If you was to tackle this fence and anything was to happen to it—'

'Oh, shucks, I'll be just as careful. Now lemme try. Say—I'll give you the core of my apple.'

'Well, here—No, Ben, now don't. I'm afeard—'

'I'll give you all of it!'

Tom gave up the brush with reluctance in his face, but alacrity in his heart. And while the late steamer *Big Missouri* worked and sweated in the sun, the retired artist sat on a

38 Twain, *The Adventures of Tom Sawyer* (see note 6).
39 Twain, *The Adventures of Tom Sawyer* (see note 6).
40 Twain, *The Adventures of Tom Sawyer* (see note 6).
41 US painter Norman Rockwell drew attention to this aspect.

barrel in the shade close by, dangled his legs, munched his apple, and planned the slaughter of more innocents."[42]

Quite often, the UoN project series or individual projects threatened to fail when cases of theft occurred, or when projects that helped to set the conditions for later projects collapsed or failed to get past their initial stages. In times like these, it is important for project structuring work to not seize every opportunity that might appear, but to instead, right then and there, find out about the requirements in the exact conditions that they are in and refer to the motive when examining them. Tom refuses to give in to the negative categories (lack of time, Aunt Polly's punishments, repressive ideas of "normal" work, i.e. the normative handling of normativity) as a means and approach to reality, and gives preference to what is positive and multiple; he builds upon the provisional and mobile aspects of the security regime. It is an exercise only for those who observe (even if they do it afterwards).[43] It is hardly possible for the individual to accept the basic conditions for committing to such a complex process without generosity, which was conveyed by the example of the UoN through its project-structuring work. It is also clear that risky practices are simply a fact. Without generosity, the project workers can't achieve a thing, are constantly at work, and ask themselves questions before falling asleep without knowing what those questions are. Nobody can withstand that in the long run.

How does generosity begin to function? In order to answer this question, we have to bring the essay's element back into play. The way in which the project makers and workers—the distribution of roles is always provisional—divide up the world, i.e. where they place the fence, tear it down, walk past it, or jump over it, always implies meaning, which often extends into the political realm. In this self-reflective, performative structure of experience, having conversations "over the fence" can be a profitable form of practice. The project makers do not stop at aspects of the form, nor the material, performance, and certainly not at understanding. They design generosity with the motive of producing livable bodies for the project's participants—on and on. The force that affects the project actors' bodies through project management is obvious in Mark Twain's adventure, and is inherent in project management.

The UoN project offered formats in which reflections on the project management can occur: these ranged from taking someone aside in an ongoing project, to roundtables and doctoral dissertations or other forms of structured reflection and analysis by actors in retrospect. Projects with the

42 Twain, *The Adventures of Tom Sawyer* (see note 6).
43 Menke, *Die Kraft der Kunst*, 98.

motive of "enabling architecture for the learning city" aimed at giving the exorbitant (anything inherent in over-burdening and the overarching organization) a strategic location. Archiving and questioning project management by redesigning the notations—we can also agree with Hans-Jörg Rheinberger[44] and Bruno Latour[45] that anything can become a notation—made some aspects of the practice seem inexplicable, unplanned, uncertain and thus a trans-gression of normative orientations, enabled by document-ing the discrepancy between what organizations say or claim and what they actually do. By tracing the actors in the notations, the project-structuring work reached pre-cisely those relevant places where urban design could be put into play.

Postscript

The word "fence" also means a receiver of stolen goods.[46] Dealing in stolen goods, or "fencing," is a criminal offense according to §259 of the German Criminal Code (Strafge-setzbuch, StGB). This type of fence or receiver distributes more than he or she can take responsibility for. A person like this is supposed to be understood merely as a political figure in the interspace, and above all, make clear once again what agents in projects can work toward, and what they are being refused. It is important to handle facilitation with care. Designing the general conditions of an enabling architecture for a learning city is not an easy task for pro-ject managers (or whoever is going to fill these positions), nor can it be done without research. Whoever wishes to manage the organization of the organization by handling the normative non-normatively must deal with the motive openly. Questions about authenticity, autonomy, agency, and honesty will always be an issue. Still, this is exactly what the methods of practicing project-structuring work are about.[47]

When I compare how relevant professional publications such as the AHO series,[48] the practical guide to the HOAI,[49]

44   Hans J. Rheinberger, *Experiment, Differenz, Schrift. Zur Geschichte epistemischer Dinge* (Marburg an der Lahn: Basilisken-Presse im Verlag Natur & Text, 1992).

45   Bruno Latour, *Eine neue Soziologie für eine neue Gesellschaft* (Frankfurt am Main: Suhrkamp, 2010).

46   The graphic designer of this book brought this to my attention in one of the first meetings about the book's structure. Thank you for this.

47   Michel Foucault, "The Ethic of the Concern for the Self as a Practice of Freedom," in *Ethics: Subjectivity and Truth*, ed. Paul Rabinow (New York: The New Press, 1997), 281–301.

48   Arbeitskreis PPP des Deutschen Verbandes der Projektmanager in der Bau- und Immobilienwirtschaft e.V., *Interdisziplinäres Projektmanagement für PPP-Hochbauprojekte*, Untersuchungen zum Leistungsbild Heft 22 (Bundesanzeiger Verlag, 2006). AHO (Ausschuss der Verbände und Kammern der Ingenieure und Architekten für die Honorarordnung e.V.) is a professional association of engineers and architects in Germany which represents their competitive interests, especially as regards fees.

49   The HOAI (*Honorarordnung für Architekten und Ingenieure*) is a govern-ment regulation of the fees for architectural and engineering services in

and the Baukultur Report[50] represent the way in which project management is practiced, I notice that only a few years ago, those representations still indicated streamlined processes from A to B, which above all demanded a way of practicing project management as a forward-looking paragon of virtue[51] with a desire for safeguards. Today, other points of reference are used more often. For example, the 2019 Baukultur Report used a Penrose tribar and an illustration by M. C. Escher. I suspect that this foreshadows the fact that supposed "business as usual" or "safe" project planning is not any more consistent than the experiment described in this book. Management standards may be universally appealing because they are largely meaningless.[52] Commitments can shift, and in practice they do. The problems always come during implementation. Aspects of a project that relate to its theme in diverse ways lead project managers to arrive at a liminal, enabling method of carrying out that project. On the basis of descriptions, they organize the means by which the individuals, groups, and collectives that present themselves come into play.

Germany. See Klaus D. Siemon and Ralf Averhaus, *Die HOAI 2013 verstehen und richtig anwenden. Mit Beispielen und Praxistipps* (Wiesbaden: Springer Vieweg, 2014).

50   Reiner Nagel, "Planning Culture and Process Quality," in *Built Living Spaces of the Future – Focus City* (Potsdam: Bundesstiftung Baukultur, 2015), 92–111, www.bundesstiftung-baukultur.de/sites/default/files/medien/967/downloads/baukultur-bericht_2014-15_e.pdf.

51   Irma Rybnikova, "Management as 'Purity Apostle': A Cultural-Anthropological Approach," in *ReThinking Management: Perspectives and Impacts of Cultural Turns and Beyond*, ed. Wendelin Küpers, Stephan Sonnenburg, and Martin Zierold (Wiesbaden: Springer VS, 2017), 59–77, doi: 10.1007/978-3-658-16983-1_3.

52   Keller Easterling, "Management," in *OfficeUS Agenda*, ed. Eva Franch i Gilabert, Ana Milijački, Ashley Schafer, Michael Kubo, and Amanda Reeser Lawrence (Zurich: Lars Müller Publishers, 2014), 148.

THE BEST UNIVERSITY IN THE WORLD
Jan Holtmann

Jan Holtmann works and researches
artistically in the field of
presentation, mediation and working forms of object and action art.
He worked at the UoN in various
teaching and practice formats.

In times of evaluation and excellence programs, it is easy and
necessary to congratulate the University of the Neighbourhoods on
its status as the best university
in the world. Yet it is not the
titles and awards, but rather the
deviating, constantly evolving
methods, the ever-loosing modes
of study that not only expand the
mother ship of university research,
question it, but support it.

As a satellite of a university,
the University of the Neighbourhoods is also always the antithesis, antagonist and corrective
to regular study.

What has not yet been clarified:
Can there be a BEST UNIVERSITY
IN THE WORLD even without a connection to an existing university
or is it always satellite?

THE BEST UNIVERSITY IN THE WORLD
is not an ivory tower — it opens
up to society. In this respect,
society is not an abstract entity,
but a concrete place in a city, in
a city quarter or a neighbourhood.

THE BEST UNIVERSITY IN THE WORLD
is not universal, but local,
contextual and specific.

THE BEST UNIVERSITY IN THE WORLD
is a concrete place that is open
to the public and is committed by
the public and used as a space
for action. THE BEST UNIVERSITY
IN THE WORLD opens spaces for the
possibility of encounters.

At THE BEST UNIVERSITY IN THE
WORLD it is never clear what it
means to go out as a university.
The practices of the Best University of the World are always fields
of action and never auditoriums,
lecture halls, demonstrations or
theaters, because they are open to
action and results.

THE BEST UNIVERSITY IN THE WORLD
never has to deal directly with
art, but it will always come into
contact with questions of artistic
practice, since it raises initial
questions that are always constitutive for artistic action. And it
will always attack, touch, start —
observe the moment when contact is
made just before the grip becomes
firm.

In THE BEST UNIVERSITY IN THE
WORLD, the question of the place of
performance is also particularly
important: in which areas does THE
BEST UNIVERSITY IN THE WORLD have
an influence (in the best case),
on the archive of knowledge, on
teaching, on research, on the
ability to act, on neighbourhood.

As in every university, a central area
of practice is the archive. In the
University of the Neighbourhoods,
however, this is not the work in and
at the library, but in the development
of enabling spaces.

THE BEST UNIVERSITY IN THE WORLD
is itself under constant observation. THE BEST UNIVERSITY IN THE
WORLD is under the observation of
the neighbourhood. Observation
by the neighborhood indicates its
success — which is reflected in
the public canteen, the CAFÉ STORY,
among others. Making history —
telling stories and listening.

THE BEST UNIVERSITY IN THE WORLD
is not built on tradition, but on
the future. And yet the University
of the Neighbourhoods is a program
— not a building — a program that
wants to be used again and again.

The best thing about the University
of the Neighborhoods is that it can
be universal in the sense that it
wants to be used again and again in
different places.

The results of THE BEST UNIVERSITY
IN THE WORLD are open in any form.

At THE BEST UNIVERSITY IN THE
WORLD, students receive their
diploma on the first day of their
studies. This is celebrated in
the evening. From the second day
on, students study.

THE BEST UNIVERSITY IN THE WORLD
is torn down at the end. It makes
way. What is emerging in its place
remains open as long as possible.

The University of the Neighbourhoods is aware of the fragility of
its status of excellence. Minimal
changes have a big impact. Even
as the second best university
in the world, the University of
the Neighbourhoods could disappear
into insignificance.

STOVE

Ben Pohl
Christopher Dell
Bernd Kniess

There are cooks without tongues.
It is probably worthwhile to cultivate a
pleasure that can be enjoyed daily.[1]

Come, wake up everybody! Come, cour-
age, my good people! We want to have a
good time; we want to laugh and joke.
To the ballroom now lead everybody and
see to it that refreshments are served
in plenty.[2]

A history of dwelling is unimaginable without the history of the kitchen. What's more: the kitchen stands out in the context of the history of spatialization processes in dwelling. The kitchen neither develops out of nothing, nor will it ever be completely eliminated. Similar to a spatio-temporal core structure or a biotope island in a sea of spatial activities, the kitchen forms a compass and activates imaginations, places, and economic conditions that already exist in their respective epochs, but are constantly played over by evolving body and representation technologies. What distinguishes the kitchen is its ability to create relationships between various spatial uses. It is precisely this skill that is staged by the modern era—in the most contradictory way—and held up as the driving force of a new production of housing space. The performative influence of new media representations as they appear with photography, women's and housing magazines, advertisements, product catalogs and television in the twentieth century must be emphasized here. It is precisely the medial display of the kitchen that outlines how the modern aspect of modernist architecture is not only reflected in the functional separation of spatial organization or in the novel use of material, but also in the relation between the constructed and its medial conveyance. It is the visual culture of newly arising mass media that relates a biopolitical gender-fication[3] to urbanistic gentrification, which architecture uses to reveal itself in the kitchen as a machine for the normative production of meaning. From now on, the kitchen confronts the discussion about the order of society—and that of genders—with a space oscillating between light and dark, between active freedom and reproducing necessity, which no longer knows what the outside is anymore.

KITCHEN TROUBLE: SINGING THE DOMESTIC UNCONSCIOUS

In light of this, one may call the kitchen the beating heart of modernist architecture, the engine of the living machine, as well as the subconscious of male hegemony in the discipline itself. The kitchen creates a space and an ensemble of practices that are instrumentalized by the so-called "housewife" as bodily techniques of self-reassurance. The kitchen's transformation presupposes not the invention of an alternative to the suburban single-family home, but rather its miniaturized though technically overloaded modulation into the urban apartment. In the kitchen, the modern era has found its normative path to an approach. Here, it vehemently invades the family's privacy, using magazines at first, and later radio and TV in order to inculcate an imaginary space that stages the housewife as the efficient control center of the home, but not without letting her workforce disappear at the same time. The kitchen is the center of her work—unpaid, unregistered, unrepresented and without any acknowledgment, but with increasing upgrading and optimization. Just think of the magical world of

1   Immanuel Kant, cited in Jens Kuhlenkampf, *Immanuel Kant: Köche ohne Zunge* (Göttingen: Steidl, 1997).
2   Wolfgang Amadeus Mozart, *Don Giovanni*, Libretto (English), www.murashev.com/opera/Don_Giovanni_libretto_English_Act_1

3   Anne Harris and Stacy Holman Jones, "Genderfication," in Nelson Rodriguez, Wayne Martino, Jennifer Ingrey, and Edward Brockenbrough, eds., *Critical Concepts in Queer Studies and Education: An International Guide for the Twenty-First Century* (New York: Palgrave Macmillan, 2016).

the Kaiser Cargo Fleetway Dishwasher,[4] which was used in the first case study houses, or the Thor Automagic,[5] which, in the spirit of old kitchens, was able to wash both laundry and dishes, or solitary freezer units of cylindrical shape. Equipped with these, the housewife catapults herself into the identity of "Mrs. 3-in-1," invented and formulated earlier in the 1920s by Emily Post in her book *Etiquette in Society, in Business, in Politics, and at Home*.[6] "Mrs. 3-in-1" is a lover as well as maid and cook, thus the perfect addition to the handyman "Mr. Fix-It." Together, they are the answer to the "servant problem"[7] that the middle class of the Western world is dealing with at this time.

While the focus is on facilitating kitchen work through technical tools and rationalization, since the beginning of the twentieth century it has been the crisis of domestic workers—which many families can no longer afford—that acts as the essential challenge of new living space arrangements of the middle class. The modern kitchen as a place of debate is consolidated around the minimum subsistence level, essentially around that which is in affordable in relation to the income of the lower-middle-class nuclear family within the reproduction machine it knows as an apartment.

The modern era understood it. They brought the primitive hut, which combined fire and soul at the hearth, back into the designed habitat in order to save the modern soul at the busy kitchen unit. In a letter to Charlotte Perriand dated March 17, 1950, Le Corbusier formulated this accordingly,

stating that the conception of the Marseille housing unit was based on the fireplace and the fire, thus making the kitchen part of domestic life; as per the oldest popular or archaic … traditions, it even functions as the heart of domestic life.[8] The kitchen reveals that it is precisely the rediscovery of the archaic that forms the core of the modern. Its goal is nothing less than to rekindle "outdated" traditions in the form of techniques, machines, and organization.[9] Paradoxically, this renaissance of the kitchen marks a return in the Nietzschean sense as an untapped subconscious, and appears (highly technologized) as an animistic shadow of architectonic enlightenment. Accordingly, Bruno Taut explains in his book *Die neue Wohnung. Die Frau als Schöpferin* that the kitchen is the nerve (center) of the apartment, where the housewife's housework is performed in the small household.[10] However, Taut is unable to explain the kitchen in detail, whose prototype (the haybox) he counts among the greatest inventions of the modern era—"Women know more about that," he claims.[11]

Nowhere does Bruno Latour's dictum exemplify that "we have never been modern"[12]better than in the kitchen. This technoid spatial structure, which historically appears just as saturated with utopia as with radiotelegraphy and airplanes, reveals the modern era to be a great misunderstanding that is constantly interfering in our contemporary theories of architecture as a rationalizing force. Their primary legacy proves to be the separation of facts and assumption, object and observer, nature and politics. This suggests that one

4   kaiserpermanentehistory.org/tag/kaiser-cargo/, accessed on May 28, 2018.
5   Museums Victoria Collections, *Combination Clothes & Dish Washing Machine – Thor, "Automagic" 1940s–1950s*, accessed April 8, 2019, collections.museumvictoria.com.au/items/402795.
6   Emily Post, *Etiquette in Society, in Business, in Politics, and at Home* (New York: Cosimobooks New York, [1922] 2007).
7   Post, *Etiquette*, 156.
8   Le Corbusier, cited in Elfie Miklautz et.al., *Die Küche* (Vienna: Böhlau, 1999), 81.
9   Le Corbusier, 81.
10   Bruno Taut, *Die neue Wohnung. Die Frau als Schöpferin* (Leipzig: Klinkhardt & Biermann, 1925), 67.
11   Taut, *Die neue Wohnung*, 67.
12   Cf. Bruno Latour, *We Have Never Been Modern*, trans. Catherine Porter (Cambridge: Harvard University Press, 1993).

could design and control all areas of an antecedent and externalized reality with the help of rational planning. The requirement for this is to interpret reality, and as part of that space, too, as passive constants.

BREAKFAST SESSION

Rrrrrrrrrrr, rrrrrrrrr, rrrrrrrrrr ... chh-chh-chh ... the last coffee bean has made its way through the grinder, followed by silence. At the moment, all that can be heard from the rhythmic rattle is the squeaking drone of the metal crank handle. I get up. I can hear the shower burble—occupied—and walk past the bathroom toward the kitchen. "Good morning! Would you like some coffee, too?" "Good morning! Yes, please." The stove glows red under the moka pot in the midst of the blue dusk creeping into the kitchen through the roof and windows. It is still quiet, and I watch the morning gather itself. Hand, crank, coffee bean, grinder, moka pot, water, stove. The steam noisily makes its way through the ground coffee—its aroma spreads throughout the whole house. The lock on the outer door is opened from the outside, and someone steps in with a bag of Simit bread. "Good morning! Oh, nice! There's coffee." Opening and closing the refrigerator doors, coffee, bread, butter, jam, cheese, plates, knives, mugs, chairs, tables are moved and set for breakfast. Gradually, other residents and guests of the house show up. "No, no, not the ultra-pasteurized milk! There is fresh milk in the other fridge." The ultra-pasteurized milk is excluded from the breakfast session and remains in its cabinet. The homemade jam finds its place on the table, as does the bread from the "Kismet" Turkish bakery around the corner. The cheese is said to come from France, the coffee from Central America. Only the stove's electricity

hesitates to reveal the fact that it stems from a hybrid network, now appearing as a glowing red ceramic hob. I take a small sip of my hot espresso and follow my thoughts as they wander and pursue further traces of this breakfast gathering. The coffee refers back to the Hamburg harbor with its containers, and from there, to the boats and across the oceans all the way to the coffee plantations in the hills of Costa Rica. The stove's electricity points to a conglomerate of cables, masts, boilers, turbines, sensors, pipelines, coal, wind, uranium, sun, gas, contracts, laws, and conflicts. The cheese can be traced back to supermarket shelves, highways, and refrigerated warehouses, all the way to the French Pyrenees, while the ultra-pasteurized milk from the discount supermarket hints at low milk prices, EU subsidy policy and Louis Pasteur's old laboratory in Paris, and further to the watering holes where the first cattle were tamed in the Neolithic revolution. And the bread? The bread points to agriculture and its beginnings, to the first cities of the Neolithic age, like Çatal Höyük, and still to the stove, the embers and to the fire places—the earliest centralities of our urban ancestors, who warmed themselves and invented language there. I sip my profuse container-ocean-ceramic espresso and think about the vast gathering of human and nonhuman actors who are put into relation with us by merely drinking a sip of coffee for breakfast.

The door opens, and a group of students in blue overalls and yellow construction helmets enter the kitchen, giggling loudly. Cable reels and cordless screwdrivers are brought from the tool room, while further preparations for the day are made. The ultra-pasteurized milk from the discount store now finds a spot as well, next to the filter coffee, which gurgles into the pot. Two residents with towels wrapped around their wet hair stroll through the kitchen in their flip-flops and back to the rooms at the end of the long hallway. In the big room, a lecturer, dressed in a suit, is setting up the projector, while someone next to him is picking up empty bottles from yesterday's party and putting them back into the boxes and a handyman is standing enquiringly in the entrance with a delivery note in his hands. "I'm supposed to check the fire extinguishers here." The window screens facing the park are removed. The neighbor with his dog waves his cane and shouts, "Moin, Moin!"

STOVE – FOCUS – FOYER

The stove has many semantic levels. In Alemannic German, *solum* refers to the ground and the earth as a fireplace. In Old High German, *focus* represents the furnace, the domestic hearth and cookery, which consists of compressed soil in the middle of a room and serves as the center and symbol of human habitation. In Middle High German, it is also described as *Haus* and *Wohnung* (house and home). The English word "stove" has Middle Low German origins, describes the heated room and refers to the parlor, in German *Stube*, which, according to Wilhelm Grimm's German dictionary contains the verb *stoben*, meaning "to braise, to steam." The idea of giving off heat has always been the essential element of the term, as it describes the warming oven, a warm room, or bathroom; it may even describe a pub room.[13] Historian Albrecht Cordes suggests that the early meaning of the *Stube* (the parlor) indicates a place of gathering for a society or a whole community, with public functions,

where people meet regularly or often to drink and socialize, to take care of other official duties for the cooperative, as well as to celebrate special celebrations of members and their families, particularly weddings, where people are being hosted in one way or another.[14] The Latin word *focus* for the stove and hearth reveals this motive of a gathering place as well. Its French expression, *foyer* (from Latin *focarium*, focus), the fireplace as the heart of the house and the family, adds another nuance of meaning. Thus, the French foyer develops from a heated meeting place for the family[15] to an open reception area and the central functional place in a largely public building, such as a theater, cinema, museum, or university. This shift then raises the question of different levels of publicity, its boundaries, and rules of access.

The etymological paths of the stove sketched out here shed light on relevant dimensions of the "kitchen foyer" at the UoN. First, the semantic level of the terms "stove, focus, foyer" refer to frequent gathering activities around fireplaces, and second, these activities seem to involve movements of extension. That which is being gathered always expands and changes in the context of the physical and material enclosure,[16] in relations and dependencies of resources and fuel, as well as in interpersonal connections and through the movements of those who gather. It increases and becomes more diverse.

The question of what is to be gathered in kitchens and around the fireplace raises "matters of concern"[17]

13   Jacob und Wilhelm Grimm, "Stube," in *Deutsches Wörterbuch*, vol. 20, 157; Grimm, "Wirtsstube," in *Deutsches Wörterbuch*, vol. 30, 704.

14   Albrecht Cordes, *Stuben und Stubengesellschaften* (Stuttgart: Fischer, 1993), 10ff.

15   Andreas Blank, *Prinzipien des lexikalischen Bedeutungswandels am Beispiel der romanischen Sprachen* (Berlin: de Gruyter, 1997), 433.

16   Cf. Gottfried Semper, *Die vier Elemente der Baukunst* (Braunschweig: Vieweg, 1851).

17   Cf. Bruno Latour, "Why Has Critique Run Out of Steam? From Matters of Fact to Matters of Concern," *Critical Inquiry: Special Issue on the Future of Critique*, vol. 30, no. 2 (Winter 2004):

that have to be negotiated. Whether the discount milk finds its place at the table, whether the associated remote fireplaces in power plants are supposed to generate coal-fired, nuclear, or solar power, whether our apples are grown in a nearby region or the coffee is shipped across the ocean, and who is given access to the theater hall or tea parlor, is in this sense a political decision. In parlors and foyers or in front of the stove, we observe "matters" in Latour's sense. They form the context of action that steers the perspective to the many human and nonhuman connections that gather and evolve as socio-material structures of living. The terms stove, focus, and foyer, however, highlight not only the gradations of indeterminacy in regard to functional and performative superimpositions between work, living, and enjoyment, but also the expanding spectrum between the private and the public.

The case of the UoN kitchen foyer reveals and questions these dimensions on the micro level as urban dimensions. The kitchen foyer is thus understood conceptually as a fireplace. It is the core around which the complex socio-material context of action develops. In terms of research and living as part of this spatial production, we understand this order as an experimental set-up, procedure, and result of a research and design practice embedded in everyday urban life.

THE CENTRALITY OF THE FIREPLACE

Henri Lefebvre calls the gathering process of separately discovered objects in nature and the respective regathering in one place as centrality. The act of regathering represents a social practice, as it addresses a rational aspect of spatial production, namely that of compression and accumulation. Although the latter are not part of the production activity itself, they cannot be separated from it. Where urban space increasingly pushes shifts in and de- and reterritorializations and modulations of centrality, differential realities and their own negation, the concept of *city* dissolves and is replaced by that of the urban.[18] To Lefebvre, the urban serves as processual, "pure" form[19] from now on, which doesn't provide any specific content, but which instead conveys, gathers, arranges, and transforms content.[20] Moreover, it is this pure form of the urban that Lefebvre captures in the concept of centrality. As it turns out, any moment can become a focal point of the urban in a dialectical and contradictory way, and that urban space is concentrically and poly(multi-)centrically[21] movable. Centrality, thus understood as a mental and social form, can be depicted neither on the general societal level nor on the private level. Defined in this way, centrality reveals itself as an intermediate level that develops in the span between the global and private levels.

This sense of centrality as a formal medium is reflected in the arrangement of the UoN's kitchen foyer. We understand this to be a moment in which the gathering of human and n onhuman actors yields an intermediate level that allows heterogeneous and differential aspects to come together.

CUCINA MISTA

"Yes, we can do that, but it will cost you. We won't do it for free." "Yes, of course. We were planning on paying for it. How much is it?" "Well, that depends. How many people did you say?" A woman in her late forties energetically marches into the kitchen

18   HenriLefebvre, *Die Revolution der Städte*
      (Dresden: Dresden Postplatz, [1972] 2003), 63.
19   Lefebvre, 156f.
20   Cf. in detail: Christopher Dell, *Das Urbane*
      (Berlin: Jovis, 2014), 67.
21   Lefebvre, *Die Revolution der Städte*, 57.

25–248. Republished in *Harper's Magazine*,
April 2004, 15–20. Republication reprinted in
Bill Brown, ed., *Things* (Chicago: The University of Chicago Press, 2003), 151–74.

foyer and into a group of students. Visibly stressed, she is carrying a heavy green basket with kitchen utensils in her hands. "All right. Where can we put this down? Is the colleague we talked to last week still there—the one who was with us? What was his name again? Ah, hello. Yes, that was you. Sorry, dear." There is a young man behind her, carrying pots and more appliances in his strong arms. "Giovanni … !" the woman calls to him, then orders him through the kitchen in Italian. Giovanni follows her gestures and stacks more equipment and boxes of vegetables in the kitchen. "My dear …,"— she's talking to me—"you said something about students helping out? They should come now, otherwise we won't finish by eight o'clock." In no time four students, the chef, and Giovanni are standing around the large kitchen isle. "Giovanni, would you mind demonstrating how to cut?" The chef from Don Matteo has taken over the kitchen and conducts it, like the captain of a barge on the Elbe, through the evening. For now, the cold room with its high ceilings has become the vibrant center of an Italian restaurant. Steam rises from the big pots; the oven produces a delicious smell and a warm glow. Giovanni shows a student how to quickly chop onions and tomatoes into small cubes. Others watch, and gradually, the workshop teams return from their expeditions across the Elbe islands. The kitchen fills up with pleasant smells and curiosity, with food, skills, and knowledge, with people, conversations, and discoveries. It becomes a stage for one or two tricks on the cutting boards and for reciprocal observations. The movements are precise, while still allowing time for chats and jokes. As the chef pulls a steaming lasagna from the oven, she asks me, "My dear, now you have to explain to me again what exactly you

all are doing here. Wasn't this the old public health department? I think I was here once when my daughter was little." I'm searching for the right words to translate the title of our workshop, "Made in … local practices of urban production," I say, adding: "Technically, it's about finding out what is being produced in Wilhelmsburg and by whom. For instance, we're interested in what kind of work people do; the same goes for you and your restaurant. But also, for example, how trust is generated and what spaces are being produced."
"Spaces? Okay, interesting. Well, we haven't been working at Don Matteo for very long, and I technically never trained to be a chef, you know? It's exhausting, especially in the beginning, but it's coming along. We're planning on renting the rooms next door, too, and want to renovate. But explain to me, what kind of university is this? I mean, looking at it from the outside, I wouldn't have expected this, with the kitchen and whatnot."

Good question. What kind of university is this? The tables are set in the large room, two colleagues are hanging Post-its on a wall, others are bringing in an old traffic sign, car tires, and rocks that they need for an installation. Then the sound of a bell: dinner is ready. Someone rises to speak. Eating, drinking, small lectures and presentations merge into each other. Don Matteo's chef listens to the young urban researchers' stories and discoveries for a while. She says goodbye by saying, "Hey, thanks. That was interesting with all these different people here. In terms of the invoice, you can just come over next week. Bye, my dear. We'll get the stuff tomorrow!"

From then on, we stay in touch. We greet each other in the street, talk about the latest gossip, and then go for dinner at Don Matteo. The manager handed over the restaurant to her sisters. They want to hold off on renovating and expanding it until visitors come to the garden exhibition in the summer. People call it a "gold-digger atmosphere," and Wilhelmsburg is the new gentrified district of Ottensen, according to the press. In the course of our stove research in Wilhelmsburg, we will probably meet Giovanni again. In his kitchen, we find out that he actually learned Italian here. He is originally from Romania, but here in Wilhelmsburg everyone knows him as Giovanni, the Italian chef.

A SHORT TALE ABOUT THE FIRE AND THE STOVE

It all begins with the use of fire. People come together and gather around the fire. The "controlled" fire culturalizes nature. It is a sign of protection, of community and warmth, as well as of devastation and destruction. Building regulations have mentioned it since the time they came into existence.

Aristotle considers the fire to be the companion of the soul. While the soul in its power to create growth cannot be limited to materiality, the fire remains a contributing source of growing and nourishment.[22] The fire is welcoming. Being invited by a collective to sit down by the fire means being accepted as a guest, belonging to the circle of the community. In Vitruvius's founding myth of architecture, it is the meeting place where language starts, and with the exchange of experiences the development of dwellings begins.[23]

In the beginning, the fire is an open one. The first architectural cultivation comes with the enclosed fireplace, and leads to the closed cast-iron stove in the nineteenth century. Throughout this time, the tamed, culturalized fire is part of the whole house in rural areas of Europe. Marked by means of a tiled pattern in the interior, the hearth is the house within the house—it has a covered roof for girding the fire upward. This roof itself is again an object of culture. Ornaments are attached to it, or, in wealthy houses in northern Germany, for example, what's called a *Hal*, a broad-toothed piece of metal. At its lower end hangs the spring jaw, which clicks into the teeth of the *Hal* and holds a height-adjustable cauldron. Furthermore, the *Hal* is a recording device, a material memory for events. Ornaments engraved on it recall important episodes of family history, such as the building of a house, weddings, or childbirth.[24]

Not only is the fire a place where cooking takes place; it is also the defining location for cohabitation. The use of fire has always been the core axis of the various spatial forms of living that evolve around the kitchen; it is a place where the source of heat used for cooking is situated,[25] and the word "kitchen" suggests a complex set of cultural rules[26] that relate to the ways in which food is prepared.

The introduction of technology into the kitchen as we know it today began relatively late in terms of cultural history. It wasn't until the late eighteenth century that the invention and marketing of new kitchen equipment began, which set off the kitchen as a metaphor and model for technological development in living. The kitchen became the subject of design in the twentieth century, exemplified by the Frankfurt

22   Aristoteles (Aristotle), Über die Seele, Book II, 4 (Berlin: Akademie-Verlag, 1959), 31.

23   Vitruv (Vitruvius), *Zehn Bücher über Architektur*, translated and with comments by Curt Fensterbusch (Darmstadt: Wissenschaftliche Buchgesellschaft, [1964] 2013), 79ff.

24   Alfred Faber, *1000 Jahre Werdegang von Herd und Ofen. Ausgewählte Kapitel aus ihrer technischen Entwicklung bis zu Beginn des 19. Jahrhunderts* (Munich, Oldenburg, and Düsseldorf: Deutscher Ingenieur-Verlag, 1950).

25   Eva Barlösius, *Soziologie des Essens. Eine sozial- und kulturwissenschaftliche Einführung in die Ernährungsforschung* (Weinheim: Beltz Juventa, [1999] 2016), 123.

26   Barlösius, *Soziologie des Essens*, 123.

kitchen;[27] it was proof of the efforts made to optimize the dwelling machine itself, which is at least equally oriented toward the androcentric order. In accordance with Taylor[28] and Gilbreth's economic studies,[29] motion sequences and their economy of time and space were measured, recorded, and optimized. This small, 6.5-square-meter "kitchen machine"—the basic version of which excludes the maid in middle-class households that are better off financially—offers space for only one person. Freed from the interdependencies of family life as well as social struggles for better working conditions, the optimized workflow in the kitchen disregards the division of labor, probably the most effective, albeit unexplored, means of increasing productivity.[30] Such gender division of spaces in terms of domestic and gainful employment manifests itself in the functionalist layout of the apartment and the city and in urban areas, such as production, reproduction, and regeneration.

KITCHEN TROUBLE II

Perhaps it can be said that Charles Fourier was the first person to denaturalize gender and to identify it as a product of social relations.[31] Conversely, this meant to him that any change in these relations cannot be achieved without including the question of gender. Fourier was convinced that the expansion of women's privileges is the basis of all social advancements.[32] Fourier did not stop at relentlessly exposing the material and moral misery of middle-class life;[33] he suggested concrete measures to counteract the construction of gender differences. The guiding principle that he thus propagated spoke of a "harmony of differences." The spatial proposal of a rural-cooperative settlement, the *Phalanstère*, is particularly relevant here. The spatialization of an association of creative diversity, launched by Fourier, should accommodate the ideal of a harmonious synergy of various skills, needs and passions.[34] The right to work plays a paramount role—it is not any occupation, but attractive work, that suits the affinities of the working population.[35] Economically secured by a right to basic income, all members of the community are to improve their social behavior in the context of new concepts of production and reproduction, communitized housework, parenting, and adult education.

As we know, Fourier's ideas were and still are highly controversial. While his perhaps harshest critics were Marx and Engels,[36] his theories are experiencing a generous reception and constructive renaissance in today's Commoning debate, whose most prominent example is the voluminous study *Commun. Essai sur la révolution au XXIᵉ siècle*.[37]

While Fourier was unable to implement his ideas during his lifetime, his criticism of the conditions of society

27 Ernst May, ed., *Das neue Frankfurt: Internationale Monatsschrift für die Probleme kultureller Neugestaltung* 1 (Frankfurt am Main: Verlag Englert und Schlosser, 1926/1927): 120 ff.

28 Frederick Winslow Taylor, "Shop Management," *Transactions of the American Society of Mechanical Engineers* 28 (1903): 1337–1480.

29 Frank Bunker Gilbreth, *Motion Study: A Method for Increasing the Efficiency of the Workman*, with an introduction by Robert Thurston Kent (Michigan: D. Van Nostrand Company, 1911).

30 Cf. Walter Siebel, *Die Kultur der Stadt* (Berlin: Suhrkamp, 2015), 149f.

31 Leslie Goldstein, "Early Feminist Themes in French Utopian Socialism: The St.-Simonians and Fourier," *Journal of the History of Ideas* 43, no. 1 (Jan.–Mar. 1982): 91–108.

32 Charles Fourier, "1846: 132–133," in Martin Burghardt, *Charles Fourier. Der Philosoph der Kleinanzeige* (Berlin: Semele Verlag, 2006), 107.

33 Friedrich Engels and Karl Marx, *Werke*, vol. 19, 4th ed. of the unrevised reprint of the 1st ed. 1962 (Berlin (GDR): (Karl) Dietz Verlag, 1973), 177–228, here 196.

34 Alexander Neupert-Doppler, *Utopie. Vom Roman zur Denkfigur* (Stuttgart: Schmetterling Verlag, 2015), 32.

35 Neupert-Doppler, *Utopie*, 33.

36 Engels and Marx, *Werke*, 196.

37 Pierre Dardot and Christian Laval, *Commun. Essai sur la révolution au XXIᵉ siècle* (Paris: La Découverte, 2014).

was taken up and developed further by social democrats. For example, August Bebel based his concept of a new society on the total social equality of women[38] at work and in society, as an equal coexistence of practical wage labor (with free choice of occupation), education, or care, and artistic or scientific activity. Domestic life should be reduced to a minimum, traditional activities in terms of housework and parenting should become a societal task, and social life should increasingly become public. Clara Zetkin proclaims the necessary rejection of the familiar domestic and parenting work, which she connects to the demand for economic, political, and social independence from men.[39] A few years later, Lily Braun also seizes upon this double burden of wage and housework. In her theory for a concrete, communal form of living, economic cooperatives play a decisive role as a solution to the problem.[40] All these approaches for dissolving the private household are unsuccessful. The "revisionist discussion" in the Social Democratic Party (SPD) leads to postponing any kind of attempt at reform that would benefit the traditional, middle-class form of single-family housing as the appropriate and private retreat for the family, as well as the promotion of garden cities and building cooperatives.[41]

The topoi of communitized housing functions and women's equality come into effect once again in the post-revolutionary Soviet Russia. The new human being is placed at the center of living standards, the collectivization of life, and women's emancipation by abolishing the household and the family.[42] Freed from private housework, the act of cooking is to be shifted from the individual kitchen to the communal cooking laboratory, meals are to be eaten in public dining halls, and children are to be educated in kindergarten and schools. Still, the same applies here: despite many communal houses being part of countless competitions and designs, thereby gaining a symbolic status in terms of so-called new dwelling, only few projects were actually realized.

SEMPER: STOVE AS
FUNCTIONAL PERFORMATIVE
Gottfried Semper's book *The Four Elements of Architecture*,[43] published in 1852, in which he distances himself from the Vitruvian triad *utilitas*, *firmitas*, and *venustas* represents one of the first functionalist spatial approaches. Inspired by the example of the Caribbean hut, which he saw in 1851 during a visit to the Great Exhibition in London, Semper turned to a genetically empirical examination of simple archaic buildings and their basic functions. The model that Semper derived from this shift is based on the division of the building into the functions of hearth (cooking, eating), mound (topographic mass of the establishment), roof (protection), and enclosure (separation). In this context, Semper feeds the "stove" both archaically and morally. He considers the fireplace to be a type of *cultus*, a spatially composed starting point of all cohabitation, which in later epochs becomes the artifact of ritualization and constitution. Just as Semper places the stove at the center and arranges the three other elements of protection around it, he is attached to George

38   August Bebel, *Unsere Ziele. Eine Streitschrift gegen die "Demokratische Korrespondenz"* (Berlin: Expedition der Buchhandlung Vorwärts (Th. Glocke), [1869] 1903).

39   Clara Zetkin, *Die Arbeiterinnen- und Frauenfrage der Gegenwart* (Berlin: Verlag der Berliner Volks-Tribüne, 1889).

40   Lily Braun, *Die Frauenfrage* (1901); *Frauenarbeit und Hauswirtschaft* (1901/02); *Was wir wollen* (1902).

41   Thomas Hafner, *Kollektive Wohnreformen im Deutschen Kaiserreich (1871–1918) – Anspruch und Wirklichkeit* (Stuttgart: Universität Stuttgart, 1992), 119.

42   Thomas Möbius, *Russische Sozialutopien von Peter I. bis Stalin* (Berlin: Lit Verlag, 2012), 365.

43   Gottfried Semper, *Die vier Elemente der Baukunst* (Braunschweig: Vieweg, 1851).

Cuvier's functionalist model of biology. Cuvier's anatomical system of correlative organs and the hierarchization of characters includes removing the characteristics from subordination through taxonomy, in order to "introduce it, prior to any classification that might occur, into the various organic structural plans of living beings."[44] Not only does Cuvier point out the fact that bodily structures are interdependent, but from now on the relation itself appears to be based on correlative contexts.

The body thus emerges as a complex composition of abstract elements that can take on countless forms. These elements are called organs. Architectural theorist Ute Poerschke holds the view that in Cuvier's theory of the organization of totality, the active functions are determined. This means that organisms are founded on an inner principle of self-preservation, and functions are used only to maintain the body's organization.[45] Functions are considered reciprocal processes of organs, which all work toward a common purpose in the state of life.[46] Now, the crucial point is that the function of the organs is given control over their disposition: one has to focus more on the performance itself, rather than its organs.[47] Taking up Cuvier's model, Semper not only expanded the prototype by functions; he also modulated the spatial function according to the activity by relating it to social prototype activities, such as weaving or pottery, thus causing the form to become performative.

TASTE AND COMMUNITY
While Semper was in line with the biology of his time (without biologizing or

naturalizing architecture, as Laugier had done), he also agreed with the physiologization of the concept of taste, as undertaken by jurist Jean Anthelme Brillat-Savarin in the early nineteenth century. The posthumously published book *La physiologie du gout, ou méditations de gastronomie transcendante*[48] (The Physiology of Taste, or Meditations on Transcendental Gastronomy) describes the form and culture of societal gathering. Savarin focuses on the dinner party and develops a new term: *convivialité*. While understanding social behavior with food and while eating, Savarin develops a historical philosophy of the kitchen, using *convivialité*, which seeks to enhance the art of cooking to becoming science. This kind of philosophy is supposed to help explain how basic needs such as hunger and appetite interact with the human soul, with notions and ideologies of taste as a cultural practice. In terms of conceptual history, Savarin's book was the first to define the concept of conviviality. Eva Bärlösius highlights three institutions of eating which apparently occur in most societies. According to her, these are the cultural definition of edible and inedible, the kitchen as the cultural set of rules for food preparation, and the meal or act of eating as a social situation.[49]

LAMBS IN THE PARK
Time for a break. I get up from my desk in the kitchen, check the residents' drawer in the kitchen furniture for tobacco, and step outside into the midday sun on the terrace. Everything smells like summer. Blankets and rugs are laid out on the Rotenhäuser Feld meadow. A colorful and dense throng, just like at a public swimming pool. Several barbecues and fireplaces have been lit,

44 Michel Foucault, *The Order of Things: An Archaeology of the Human Sciences* (London: Routledge, [1966] 2006), 287.

45 Ute Poerschke, *Funktionen und Formen. Architekturtheorie der Moderne* (Bielefeld: Transcript, 2014), 95.

46 Georges Cuvier, *Vorlesung über vergleichende Anatomie*, vol. 1 (Leipzig: Paul Gotthelf Kummer, 1809–1810), 39.

47 Cuvier, *Vorlesung*, 52.

48 Jean Anthelme Brillat-Savarin, *Physiologie du goût, ou méditations de gastronomie transcendante* (Paris: A. Sautelet, 1826).

49 Barlösius, *Soziologie des Essens*, 48.

surrounded by baskets and bowls with food, women, children, and men gathered in concentric order. The entire household of the neighborhood seems to have spread out here. Pale blue columns of smoke rise and drift through the park. The hearth assembly transforms the meadow into a large summer kitchen and the living room of the district. I walk along the gravel path for a while. The instant blending of the smell of lamb meat with odor of a joint greets me from a shaded corner. "Excuse me. Do you have a light?" A little further down the path, protected by surrounding bushes, two boys sit on small Persian rugs next to two impressive lambs they are roasting on a spit. Clearly bored, they seem to have stopped caring about watching over the embers and meat.

Back on the terrace, I sit down in front of the kitchen in the partial shade of the trees. A woman with five children in tow is walking from the park toward me. "Can we get some water from you?" "Yeah sure, right here in the kitchen." The children use the tap to fill up crumpled plastic bottles. "Do you happen to have a bathroom as well?" "Yes, first door on the left." The children wait while observing and exploring the room with their eyes. When their mother returns, they kindly say goodbye and disappear toward one of the pillars of smoke.

Whether in houses, gastronomic establishments, or here in the park, whether stacked on top of each other or scattered far and wide, the stove belongs to the household. By this implication, we can conclude that a city consists of many hearths. What is interesting about this gathering of stoves at the park is that in this case, everyday life is not hidden in the domestic kitchen, but is visible and negotiable as a relational diagram of human and nonhuman actors, their practices, languages, sounds, and smells. We, too, are among the users of this urban space. With the dismantling of the fence, the strictly defined border (physically, though not in its effectiveness) is set aside. We make use of the open resource and emulate the "lamb on the spit" or begin conversations and mingle with the neighbors by talking about herbal gardens and tree houses. Conversely, we are also appropriated by the park users. The children surround the house, sway in the fabric tree houses, and snatch a soft drink when they get the chance, and soon the word is spread that we are also a kitchen, watering hole, and bathroom.

The Rotenhäuser Feld becomes the territory of summer gatherings and encounters that extend all the way to the terrace and the house and, when the big gates are opened, expand and spread into the kitchen and thus the house. Although careful at first, the urban blasé[50] turns into an act of appraisal and respectful realization; respect and pragmatic calculation account for initial approaches: "Do you have any water?," "May we use the bathroom?," "Can we have another Coke?," "Do you have a light for me?"

The state of not being able to do, know, or have—in other words, human deficiency—appears here as the resource of social interaction and association. We set out with our deficits, our lack of knowledge, and our curiosity to build new connections: "Hello. We're planning on making a book about the gastronomic scene in Wilhelmsburg. May we ask you something?," "Hello. We want to celebrate an event in the old public health department. We're still looking for dishes and cutlery," "Hello. We're

50   Cf. Georg Simmel, "Die Grossstadt. Vorträge und Aufsätze zur Städteausstellung," in *Jahrbuch der Gehe-Stiftung Dresden,* ed. Th. Petermann (Dresden, 1903), 185–206.

trying to set up some sort of restaurant and are still looking for someone to cook for us," "Hello. We want to roast a lamb. Where can we get one here in Wilhelmsburg?" These questions open up and expand the repertoire of possibilities and local knowledge. At the same time, new and also economic connections develop, which, however, elude the simple logic, "solid for solid, substance for substance, and meal for coin of the realm,"[51] as Michel Serres describes it.

STORM OF COMMUNITIZATION

Two weeks later at the tree house party, a lamb is roasting on the grill, which we borrowed from a neighbor in the restaurant business. Actually, we wanted to roast it over the fire, and it was supposed to be a sheep from the dike, one that had become round from eating all the grass on the Elbe islands, but the process of slaughtering it turned out to be more difficult and expensive than we'd thought, and a whole sheep roasted over the fire was too risky of an idea in the end. Hence the lamb arrived frozen from the ends of the Earth, with the spit already in its place. Twenty kilograms, ready to barbecue, no head or innards; the barbecue is electric.

A long table is being set on the terrace. The children from the tree house camp are enjoying campfire bread by the fire in front of the kitchen. In the park, the barbecue areas are lit again and the sky is closing in, covered in thunderclouds. It gets dark, the first raindrops fall, and the families hurriedly gather their belongings. We carry the table and the electric lamb inside, too. When the rain starts, the room fills with the warm, rushing sound of raindrops

hitting the roof. The kitchen now resembles an open tent, which has become a shelter for a bright jumble of people and things. The large room next door fills up and everyone moves together at the tables: children from the neighborhood, fathers, mothers with and without headscarves, neighbors, friends, and other fugitives from the park.

The lamb is ready to be carved, and together with all kinds of grilled vegetables and salads it creates a lush buffet. Now I recognize the mother who'd asked for water; her children have eagerly participated in building the tree houses. We sit facing each other, me with my own children, she with hers, as we eat vegetables and lamb with, due to a lack of knives, a spoon and fork.

The thunder has turned the multitude of barbecues and fireplaces that had sprung up near and next to each other in the park into an incidental tableside fellowship. The concept of this kind of community includes an aspect of separating as well as of collecting. Max Weber, among others, primarily understood it as practices of difference, the formation and confirmation of a community in relation to its constitutive exterior. These practices include food-related taboos (e.g. halal or vegan) as well as an affiliation with the community of eaters.[52] Eva Barlösius points out that in many languages, eating and community had been combined into one word, i.e. one word to symbolize the other, because the collaborative sharing of food is considered the first social act.[53] On the one hand, the thunderstorm is ruining our summer party; on the other hand, it is becoming the impetus to unite the barbecue and fireplaces on the meadow to form a

51   Michel Serres, *The Parasite*, trans. Lawrence R. Schehr (Baltimore: Johns Hopkins University Press, 1982), 35.

52   Cf. Max Weber, *Grundriß der Sozialökonomik III. Abteilung Wirtschaft und Gesellschaft* (Tübingen: Mohr, 1922), 247.

53   Barlösius, *Soziologie des Essens*, 174.

tableside fellowship for the moment. Similar to the famous scene described by Clifford Geertz in *Deep Play*,[54] in which he and the Balinese cockfight participants run from the police into a family's courtyard, the UoN's kitchen becomes the refuge and a moment of communion opposite the outside world. The symbolic, imaginary, and physical thresholds are overcome by the incipient rain; humans and objects gather under the protective roof in the kitchen foyer.

CONVIVIALITY AS A FORM OF EATING AND COOKING

In her historically informed architecture manual *Designed to Live in*,[55] Elisabeth Beazley calls the relationship between the kitchen and other rooms the key to the layout of the modern house. Where there is no attending chef, the housewife works there. She spends most of her day working in the kitchen or navigating between it and other rooms. The kitchen is thus the "working hub of the house,"[56] which in the modern era can appear in of three types: the "working kitchen," the "dining kitchen," and the "living-room kitchen."[57] The last two kinds in particular remind us of the fact that the kitchen is, unlike any other architectonic structure, linked to the question of cohabitation and its respective reproduction.

Throughout the nineteenth century, industrialization, progressive trade and the development of administrative political organizations paved the way for the *embourgeoisement* of society. In that respect, the new role of the woman is the housewife, who single-handedly enables cohabitation. This core of division of labor sets off a conflict between individualization and communitization that runs through the entire twentieth century and whose problem structure also defines the guiding principles of urban development. But what does cohabitation mean?

Ivan Illich made this an issue in the 1970s, particularly with his book *Tools of Conviviality*,[58] and reintroduced the concept of conviviality into the discourse. Here, the term mainly represents an anti-reductionism directed at the one-dimensional notion of industrial productivity. To Illich, switching from productivity to conviviality means replacing technical values with ethical ones, and materialized values with realized ones.[59] He considers conviviality as the individual freedom that is realized in a relation of productivity embedded in a society equipped with effective tools.[60] The issue of reproduction in light of the use of resources is thus addressed and—in his day—a critique of both capitalist and real socialist behavior towards the needs in question: no inflation of production, however vehement, is capable of fulfilling the multiplied needs of a purely production-oriented society.[61] The requirement here is to formulate new criteria of good living and prosperity that negate any restriction on economic growth. The traditional method of understanding the statistics regarding gross domestic product (GDP) as a criterion for growth becomes obsolete, thus calling for a redefinition of the concept of wealth.[62] This argumentation is later used for the discursive position of post-development, which criticizes the modernization of the global South along the logic of Western economic growth and development.

Urban conviviality is the social communitization for the needs of urban actors. Physical structures and

54   Clifford Geertz, *Deep Play: Notes on the Balinese Cockfight* (Münster: Daedalus, 2005).
55   Elisabeth Beazley, *Designed to Live in* (London: Allen & Unwin, 1962).
56   Beazley, *Designed to Live in*, 182.
57   Beazley, *Designed to Live in*, 182.
58   Ivan Illich, *Tools of Conviviality* (Glasgow: Fontana, 1975).
59   Illich, *Tools of Conviviality*, 32.
60   Illich, *Tools of Conviviality*, 32.
61   Illich, *Tools of Conviviality*, 32.
62   Serge Latouche, *Farewell to Growth* (Cambridge: Polity, 2009, 2011).

conviviality are tightly interlocked therein. Relationally, they allow urban space to emerge in complex and highly variable ways. Throughout the daily physical and social recreation of the self—which also includes joint cooking, eating, and sharing of food—conviviality is situated as a producing part of the urban body. Instead of referring back to closed identities, conviviality expresses a specific and nuanced mode of spatial production that orders and anchors open encounters between actors around motives.[63] One may also describe this mode as an assembly that aims at collectively overcoming material and symbolic questions.[64] Many cultures have ritualized or institutionalized precisely this question in spatial structures.

Therefore, one may understand conviviality as a theoretical framework that makes it possible to describe the spatiality evoked by the stove and, with it, the kitchen as a place for nutrition and assembly in urban agglomerations. Focused on reproduction, the spatial structures of the kitchen affect urban constellations by configuring, restricting, or enabling everyday practices. Social activities that evolve around food turn common materials of life into special occasions or events, ranging from shopping at the market to shared coffee or a meal. These everyday rituals and practices regarding food are embedded in urban geography. They span a topological net over the *city*, sometimes located within a neighborhood, and sometimes across and beyond city districts.

Wherever conviviality remains an economic matter, its social and ritual character always transcends linear market strategies, as sociologist Marcel Mauss illustrates with the concept of the gift. Mauss sets the principle of *convivialité* against the logic of economy, which he connects to the practice of giving. To Mauss, conviviality is a form of mutual acknowledgment through the exchange of gifts, which is based on social relationships.[65] Conviviality is thus directly linked to the issue of how space is used and the question of what kind of boundaries are drawn between public and private property. However, within the regime of neoliberal biopolitics, conviviality is exposed to the commercialization and marketing of the space as a product, leading to the branding of hospitality and the commodification of urban lifestyles.

As simple and effortless as the moment during the storm may seem, the strategies and tactics for overcoming thresholds are as varied as the thresholds themselves. After all, the kitchen of the UoN is not a public space. Unlike the removal of the fence, where the border opens up a threshold, the large window screens—given the right conditions—offer the opportunity to adjust the threshold and point of transition from the outdoors to indoors. Just as with the dining rooms of the pubs or the families' barbecue areas on the meadow, these centralities develop rules of access as well which are not revealed to or opened up to everyone. What is needed in order to explore or overcome these thresholds is initially an interest.

63   Paul Gilroy, *After Empire: Melancholia or Convivial Culture?* (London: Routledge, 2004).
64   Claude Grignon, "Commensality and Social Morphology: An Essay of Typology," in *Food, Drink and Identity: Cooking, Eating and Drinking in Europe Since the Middle Ages*, ed. Peter Scholliers (Oxford: Oxford University Press, 2001), 24.
65   Marcel Mauss, "Die Gabe. Form und Funktion des Austauschs in archaischen Gesellschaften," in *Soziologie und Anthropologie*, vol. 1 (Munich: Ullstein, [1924] 1978).

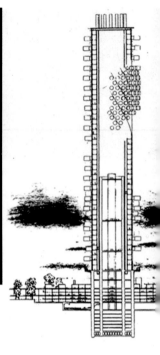

b)   2 x 3 (F2 = c+d+e)   2 x 5 (F5)

a	Herd
b	Bett
c	Fenster
d	Zaun
e	Dach

2 x 4 (31)

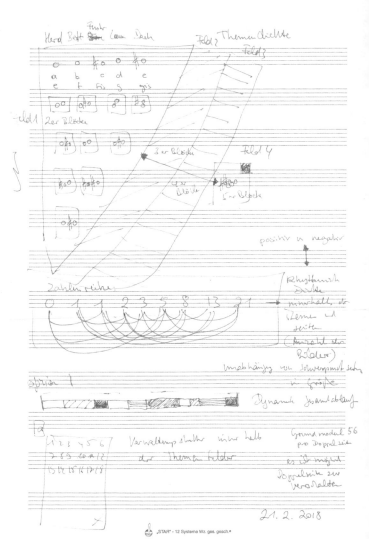

genden Sparren auf Lagerhölzern aufliegen, welche unmittelbar auf tragenden W..
ruhen. Abstand und Lage der Sparren sind dann allein von der Art bzw. dem Gewicht der
Dachdeckung und dem Gebäudegrundriß bestimmt. Lediglich die Durchbiegung der Sparren begrenzt hinsichtlich der Spannweiten die Ausführungsmöglichkeiten (Bild 1.25).

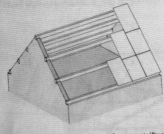

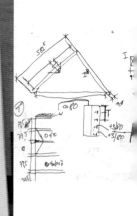

1.25 Ausgangsform des Pfettendaches:
Pultdach mit Sparren, die auf Mauern aufliegen (kleinformatige Dachdeckung)

1.26 Pfettendach mit Pfetten auf ausgesteiften
Giebelwänden in Verbindung mit großforma-
tiger Eindeckung ohne Lattung (z. B. Faser-
zement-Wellplatten)

In der Regel werden die Sparrenauflager durch tragende „Pfetten" gebildet. Sie können bei
kleineren Gebäuden mit einfachen Grundrißformen frei zwischen ausgesteifte Giebelwän-
de oder sonstige hochgeführte Querwände gespannt werden (Bild 1.26).
Dachdeckungen aus großformatigen Bedachungsmaterialien (z. B. Faserzement-Wellplat-
ten) können direkt auf Pfetten aufliegen, wenn diese im erforderlichen Abstand frei zwischen
ausgesteifte Giebelscheiben gespannt (Bild 1.26) oder auf anderen Unterkonstruktionen wie
z. B. unverschieblichen Dreiecksverbänden aufgelagert sind (Bild 1.27).
Mit derartigen Pfettendachkonstruktionen können jedoch nur einfache Satteldächer über
kleineren Rechteckgrundrissen gebildet werden.

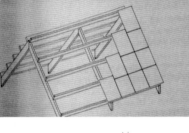

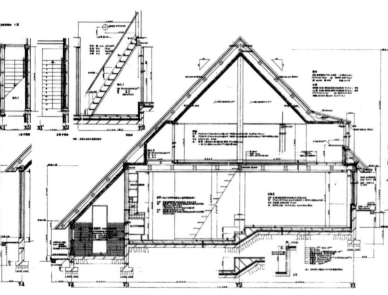

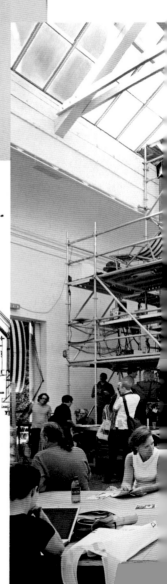

Handwritten notes:

$c = 5,825\,m$

$3,12\,h$

$4/2 \quad 10,11\,m$

$5825 : 60 \Rightarrow 9,71 \approx 10 \text{ Tage}$

$I \quad 8 \rightarrow 640 + 80 \Rightarrow 720$

$II \quad 12 \rightarrow 960 + 110 = 1070$

Fläche $I_a \rightarrow 720 \times 5.82,5 \rightarrow 419400\,cm^2$
$\approx 41,94\,m^2$

$II_a \rightarrow 1070 \times 5825 \rightarrow 623275\,cm^2$
$\approx 62,3275\,m^2$

$5,825^2 = 5,55^2 + h^2$

$5,825^2 - 5,55^2 = h^2$

$\sqrt{(\quad)} = h$

$c^2 = a^2 + b^2$

$c^2 - a^2 = b^2$

I_8
80
I_{12}
20

Gibs

So wird gedämmt

[k] **KAMPNAGEL HAMB**
JARRESTRASSE 20 /22303 HAMBURG
WWW.KAMPNAGEL.DE

God's Entertainment (Wien)
Universität der Nachbarschaften (Wilh

SHIVERS

Fr-12.06.2009 /13:00 Eröffnung
Weitere Termine: Sa-13.06. bis Di-16.06. zwischen
im ehemaligen Gesundheitsamt /Rothenhäuser Damm 3
Eintritt frei

[VON UND MIT] God's Entertainment und Wilhelmsburgern

Am Freitag, den 12.Juni 2009 um 13Uhr startet im ehemalige
Gesundheitsamt die "Universität der Nachbarschaften", ein G
der IBA, HCU und Kampnagel, mit einer Performance der Wien
God's Entertainment. Aus Motiven des Films SHIVERS von Dav
entwickelt das experimentell arbeitende Performer-Kollektiv
Reise in die eigenen inneren und andere unbekannte Welten e
bis zum 16.Juni jeden Abend gemeinsam mit Wilhelmsburgern e
ehemaligen Gesundheitsamtes.
Dort gibt es u.a. einen Erlebnis-Raum, der "Meet the Shive
ist. Ein Angst-Detektor zeigt, ob die Angst, zum Beispiel
so stark ist, dass die Nachbarn aus dem Wilhelmsburger Afro
yourself"-Raum hilfreich unter die Arme greifen müssen - o
zur "Anti-Ismus"-Impfung greifen sollte. Im „Interview"-R
bei Wilhelmsburg-TV den Fragen der Performer stellen oder
äußern.
Draußen im Garten können die Besucher im "Strand-für-alle"
entspannen mit einem Drink der "Cocktailbar für nette Mens
Statumenpark entdecken. Es werden außerdem Fahrradtouren, o
Busfahrt durch Wilhelmsburg angeboten.
Am Sonntag, den 14.Juni, spielen um 20:00 Dirty-Disco-Youth

Die »Universität der Nachbarschaften« (UdN) ist eine Kooperation
Universität Hamburg (HCU), der Internationalen Bauausstellung Ham
Kampnagel.

Presse: Mareike Holfeld, T: 040 270 949 17, t: mareike.holfeld@k
Sarah Rosemau, T: 040 270949 347, t: sarah.rosemau@kampnagel.de
KARTEN: 040 270 949 49   Mo-Fri / 13-19Uhr, Sa. Su 16-19Uhr
Kampnagel Hamburg, Jarrestr. 20, 22303 Hamburg, www.kampnagel.de

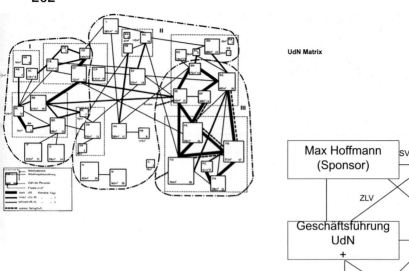

UdN Matrix

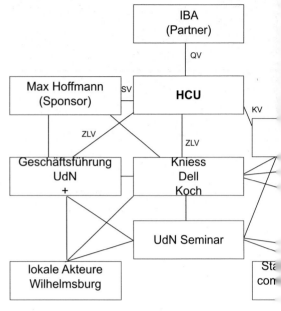

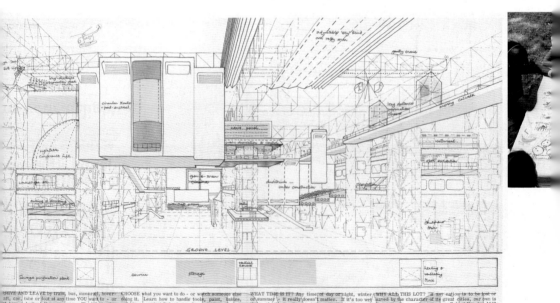

GROUND LEVEL

DRIVE AND LEAVE by train, bus, monorail, hover-aft, car, tube or foot at any time YOU want to - or at have a look at it as you pass. The information reens will show you what's happening. So need to ok for an entrance - just walk in anywhere. No doors, yers, queues or commissionaires: it's up to you how to use it. Look around - take a lift, a ramp, an esca-tor to wherever or whatever looks interesting.

CHOOSE what you want to do - or watch someone else doing it. Learn how to handle tools, paint, babies, machinery, or just listen to your favourite tune. Dance, talk or be lifted up to where you can see how other people make things work. Sit out over space with a drink and tune in to what's happening elsewhere in the city. Try starting a riot or beginning a painting - or just lie back and stare at the sky.

WHAT TIME IS IT? Any time of day or night, winter or summer - it really doesn't matter. If it's too wet that roof will stop the rain but not the light. The arti-ficial cloud will keep you cool or make rainbows for you. Your feet will be warm as you watch the stars, the atmosphere clear as you join in the chorus. Why not have your favourite meal high up where you can watch the thunderstorm?

WHY ALL THIS LOT? "If any nation is to be lost or saved by the character of its great cities, our own is that nation" - Robert Vaughan 1843

We are building a short-term plaything in which all of us can realise the possibilities and delights that a 20th Century city environment owes us. It must last no longer than we need it.

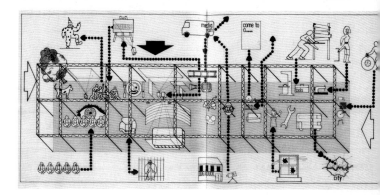

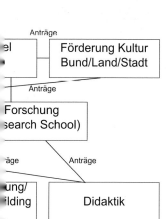

Anträge

| | Förderung Kultur Bund/Land/Stadt |

Anträge

Forschung
search School)

äge   Anträge

ung/
ilding   Didaktik

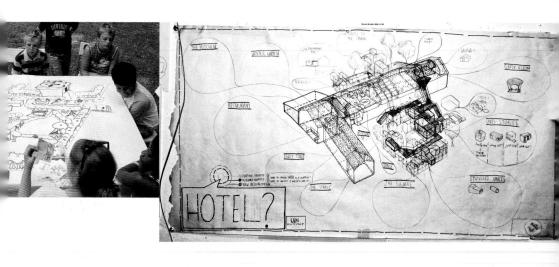

Ansicht Süd

Ansicht West

Schnitt B-B

Schnitt A-A

Ansicht West

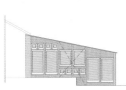

Ansicht Nord

Teerpappe/Dachpappe 200mq

Schalplatten/OSB -Platten (250x125x22mm, 32 stk)

Kantholz 10 x10cm x 4m (38 stk)

doka Träger h20 (4m, 15 stk)

doka Deckenstütze Eurex 20 top 400 (16 stk)

Kantholz 10 x10cm x 2,5m (65 stk)

Gehwegplatten 50 x 50cm (84 stk)

L-Steine h 80 b 45 14m (für Höhenausgleich im Gelände

Lochplattenwinkel/Schwerlastwinkel 8cm 250 stk

Lochplattenwinkel/Schwerlastwinkel 6cm 250 stk

Holzkeile/Montagekeile

Diverse Spax-Schrauben
- 4x40mm 500 Stk.
- 4x60mm 500 Stk.
- 4x80mm 1.000 Stk.
- 4x100mm 1.000 Stk.
- 5x80mm 500 Stk.
- 5x100 mm 500 Stk.
- 5x120 mm 1000 Stk.
- 5x140 mm 500 Stk.
- 6x120 mm 500 Stk.
- 6x160 mm 200 Stk.

2,30

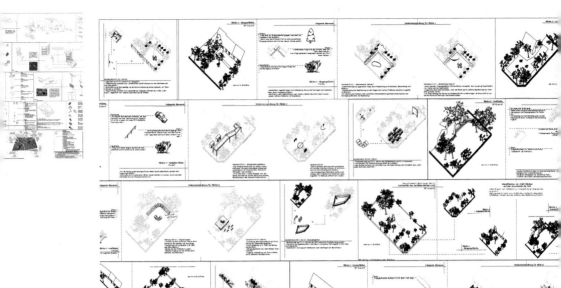

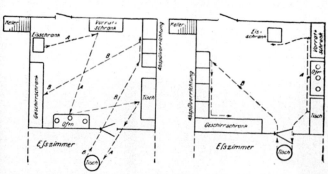

Abb. 47. Christine Frederick: Ganglinien in der Küche bei falscher (links) und richtiger Einrichtung (rechts)

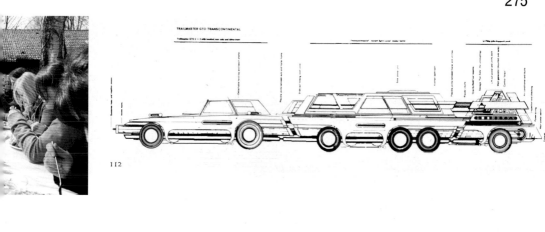

TRAILMASTER GTO TRANSCONTINENTAL

112

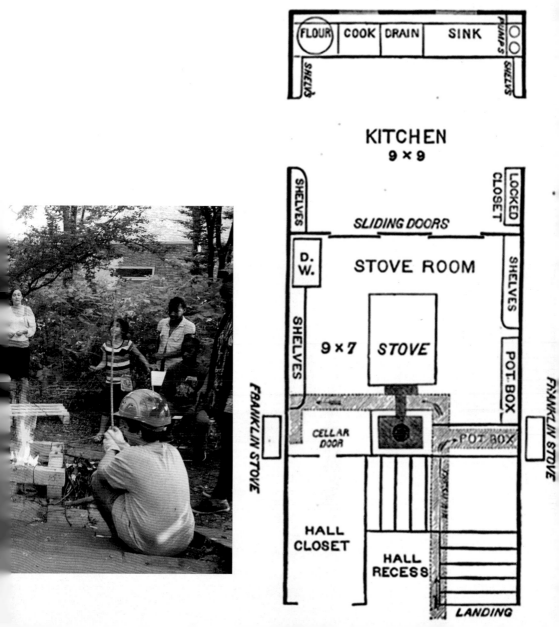

FLOUR	COOK	DRAIN	SINK

PUMPS

SHELVS

SHELVS

KITCHEN
9 × 9

SHELVES

LOCKED CLOSET

SLIDING DOORS

D. W.

STOVE ROOM

SHELVES

SHELVES

9 × 7   STOVE

POT BOX

FRANKLIN STOVE

CELLAR DOOR

POT BOX

FRANKLIN STOVE

HALL CLOSET

HALL RECESS

LANDING

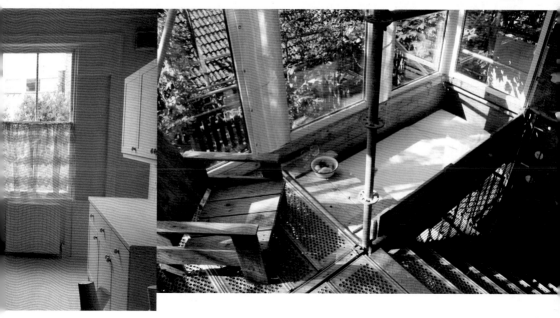

WINDOW

Maja Momic
Christopher Dell
Bernd Kniess

Maja Momic came to the UoN as a project assistant. She lived on site for a while and dealt with the UoN in her master's thesis.
For more information on the contributors, please see the chapter Three Questions to the Contributors on page 415.

Instead of being considered a painter, I would have liked, on this occasion, to be thought of as a fenetrier … I was led by the idea (always) to make something that could not be called a picture (in this case 'make windows').[1]

… after all, you never know who is going to walk through the open door next.[2]

On sunny days, the building now finds its expansion to the terrace and the park for most of the day, usually until late in the evening. Opening and closing the windows is the first and last act of the day. House, terrace, garden, and park are merged into a continuum of action spaces in which functions no longer determine the use of space. What appears to be a living room one moment can be used as dining room, study room, or classroom, a stage or event space the next—simply following the whims of its users.

> *Sunday. It's noon already. Everyone got up late again! And we really have to hurry up. The coffee isn't ready yet, the cream isn't whipped, the cake is still in the oven, and nothing is prepared on the terrace! As soon as we open the kitchen window to start tidying up the terrace, the first IBA guide is standing there with his group of visitors and asks if there was no coffee today. There will be in half an hour, we tell him. Good—they are supposed to go to the bunker.*
>
> *An hour later, the homemade hotel counter is set up to the left of the kitchen window. On top of it are the dishes that Ton Matton had acquired as props in the course of his film shoot for* Broad Welfare Hotel; *there's coffee, milk, cream, three types of cake, water with mint leaves, flowers from the park. Everything is shielded by the red parasol left over from last summer's construction camp. The tables and chairs that are set up create the atmosphere of a café, the mood is casual on the lower level, similar to that of a living room: deck chairs and stools are arranged around the improvised table next to the fireplace, in which fire was burning the night before. A black board leaning against one of the trees in the park reads, "Sunday Café University of the Neighborhoods."*[3]

WINDOW – FRAMES

We base our story on the characteristic of the window as a connecting interface between inside and outside. We do this by trying to understand the tale through different frames. Each frame draws attention to a certain situation or snapshot from the five-year duration of the project. One can compare this procedure to the interplay of element and *dispositif* that Michael Foucault made useful for analyzing discourse. According to the French philosopher, among

---

1   Marcel Duchamp.
2   Julia Lerch Zajączkowska und Kathrin Dröppelmann, *Wie zusammen leben*, Urban Design Project, 2013, 21.
3   UoN resident, summer 2013.

"elements, whether discursive or non-discursive, there is a sort of interplay of shifts of position and modifications of function …"The appearance of elements in the discourse depends on the reading and the lens under which they are placed. This lens is the *dispositif*, "the system of relations that can be established between these elements."[4]

By referring to the concept of the *dispositif*, we highlight and use a double resonance of the window in architectonic practice itself: What can be said about imaging displays of architecture—be it a floor plan, cross section, view, an isometry, or rendering—is that their *modus operandi* includes defining the segments of what is visible about architecture. The same goes for the window in terms of construction: it determines what can be seen from a building. So what we are doing in this text is circling around the structural dispositive *window* as a discursive and representational dispositive, with the use of the displayed relationship between structural transformations of a window and various uses of a building. We want to use this to illustrate what we were searching for in the UoN's procedures: namely, to constructively keep open the processes of potential activities that may emerge.

FRAME 4 – FROM ALBERTI'S WINDOW TO PEEPING TOM

It is well known that the spatial code of the Renaissance takes up that of Vitruvius, but with new auspices. Instead of experimenting in order to structure the reality of the city into ordered systems, the focus is now shifted to the practices of how this order is projected. As a tool of this projection, a perspective inscribes itself in the epoch's architectural spatial production. As architecture operates from code to space, it sets in motion politics of a representation, i.e. a scopic regime,[5] which produces a new spatial reality and discourse. The space of representation now provides the framework for an understanding of the urban that no longer stems from the contingent urban reality, but from abstract, logical compositional codes of the universal. From now on, this will be the lens through which *city* is seen, with whose aid *city* is understood. Along its lines, whose horizon opens up to infinity, a logic of the visual extends across the city with the perspective.

Leon Battista Alberti, whose *De Re Aedificatoria* from 1485 can be considered the most important treatise of Renaissance architecture, emphasizes the teleological orientation of the new order. According to Alberti, we are dealing with rules of composition that can be interpreted from a metaphysical universal law. This aesthetic concept, known as *concinnitas* (harmony), has to "put

---

4   Michel Foucault, "The Confession of the Flesh, 1977," in *Power/Knowledge: Selected Interviews and Other Writings*, ed. and trans. Colin Gordon (New York: Pantheon, 1980), 194–228.

5   Christian Metz, *The Imaginary Signifier: Psychoanalysis and the Cinema* (Bloomington: Indiana University Press, 1986), 61. Georges Teyssot, *A Topology of Everyday Constellations* (Cambridge, MA: MIT Press, 2013), 252.

together members differing from each other in their natures, in such a manner, that they may conspire to form a beautiful whole."[6] Here, he significantly differs from Vitruvius, who distinguishes between the architectonic form and its applied *ornamentum*. From now on, the compositional goal of a building is that "all the parts should be made to correspond so exactly, that let us consider which of them we please, it may bear its just proportion to all the rest."[7] In this, the composition is the proportional representation of visual reality; it is directly linked to the rule of perspective construction.[8]

In his book, Alberti derives the origin of building purely from the functional requirement of offering protection from the weather. Vitruvius' idea that the development of inventions and the training of taste is based on rivalry, mutual emulation, and learning and improving through reflection, observation, and calculation[9] is reduced by Alberti to the satisfaction of comfort and pleasure.[10]

In doing so, Alberti differentiates between the place of rest, which people sought in safe areas in order to take possession of it, should they like it, and its design in accordance with functional aspects.[11] Alberti derives six elements of architecture from these requirements: region (*regio*), ground (*area*), partition (*partitio*), wall (*paries*), ceiling/roof (*tectum*) and opening (*apertio*).[12] Alberti differentiates two types of opening, "the one serving for admission of light and air, and the other for the entrance and passage of the inhabitants."[13] The opening, as an element of transition, must be understood as the logical keystone of Alberti's spatial approach to architecture,[14] which is what places the other elements into a meaningful order. The opening not only connects the spatial parts consisting of wall and ceiling, but also relates them to the spatiality of the ground inside and outside of the building and area. Only through this connection does the significance of Alberti's understanding of architecture become apparent: the house is more than just a spatial differentiation of functional arrangement in one place. Rather, at its openings, it outlines itself as part of a conceived whole in the spatio-temporal dimensions of nature, city, and society. Thus, the openings allow Alberti to interrelate city and state with each other by means of the elements *regio*, *area*, and *partitio*, or house, city, and state. The order of urban society is reflected in the spatial order of the house, while, following ancient ideals, the idea of *city* and state is one and the same to Alberti.

6   Leon Battista Alberti, "De Re Aedificatoria," in *The Ten Books of Architecture*, Book IX (New York: Dover Publications, 1986), 195.
7   Alberti, "De Re Aedificatoria," Book VII, 140.
8   Kurt W. Forster und Hubert Locher, *Theorie der Praxis. Leon Battista Alberti als Humanist und Theoretiker der bildenden Künste* (Berlin: De Gruyter, 1999), 97.
9   Vitruv [Vitruvius], *Zehn Bücher über Architektur* (Darmstadt: Wissenschaftliche Buchgesellschaft, [1964] 2013), 79.
10   Alberti, "De Re Aedificatoria," Book IV, 64.
11   Alberti, "De Re Aedificatoria," Book I, 2.
12   Alberti, "De Re Aedificatoria," Book I, 2.
13   Alberti, "De Re Aedificatoria," Book I, 17.
14   Uwe Schröder, "Die Wand. Grenze der Architektur – Architektur der Grenze," *Der Architekt* 4 (2016): 23.

The fact that Alberti thinks with a filter of representation is mainly due to the function and technology of the window. In his treatise *De pictura*, incidentally the first textbook on painting, Alberti defines the painting as an open window (*aperta finestra*). This window is the medium through which the object to be painted (*historia*) is visible.[15] While the world becomes the image here, the window attains the status of the central means of access to the world. Though the window works functionally for Alberti in terms of light incidence and ventilation, it also serves the purpose of giving objects and people access to the house,[16] and is thus the gateway to the world: "The window is an 'architectural' feature that serves both as useful, hygienic device connected to the body's needs, and as an 'optical' apparatus, a kind of magnifying glass or pair of spectacles."[17] The window constitutes a threshold space that is arranged in two ways: On the one hand, it is an instrument that breaks up the continuity of space, thus generating asymmetrical distance, which enables the invention of perspective. On the other hand, the figure of the subject uses this frame to enter the stage of modern times as an observer of the world. The ability to see through the window without being spotted and to abstract the outside world into a geometrized image divided into sectors is one of the founding practices of the modern subject. The spatial cultural technology of the window further uses the possibility of hidden observation to explain what is understood as intimate in modern times. The Latin word *intimus* and its comparative form *interior* describe what is hidden from the gaze of others. The term "intimate" thus reveals itself to be a stronger concept than "private," which is borne by the discretion not to look or peep. Accordingly, every glance is potentially indiscreet—when it enters domestic interiors, it becomes intrusive, hurtful, even forceful: "To look inwards through the window is tantamount to entering a forbidden body."[18] Moreover, "as the gaze penetrates inside, a new *jouissance* is born: to look at the forbidden. The prohibition always contains its opposite—its violation."[19] A door that can be closed can also be opened. This theme is perhaps best exemplified in Michael Powell's meta-film *Peeping Tom*. This piece about filming plays with the negative implications of cinematic voyeurism. *Peeping Tom* is the story of murderer Mark Lewis, who films not only the victims he kills, but also the police investigations of those murders. What this film does is give a powerful platform to the "distance machines" of camera and projector and the possessive and spatial demarcation they make between the person looking and the one being looked at. The mobility of the camera is thereby staged as the symbolization of a transcendental subject that emerges only from scopophilia—the pathological desire to look.

15   Leon Battista Alberti, *Das Standbild – Die Malkunst – Grundlagen der Malerei / De Statua – De Pictura – Elementa Picturae* (Darmstadt: Wissenschaftliche Buchgesellschaft, 2012), 225.
16   Leon Battista Alberti, "De Re Aedificatoria," Book I, 17.
17   Georges Teyssot, *A Topology of Everyday Constellations* (Cambridge, MA: MIT Press, 2013), 254.
18   Gérard Wacjman, cited in: Georges Teyssot, *A Topology of Everyday Constellations*, 258.
19   Teyssot, *A Topology of Everyday Constellations*, 258 f.

FRAME 2 – OPENING

With the tasks necessary for the recommissioning of the building, the development of a performative project was set in motion, with the expectation that the process would provide information about its possible further use. In terms of its framing, one may refer to Roland Barthes' representation regarding the history of visual space as experiments that have been less about removing or breaking a frame than about undermining or overcoming it. Starting the project can also be understood as an undertaking that does not replace a form (not yet given) with a contrary one, but that instead aims at keeping the form and exposing it in a play of overlays, suspensions, and transgressions.[20]

To architecture students, this way of "making space" is at first an unusual way to approach spaces. This may be due to the fact that it has little in common with the usual design or planning activities. To transcend this habitual practice, the performative course of the undertaking and its continuous practice are seen as an attempt to make use of one's own movements, to approach and appropriate circumstances in order to create new modes of dealing with the spatial conditions. In doing so, traditional parameters of architectural production are in no way eliminated. With reference to Alberti, these would perhaps be the location (*regio*) and visual relationships, the incidence of light, and the possibilities of entry and exit (*area*), the external conditions of the building structure (*partitio*), and different dimensions of the spaces (*paries* and *tectum*) and their connections (*apertio*) as well as the internal, functional conditions. In addition, there are parameters that retroact with the space by means of appropriation and use by its occupiers. The interplay of all parameters on a pragmatic level of proceeding determines the order in the same way as we spatialize requirements that are initially provisionally conceived—which means nothing other than spatially implementing and practicing the experimental arrangement we call an "opening."

FRAME 6 – THRESHOLDS

During the opening ceremony, a temporary situation resulted in two kitchens, connected as well as separated by the window. The kitchen window not only served as a source of light and air; it also offered views inside and out and served as a hatch and counter, forming a zone of exchange—threshold space. The design of thresholds stems from the need to not only separate and connect space, but also to create it. The term "threshold" draws attention to the fact that it is only through the existence of openings in the walls that the inside and the outside of a building, and thus the interior and exterior of our existential

20   Roland Barthes, *Wie zusammen leben: Simulationen einiger alltäglicher Räume im Roman. Vorlesung am Collège de France 1976–1977* (Frankfurt am Main: Suhrkamp, 2007), 191.

spatiality, is possible at all.[21] Accordingly, literary scholar Rüdiger Görner refers to the etymological meaning of the word "threshold" as alteration, flooding, transition—thus, transition is also the transient place where the unexpected and unusual may take place.[22] In his seminal essay *Bridge and Door*, sociologist Georg Simmel also discusses thresholds as defining elements of human space. He notes that the window—as a connection between the interior and the outside world and as an element that enables a continuous exchange—is related to the door. Just as the door places a hinge between human space and everything outside it, it removes the separation between the inside and the outside. Especially since the door can be opened, the state of it being closed evokes a stronger feeling of isolation from everything beyond this space than the mere unstructured wall.[23]

Doors and windows connect and separate. Where Simmel differentiates between human space and everything outside it, architectural theorist and historian Georges Teyssot describes a new everyday experience that, with the rise of global networks and new "virtual realities," includes a network of interactive social life and marks a threshold in the transition from "intimacy to extimacy." Teyssot describes humans as "animals with windows"—which he understands as the mediator between the subject and the world, "the exterior and the interior; the illuminated and the adumbrated; the visible and the invisible; the manifest and the hidden."[24] Although thresholds can be considered as markers of the boundaries between these opposites, they are also the means of bridging them. Separation and communication are ultimately connected aspects. After all, the former creates the condition for the latter. Teyssot does not think of thresholds as clear boundaries, but rather as zones for inhabiting a space. In his opinion, the threshold is a topography of the intermediary, the relationship between the individual and the communal—threshold spaces in which inside and outside meet, and public and private find their common ground.[25]

The UoN's actors did not simply consider the crossing of the door and window threshold into the building to be the framework for the performative actions of the opening. It was also about overcoming the boundaries between the academic, the administrated and the experienced world. The goal was to enter a threshold space, a gradual process that began with encounters in the kitchen and on the terrace, in which it became clear that the threshold is not only a spatial, but also a temporal, figure.[26] The "UoN" construct should be considered

---

21   Cf. Chan-Fai Cheung, "Separation and Connection: Phenomenology of Door and Window," in *Space, Time, and Culture*, ed. D. Carr and Chan-Fai Cheung, Contributions to Phenomenology vol. 51 (Dordrecht: Springer, 2004), 253–62, link.springer.com/chapter/10.1007/978-1-4020-2824-3_17, doi: 10.1007/978-1-4020-2824-3_17.

22   Rüdiger Görner, *Grenzen, Schwellen, Übergänge. Zur Poetik des Transitorischen* (Göttingen: Vandenhoeck & Ruprecht, 2001), 10.

23   Georg Simmel, *Brücke und Tür* (Stuttgart: F. H. Koehler, 1957), 3–4.

24   Teyssot, *A Topology of Everyday Constellations*, 255.

25   Georges Teyssot, "Mapping the Threshold: A Theory of Design and Interface," lecture, 2007, www.youtube.com/watch?v=HETAowHaetU.

26   Teyssot, "Mapping the Threshold."

a threshold space from the start, a liminal place of "not anymore" and "not yet"—
no longer a single women's residence hall or health department office on the
one hand, and not quite yet a university on the other. The UoN seemed to be
transformed into a kind of machine that condensed and overlapped time and
space to a form in which past, present, and future merged in a process of be-
coming-house as well as becoming-*city*. Where, apart from representational in-
tentions of respective institutional actors, it was not (yet) clear who was going
to have to do what, nothing was more obvious than to make use of the temporal window that opened up to awaken the potential of the yet-unconscious
knowledge of the past.[27]

FRAME 7 – BAUDRILLARD'S GLASS

While it opens up access to the universal for Alberti, the window transforms
into a motor of the particular in Jean Baudrillard's postmodern view, one that
simultaneously participates in the production and decomposition of the universal. The glass window thereby becomes the "focal point of matter." For the
modern age, glass still offers a materialized entry into the world as an image.
Before the ruins of history, however, it now appears as a membrane of the enclosure, which casts doubt on the universal as illusion. The glass manifests "at
once proximity and distance, intimacy and the refusal of intimacy, communication and non-communication"[28] of societal processes of singularization. Surely,
just as the window is the architectural medium that enables views that cannot
grasp anything, the cultural technique of looking out the window gives rise to
a space of knowledge; only through this space is it possible to interpret contexts as "universal and abstract."[29] At the window, the world becomes the stage
that maintains a long-distance relationship with the viewer. The onlooker
watches without being seen. This is where the material of the glass has the property of providing maximum visual contact between the inside and outside.
However, and this is the crucial point, glass also establishes a wall of the invisible, "which prevents such communication from becoming a real opening onto
the world."[30] Baudrillard emphasizes the fact that this distance is the price and
requirement for any pictorialization of the world, in which the perspective as
the constructive principle of looking through something (Latin: *perspicere*)
found its equivalent.

---

27   Walter Benjamin, *Passagen-Werk* (Frankfurt am Main: Suhrkamp, 1982), 1014, para. H°, 17

28   Jean Baudrillard, *The System of Objects*, trans. James Benedict (London and New York: Verso, 1996), 41–42.

29   Baudrillard, *The System of Objects*, 42.

30   Baudrillard, *The System of Objects*, 42.

FRAME 8 – BARRICADING
FRAME 10 – FRAMING WINDOWS
FRAME 11 – GLAZING WINDOWS

The house was increasingly being used again but, initially, could only be used in warmer seasons due to the lack of heating. In times of absence, its windows remained not only impenetrable, but also closed. Unbidden visits and their resulting consequences turned barricading the house into a necessary obligation, which significantly highlighted the states of use and non-use. Various forms of makeshift burglar protection were developed by using plywood panels found on site, the most recent of which were optimized in such a way that the scattered holes in the panels allowed sufficient light to enter the interior, even when closed. This was done in a way that allowed for shorter (seminar) sessions to take place without spending much time on preparation and follow-up.

The provisional arrangement of the plastic sheet windows in the event room and kitchen had been with us throughout the first one and a half years. Activities in the house were, apart from continued construction work, increasingly characterized by the university's use of the building for summer schools, seminars, and events. With the summer schools came the first dwelling functions; people stayed overnight, cooked, ate, celebrated. At first, everyone made do with simple means, but we quickly learned how to get settled in the house and to not only meet various and self-imposed requirements, but to also make it pleasant for everyone involved. The objects needed for activities stopped following purely functional requirements, but increasingly focused on the criteria of abundance. Furniture, lamps, dishes, tablecloths, and yes, even flowers often helped to embellish life in the house.

One characteristic of the temporary arrangement, namely to stabilize itself over the course of its intended short duration, became visible in the case of the plastic sheet windows; they highlighted the different effects on the interior as well as the exterior and an openness that one would have expected from the planning-related solution. However, the (technical) solution led to an unsatisfactory result due to the geometric openings in the wall, as only one of the three sliding windows could be opened as a sliding door; moreover, the costs were hardly proportionate to the result. The question arose as to why one should give up once-gained benefits because of a less practical solution? It was easy to unscrew the plastic-covered wooden frames of the windows, which were at least nine square meters in size, from their outer structures to put them aside in summer. Details were developed, which refined the temporary windows into a more permanent solution. The wood of the frames was replaced by aluminum sections, the plastic foil by polycarbonate light panels. With support from the metal workshop of Arbeiten Lernen Hamburg (Working Learning Hamburg, a social institution with workshops and competencies in metal construction), three large gates were built by students during a building internship. The outer frames were anchored into wall jambs, to which casement frames were fastened using wing nuts. In the end, the cost of the three windows amounted to a third of the estimated sum for the sliding gate alone. The luxury of the solution that was found did not emerge from financial overhead. Luxury means enjoying the freedom to keep the planning process open until the performative qualities of the architecture to be designed can be ascertained through their use.

In terms of cost-benefit calculations, it is impossible to imagine how senseless it would have been to adapt the building to the current Energy Saving Ordinance for new buildings. Instead, our approach was to maintain the building with necessary measures in its existing standards, or to improve them if possible. When the heating system was put into operation, there was the necessity—in addition to the measures already implemented in the foyer—of replacing the remaining single-paned windows. Within the overall recommissioning and further expansion of the building, the decision to turn makeshift construction by the students into the task of the project itself was crucial. This, however, also meant that services we were unable to provide ourselves had to be included in the planning. The funds we managed to save through our approach of home-made construction made it possible to include the types of work that would have been overwhelming in terms of time and capacity. In this case, the cost-reducing personal contribution consisted in the removal of the metal ventilation sashes and other preparatory measures. The devitrification of the single glazing held in place with putty and the subsequent insertion of the new insulated glass panes was taken care of by the commissioned company. The new panes were then fixated in the old window frames with simple wooden strips.

FRAME 18 – OPENING THE FORM

In his concept of nomadism, Gilles Deleuze initially differentiated between a nomadic and a sedentary *nomos*. In subsequent texts, he aimed at reinforcing the opposition of *nomos*, the legal distribution of things, to the nomadic, as an aleatory distribution. He defined two opposite ways of occupying spaces: spreading out in an open space, and dividing a sedentary and closed one.[31] As important as Deleuze's conceptual outline of the space was, its impact was short. The UoN proves that it cannot remain a matter of playing *nomos* and nomadic elements off against each other. Rather—and this is primarily exemplified by the interlacing and nomadic appropriation of the living spaces in the course of the UoN, from its initial development to the massive protrusion of the Hotel Wilhelmsburg—there are always negotiations between *nomos* and the nomadic. The nomadic distribution concept is not possible without any properties, housing or dimensions, as can be seen in negotiation processes in various spatial orders.

---

31   Gilles Deleuze, cited in Teyssot, *A Topology of Everyday Constellations*, p. 16.

The project was designed to be developed from the process. Only a few adjustments were needed to generate experimental arrangements that would produce the next one, derived from the course of events and actions. The problematization of its processes in comparison with the motivations and interests of participants usually produced the relevant questions that led to the next project; even if the decisions were different than the ones that led to the resolution not to occupy a "finished" building in the sense of a sedentary *nomos* (Deleuze) and to divide a thereby given closed space, but rather to open up the given space according to a nomadic *nomos* in a way that allows its actors to spread out into an open space. What existed and what was perceived as closed, therefore, had to be opened. The prospect of demolition having been decided upon provided the instructions for action: it should not be a matter of (forward) building, but rather of continuous dismantling and thus the continued perforation of a space open for action.

It seemed that we were correct in our thesis that continued structural changes could keep the space open and allow unplanned activities. In doing so, it was not necessary to rigorously stick to decisions already made until they were completely implemented. Sometimes plans remained unfinished and thus expanded the possibilities. The large terrace, which was planned as a conservatory, for instance, was to serve as a communal dining hall to meet the needs of a larger number of users. The plan was never carried out, and the "harvested" building material of windows and doors from condemned houses was used for other purposes. The resulting interim situation not only corresponded to the once-intended purpose as a meeting room; it was also the catalyst for the creation of the UoN's Sunday Café. The process of establishing such a café again illustrated the influence of spatial parameters. The completed floor of the conservatory, its roof-like structure of torsional stiffness and formwork beams in between the park and the interior of the building opened the space to spontaneous activities by the students. Moreover, further factors such as accessibility and the specifics of the situation allowed some uses to flourish, while others quickly disappeared.

The project of the UoN as an experimental arrangement of the teaching and research field of UD understood architecture and *city* to be a collectively produced space—as a space for negotiating the everyday processes of being active. The juxtaposition of unspecific and unconnected rooms in one part of the house created a sequence of rooms of varying sizes that were interrelated and whose use could be adapted to meet changing requirements by means of expansions. The other part of the building continued to contain rooms accessible via the hallway, which provided space for working and/or sleeping.

The building procedure reflected the research approach of the project: it was not a matter of confirming or refuting a hypothesis or developing a solution—after all, there was no problem that had to be solved. It was rather about keeping both research and building processes open in a way that allowed a specific program to be developed from them within the given framework that would assure the project's use. This was about turning improvisation into a technology, i.e. developing the ability to constructively deal with indeterminacies and unexpected results, about cooperatively adapting to changing situations, recognizing their potential and using them. One could say that the whole building and research process was characterized by constantly changing parameters—the availability of resources (manpower, building materials, etc.), the university context, institutional and financial dependencies.

The project's process of transformation was never understood to be completed, but still, or especially because of this, it was understood to be an outline. This may sound paradoxical, but it can be deduced from the way it was conceived. The concept of use is solely based on the underlying motives and interests of its actors. Interplaying with the material conditions of the location, of objects, discourses, and actions, causes these to shape the structure in order to play on the dynamic and constant overlapping that derives from it. In other words: the building is continually being programmed, and the program of the building and its processes of change are continually being developed. The structural substance, integrated into the networks of human and nonhuman actors, becomes a catalyst. Opportunities and possibilities emerge from it and also bring forth architecture as well as its options for further development: "enabling architecture" is what we called it. The building as a structural and constantly transforming object plays a significant role. However, the focus is on the performativity of processes that set out from this point, and whose vectors affect the neighborhood, which in turn incorporates them.

FRAME 19 – PERFORATION

Usually, the vision of architecture is focused on new buildings, but in doing so, it primarily looks at what is called "Architecture" with a capital "A"—the Art of building (*Baukunst*). Still, the Art of building also includes that which does not correspond to this understanding but which offers spaces for daily negotiations and appropriations in the actions of its users. Along with unnoticed everyday architecture, three quarters of all construction services in Germany go similarly unheeded: work on existing buildings.[32] Even though it seems sensible to let changes in lifestyles influence the built spaces as well, as proven by Druot, Lacaton, and Vassal in their transformation of Tour Bois-le-Prêtre.[33] The visualization of their concept reveals the underlying idea, namely the overlapping of the unpopular prefabricated high-rises of the 1960s with the spatial qualities of the case-study houses from the preceding two decades in the US. The crucial decision that led to the proposal by Druot et al. is based on their

32   *Baukultur Report 2014/15* (Potsdam: Bundesstiftung Baukultur, 2015), 24.
33   Frédéric Druot, Anne Lacaton, and Jean-Philippe Vassal, Tour Bois-le-Prêtre, 2013.

study *Plus*,[34] in which they confront the maintenance and conversion of existing buildings by preserving gray energy through demolition and new construction in calculations and planning procedures. The pilot project Tour Bois-le-Prêtre illustrates the transformation process. Panels with small openings were cut to create generous openings, which, by aid of a second façade and the resulting glasshouse not only enhanced the living space, but also extended it to the outside. The apartments were not only larger and brighter, but new visual references to the city were established as well, creating a new relationship between inside and outside. In addition to that, the floor plans of the apartment were adapted to the occupants' needs while still maintaining stable rent levels. The principle of subtraction produced luxury in low-budget circumstances.[35]

In our project, however, the demolition was a foregone conclusion; we took advantage of the initiation of the process and its extreme deceleration to explore the possibility of partially demolishing the building for the sake of a project that was neither necessary nor based on any program—an experimental set-up. How can the architecture of the 1950s, which was developed out of necessity and the limited availability of materials, which was overwritten with the functional requirements of a public health office without any value on the quality of stay, manage this by subtraction? How does one succeed in cutting rooms out of the existing substance that weren't planned to exist in this form? The positioning of the many openings and thresholds around the kitchen foyer contributed to the formation of a core. Where there used to be a dark entrance area, there was now a central gathering room created by cutting out parts of the walls and the ceiling.

The further perforation of the building structure and the resulting interconnection of previously small rooms in the working and exhibition wing resulted in spacious rooms that merged into one another, offering a high quality of stay and multiple possibilities for use. The recently created openings enabled new and varied views in, out and through: windows to the sky, windows to the park, visual connections between the kitchen foyer and the gallery, between the gallery and the event room, the event room and work niches, etc. Moreover, this perforation of the interior provided opportunities of transition and interconnection—different activities could take place simultaneously.

Each window had its own qualities and offered different services. For example, the openings to the park could evoke different atmospheres through their seriality and interconnectivity; they could add a different character or qualification to the rooms: they could invite or repel, let light and views in or out, enable different space usage or connections, even fundamentally change the whole orientation of the building. If the windows/gates are open and all activities take place on the terrace, is this the back or the front of the building?

34   Frédéric Druot, Anne Lacaton, and Jean-Philippe Vassal, *Plus: Large-Scale Housing Development* (Barcelona: Editorial Gustavo Gilli, 2007).
35   Druot et al., *Plus: Large-Scale Housing Development*.

Still, this perforation was not only physical. "Home-as-one's-castle with its roof, walls, windows and doors now only exists in fairy tales. Material and immaterial cables have knocked as many holes in it as in a Swiss cheese: On the roof, there is the aerial, telephone wire comes through the wall, the television takes the place of the window, and the door is replaced by the garage with the car. Home-as-one's-castle has become a ruin with the wind of communication blowing through the cracks in the walls."[36] At the UoN, a medial perforation took place as well—studying, working and all other everyday practices are inconceivable without the screens and eyes of mobile devices. Thus, every day, various virtual windows open up references to the world. Teyssot describes the social practice that helps to live in disembodied connectedness and the effects associated with the transition from intimacy to extimacy.[37]

OUTRO: SYNTHESIS OF THE OPENING

Vilém Flusser defines the window as an instrument for looking outside from the inside without getting wet; to the Greeks, *theoria*—harmless and inexperienced recognition. "The phenomenological question raised by this is: Are experiments carried out through the window (i.e. in theory) valid? Or does one have to go out the door to experience things?"[38]

At the UoN, we may have gone out the door after all—from the protected space (of the university and studio) out into the field, and not just for a short stay, but for five years, to test and explore the questions that moved us in our (theoretical) dispute with the *city* in a real urban context on site: dealing with what is existing, with the relation between the private and the public, between living and being occupied, and possible ways of overlapping functions, and so on.

Throughout this process, however, it has always been an alternating motion between theory and practice, the *city*, the *space*. A transformational dialectic, according to Lefebvre, insofar as both interact with each other and thus change and become means of description.[39] Although we have often assumed the role of the neighbor, the host, the innkeeper, the guest, and so on, we have always remained first and foremost students and researchers who were able to withdraw from the given situation to interpret connections, frame the questions that were relevant for our research from them, and set the framework. Is it possible though that we were, perhaps, standing by Baudrillard's window the whole time, which provided us a space for being close and distant, intimate and cold, communicative and reclusive?[40]

---

36 Vilém Flusser, *The Shape of Things: A Philosophy of Design* (London: Reaktion, 1999), 82–83.
37 Teyssot, *A Topology of Everyday Constellations*, 283.
38 Flusser, *The Shape of Things*, 82.
39 Stefan Kipfer, Parastou Saberi, und Thorben Wieditz, "Henri Lefebvre," in *Handbuch Stadtsoziologie*, ed. Frank Eckardt (Wiesbaden: Springer VS, 2012), 167–83.
40 Baudrillard, *The System of Objects*, 41–42.

At the very first seminar, we had decided that the building, or rather the project, had to be "opened" first for the work to begin. Our intention was to get a sense of what the place could be like. Only through an open approach were we able to base the programmatic setting of the University of the Neighborhoods on the context and motivations of the participants continuously expanding and reconfiguring it over time and through interactions with the environment and various actors. From this perspective, the house was no longer considered "an artificial cave; it is more a warping of the sphere of interpersonal relations."[41] On top of that, the house itself (as a research station and thus the starting point for student research projects) technically also served as a window through which the researchers could look out into the *neighborhood/city/world*. A final opening is taking place here and now: the reflection and evaluation of the project—disclosing the procedure (not without resistance!) in this publication as well. By observing the interaction between structural transformations and use of the building, we tap into openness and indeterminacy as resources that will, again and again, open up a window for us.

---

41   Flusser, *The Shape of Things*, 83.

BED

Katrin Borchers
Sebastian Bührig
Janna R. Wieland
Julia Lerch Zajączkowska
Christopher Dell
Bernd Kniess

Katrin Borchers, *Sebastian Bührig*, *Janna R. Wieland* and *Julia Lerch Zajączkowska* studied in the Urban Design master's program and were responsible for various formats at the UoN, such as the Wilhelmsburg Orchestra, the hotel, restaurant, café and bar, schools, workshops, and theater groups. Sebastian, Julia, and Janna occasionally resided at the UoN.
For more information on the contributors, please see the chapter Three Questions to the Contributors on page 415.

"What Proust intends with the experimental rearrangement of furniture ... is nothing other than what here is secured on the level of the historical, and collectively. There is a not-yet-conscious knowledge of what has been: its advancement has the structure of awakening."[1]

The history of this essay is one of many detours. It begins with a sketch that depicts various sleeping positions, which the author had taken himself while staying at the University of Neighborhoods as an occasional resident.[2] His episodic memories relate to sleeping individuals who, like him, were using the impromptu sleeping accommodations; visitors who held a more formal status as guests; and those who had made this their permanent place to sleep. Certainly, such memories are not able to tell us much about sleep itself. They rather deal with its conditions and framing, with appropriation and negotiations that take place around the piece of furniture commonly known as the bed.

It's September 2008. Students of the first Summer School are gathering in the recently reopened building. Their rooms were finished in time, the walls were white-washed, and with the help of people from Arbeiten und Lernen Hamburg (ALH)[3] it was even possible to install new OSB flooring. Folding cots borrowed from the Federal Agency for Technical Relief will serve as their place to sleep for the next few days. Each room contains four or five cots, a living room lamp, and a rug.

It's July 2009. A construction trailer in the parking lot. A young man is sitting on the doorstep that he has built out of pallets. A big dog sits next to him. This night will be their first in the mobile home at its new location. It's their own home, one that can be parked right in front of the ocean, in the middle of a forest, or anywhere else. Another option is to find a nice spot, settle down, build an extension, re-build again. Going on vacation while knowing that there is a home waiting to be returned to. The bed is made: two wooden pallets, a mattress, sheets, pillows, and a sleeping bag. That should do for now.[4]

It's October 2012. The fact that people have started living here permanently has changed the site. At first, I thought these were only workspaces, but as it turns out, people live here, too. Compared to conventional dwellings, there is

1   Walter Benjamin, The Arcades Project, trans. Howard Eiland and Kevin McLaughlin (Cambridge, MA, and London: Belknap Press of Harvard University Press, 1999), 883.

2   Cf. Sebastian Bührig, "Bett," UoN Project Archive, 2016.

3   Working and Learning Hamburg, a provider of education and qualifications focusing on the skilled trades.

4   Cf. Matthias Möckel, "Bauwagen Zwischenbericht," UoN Project Archive, 2011. In the experimental setup of a "construction trailer," Matthias Möckel was a partner in this neighborhood project. From June 21 to July 19, 2011, he lived and worked in his trailer on the UoN grounds. He recorded his activities and experiences and made them available to the UoN lab. He stayed until early 2013.

constant background noise: no privacy in the proper sense, but instead, there is only the divided and shared space. The chances of experiencing individual seclusion are relatively slim. Two aspects account for this: the arrangement and size of the rooms—i.e. the architecture—within the building, but also their use.[5]

BUILDING BEDS

It's March 2012. So far, we had helped ourselves to the cots for sleeping. They were borrowed whenever we needed them. The cots were flexible in regard to use and handling, and instead of lying on the hard floor, you could sleep on a stretched panel of fabric. The size and construction alone limited your urge to move around while sleeping. However, a proper bed was cumbersome. With its dimensions, it contradicted the etymological definition of the word furniture; the German word Möbel derives from Latin mobilis, meaning movable goods. Mobilis was what we needed, i.e. a bed that is flexible in its use. The stacking beds by designer Rolf Heide seemed ideal for this purpose, as they could be stacked atop of one another when they was less needed and still be used regardless of how many there were. The setup is fairly simple; one bed consists of four boards, one slatted frame, and a mattress, while the frame can easily be joined with screwed steel brackets. The production of its curved cheeks, which ensure stable stacking and at the same time stand for its distinct design quality, proved to be a technical challenge in terms of craftsmanship, which we tried to tackle with our (simple) means and possibilities. Those beds not only served us well; they are still in use by the occupants of the residence for single men in Rehhoffstraße.[6]

DISPOSITIF BED

There are two things that account for the fact that "housing" went from being an inferior purpose as "use authorized as an exceptional case,"[7] and thus an unplanned component of the UoN's program, to becoming the project's main focus, namely the subject of *bed*. For one thing, it might have been due to a concatenation of various, supposedly coincidental, circumstances. However, at the same time, it was the logical development of an experimental arrangement, something that had already become apparent in the performative setting of the opening event.

5   Cf. Janna R. Wieland, "Die Universität der Nachbarschaften – Erfahrungen ihrer Nutzerinnen. Urban Design Project 2," UoN Project Archive, 2014, 35.
6   Cf. "IBA Bericht 2012," UoN Project Archive, 2012.
7   In accordance with the "application for a building permit in accordance with the simplified authorization procedure pursuant to §61 of the Hamburg Building Code (HBauO)," filed on March 19, 2009 as a conversion and alteration of use of the former Health Department building into a "university educational institution and apartment for a supervisor."

An unfinished space requires trust in change. Here, unlike in a seminar room, only the process of becoming can orient the dealing with space. Apart from the special working atmosphere that prioritizes the actors' actions (the same goes for actions following other actions), it was also the dwelling experience, at first initially makeshift, that initiated collective actions and the respective drawing of spatial boundaries.

With that said, the bed should be understood as a central *dispositif* that created arrangements of time and space within the UoN. Throughout the experimental setup, those arrangements have revealed themselves to be questions and problems, potentials and adversity. By interlinking theory, research, and practice, we tried to challenge and effectively conquer them.

The bed is generally considered the innermost core of privacy and a space of retreat. By drawing boundaries, however, the UoN made the dichotomy between private and public space fragile. Rather, it was more a question of how the performativity or the separation of rooms co-determine the configuration of dwelling. Such a shift can help conclude that the bed could be more than a piece of furniture for internalization, namely an attractor for societal spatial configuration, where alleged opposites such as public and private, subject and abject, state and individual, prohibition and enjoyment, are close to each other and interfere with as well as promote one another.[8]

We should therefore focus a history of the bed less on the development of the object itself and more on the analysis of its genealogy. There, the bed, through its function of spatializing the intimate, manifests the restructuring and differentiation of the topology of living. It may be assumed that the historical withdrawal of the individual from the public sphere and the unlocking of his or her intimacy lay the foundation for what we understand by living or housing today. The complex social and functional differentiation mechanisms of housing could be traced in the tedious and lengthy process of making living space more intimate, as well as its arrangement of everyday activities in the formation of normative regulatory mechanisms. Within this, it is important to point out once again that it is the activities of housing that provide the activation of the living space— opening and closing doors, sitting on a chair, cooking at the stove, and going to bed. These are all gestures that demonstrate a chain of serial events that embed the history of living in structures of repetition and difference. Not only do they inscribe themselves into cultural memory; they also form the normative framework of the complex of living. In this respect—in addition to its practical function—the bed in particular has a normalizing function, whether as a distinguishing feature of stately property, as an orthopedic instrument, as a hygiene machine or torture utensil. In other words: every survey of the social begins with the normativity of the bed.

8   Kathrin Heinz and Irene Nierhaus, ed., *Matratze/Matrize* (Bielefeld: Transcript, 2016), 16.

There are two axes along which one can map out a bed's genealogy: one, between intimacy and exposure, and the other regarding the shift of the two words *sala* (hall) und *camera* (chamber). In this respect, the invention of hospitals marks an important milestone. With the birth of the clinic in the eighteenth century, the disciplinary *dispositif* of serializing sleep came into effect. One characteristic aspect of surveillance of the hospital bed is connecting it to further circulation *dispositifs*: "with military control over deserters, fiscal control of commodities, administrative control of medicine, rations, disappearances, cures, deaths, simulations."[9] The hospital bed arises to become the origin and destination of a governmental *dispositif* that, for the first time in history, connects the interest of the state to the condition and behavior of the collectivized bodies of the population.

Against this background, the rise of intimacy in the nineteenth century manifests as an effect resulting from the process of differentiating and separating. It articulates this demand for the possibility of retreat, the need for shelter from audience and public opinion, which eventually brought about the closed bedroom zone in middle-class homes. The condition of such a strategy of seclusion being possible stems from experiencing your body as something private, as your own property. This is a multilayered veiling in which the *camera*, the bedroom, separated from the apartment, the *sala*, has yet another inner veil, namely the bed. Here, more than in any other place of living, the individual of the modern age practices being by him- or herself, in order to share this condition with others in total intimacy or to endure urban alienation.

In her essay "The Century of the Bed,"[10] Beatriz Colomina showed impressively that there is little left of the bed as a refuge in late modernism. With the entrance of portable computers into the living space, the bed has advanced to become a control center of globalized communication and work: "The whole universe is concentrated on a small screen with the bed floating in an infinite sea of information. To lie down is not to rest but to move. The bed is now a site of action."[11]

It's June 2013. My room at the end of a long corridor seems vast. I will have to share it temporarily, either with one person or, in an extreme case, with six more overnight guests. That's the deal. On my moving day I bring a bedside lamp, a clothes rack, curtains and a rug with me. I also find a sled at the UoN, which I use as a nightstand. I sleep in one of the many stacking beds and use a few wooden boards and bricks to build a small shelf.

By now, it's October. After nearly four months of sharing a room, I am craving more privacy. Rarely are you undisturbed, but you also never get bored. There is often an

---

9   Michel Foucault, *Discipline and Punish: The Birth of the Prison*, trans. from the French by Alan Sheridan (New York: Vintage Books, 1995), 144.

10   Beatriz Colomina, "The Century of the Bed," in *The Century of the Bed*, ed. ARGE curated by_vienna (Vienna: Verlag für moderne Kunst, 2014), work-body-leisure.hetnieuweinstituut.nl/247-bed.

11   Colomina, "The Century of the Bed," 11.

exchange of thoughts, most of the time with people you didn't know before. Living at the University of Neighborhoods means: sharing rooms, having to negotiate boundaries, working and living together (in a big group). Welcoming guests, being a guest yourself, cleaning up if others use the space, explaining, giving tours, being present and always approachable even if you want to retreat, being able to retreat, building, washing, cooking, talking, listening, watering the plants, scaring children away from the hotel scaffolding, and keeping teenagers from smoking in the attic, trying to weigh in, finding your place, wanting to stay for only two months and then not leaving.

Sunday morning. I wake up and Sophia is not in her bed. I heard her laughing and talking loudly in the kitchen at around half past eight, though—she had probably just gotten home. I fall back asleep and wake up about two hours later— I hear voices from the kitchen again, this time an IBA group— some forty people are standing in front of the entrance while someone explains the hotel? to them. And now, half of the group has to use the bathroom, too. I'm standing behind the door in my pajamas, a door that separates the UoN's private part from the public one. Private? Good morning—it is Sunday, 11 a.m., and I'm not up for visitors. I can see the prepared breakfast waiting on the kitchen table through the cracked-open door, and again, more guests with the urge to empty their bladders. I go back to my room to quickly put on something halfway appropriate, but I leave my sweatpants on. Now, fifteen minutes later, I don't care about people looking or asking to use the bathroom anymore; instead, I grind beans to make coffee for myself and the others. I sit down at the set table, read a newspaper that's lying around and let myself not be disturbed by the visitors who keep dropping in.[12]

Technically, there is always something going on here, especially if you work together for several days at a time. In spite of the many people, it is pleasant because the activities always move around, never getting in each other's way. I know I can always escape the hustle and bustle. After all, there is always a room somewhere in which I can seclude myself to sleep or to work. If I seek conversation, I just go to the kitchen, as it is the communications hub. Here, you can sit down at any time and you'll always find someone to talk to. The focus is neither on the private nor the public aspect, but mainly on the personal. There used to be an alarm system, but since we live here now, we don't need it anymore. In a way, it was replaced by social control, someone constantly

---

12   Katrin Borchers and Julia Lerch Zajączkowska, "Wie zusammen leben – eine Momentaufnahme. Urban Design Project 2," UoN Project Archive, 2013, 25ff.

being there, and the fact that everyone knows the neighbors who look after the place as well.

Living in a university is unusual: public and private spaces are mixed in so many ways. Moving back and forth between them is exciting. It shifts boundaries, which makes the transition from one to the other easier. In this space of in-between or transition, one need not fear for one's own privacy; it becomes easy to share. It is something one can practice here. However, how much publicity can one endure in one's living spaces? How much privacy does one need? This is an experimental arrangement, living and working, private and public, both being defined by one's actions. Can you imagine dwelling independently of a permanent residence or apartment? What does the future of living and working space look like? These are questions (among many others) that we automatically deal with as we spend more time here or even temporarily live here.[13]

HOTELHOTEL

Since the twentieth century, the spatial disposition experienced by someone lying in bed has been a microcosm of the urban credo that is probably most evident in hotels: the concurrent private seclusion of a carrying case and being located in the midst of metropolitan density. Historian Habbo Knoch describes the hotel as a place of estrangement and objectification of human relationships, the mediatization of public life, and the spread of a multifaceted culture of entertainment, which come with the development of the city. Repositioning oneself means first and foremost embedding oneself in places that are constantly changing. The hotel has become an emblematic place of modern nomadism, a sign of the constant *disembedding* and *reembedding* of people who are no longer bound to a habitat or home.[14] While Joseph Roth saw the hotel as a utopian place, hybrid and precarious in between affiliation and loneliness, but revealing the inevitability of this new way of life of his time,[15] the fleeting togetherness of modern hotel society was to Simmel already a sign of the diminishing intensity of socialization. This intensity arises from the complexity of cities at the expense of those ties and arrangements that were familiar from the countryside and are now lost. From now on, the individual was inevitably challenged to deal with contingency, the problems it brings, insecurity, as well as options and leeway.[16]

The spatial configuration of hotels proves to be a hybrid space of public privacy and a projection surface of both existing and possible social orders, where metropolitan perception and consumer practices intensify. As a temporary home, it is oriented toward the expectations of comfort of

13   Janna R. Wieland, "Die Universität der Nachbarschaften – Erfahrungen ihrer Nutzerinnen. Urban Design Project 2," UoN Project Archive, 35.
14   Habbo Knoch, *Grandhotels* (Göttingen: Wallstein Verlag, 2016), 12.
15   Knoch, *Grandhotels*, 14.
16   Knoch, *Grandhotels*, 23.

private living. As a transitory place, it creates an affiliation between stability and fluctuation. As a threshold of the urban public space, it disassociates itself from that by using a finely graded entry system, and as a stage of performative exchange, its operation is based on observing as well as on breaking complex rules.[17]

You can say that hotels, with regard to the bed, open up an intimate space of individual retreat. A hotel is a multifunctional switching relay that opens its differentiated gradations and transitions into spaces of the community. Whether a suite, a room or a pod, the starting point is always the immediate surroundings of the bed that reveals urban living.

It's Summer 2011. Together with the Kulturfabrik Kampnagel, we are working on a proposal to transform the river isle of the Elbe into a performative *city* lab. "HOTEL TOKYO – L'Habité Intercontinental" should make basic functions of living (eating, drinking, warmth, the need for shelter, hygiene, work, sleeping, sexuality, etc.) and their respective contemporary connections to urban space possible through shifting and exaggerating in order to create new ways of interpreting urban living. In a real setting, the "boxes for living in"[18] should be questioned once and for all. It never happened in that sense; the application was not accepted. However, the hotel will accompany us as a metaphor and an experimental arrangement.

It's May 2012. A hotel guest in Hamburg-Altona crosses the hotel hallway, or street, to get to his hotel room. He is a guest who is temporarily offering his room or apartment to another person: welcome to the Hotel Hamburg. Imagine putting yourself in the role of a hotel guest while at the same time being the hotelier/host; exploring living within its temporal and spatial limits, within the social and societal dimensions of the space, while asking in what kind of public, communal, and private spaces residential capacities can be realized. Artist Jan Holtmann developed this component of the project, in which he considers the whole *city* a hotel. The rooms of the Hotel Hamburg are also the apartments of the guests/hosts. They are spread across the city; the streets are its corridors; vehicles are the elevators; the reception desk is the daily meeting point for the exchange of room keys and helpful information, which is set up in a central spot at a fixed time. On a scale of 1:1, guests/hosts use practical experimental setups to explore work and functions of temporary living, which they will later transfer to a spatial setting.[19]

17   Knoch, *Grandhotels*, 26.
18   Henri Lefebvre, *The Production of Space* (Oxford and Cambridge: Blackwell [1974], 1991), 98.
19   Cf. Derya Aguday, Katharina Böttger, Aleksandrs Dembo, Anna Hirsch, Tamara Kalantajevska, Felix Müller, Didem Saglam, Viktoria Scheifers, and Tutku Sevinc, *Hotel Hamburg | [k]-stage, UdN-Pension Wilhelmsburg*, Hamburg: Urban Design Project 2, Wohnen als Praxis (Hamburg: UD, 2012).

Jan Holtmann followed up on the project, realized two years later as "an art and theater project somewhere between environment, urban art, and applied Fluxus."[20]

It's June 2012. A temporary sleep installation is being set up in the atrium of the Kulturfabrik Kampnagel. In the context of the Live Art Festival, seventy performers will spend the night in a kind of camp. Students are designing, building, and operating the [k]-Stage project in the lobby here. They are neither guests nor hosts, and they have a clear purpose. In their role as receptionists/concierges, they can track the use of what has been planned and built, and implement it according to the built environment. Welcome to [k]-Stage.[21]

It's October 2012. Sixteen guests gather on the UoN's terrace, facing the park. For eighteen hours they will make themselves at home in the Zweite Haut (Second Skin) and spend the night there. They have a budget of 100 euros. There are no rooms, no kitchen, no toilets, and no water, but at least there's electricity. Tents are not allowed; the house is off-limits. They make a provisional kitchen out of pallets and a camping stove; they create a shared sleeping area with a roof; they set up a bar; they cook, build, research, make plans and then scrap them; they get water from neighbors and bread from the bakery around the corner; they get groceries from the supermarket and perform transactions with the owner; they network with each other inside and outside; they share their work and their beds; they take photographs and document things; they become one group. Welcome to Hotel?Wilhelmsburg.[22]

It's January 2013. A rainy Wednesday afternoon. The restaurant is preparing for business, as it does every Wednesday. Jan Holtmann came up with the rule, which is quite simple: "Bring a cook, a musician, a guest from the neighborhood. Make it happen. Plan B: if no cook & no live music & no guests: we cook; we sing a song." A seminar comes to end in the event room, and in the rooms behind it students are working on their portable computers. In the foyer, two students are discussing their project with a lecturer, while a group of students are in the kitchen preparing a meal with the chef of a neighboring Turkish restaurant.

20   "HOTEL HAMBURG – Das größte Hotel der Stadt" (HOTEL HAMBURG – The City's Largest Hotel), Hotel Hamburg, accessed May 12, 2018, www.das-hotel-hamburg.de/hotel-hamburg/das-groesste-hotel-der-stadt/.
21   Aguday et al., 2012.
22   Cf. Julian Bauer, Tim Koblun, Melih Kös, Magdalena Maierhofer, Valeria Micara, Martin Muth, Jenny Ohlenschlager, Dominique Peck, Christopher Phiphak, Paul Raupach, Michelle Renz, Mariana Rösel, Viktoria Scheifers, Vedran Skansi, Tina Steiger, Janna R. Wieland, and Julia Lerch Zajączkowska, *Interdisziplinäres Projekt Hotel Wilhelmsburg* (Hamburg: UD, 2013).

Around the corner, a resident is repairing the shopping cart, which was damaged after transporting food from the store today. Drinks are delivered; tables and chairs must be moved aside in order to allow access to the storage and bar room and to stow the beverage crates. The heavy molleton curtain that separated the work space from the kitchen is drawn; it's a signal for the restaurant group to start converting the space into a place to eat. Tables, chairs, a stage for the band, and the bar are set up. Welcome to the restaurant!

It's Sunday. The café has opened. It consists of a self-constructed and self-designed format, where spatial arrangements can be tested while neighbors and hotel guests have conversations over homemade cake. The windows facing the park are open and the kitchen turns into a park café. Welcome to the café!

It's December 2013. A thirty-foot trailer is parked on the courtyard; sweaty people are sitting inside while the exterior of the mobile sauna is finalized. Welcome to the spa!

The hotel in this sense is an assertion that becomes reality once a guest knocks on the door. The hotel is open! Someone will eventually react, open the door, and take on the required role. There is no booking system in place. No stars, no bellhops, no garage, no valet service, no advertising, no official sign, no room service, and no keys. The red carpet is rolled out for only a short moment, before being put aside, lest it become dirty from the construction site. People walk past the reception desk and through the lobby to the rear working area in order to get tools, building supplies, groceries, or visitors through. At night, the rooms are transformed: sometimes into a conference room where lectures are held, sometimes into a cinema, a stage, and afterwards into the restaurant with bar and a hotel band. There is one plan in place: namely, that there is no plan.

In the front yard of the UoN is a scaffold with 18 sleeping pods and 21 berths. Inside the building is the reception desk, a makeshift counter made from carefully positioned leftover wooden boards. A bell has been drawn on a small foam board. Most of the time, there is no one at the reception desk. Handwritten brochures lie between stacked-up wooden boards, explaining the concept of the hotel; alongside them are flashlights, so that guests can find their rooms in the dark. In the closet next to the reception desk, bedsheets and towels are piled up, constantly pushing the glass doors of the wooden cabinet open, because someone didn't stuff the pillows in properly, causing them to keep falling out.[23]

---

23   Borchers and Lerch Zajączkowska, *Wie zusammen leben?*, 47.

Calling this a program helps, as this box, still under construction, can be programmed in many different ways. Everything is up in the air. The hotel has to be developed with a flaw, as the real hotel business is unaffordable and isn't appealing anyway. The space makes us understand how it would like to be used, and at the same time we deliberately decide what actions to take in it. The pretext of the university protects the project and, at the same time, provides an avenue for trying things out. Apart from the ideational conditions, it is also the seemingly inexhaustible stock of materials that enables us to realize different settings here.[24]

Spaces aren't just empty containers, even if their implied use can oftentimes be inferred from their architecture. This means that possible actions always have to be considered in the space that is to be designed. There are big, small, transformable, bright and dark spaces, interspaces, as well as transitional spaces and so on. There are many rooms at the UoN: rooms for working, researching, gathering, sleeping, eating, cooking, celebrating, storing, and building. Here, rooms are not assigned individual programs or functions. Depending on the circumstances and the setting, existing rooms are used according to the situation. The respective function always results from the use: as a lecture room, bedroom, dining room, quiet room, private space, living space, public space—hotel? For this use, there is always the need for actors who recognize the open space and make it accessible and available for their purposes. This works because the spaces are empty in their own way (even though they are anything but empty). They were robbed of what creates uniqueness and defines a function. This is good for the different actors, as they can exploit the defect for their own benefit. Apart from the physical conditions, it is the precisely the simultaneity (working, researching, gathering, sleeping, eating, cooking, celebrating, etc.), i.e. the maximal overlapping of programs, that determines the UoN's image and potential. Despite there being chaos, this place functions well, because everyone involved, whether for their own sake or the sake of the community, ensures that the space is functioning well.[25]

The reports of residents show that it was the perception of possibilities within the framework of university offers that had opened up the space for residential use. The persistence of the bed underscores this development, and the intensification of its communal use—despite all empathy for this exceptional situation—makes long-term residents be the first to recognize the loss of this individual space for retreat. They compensate for it

24   Cf. Borchers and Lerch Zając̨kowska, *Wie zusammen leben?*, 39ff.
25   Cf. Borchers and Lerch Zając̨kowska, *Wie zusammen leben?*, 65.

performatively, by making use of opportunities and situations when sleeping alone or taking care of personal hygiene are possible. The focus of this consistent intermittent living lies on actions that account for community, when working, cooking, eating, celebrating, and designing the immediate living environment collectively. Even though the confluence of public use of the university and interested professionals is described as inspiring with its possible encounters, it also appears to be situationally disruptive. Having one's own room as an area of retreat within and from the community becomes a need. It can also be said that with the increasing use of the initially open space by its different actors, the precondition for the formation of the vector for the articulation of and desire for intimacy has only just emerged. The final experimental arrangement—as a play—sought to problematize, display, and put up for discussion the boundaries of the intimate on the basis of the cultural genealogy of the protective space between performative respect and spatial envelopment.

At the Hotel?Wilhelmsburg, experiences that carried the project in regard to the question of "how to live together" were intended to open up a space for reflection on the present and future of living. However, the plan was not to present finished results or solutions during the presentation year of the IBA Hamburg, which serves as one of the most important institutional frameworks for the project. Instead, rounds of questions that had developed from the experiences of previous years were to be applied to a new spatial arrangement and made clear. In terms of content and space, the aim was to turn the inside out, making spatial practice visible in order to make possible a public reflection on experimental forms of living at the interfaces of individual retreat, community, and the *city*.

HOTEL?WILHELMSBURG

Testing of intercultural practice in 1:1 mode. A lab that deals with the question of what it means to be a guest and host at the same time. The question mark in the title is crucial; it points to ambiguous and uncertain developments of the project—the results are up in the air and unpredictable. The question mark also addresses the uncertainty regarding the project's underlying resources and the collective objectives that would be pursued during work on it. The property and the house were given as a framework, as well as methods that had been practiced throughout previous years, such as being a guest or host, the performative production of the collective and intimate/private spheres, requirements of having a low budget and high-quality standards, and the assembly of various actors from other neighborhoods. The rehearsed procedures had also allowed us to follow those whose actions in different places always prompted new questions that we sought to align with discourses. In doing so, we proceeded iteratively instead of linearly; the process led us further and sometimes pushed us forward. In the course of the presentational year of the Internationale Bauausstellung (IBA, International Architecture Exhibition), the end of which was to coincide with the end of the project and the demolition of its building, we pursued the goal of making the negotiated interests public—not by specially producing an exhibition of what was or was not possible, but rather by making the project accessible to the public in the sense of representing its spatial practice.

Hotel?Wilhelmsburg. The organization of projects extending over several semesters with changing protagonists was also something we had practiced in previous years. We understood the term "hotel" to be a working title at first, which would bring together various players. The question mark serves as an open field, where different modes of living were to be questioned and tested. After all, Wilhelmsburg is the site where the IBA led to accelerated urban development as well as the home of people from 156 nations, making it one of the most ethnically vibrant and at the same time economically marginalized districts of Hamburg.

The project's more narrowly specified confines with an uncertain outcome are the Takes, in which explorative research of its various aspects is carried out. The Second Skin was about arranging conditions to meet the housing needs of the sixteen protagonists over the course of eighteen hours. The second Take dealt with the question of luxury and what difference the hotel's stars make. There was a Live Experience in five-star hotels focusing on the topics of personal hygiene/well-being, food, reception, sleeping, and socialization. Take 3 was about the hotelier's job profiles and fields of work in light of the expression "Make it happen." Taking into account the findings from Takes 1 and 2, the aim was to develop a larger context within the project under the conditions of "Low Budget – High Quality." Take 4 dealt with the development of an architectural implementation, using earlier findings and applying those to the existing building and resources, taking underlying rules into account. The spectacle of the Big Idea, with its everyone-can-agree image of Iconic Buildings,[26] mirrors its own pitfalls: it is conditioned by the translation of the imagination of a possible future into a single image. Such a process can only be made possible by sacrificing the complexity of the project's actual conditions. Indeed, differentiating between the capacities of diagrammatic representations (understood as visualizing relations and potentialities) and planning (understood as an intended goal and object to be fulfilled) is a central epistemic practice of our discipline which we will experience again, not least because of our own failing.

Setting up an "architectural office" requires organizing the necessary steps toward implementation, drawing up plans, having preliminary discussions with the authorities whose approval is needed, sponsoring campaigns to acquire materials, and having the support of staff. It is a race against time. Possible difficulties with (institutional) actors and current regulations will be (as in real life) averted by first adjusting the plans. For now, reality puts the plan into motion again, first by adhering to the idea, then by reworking the XXL version into an XL and then an L version before letting go of the plan (and the image) altogether while applying tried and tested procedures: no longer following the plan, but rather the

26   Charles Jencks, *The Iconic Building: The Power of Enigma* (London: Francis Lincoln, 2005), 22f.

motive, and operating the hotel's experimental setup based on what is available, with the aid of what is possible. For one thing, the existing building provides an opportunity to initiate the impending and complete dismantling and including it in the transformation. Furthermore, the scaffolding material of an advertising tower that was no longer required and made available by the IBA served as base material to temporarily expand the building structure.

The following Takes result from the questions that arose during the process. Breaking even. The economic factor became an integral part of further programming. Crowdfunding of restaurant evenings to explore the possibilities of economic realization. Various methods of payment came into play, and the hotel became a test site for alternative economies and their negotiation processes. Possible methods of barter are conceived and tested: Barsharing Deal, Dinner Capital, Budgeting, Finance Responsibility, Dinner Payment Systems, Payment Moments (with visible/invisible exchange currency), Bierdeckel-System (tally marks), Key-Card, Hotel-Value Currency and the Communication Deal: "Let's talk about money." Organizational processes remained a focal point of the process: what prompts a group of strangers to organize themselves? Knowing each other's strengths and weaknesses and acquiring practical experience when organization meets reality. Encountering one another during organized and non-organized situations, i.e. cooking, eating, celebrating, acquiring material, building, and planning. Scenarios are used as opportunities to develop and test the hotel's organizational models across various structures. Additionally, it is about responsibilities, possible legal entities and the deconstruction of hierarchies, public relations, branding and spatial articulations of the like.

During international workshops in the weeks that followed, the theme of *cadavre exquis* would be applied, something Ton Matton borrowed from the surrealists: process design. It has to do with making architecture: scenarios and meanings, organizing service facilities: "The beginning of an open process." Sabrina Lindemann, Hotel Transvaal, asks, "What is my role in the process?" Tim Kistenmacher, a lawyer in the field of cultural activity, deals with the internal organization, legal deliberations, and creating new job profiles and different positions within the organizational structure. Ton Matton takes us outside our comfort zone and creates his notion of "Well-Being in a Broad Welfare Hotel." Based on their empirical research, Ana Rosa and Valeria follow the "Storyteller Idea"— something they will inscribe in the building with the Speaking Walls, which will also lead to spatial articulation in the form of the Gypsy Room and later the Washing Machine Bar in the attic, a name given by Alex Römer. What could an open-process hotel look like? With the International Building Workshops, the new exploration of the area and its specific (hidden) potential had started with Véronique Faucher of Atelier le Balto. Martin Kaltwasser restructures Ton Matton's first scaffolding attempts: "Just build it" and "Teaching how to dig a hole." Benny Förster Baldenius from raumlaborberlin again explores the hotel's identity, which is progressing with the penetration of the roof and the construction of a Smokers' Room, the open-plan bathroom of Florian Tampe, and later Alex Römer's Kids' Wellness Area, right where the terrace and conservatory are being tackled and Peter Fattinger is conceptualizing and building upon the Hotel as a City. On top of that: lectures, an operating restaurant, seminars, master's theses, concerts, movie nights, the lives of students, long-term residents, guests, neighbors, IBA visitors …

Based on the bed, each phase throughout the process reconfigured the hotel and challenged us to think of the architecture itself as the improvising organization of space—to see it as an open process of disembedding and reembedding, in which anyone can enter at any time in history to modify its direction.[27]

But let's turn this question around. When a family has left the apartment intended for them, what do they leave to the vast majority of people living alone or as couples, apart from an abundance of space? If one's own room has turned into an apartment, but there is nobody left from whom one needs to retreat in order to rest, and the bed is no longer a place of silence but one of action, what does one do with this extra space? Moreover, if the functions of living take place outside the apartment, what are the new communities that we seek for cooking and eating, for getting fit—and what are the appropriate places for them?

From this set of questions, the one to be asked the bed would be how the overall organization of living—on the scale of the room, the apartment, the house, the district, and the city—should be rethought today with regard to common and heretofore unknown forms of dwellings.

27   Cf. Bauer et al., 2013.

Inhalt

[Leurs volontés changeantes, ou leurs paroles trompeuses;
la diverse face des temps; les amusements des promesses;
l'illusion des amitiés de la terre, qui s'ent vont avec les
années et les intérêts][10]

Figure 2. Page from Mémoires (1959) by Guy-Ernest Debord and Asger Jorn (Copenhagen: Permild and Rosengreen). General Collection, Beinecke Rare Book and Manuscript Library, Yale University. Reproduced with permission of the Estate of Guy Debord.

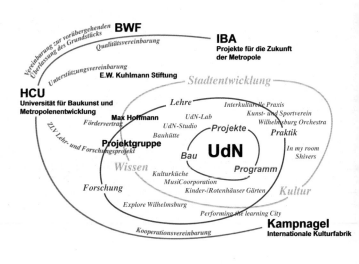

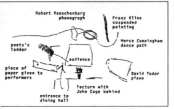

John CAGE, *Untitled Event*, 1952, Black Mountain College
obert RAUSCHENBERG, David, TUDOR, Merce CUNNINGHAM, Jay WATT,
Charles OLSEN, Mary Caroline RICHARDS

1   UD Raum-Matrizes

Funktion

Performanz, Nutzung, Aneignung, Gebrauch: „Erst die Handlung macht aus dem Ort einen Raum." (de Certeau)

Form

Urbane Form: Raum wird erst dann politisch, wenn er „in einer Stadt gesichert ist." (Arendt) Durch den Vektor Null ist die urbane Form definiert als eine Form, in der jeder Punkt virtuell alles auf sich beziehen kann. (Lefebvre)

Urbane Praxis

Struktur

Relationaler Raum: „Daraus resultiert, dass der Raum als ein relationales Geflecht von beweglichen Elementen verstanden werden kann. Er ist gewissermaßen von der Gesamtheit der Bewegungen erfüllt, die sich in ihm entfalten." (de Certeau)

Vektor

Um die Wichtigkeit der Interessen und ihre Materialität in Situationsgefügen deutlich zu machen, möchten wir Interessen mit Vektoren benennen. Vektor ist hier nicht als mathematische Grösse gedacht, sondern als Energie, die eine bestimmte Gerichtetheit aufweist und Handlungsfelder beeinflusst und umgekehrt auch durch Handlungen beeinflusst wird. Das Besondere an Interessen ist, dass sie oft nicht auf den ersten Blick erkennbar sind, von Interessengruppen verschleiert werden und sich auch in der Zeit entwickeln. Interessen sind die tacit, die "stillen" Steuerungsanteile von Interaktion. (Dell/Kniess)

2

Perzeption

Konzeption

wahrgenommener Raum (espace percu)

konzeptionierter Raum (espace concu)   gelebter Raum (espace vecu)

Projektion

Improvisation

3

Produktion (von Raum)

Heute finden sich das Mentale und das Soziale in der Praxis wieder: als entworfener, gedachter und gelebter Raum (l'espace conçu et vécu). Die Produktion von Raum dominiert heute, so Lefèbvre, die soziale Praxis. [Funktion]

Transformation

(Lebensform, Technologien des Selbst, Improvisation), Selbsttechniken können bezeichnet werden als Einwirkung des Subjekts auf sich selbst, durch die man versucht, sich selbst zu bearbeiten, zu transformieren und zu einer bestimmten Seinsweise Zugang zu gewinnen. (Foucault) [Form]

Ermöglichung

Produktionsbeziehungen

Der transformierte Modus der Produktion beinhaltet die Transformation der Produktionsbeziehungen. Es handelt sich

Macht

Performativität von Macht: sie kann kein Eigentum sein, nicht besessen werden, da sie rein operativ funktioniert. Die

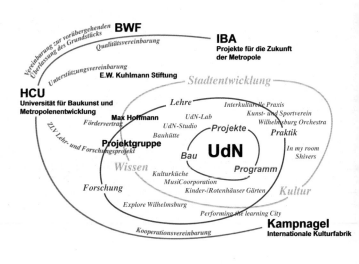

BWF
Qualitätsvereinbarung
Vereinbarung zur vorübergehenden
Überlassung des Grundstücks
Unterstützungsvereinbarung

IBA
Projekte für die Zukunft
der Metropole

E.W. Kuhlmann Stiftung

Stadtentwicklung

HCU
Universität für Baukunst und
Metropolenentwicklung

Fördervertrag

ZLV Lehr- und Forschungsprojekt

Max Hoffmann

Projektgruppe

Lehre

Interkulturelle Praxis

Kunst- und Sportverein

Wilhelmsburg Orchestra

UdN-Lab
UdN-Studio
Bauhütte

Projekte

Praktik

In my room
Shivers

Bau

UdN

Programm

Wissen

Kulturküche
MusiCoorporation
Kinder-/Rotenhäuser Gärten

Kultur

Forschung

Explore Wilhelmsburg

Performing the learning City

Kooperationsvereinbarung

Kampnagel
Internationale Kulturfabrik

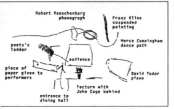

Robert Rauschenberg
phonograph

Franz Kline
suspended
painting

poet's
ladder

Merce Cunningham
dance path

piece of
paper given to
performers

audience

David Tudor
piano

lecturn with
John Cage behind

entrance to
dining hall

ITING FOR A FRIEND: 00.03.15

em-offen gehalten, um die bestmögliche Planungsbasis
einen so langlebigen Gebäudekomplex zum Leben und
nen zu ermöglichen.

Rechts oben:
Lufthalle von Yukihisa Isobe
für das Sommerhappening
von PHOENIX HOUSE

Links Mitte:
„Riesenbillard"
(HAUS-RUCKER-CO)

Links unten:
„Der ruhelose Ball"
(COOP HIMMMELBLAU)

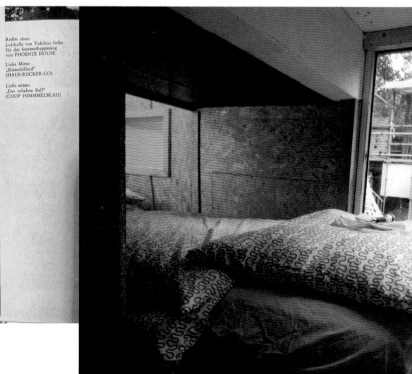

KEY FOR THE SHOWERS IN THE GYM - WARM WATER FROM 7⁰⁰ - 16⁰⁰

ALWAYS BRING IT BACK HERE!

BAUSTUFEN

DER FREIEN UND HANSESTADT HAMBURG

WILHELMSBURG

B 63

ZOLLGRENZE R
ASID CANGO 09 ED
EKA KNOPPERS
LEUCHTE NICHT I
N BETRIEB APF
ELSAFT PADERB
ORNER GRAZIL O,
1% FETT SMART

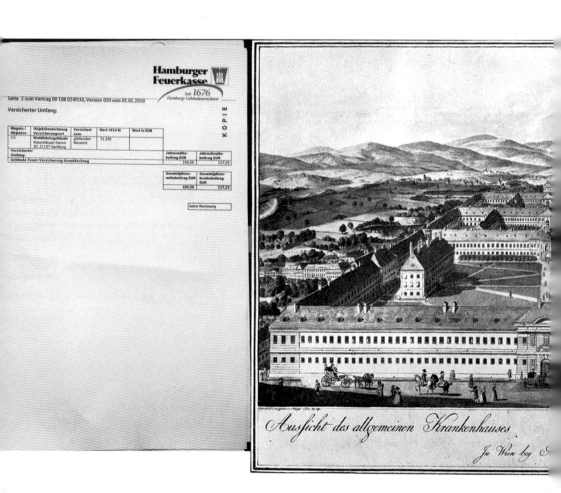

Bestandssituation	
Lage, Nutzung	- Die Fläche liegt mitten im Stadtteil Wilhelmsburg, in unmittelbarer Nähe einer Parkanlage - Derzeitige Nutzung: „Universität der Nachbarschaften" der IBA GmbH und der Hafencity Universität, ehemals Gesundheitsamt des Stadtteils
Infrastruktur	- Nahversorgungseinrichtungen in unmittelbarer Nähe am Veringhof und in der Zeidlerstraße, - ÖPNV: Über Bushaltestellen Neuhöfer Straße / Georg-Wilhelm-Straße Anschluss zu den S-Bahnstationen Wilhelmsburg und Veddel - Schulen, Kitas und Sporteinrichtungen sind in unmittelbarer Nähe vorhanden - Überörtliche Anbindung über B4/75 an die A1
Interne Erschließung	- Nicht notwendig
Bestehendes Planungsrecht	- Baustufenplan Wilhelmsburg von 1956 - Festsetzung: Fläche mit besonderer Nutzung, W, 3-geschossig

Aktuelle Planungsüberlegungen	
Städtebauliches Konzept	- Abriss des Bestandsgebäudes - Wohnungsneubau (städtebauliche Struktur offen)
Art des Wohnens	- Geschosswohnungen - Mietwohnungsbau (anteilig öffentlich gefördert)
Zielgruppen/Haushalte	- Alle Bevölkerungsgruppen
Neues Planungsrecht	- Nicht notwendig; Umsetzung des Wohnungsbauvorhabens über Befreiungen zu prüfen
Projektstand/Handlungsschritte	- Derzeitiges IBA-Projekt „Universität der Nachbarschaften" en-

l'Hôpital General a Vienne

283

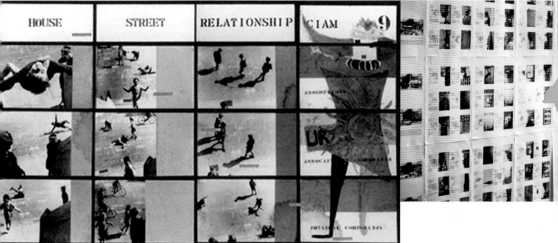

HOUSE	STREET	RELATIONSHIP	CIAM	9

PERVERSE METH

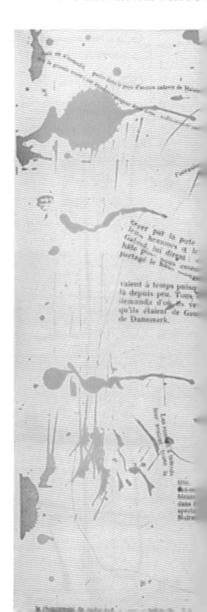

OF DEBORD

VILLA SAVOYE A POISSY 1929-31

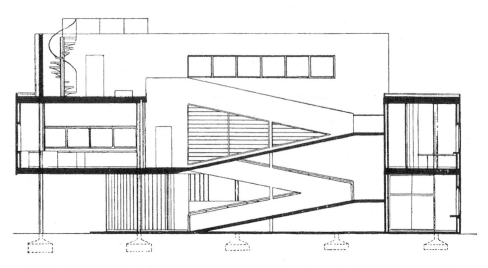

Coupe en travers. Du pilotis, on monte insensiblement par une rampe, ce qui est une sensation totalement différente de celle donnée par un escalier formé de marches. Un escalier sépare un étage d'un autre: une rampe relie

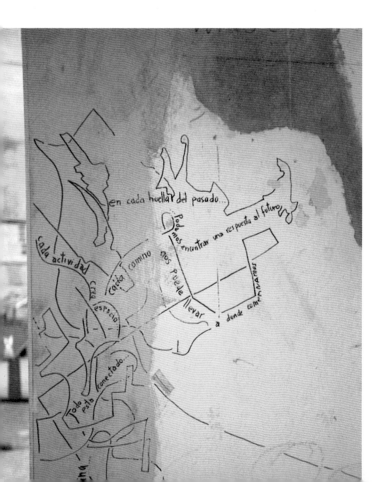

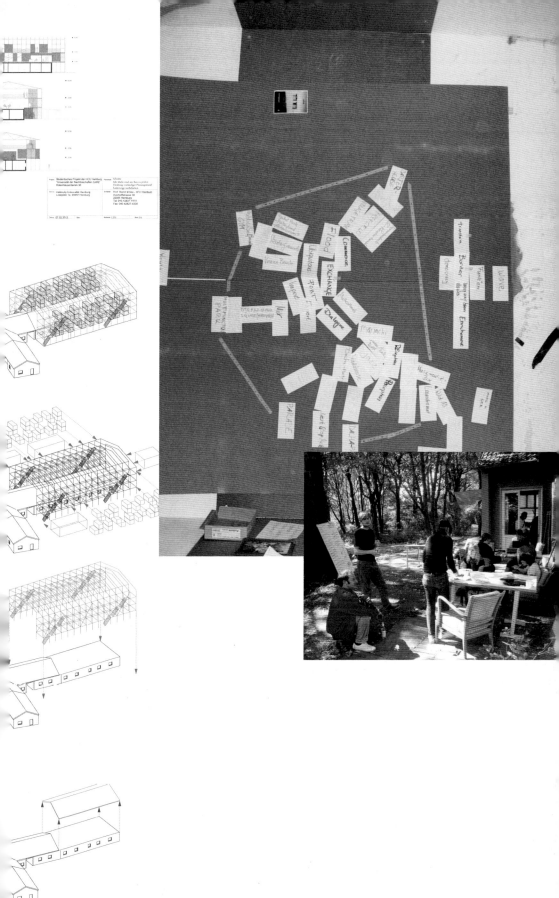

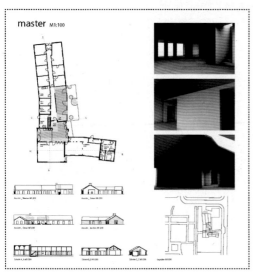

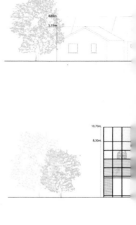

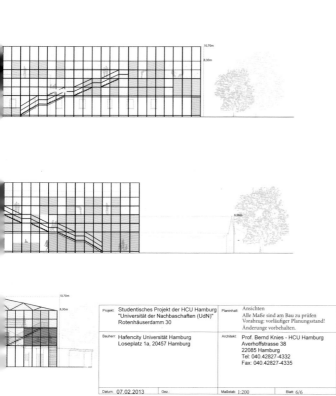

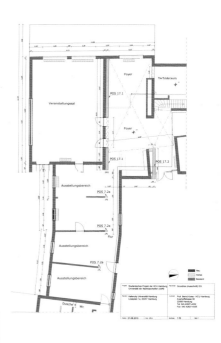

Projekt:	Studentisches Projekt der HCU Hamburg "Universität der Nachbaschaften (UdN)" Rotenhäuserdamm 30	Planinhalt:	Ansichten Alle Maße sind am Bau zu prüfen Vorabzug: vorläufiger Planungsstand! Änderunge vorbehalten.
Bauherr:	Hafencity Universität Hamburg Loseplatz 1a, 20457 Hamburg	Architekt:	Prof. Bernd Knies - HCU Hamburg Averhoffstrasse 38 22085 Hamburg Tel: 040.42827-4332 Fax: 040.42827-4335
Datum: 07.02.2013	Gez.:	Maßstab: 1:200	Blatt: 6/6

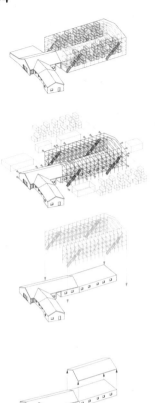

„Hotel Wilhelmsburg"

Universität der Nachbarschaften (UdN)
Exzellenzprojekt der Internationale Bauausstellung (IBA)

Projekt: Studentisches Projekt der HCU Hamburg "Universität der Nachbaschaften (UdN)" Rotenhäuserdamm 30	Planinhalt: Vereinfachte Isometrie Vorabzug: vorläufiger Planungss Änderunge vorbehalten.
Bauherr: Hafencity Universität Hamburg Loseplatz 1a, 20457 Hamburg	Architekt: Prof. Bernd Knies - HCU Ham Averhoffstrasse 38 22085 Hamburg Tel: 040.42827-4332 Fax: 040.42827-4335

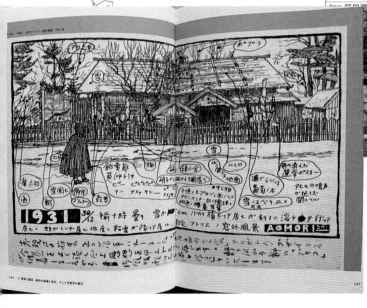

PLAY

BORIS CEKO
CHRISTOPHER DELL
LUKAS GRELLMANN
IULIA HURDUCAS
BERND KNIESS
TIM KOBLUN
MELIH KÖS
MAGDALENA MAIERHOFER
VALERIA MICARA
TABEA MICHAELIS
DOMINIQUE PECK
CHRISTOPHER PHIPHAK
BEN POHL
MICHELLE RENZ
VIKTORIA SCHEIFERS
VEDRAN SKANSI
TINA STEIGER
HANS VOLLMER

BORIS CEKO came to the UoN as part of the experimental theater performance collective God's Entertainment for the opening event.
IULIA HURDUCAS, MELIH KÖS, MAGDALENA MAIERHOFER, VALERIA MICARA, CHRISTOPHER PHIPHAK, and VEDRAN SKANSI were students at the UoN. Christopher and Vedran temporarily resided in the UoN.
LUKAS GRELLMANN, TIM KOBLUN, MICHELLE RENZ, VIKTORIA SCHEIFERS and TINA STEIGER studied in the master's program Urban Design. Tina supported the project UoN as project assistant and temporarily resided in the UoN.

TABEA MICHAELIS and HANS VOLLMER studied in the master's program Urban Design. Both were among the first people to move into the UoN as a research station. As an academic assistant at the Teaching and Research Program Urban Design, Hans also contributed to the Low-Budget-Urbanity research network that met frequently at the UoN and worked on issues related to the UoN.
For more information on the contributors, please see the chapter Three Questions to the Contributors on page 415.

"[The] play only happens when the players have a desire to play, even if it is the most absorbing, exhausting game … Finally and above all, it is necessary that they be free to leave whenever they please, by saying, 'I am not playing anymore.'"[1]

"Tt's only offside if the referee blows the whistle."[2]

The bucket's in front of me; sticks are bouncing up and down. Change the pounding movements, look for new sounds. There is a clicking sound at the edge of the bucket, and at the middle of the top, a fat beat. Jammed between the feet, the bucket can be lifted while playing, expanding the resonance chamber, deep bass tones booming. The beats coming from the bucket are compressed to a minimal spatial structure, which concentrates the beat on the essential. But that's not all; even the motive of the beat becomes apparent in its simplicity. The bucket is the central point of the motive's connection within the orchestra, which the musical spatialization of the beat itself follows. Another advantage is the fact that you can carry the bucket anywhere; you can play in front of a kiosk just as well as on the bus, at the bus stop, the ENTRÉE of the UoN, or in the park opposite it. The bucket's sound carries far. Already, passersby show up, asking what is going on here. The bucket is inviting.

Already, there is one child who wants to take a turn in playing. Already, a harmonicist from the neighborhood joins in. Play.

PLAY

In regard to its history of ideas, the term "play" was and remains some sort of wild card, which can be set up in a variety of ways of criticism of rationalism. Thus, its conjuncture is dialectically defined; it increases, especially when rigid norms are established in society. In this sense, the idealization of playing, both in early Romanticism and later on by Nietzsche, can be understood as a counterproposal for the progressive gesture of the total transparency of all being. Furthermore, Plato's dictum about humans as PAIGNION THEOU, as "plaything[s] for God,"[3] was spread in regard to representation theory, and in areas where all social life was equated to a performance in the early modern and Baroque era. This tradition found its reappropriation in sociological action and role theories of the twentieth century—for instance in Erving Goffman's classic, THE PRESENTATION OF SELF IN EVERYDAY LIFE[4]— and is continued in today's performance theory.

But even the Enlightenment itself knew how to report on the question of play. While Kant's definition of the

1   Roger Caillois, *Man, Play, and Games*, trans. Meyer Barash (Chicago: University of Illinois Press, 2001), 6.
2   Franz Beckenbauer.
3   Plato, "Nomoi 804b3," in idem, *The Laws*, transl. Tom Griffith (Cambridge: Cambridge University Press, 2016), 263.
4   Erving Goffman, *Wir alle spielen Theater. Die Selbstdarstellung im Alltag* (Munich: Piper, 1983).

PLAY

beautiful was based on the free play of the powers of cognition,[5] in which imagination and the mind interact, Friedrich Schiller claimed that man was "only wholly Man when he is playing."[6] Central to all these assumptions was a certain childhood myth which pertained to stand as legitimation for the vital characteristic of freedom associated with playing. Marx reinvestigated this issue in the famous trope of alienation, a theme that regained popularity in the industrial welfare state of the 20th century, when humans had to cope with processes of rationalization and differentiation. Consequently, the play emerged as a form that—being directed against what Adorno would call the "administered world"—was understood as an activity that withdrew from the dictation of any normativity.

Certainly, such dichotomic definitions can be regarded as outdated today. In regard to the constitutive relation between play and perception, Natascha Adamowsky, for example, has shown how performance theory in particular put an end to play and reason playing off against each other. While the performativity of play is emphasized as a fact, it comes into view that the action of playing presents some kind of meta-action; a meta-action that thematizes precisely the pre-conceptual dimension that accompanies every creation and use of concepts. Adamowsky concludes: Whoever wants to find out how epistemic spaces and dynamics are produced has to enter mental-sensory spaces of play, in which new ways of thought and perspectives can be tested.[7] The not necessarily simple art of scientific action—to paraphrase Michel de Certeau—then means giving in to the playful way of dealing with the indeterminacy embedded in the process of any exploration, knowing full well the risk of getting lost. That's the price of following the developing processes like the course of a game, of moving between the interchange of trial and error, on betting on what is cyclical.[8] If it makes any sense at all to talk about a "speculative rationality," then rather in the context of the play's hypothetical vectors.

Such a thesis of enhancing the play, however, also holds the pitfall of devaluation. Today, in times of a neoliberal release of the human capital—especially true for the imperative of the creative class ("Be yourself!")—one witnesses the ubiquitous call to turn labor itself into play. Similarly, the question arises as to whether play is really still being played in an eventization of culture that commodifies any spontaneity into the closed form of a product. On the one hand, one might agree with Isabelle Graw, who claims that

5   Immanuel Kant, *Kritik der Urteilskraft*, in idem, *Werkausgabe*, ed. Wilhelm Weischedel, vol. X, §9, p. 132.
6   Friedrich Schiller, "Ueber die ästhetische Erziehung des Menschen [2. Teil; 10. bis 16. Brief.]," in idem, ed., *Die Horen, 2. Stück* (Tübingen: J. G. Cottaische Buchhandlung, 1795), 88.

7   Natascha Adamowsky, "Spiel und Wissenschaftskultur," in idem, ed., *Die Vernunft ist mir noch nicht begegnet* (Bielefeld: Transcript, 2005), 29.
8   Adamowsky, "Spiel und Wissenschaftskultur," 29.

in times of self-exploitation, any resilience of play has been lost, and that the time of play may possibly be over.[9] On the other hand, and as Gilles Deleuze also saw it, play remains a vehicle for the production of meaning, instead of being meaning itself. Thus, play does not provide any pragmatic determinant like the economy, which in turn may appear on an ideological level. In other words, play remains a self-sufficient factor, the results of which still pose a conundrum.

DÉRIVE, SHIVERS

Down the Reiherstieg. Blackbirds in front yards. Doorsteps, fences, clotheslines, tree gratings along the avenue. Somewhere further away, a cluster of people is gathered in front of the UoN. The gentle sound of a boys' choir reaches my ear—here in Wilhelmsburg? My pace becomes faster, and I notice a group of young migrants singing while doing squats to the beat. They are carrying a banner identifying them as the Wilhelmsburg Boys' Choir. As I get closer, I realize that they have a tape recorder: they're lip-synching. Two people cut through a silk ribbon: the festivities can begin. In the foyer, next to one of the two entrances to the event hall, I notice a performative security check that seems like a humanized form of the metal detectors at airports. Two teenagers are standing at the doors, acting as surveillance staff. As soon as I try to enter, warning lights start flashing. I am a suspect. The supervisors stop and escort me to an adjoining room decorated to look like a medical officer's room.

Here, I am greeted by medical officer Dr. Blau and his assistant. They claim to have an "anti-ism immunization center." After the examination, Dr. Blau diagnoses me with "bizarre social incompetence." The only cure is a surreal treatment, which includes massive injections and imposes various social interactions. Confusion. Is this a play or is it real? What's going on here? Shouldn't this be the opening of a university? Finally, I arrive at the event hall, pass through it, and find another bizarre situation in the next room. The chancellor of the university I attend is sitting in a barber's chair, and a young woman is casually adding hair extensions. I ask and am told that a hair salon in Wilhelmsburg run by Ghanaians has moved their business to the UoN for the night. You can get dreadlocks, a fancy hairstyle or a complete hair weave for free. From here, I can feel the next creeping infection start, namely, a transformation of my hair. I quickly order a wig, put it on, and move forward. I make my way to the side wing of the UoN. There, I find an elaborately decorated television studio and can hardly believe my eyes: locally known radio and TV host Marco Alonso Reyes Loredo is the presenter and is, as always around this time of the day, especially

9   Isabelle Graw, "Gruppenspiele," in *Die Vernunft ist mir noch nicht begegnet*, ed. Natascha Adamowsky, 133.

PLAY

enthusiastic. His show is about to host an important figure in Wilhelmsburg, Johann Sebastian Bach's thirty-third-generation great-grandson and the premiere of his two-minute opera for the cello, DER BAUERNHOF (The Farm). Everyone can watch it live via a video broadcast in the event hall. Now over to the graffiti room, then on to the lounge with its stale and notorious atmosphere including a plush sofa, disco ball, glass bead curtain and dance pole.

Then out and into the event hall again, where the Bar für nette Leute (Bar for Nice People) is in full swing. I order a cocktail at a counter made out of beer crates while the lip-synched performance by the Fake Combo starts playing. People dance. I look out the window melancholically and notice the hustle and bustle in the Beach Club. Sixty square meters of sandy beach, a wading pool, beach chairs with umbrellas, and a lifeguard's chair. In this cold weather. It smells good. Around the corner, Nirmat from Iran and her friends are busy baking their wonderful flatbread. They brought the necessary charcoal oven themselves. Rap music is booming from the music room of the MusiCooperation.

In his work ZUR PSYCHOLOGIE DES SPIELS, Rolf Oertner describes the play as a basic phenomenon of human action, which can be characterized by the end in itself (action for the sake of action), the change in reference to reality, by its repetition or ritual, and its subject matter. Children use the play to process specific

problems and topics relevant to development and relationships for which they still lack other methods to overcome. The play serves the intensive exchange between individual and environment through appropriation and reification. The childlike play forms are developed from the sensorimotor and proto-social game, then are further developed in pretend play, through role play, and leading to a non-simulation play, while the construction play is developed from exploration. Forms of play build the foundation of all cultural creativity.[10]

Play as a system of action is generally distinguished from work as a remunerated occupation, which, on the other hand, is closer to sports as an activity that is competitive and generally goal-driven. Forms of play can differ in the various sorts and individual styles of playing. There are motoric, functional, productive, and constructing forms of play, role play, non-simulation and communication play. They are usually characterized by a set of rules based on free invention, development, or agreement. The rules describe the game precisely in order to differentiate it from other forms of play. They can be very complex at times, but details are always important; only they make the game playable and interesting.[11] One can play either alone or in groups. There

10   Rolf Oerter, "Zur Psychologie des Spiels," *Psychologie und Gesellschaftskritik* 31, no. 4 (2007): 7–32, nbn-resolving.de/ urn:nbn:de:0168-ssoar-292301.
11   Cf. Ulrich Schädler, "Vertreibung aus dem Paradies, über das Tempelhupfen," in Brigitte Felderer, Ernst Strouhal, and Manfred Zollinger, eds., *Spiele der Stadt. Glück,*

are puzzles, board, card, and parlor games, golf, tennis, and ball games, marbles, hopscotch, and hide-and-seek games. The playing environment can be part of the surroundings, which are separated while embedded in the course of the game; for instance, a group of trees in their natural habitat, a pile of sand on a construction site, the sidewalk as part of a traffic facility, a playground, a room, etc. The play, or game, respectively, lets people—even if only temporarily—become self-determined actors; it allows them to win sometimes, and thus defy social equitableness.[12]

TREE HOUSE – DIN[13]

A "climbing parkour" is to be planned in the neighboring Rotenhäuser Feld. The IBA's project board asks us if we would like to develop and test a tree house as a prototype, so to speak, with our students and children from the neighborhood. Naturally, we get to work, put on a prepared seminar in the Interkulturelle Praxis (Intercultural Practice) series, and organize a summer camp in the time when summer holidays and the lecture break coincide. Children from the neighborhood and students meet. There is no time for carefully scanning each other; it is immediately time to kick things off. Materials are discovered and tested, forms of construction are researched, drawings are made, and models are developed, then directly tested on a 1:1 scale. Near the proposed parkour course, a group of trees is chosen. Skillful preparations are made to protect the trees, and a web of ropes, straps, and fire hoses quickly appears between them. Interested commissioners from the district who want to take a look at the development of their idea are initially excited about the events. However, they promptly realize their own role and advise us to abide by the relevant rules and regulations. Their visit is followed by more experts (and skeptics), who eventually agree that the construction must be dismantled every night in order to comply with supervisory obligations and safety precautions. If this is not possible, a "night watch" has to be established. After all, the experts say, we are dealing with public space that is subject to certain regulations and, in view of the children's play equipment, has to conform to DIN standards. Nobody had thought of putting a self-built tree house, improvised in a certain way by means of available material, through the TÜV[14] individual assessment. Even if in the following year, research into the technical and legal requirements for approval will be the main focus of the seminars, we quickly arrive at the conclusion that this is going to remain a hopeless undertaking. So we move the construction sites of the tree houses to our own property and open up the fences to the park instead. At the same time, the

Gewinn und Zeitvertreib (Vienna and New York: Springer, 2012), 47.

12   Brigitte Felderer, "Bildchronist des Spiels," in Felderer et al., *Spiele der Stadt*, 58.

13   German Institute for Standardization.

14   Technical Supervisory Association.

professionally planned climbing course, equipped with DIN-approved playing equipment, finds its implementation at the proposed location. The children, who come from school and return to THEIR tree houses (and also to the students with whom they had worked), are asked why they are not playing on the new playground, and they reply, of course, by saying: "Because that's for children."

The experimental setup of the climbing course is an example of what is generally valid today with regard to playing, namely the connection between playing and CITY being reduced to the playground. Building codes regulate structural facilities, which playgrounds are part of, too. The combination of demand and size is deduced from the number of apartments per building. DIN standards 18034, 33942, EN 1176, and EN 1177 regulate the requirements for planning and operating playgrounds and open spaces for playing. Children's games, such as throwing and tossing balls and other objects, jumping rope, flying kites, playing with spinning tops and hoops, riding scooters or similar means of transport, as well as games with or on bicycles on the road have been prohibited according to traffic regulations since 1937—except for roads that are closed to through traffic.[15] The currently valid traffic regulations categorically exclude sports and games on the road, the shoulder, and on bike paths, as long as they are not designated with

additional road signs indicating the approved type of sport or game.[16] Section two of the paragraph addresses regulations for inline and roller skating.

However, that which constitutes play is something that the legally regulated playground with its possibilities of playing as well as experiences can hardly cover in its range.[17] Not only is the game regulated—according to its assigned locations—the children's lives seem to be, too: as children have heavy schedules and are institutionally taken care of, one practically only encounters them in public streets in specific and short windows between the start and end of school or kindergarten and at characteristic places, for instance in front of the school.[18] Play streets in residential areas remain less frequented due to the lack of time and the right group of friends in the neighborhood. On the other hand, shopping malls centrally located at traffic intersections have become more popular and serve as meeting points for adolescents to hang out at due to their urban anonymity.

Every now and then, one still comes across a hopscotch drawing, which indicates children's activities. (One of these was found at the UoN's entryway during the tree house workshop.) Hopscotch, potsy, hop-score … has been played for

15   Traffic Code – Straßenverkehrsordnung (StVO) from November 13, 1937 (Reich Law Gazette I, p. 1179, §43 Child Games).

16   Traffic Code – Straßenverkehrsordnung (StVO) I. General Traffic Rules §31 Sports and Games.

17   Cf. Cordula Loidl-Reisch, "Im Freien. Von Spielorten, Spielplätzen und der bespielbaren Stadt," in Felderer et al., Spiele der Stadt, 202.

18   Loidl-Reisch, "Im Freien," 202.

centuries all over the world, together or alone. (Legend has it that one of the oldest courts was found at the Roman Forum.) While the game, with its increasing levels of difficulty, presents a challenge for the coordination skills of children in the city, the drawn courts leave a message in the urban space: This is where I played![19] The players explore and use public areas, occupy it with relish as their territory and play according to the school of life.[20] Cordula Loidl-Reisch describes the squares of hopscotch as the city's play spaces that continue to be free zones beyond their assigned areas, which are always excitingly occupied by the players with a certain amount of civil disobedience and which render the players' game visible.[21] Ulrich Schädler mentions the right to break an arm[22] in the context of averting danger and security obligations.

AN ELBE ISLAND DÉRIVE REMIX

We make apple connections, swapping apples for stories in the Altes Land, exchanging dialogue and drinking homemade applejack. Sweet. Spicy. Now, we know the whole story. It burns. They breed horses, and have been doing it for over twenty years. They are all standing between the apple trees. Fawn. Puppy love. We find an umbrella. It's raining. We

hitchhike back to the UoN—by car? There is nobody out in the streets whom we could ask for directions. We pretend to be tourists. We ask around in St. Pauli: "How do we get to Wilhelmsburg?" Pause. From the Reeperbahn through the Elbe Tunnel. I see. So, down to the St. Pauli Piers, into the harbor area. It's getting noisy. Pounding, machines humming—the harbor. Hamburg's motor is whirring. The other side is deserted. We stop. Wait, wait for nothing. No person dressed in black or blue takes and guides us away from here. Empty buses arrive before driving past us again filled with dockworkers. The bridge in the east is the only connection to the city. A tiny eye of a needle. Nobody knows that or is even aware of the bridge itself, despite it having stood there for over two hundred years! Is that really possible? Motorized transit area. Truck after truck. Not a soul in sight. It's noisy, so noisy. Windy, so very windy. Hostile to life. No plan. A map of noise is recorded: where is stimulation, where is no stimulation. Dead ends—many of them. Streets leading to nowhere. We're stuck. Seems like part of the game. Proceeding in the process. Stagnant situation. We need new rules to play by— if nobody is going to pass by here. We have lost ourselves—we are lost, lost in urban space. We can hear the city, but there is no one there. Hello? Is anybody there? No public transport. Shit. We want to go back; we've had enough. How do we get to the island? "Hello. How are you? Can you name three things

---

19   Cf. Schädler, "Vertreibung aus dem Paradies," 50.
20   Felderer, "Bildchronist des Spiels," 58.
21   Cf. Loidl-Reisch, "Im Freien," 213.
22   Schädler, cited in Loidl-Reisch, "Im Freien," 210.

PLAY

that you associate with Wilhelmsburg?" "Um, yes: nice people, green island, good attitude." "And you, what do you associate with it?" "Well, Turks, people who don't earn well; there's just not much being done." I would say, "The flood of '62, a good attitude toward life, community." "Oh, well, there is this bunker, my kiosk; people are warmhearted." Now we're excited for Wilhelmsburg. "What facial expression comes to mind when you think of Wilhelmsburg?" Shrug, question mark. Smile. Thanks. Moving on. All we see is trash, trash, trash. Plastic bags, bottles, refrigerators, computer hardware. And other unsightly traces—remnants of everyday life. Mostly shopping carts; they're all over the place. We grab one, take it with us, fill it up. We sail. Roll over pavements and the bridges of the canals. Leisurely. We stop—next to the front yards. We look at them, observe them for a while. We try remembering our childhood, what images come and go. We imagine who lives here and what they are doing. We immerse ourselves in it, ask questions, and perceive. "How do I know that I am in Wilhelmsburg? What do you mean?" Versatile, thatched houses, old buildings, many foreigners, many beautiful spots, large areas being developed; there is generally a lot being renovated, built, and planned for the IBA, but nobody is being integrated there, FUCK IBA (as we later read on the wall of a house close to the UoN); canals, garden exhibition, people say "Mahlzeit" to each other, green areas

everywhere, a lot of green, just completely different than the city. Oh, yes, the island. But don't forget: "You will never dance alone."[23]

Rules
1. Draw a ticket with a number
2. Find your group
3. Use public transportation to get to one of the set starting points
4. Find your way back on foot with your own rules
5. Duration: open-ended
Prohibited items: maps, compass, navigation systems, etc.
Tracking of the route: scribbling, photography, sound, video, field report.
Found artifacts are desired.[24]

DÉRIVE

In general, DÉRIVE means to wander, walk, saunter, stroll, move through urban space. One may also consider it an active form of percipience. What is thus embedded in the Dérive are ways of appropriating, participating, interacting, of processing, living, designing, and transforming urban spaces. The eponym but in no way inventor of the concept, situationist Guy Debord, defined the Dérive in 1958 as one of the different situationist methods of hurriedly passing through diverse environments.[25] The concept of wandering about is inextricably linked to the exploration of the effects of a psycho-geographical nature and the claim

23   Tabea Michaelis and Ben Pohl, "Made in, Lokale Praktiken urbaner Produktion," in *Urban Design Projekt 3* (Hamburg: HafenCity Universität, 2011/2013), 96f.
24   Michaelis and Pohl, "Made in," 77.
25   G.-E. Debord, *Situationistische Internationale Nr. 2*, 1958.

of constructive play, which contrasts it in every way with classic concepts of travel and walking.

FROM FUNCTION TO USE VIA PLAY

In the fields of art and architecture, the question of play became fashionable in the twentieth century. In connection with the model of "Children in the City," play especially towards the end of the 1940s found its entrance in the art discourse. Founded in Amsterdam in 1948, the COBRA artists' group sees childlike play as a model for social change. The group, which included Constant Nieuwenhuys along with Asger Jorn and Christian Dotremants, reactualizes Marx's thesis of alienation in capitalism as a central argument, an argument which is supposed to later fuel the Situationists' activities as well. Against alienation, a child naturally indulges in experiments, freedom, and innocence. According to the founding manifesto of COBRA, written by Constant, a child knows no law apart from the spontaneous experience of life, and it doesn't feel the need to express anything else.[26] In COBRA's aftermath, architects Peter and Alison Smithson discover child's play as a model in the 1950s and use it productively for their work. Well-known is the research they undertook in the London working-class district of Bethnal Green. There, the Smithsons—together with photographer Nigel Henderson—examined the spatial arrangements of the games children played in the streets. Just as they read these structures as specific forms of street use, the Smithsons translated them into suggestions for an interconnected and clustered spatial order of the city.

TREE HOUSE WORKSHOP
(GAME SERIES)

Drawing a tree house. Stereotypes of an imagined house with a saddle roof in the tree. Reproducing common ideas and practices learned in families and kindergarten or school. But how should the house-house get into the tree, and if it cannot, what is a tree house? What would one want to do there? Supporting ideas about introducing possible building contractors with very unique needs, for instance the spider-man, the hip-hopper, the tree-climber. Painting again, drawing, cutting, making models. The rhythm—always in the same sequence—as long as the concentration and fun suffice. Swinging, building, skipping rope. Then: knit tree house. What material, how to build it? Cord, wool, rope, bicycle, and fire hose; knitting, knotting, crocheting. White construction sheets, cutting it into strips, measuring knitting needles, testing patterns, knitting prototypes. Then, how does that work again? Knitting dolly. Testing again on a small scale, then in the XXL knitting dolly. Building with the big boys. XXL knitting, indoors, in the park. For hours and days. Supporting frame: the inflated

26   Constant, "Manifest van de experimentele groep," *Reflex: Orgaan van de experimentele groep in Holland* 1 (1948), 2–11.

inner tube gives shape to the knitted tube. Different parts are assembled to form a hanging tree nest, which serves as both a swing and horizontally as an armchair. Again and again, cutting apple slices, making lemonade, chopping cucumbers, ball games, spray-painting safety helmets, swinging, skipping rope, jumping games, topping pizzas, running foot races, eating and drinking together, attending lectures.

What appears here, although not yet determined properly, is one of our fundamental lines of argumentation; it is neither about absolutizing nor negating the function, but about focusing on the application and use. The suggestion to do so comes from Michel de Certreau and his thesis of reusing. It discusses the tactics of everyday users that undermine any determination of the function: products in everyday life are always different from what they were intended to be. Koki Tanaka illustrates this with relish in his video piece EVERYTHING IS EVERYTHING.[27]

THE HOTEL PLAY.
TAKE 1 SECOND SKIN.

Bernd Kniess advertises the Hotel?Wilhelmsburg in the annual study program consultation at the beginning of the lecture period. Two choices of subject are offered in the winter before the IBA Hamburg's exhibition year: Urban Design Project for 10 credit points and Intercultural Practice for 5 credit points. As always, students

have to organize which accomplishments in the study program fit which catalogues. Kniess signals to the interested students that it's possible to postpone things. Alice Ott, responsible for all formalities in the coordination of students of the Urban Design program, will deal with individual cases later. Bernd Kniess advises everyone who's interested to visit the UoN's kick-off event and to decide then and there whether to take courses and which ones. Later on this Thursday, twenty-two students are sitting on cheap folding chairs around four seminar desks in the large room of the UoN. A little delayed, Bernd Kniess, Ben Becker, and Jan Holtmann introduce the Take: SECOND SKIN, a sixteen-hour site visit from Saturday to Sunday. That is, in three days everyone is supposed to be brought to play. In short, this is about a performative site exploration following the announcement "The hotel is already there." These few guidelines make the program possible: Kniess hands the students one hundred euros in cash for an overnight stay with half board; the UoN building is not to be entered; the UoN is a sculpture and battery; SECOND SKIN means no tents, caravans or cars, but only clothes and a sleeping pad, and is to be taken seriously. "The Take starts now," says Becker, and the documentation of its organization starts as well; collectively reflecting based on the latter is on the agenda for the project date in the coming week. In other words: Okay,

27   Koki Tanaka, *Everything Is Everything*, YouTube, accessed June 4, 2018, www.youtube.com/watch?v=ym0LaSAn5n8.

okay, okay … so we have to figure out how to organize the How and make a decision. "I have some experience. Let's try this: The person who has a proposal starts talking. If the group likes the proposal, they raise their hands and wiggle their fingers, like that, like Spirit Fingers in BRING IT ON, OK?"

This is going well. She is moderating. Someone is taking notes to later upload to Google Drive; the invitation to the online folder comes instantly. First, a few things have to be made clear. The students want to buy food from the Turkish grocery store at the end of the road; it's super-cheap, the vegetables are always fresh, and everyone there is really nice. This will be taken care of by the Food group. They are planning on making a curry; that always works, even on a small budget. A flyer would be nice, too, for the neighbors. Okay, alcohol needs to be purchased, which is too expensive, so everyone should bring their own. They also want to take care of the music. The question of whether there might be problems with the neighbors is answered with the fact that there aren't any at the Rotenhäuser Feld, and that if people should come by, they would be invited to the Hotel opening. The students list everything in their journals and in a Google Doc, which is projected onto the wall for everyone to see. The cooking has to be done on a hotplate. The moderator asks who could organize one. The first students have to leave; it's almost 8:00 p.m. They

decide to meet again on Friday evening to discuss the final details. Nobody is happy with the first distribution of finances.

The collaboration via Google Drive doesn't work for everyone. Students talk on the phone, write texts, e-mails, and direct messages on Facebook. This generates a list on many platforms. Everyone brings 1.5 liters of water with them. There are five groups: Site, Documentation, Equipment, Food, and Community. Not all students own a sleeping bag. Whoever has or can arrange more than one should bring them. The first students note that they wouldn't stay the whole night, but are happy to bring a sleeping bag. The first set points of the program have now been agreed upon as well. Setting up, cooking, eating, opening the hotel, sleeping, breakfast, cleaning everything, and students want to invite people to the event. To do that, there will be a flyer for the announcement. Individual students are skeptical. What if too many people show up? The Site group meets the night before the event and designs all plans after a first tour of the site. The situational opportunity structures should be sufficient for the hotel opening.

"Anyway, the play as I see it is exciting."[28] The groups all arrive at the UoN a little too early. In front of the door, the members of the Documentation group lay out a sheet and set up a camera on a tri-

28   Gertrude Stein, "Plays," in Gertrude Stein, *Last Operas and Plays* (Baltimore and London: Johns Hopkins University Press, 1995), xxix–lii.

pod. They ask all arriving hotel guests to place their luggage on the sheet and take a photo of it. The Foodies push a full shopping cart up to the UoN's entrance. They were asked at the checkout in the nearby Turkish supermarket what they were up to. The woman offered the students to take the cart with them and bring it back in a few days. The owner of the supermarket hears the conversation and gives them grapes, lentils, and bananas, everything past its sell-by date but still good. His children had participated in the tree house workshop last year. The dining car is filled. Where is the kitchen?

"Should we go to the Wilhelmsburg Corner across the street to wash the vegetables?" Three students take a flyer with them and start walking. Meanwhile, the rest of the Food group can begin setting up the stove. After an unsuccessful search for an extension cord, they install the hotplate on a small bench in front of the window. One of them can now sit while stirring, using the cooking spoon that was brought along. The students build a work surface from three pallets, one with the supporting surface to the ground as the foundation, two standing upright, and a wooden board on top. Nobody has brought any tools or screws. At 8:50 p.m., the food is cooking. The lentils take longer than planned. In order to protect the kitchen from falling autumn leaves, the students span a construction tarp into the trees in front of the UoN window. One student who recently worked on a campground in Berlin has set up an outdoor toilet by the property line: toilet paper hangs from a tree next to, only an arm's length away, an empty shopping bag. Along the plot boundary, the bushes are dense. A few meters away is the shower: a watering can mounted on a branch. You pull on another string, and water starts running.

Food is ready. The students quickly put coriander, lemons, and chili out on the work surface, which has now been converted into a dining table. Things start moving, getting in line, taking a bowl, spoon, curry, toppings, putting the meal together. The students use cobblestones from the UoN's material stock to form a circle and light a fire that warms, illuminates, and smokes everyone's clothes. Then the opening begins. All of the students line up in front of a black and yellow barrier tape. One of them gives a speech. Could be worse. This is going to go on until 2:00 a.m. Students are playing music on a miniature piano and with rattles. Everyone has stories. The hotel landscape is in operation. Afterwards, everyone lies in their sleeping bags on cardboard boxes, on top of the pallets. There are enough after all. Some students have taken the last bus home. The sleeping camp is right around the corner from the kitchen and bar, along the path from the Rotenhäuser Damm to the Rotenhäuser Feld.

In the morning, almost all the bottles are gone. The Food group sets off in search of breakfast. Because there was still money left over and special emphasis had been placed on the importance of good breakfast rolls, sixty bread buns were ordered from the kiosk. However, on Sunday mornings, the kiosk is still closed. The group asks a woman watching the street from the window of her apartment if she knows what time the kiosk opens. The woman doesn't understand. Moving on towards the bus stop. Apparently, there are bakeries and restaurants there. The students ask a man whether he knows where they could get rolls. He is also on his way to the bus stop and invites the students to follow him. In front of the bakery, he invites them to attend the worship service.

Meanwhile in the hotel, the first students to wake up are cleaning. In the lobby, they lift the white sheet from the documentation installation off of the ground, shake it out, and roll it up. In the kitchen, they pack the unused groceries that are still good into a big box and the other leftovers into a large trash bag. They take down the tarps and shower, dispose of the toilet, dismantle the work surface, and bring individual pieces back to the UoN shed. All of the kitchen equipment is lined up so that everyone can take theirs back home with them.

TALENT FOR IMPROVISATION

Felix had noted the term "talent for improvisation" in his field log and opened a discussion with it: Can people have a talent for improvisation? Isn't everything we use or apply in improvisation a reference to knowledge that's already been attained? Let's return to the initial plans of the planning group once more, which—in their concrete form of location choice, group division, the bread roll preorder—quickly proved to be outdated. When considering the practical planning, students saw themselves as representatives of a group whose collective action was prepared in such a way that the planning could be carried out successfully. Following the usual procedures, they separated active planning and planned actions as well as respective materializations. The framework in which something can take place is always set, similar to the predetermined actions in the plan that are necessary in order to achieve a goal. What they had not considered in their plans, however, was the fact that the collective actions of people, predominantly strangers, and their various resources of knowledge and creativity inevitably affect organizational structures. This automatically suspended the separation of active planning and planned actions. What one might call the performative plan came onto the scene: a plan that, on the one hand, emerges from acting and, on the other, provides the framework in which actions can only appear to generate structure. However, the actual, teleological plan and the active planning that led to it were in no way obsolete in this process. They had contributed to the clarification of general conditions on site and related them to the requirements of the task in an initial scenario, which—in order to establish planning security in preparation for the action—was then understood as a plan. It was important to not understand the plan as a teleological posit, as finalistic and closed, but rather, as already suggested in the SHIVERS example, as an open frame and score that provides available structures for further playing. This also implied an epistemological turn: One can only read open moments of forms and develop performative ones from a common plan if one takes an improvisational perspective that allows interpreting forms in their state of becoming and having become. This means that the kitchen group's choice of location, the terrace, merely brought the parameters into a new arrangement, reassembled the actions of the actors in new places, and thus brought the new experimental set-up into effect. The organization of the project group had developed through smaller groups, formed according to their interests, and did not stick to a linear pattern, but was characterized by performance, organized improvisation, and interactivity. A certain level of trust in improvisation as a reliable factor of organization had been established, but had not yet been proven. At this point, the students hadn't seen improvisation as a method; no decision was made to do things this way for their own sake. Their methods had rather developed from the dynamics of the group, in whose coordinated actions they became aware of their own skills and gained confidence in them. Consequently, the improvisational perspective was developed from a situation in which it was important to combine 1:1 oriented improvisational action with a form of knowledge, i.e. to gradually turn it into a technology.

In the case of the setup for the night, improvisation proved to be a recourse to pre-existing knowledge and experience combined in heterarchical interaction and performance within the group, in order to acquire new knowledge and apply it directly to the field. Just as the construction site group was improvising with the materials of the UoN to build sleeping structures, the kitchen crew improvised the main course and dessert, which was prepared using valuable and substantial foods based on the neighbors' local knowledge.

This form of organization in work groups was to prevail throughout the entire course of the project. Decisions regarding specific tasks, such as preparing dinner, would be made within the work group but in relation to the community. Overarching problems (such as the need for a stove) were solved by involving the whole group. The design of the bar revealed an attitude among the group that would be observed again and again: the urgent need to participate and the willingness to make a decision.[29]

29   Tim Koblun, Melih Kös, Magdalena Maier-hofer, Valeria Micara, Dominique Peck, Christopher Phiphak, Michelle Renz, Viktoria Scheifers, Vedran Skansi, and Tina Steiger, *Sampling aus der Projektdokumentation Hotel?Wilhelmsburg* (Hamburg: HafenCity Universität, 2012/13).

ART AND SPORTS ASSOCIATION

(E-mail from Iulia Hurducas from June 29, 2010) "Dear SU-PERKICKERS, as previously announced, here is some more information about the tournament. We will meet on July 4 at 10:30 a.m. on the big meadow in the Rothenhäuser Feld behind the University of the Neighborhoods. This is also the catering point for the tournament. There will be lunch around noon, and at night we plan on having a barbecue. We will play in six different locations, which are easy to reach on foot or by bike. Six variations of the game will be played on different surfaces (concrete, wood, grass), so bring appropriate shoes if needed. On Sunday morning, you will be given a map showing an overview of all locations and your personal course. Please send me the names of your teams and players by Saturday morning. Also remember the jerseys; we will award points for them as well as for rally chants."

(re: Iulia Hurducas) "Dear Berat, it's a pity that you won't be playing. Sunday will be a lot of fun. Maybe I can still convince you if you hear more about the games: in the container terminal, we will play 'XXL container soccer,' in the soul kitchen hall 'disco soccer,' in the park at the Vering Canal 'wave soccer,' in the park at the Rothenhäuser Feld 'one-goal soccer' and 'basket soccer,' and on the Vogelhüttendeich sports field, we will play 'Guantánamo soccer.' It will be five against five."

(re: Jan Holtmann) "Tell them that five players are enough and that there will be a cold shower room and lots of drinks …"

(re: Iulia Hurducas) "I already did …"

(re: Jan Holtmann) "Hi Iulia, attached is another registration. Also, the fishing department has registered with me by phone. Anton will take care of that …"

(ff: Marco Antonio Reyes Lorede June 29, 2010 10:03 a.m.) "Dear Mr. Holtmann, I am pleased to inform you that the Konspirativen KüchenKicker (Conspiratorial Kitchen Kickers) would like to honor your tournament and hereby commit to attending. We have only a few conditions, which are easy to fulfill: 1. we win from the start, 2. if the first condition is not guaranteed, we can cheat as we please, 3. coffee! whenever the chef requests it! …"[30]

Before the tournament begins, six official registrations are received: nine teams with a total of seventy-five players will play six variations of one game. The teams: Chicago Bulls, Fortuna 1817, Konspirative KüchenKicker, Die Ausländer (Foreigners), Bayern Kebab FC, Abi 2013, Hafencity bleibt (Hafencity remains), Rhino, Anglo.

SHIVERS REWIND

"We methodically approach the adaptation of SHIVERS like an

---

30 Iulia Hurducas, Lukas Grellmann, and Hans Vollmer, *Sampling aus der Projektdokumentation Interkulturelles Fußballturnier, Interkulturelle Praxis Seminar* (Hamburg: HafenCity Universität, 2010).

action painting. As action performers, we turn our bodies into the starting point of our work and practice contagion by creating liminality.

'The strategy of our work is, for one, to work on site. What do you find and how do you deal with it? The challenge is not knowing what to expect, what to do with this place. Second, it would be important to have an ulterior motive. At this point, we were extremely affected by the parasite metaphor that Cronenberg had first used in Shivers in connection with a scientific experiment that had gotten out of control. The location and the given situation of the IBA practically challenged us to take up the topic and creatively work with it. And then, finally, there is a set date, a date to work towards, where things and actors collide and the piece comes into action.'

The metaphor of the parasite allows us to dismantle the boundaries between audience and performer more subtly than before. The viewers should be involved in the events both mentally and physically, so that (cf. movie template) no separation of performers and viewers is possible. Total symbiosis.

'The question that we always deal with in our projects is how to enter existing structures without significantly influencing or disturbing them by our presence. The parasite seemed appropriate, as it doesn't appear at first, so it does not produce disapproval or cause aggression, which would hinder any further development. The parasite sneaks in unnoticed. One could call it parasitic strategy to attach itself onto certain contexts, formats, events or structures, to tap into the resources, make them usable and translate the motive. The translation is up to us. This means that we choose from these structures and pick exactly that which is available but not yet translated. The structures as we found them in the city district seemed relatively 'tough' at first and sometimes very self-contained; a heterogeneous migrant district with various communities—it is extremely difficult to get close to people. Plus, there had been rigorous reservations about the IBA, art in general, and gentrification artists. Kampnagel was virtually unknown; the only point of connection was the location of the former public health office—people knew that. We also put up pieces of paper and used existing contacts. It was about getting people to participate. And, of course, it was always about what the object of a possible exchange might be. Money was one option. However, the difficulty with that is preserving those energies that the characters bring to the table, without tempting them into supposedly professional work, i.e. into acting, by paying them in return.

Subsequently, we developed the program using the spatial arrangement of the building, such as its rows of rooms. We then worked out individual storylines together with everyone, thus creating individual situations: the reception and lobby with the Bar für nette Leute

(Bar for Nice People). Then there was a couple from Africa. While busy with preparations, we had some beer in their bar across the street a few times. Super-cheap—I think a beer cost one euro—and it was really nice there. We told them, 'You just have to come on over and set the bar up with us.' And, well, the vaccination room to fight -isms, against all prejudices and fears. 'Respect yourself': that was the beauty salon. We had discovered the African hair salon in the Veringstrasse, and the deal was for them to move their salon into our building. We would prepare everything and pay them their usual daily income. Marco was in charge of the TV studio, with live coverage in the lobby. During the preparation stage, we had three very long sessions there. The project really had to be justified, and we had to state what had to happen when. And, above all, why: no, we are not from the IBA. At the same time, it wasn't about playing on something random, but also about making a difference. Of course, you only win on this political level by telling someone clearly, 'That's how it is!' You enter a discourse and try to work it out with them. Yes, and then there was the disco room, completely plastered in gold. With a shiny disco ball and a pole, i.e. a stripper pole. There you could also sign up for a private dance. Then the concert room with a stage; we arranged that with the students. The kitchen worked extremely well. We built it in collaboration with another group of students. They cooked very well every day, and sometimes we took care of it as well. The room with the DIY courses, street art, spraying and stuff—failed, I'd say. And then there was the bike tour: you basically went for a ride with a tour guide through the whole of Wilhelmsburg for an hour. The guide was twelve years old, an extremely bright boy in the volunteer fire brigade. People really liked that. The Yoko Ono Garden and the Shivers Cinema outside were meant to be a meeting point, to start every day at 12:00 p.m."

Technically, the viewer serves as the carrier of the parasite, transmitting it to us. We try to mirror this transmission performatively in such a way that the viewer becomes aware of his or her role as the vector. In the course of the performance, it becomes clear that they themselves are already infected and that they have contaminated performers by being present. There are no rules or formulas yet for this type of interaction and reception: they have to be generated first, in order to be described and established in the next step.

'To play the stage, the location, by yourself is boring and technologically impossible when you enter such a situation. We have no expectations; there is no need for them. It's an experiment. You try to see who or what is radiating energy and where. We ended up with more than thirty actors, I think, and someone had to coordinate them. Coordinate, not control. Although: you even had to keep the children under

PLAY

control; they have an energy
that at a certain point they
can't control themselves.
That's what we did with the
vaccine. They were extremely
scared of that. That was such a
nice situation, too.'"[31]

PLAY URBAN DESIGN

To us, the aspects collected
above show that the comprehen-
sibility of the question regarding the logic of spatial
production can only be understood in light of spatial actions, i.e. use and application, which in turn ask about
the practice of medial-rep-
resentational statements that
make them plausible. What is
made possible here in terms of
planning is that the connota-
tions, which have historically
brought a form of planning
classification for spatial situations shaped by a bird's-eye
view and externalization, are
separated from the question
of a possible reason for the
use of space. The prospect now
is to see design and use in a
complementary relationship
rather than in a dependent one.
Everything points to the plan's
shift from a closed form to
an open form of relational,
hybrid, and network-like forms
of representation. Such representational forms or open notations measure themselves
against the criterion of always
developing anew on the representation of the actual use.

The fact that they are never
successful in fixating the use
conclusively is part of the
game. We constantly have to
deal with the game and its insertion into the form of spatial production with a specific
difference, namely that between
the perspective that regards
use as incomplete, and that
which understands it as a complete unit of meaning. If you
want to know what potentials an
urban situation offers in terms
of structure, do not simply
rely on what you supposedly
see—because there is nothing to
see, really—but instead, show
how the materials and constellations of the situation are
used and what applications and
uses are part of the situation.
This kind of insistence on use
is certainly not the end of
research design, but surely its
beginning. It is about dismantling the trend of those forms
of representation—renderings—
whose purpose it is to make
people believe in something
they allegedly see through suggestion. Finally, we have no
choice but to be naive and to
admit to ourselves that we do
not understand urban situations
for the time being, in order
to playfully approach the uses
of the urban. In other words:
work begins with the acceptance
of not knowing.

31   God's Entertainment, "Shivers – Die para-
      sitäre Reise in Innere der Umgebung," God's
      Entertainment (2009), accessed June 4, 2018,
      www.gods-entertainment.org/index.php/
      arhiv-ge/2005/item/36-shivers. Regathering of
      the project display on the website and a Skype
      call with Boris Ceko, God's Entertainment, on
      March 7, 2017.

Round Table Redesign: What is Urban Design to Do in the Age of Uncertainty?

Ben Becker
Christopher Dell
Constanze Engelbrecht
Stefanie Gernert
Bernd Kniess
Philipp Löper
Ben Pohl
Moderation and preparation:
Dominique Peck
Julia Strohwald
Robert Stürzl
Dorothea Wirwall
Yannik Hake
Jakob Kempe

Ben Becker was an academic assistant at the Teaching and Research Program Urban Design and as such responsible for project development and construction at the UoN.
Constanze Engelbrecht was an academic assistant to the Chair of Urban and Regional Science at HCU Hamburg and a frequent visitor to the UoN.
Stefanie Gernert was an academic assistant at the Teaching and Research Program Urban Design. She was responsible for project development and management at the UoN.
Philipp Löper was a lecturer at the UoN.
Yannik Hake and *Jakob Kempe* supported the project Tom Paints the Fence as student assistants.
For more information on the contributors, please see the chapter Three Questions to the Contributors on page 415.

Construction sites in their final days of use are suitable confines for making actors and relations in collectives tangible.

What we'd like to discuss is: How does an experiment turn into practice? Bernd, maybe you can start by explaining how you came to the UoN project.

Bernd Kniess: It was one of my first days working here at the HafenCity University when Martina Nitzl, research assistant of Michael Koch, asked me whether I would like to contribute to a grant application she was currently working on. Turns out it was about a follow-up project regarding what was called Experiment auf der Insel (Island Experiment), a student competition that had already dealt with the area that later was to become the University of Neighborhoods. The main focus of the application for the follow-up project was supposed to be raising an additional EUR 540,000, thus doubling the existing budget. I thought the concept of the application, at least the state it was in back then, was not specific enough, however, and apart from several fundamental thoughts about how I would approach such a project, I couldn't contribute much to it. That was my first encounter with the project.

It wasn't long until I was indeed asked if I would like to lead the project. How and primarily why they came to me are things I only realized much later. The reason why we very quickly chose this option was mainly the given conditions: our general task was to develop the new Urban Design master's program, make it eligible for accreditation *and* ready for launch in the winter semester, while at the same time defining and establishing a new field of research. The third aspect now emerging—a field of practical experience—seemed to be the ideal complement to this possible triad.

Christopher Dell: It was Bernd who took me aside after it was clear that I would be responsible for the theory of the new program. He told me that there was something else and asked whether we'd want to do it together. It was clear from the start that it would be an add-on, something on top of the basic teaching. Anyway, we opted for it. And we did it because we were interested in trying out something that's usually a mere hypothesis: that the *city's* future will play out mainly in terms of working with what already exists. One could say that at the time—especially regarding the actual economic, demographic, and political situation of the *city*—the understanding of urban design shifted conceptually from design to redesign. However, this idea would remain abstract as long as we were not getting to concrete examples and testing it. That's why the possibility of doing the project here was very attractive to us.

During that time, we often ended up talking about theater when we discussed the progress in urban production and design.

We quickly agreed that the professional urban design discourse left little room for negotiating what really interested us. In theater, by contrast, there had been new developments for a while that suggested a different understanding of city and space. Terms like "experts of the everyday," coined by the performance group Rimini Protokoll, or the idea that *city* can be relationally organized as a field for negotiation; that *city* can only then be epistemologically grasped—as a relational arrangement of actions. This led to the basic idea of collaborating with theater and performance groups in the context of our projects. Shortly afterward, we wanted to get in touch with the Kulturfabrik Kampnagel, an internationally acclaimed platform for the performance arts in Hamburg with many international connections and advanced forms of theater and performance in its program. At the time, Amelie Deuflhard had started to work as Kampnagel's intendant, so we were all new here. In Berlin, Amelie Deuflhard had supervised the Volkspalast project at the Palace of the Republic together with Sophiensäle and Matthias Lilental from the HAU.

The most notable historical reference for a coalition of architecture and theater was Cedric Price's famous Fun Palace of the 1960s. Unlike the protagonists of plug-in machines of the time, Price designed what one could call a machine for making learning experiences possible. Price did so while also accounting for—and this was radically new for modern architecture—the remaining life of the building. The Fun Palace was intended to have a life span of five years before being completely dismantled. Along these lines, the Fun Palace unfolded as a new form of research by specifically confronting architecture and theater in terms of the performative: over the course of ten years, the Fun Palace was part of extensive interdisciplinary cooperation; it never made it into construction. However, without the experiences of its contractor and initiator, theater director Joan Littlewood, the Fun Palace cannot be understood in full. It is action theater's performative experimental setups—which Littlewood had already practiced in the 1930s—and adapting them to a University of the Streets that made the concept of Price's plug-in machine concrete. The Fun Palace gave us the image that inspired and empowered us in our proceedings. At the same time, however, we all agreed that it would have to be more than a University of the Streets that delivers the conceptual and performative backdrop for Price's plug-in machine. The street that had been essential for certain reasons back in 1960—for the Smithsons, for example—was swapped for the neighborhood: a relational term, which we looked at in a multi-scale way from the very beginning.

Dominique Peck: So your starting point was the realization that you could no longer go through the archives of your own discipline and find what you needed in order to proceed further? What other people do you need to start a project like this? And what curricular frameworks are required in order to make something like this even possible?

Bernd Kniess: Confused by the results of the planning competition *Experiment auf der Insel*, which was meant to kick off all future project work, we soon realized that the project had already failed in a certain way in its early stages—not only because the conceptual scope of the task had not been grasped, but also because none of the proposed projects would have been feasible with the given financial resources. We thought the question had to be shifted in the direction of what task for a university could actually be set in this area around the Elbe islands. It must be said that the HCU had just been newly founded by merging individual faculties and departments from various universities. Everyday academic life suffered from organizational difficulties, weak connections, and little room for face-to-face communication. And now there was yet another location to be added. Thus, we first had to discuss what we wanted to do there, how that could be promoted through the architecture that was to be created, and conversely, how the architecture could be grounded in what we were doing. That was important, not least in order to counterbalance the aspects that argue against this additional and remote location with its possibilities. We thought: if this new university is committed to the built environment and metropolitan development and we are educating young people here whose future careers will be embedded in the professional fields of architecture and *city*, why should we then commission a *real* architect who will deliver a house that's vague in terms of its purpose, but "finished" in its form? Why shouldn't we give our students a derelict building that's supposed to be demolished in five years anyway to use as a tool and test setup from which to gain experience at a scale of 1:1? Who could, in addition to that, use their activities to elicit the initial uses of the building? We wanted an epistemically justified doubling: what kind of research results can we get about *city* if we keep both the usage and the construction contingent? The requirements for that were, however, to start the process differently than one normally would in conventional architecture and urban design projects. Not to start with a plan or objective for a finished object, but instead by actively interpreting step by step and by reactivating existing material. We wanted to achieve an interrelation between our own construction and design activity while reflecting on the space's possibilities, in order to induce the active redesign of the building. In doing so, we also wanted to find out what construction and design activity mean today.

The forced openness required an especially solid framework because of the different actors who were to be involved. On the one hand, it was those, as Christopher has already conveyed, who know the performative production of space extremely well: theater people who, like us, had the goal of reaching the "experts of the everyday" as those who know their immediate living environment incredibly well, an environment that was strange and new to us. And on the other hand, we needed people with the appropriate skills to bring the whole thing together and keep it moving; those who are able to shape the interfaces that turn up while managing the much-needed translation between various actors, something we also call diagrammatic practice. In other words, the first step for me was to find research assistants for the construction's project management and controlling.

Ben Becker: In August I came back from development work in West Africa, stepped off the plane and marched into Bernd's office in September. He told me about this project and its issues and explained to me that now it was about approaching the project without a definite program, and having amateurs technically modify the house. The program was to be developed from dealing with the neighborhood and with what was to be found there. It really reminded me of my work in West Africa. I thought it seemed exciting, so I happily entered the project. Nobody knew how to do it. How do you build such a house with students and amateurs from the neighborhood? You basically had to reinvent everything to launch an infrastructure that made construction even possible. Over the years we carefully approached the project and developed a sound structure that enabled us to permanently continue building the house.

Stefanie Gernert: I joined a bit later, in 2010. At the time I was also involved in teaching and research, so I was intrigued by the project, as it could lead me back to practical work. In the interview, Bernd described the project to me and it was the exact same problem I had already dealt with in my master's thesis on "counterspaces." But then, Ben took me aside at the end of the conversation and told me, "Just so you get the right picture, this is a really complex project and your part will be its coordination. There is so much to do, and you'll have to deal with it by yourself— so choose wisely."

I joined the team when the first construction phase was underway, and I first had to get an overview. Obviously, there was an administrative structure from the university. I needed to work my way into that and see which paths were predefined. And there was also the case with the construction site itself. It wasn't clear how to organize this form of work. In traditional project management, you deal with products or at least explicitly targeted results, and the goal is clear from the beginning. However, what we wanted to develop at the UoN was not foreseeable. So I had to check what was happening on site first and see what was needed, while figuring out what administrative work was even necessary to do and how to organize all that relationally. My top priority was, however, to get the budget for the construction site.

[see p. 398 – Materials]

Bernd Kniess: Here we can see an example of the project's structures: there are various constellations, essentially regarding mainly investors and their respective interests. Uli Hellweg, former executive director of the IBA GmbH Hamburg (2006–2015), was the initiator of the cooperation and the project. His goal was to win over the university as a partner for IBA's exhibition, and it made sense to look for that in the newly founded University of the Built Environment and Metropolitan Development. Then, IBA said they would provide us with a project budget of EUR 200,000, which should be sufficient to use as the project's foundation. Of course, this was linked to requirement that the partner contribute the corresponding co-financing funds.

With this initial step, IBA reached out to launch the project and start the process. The basis was an idle urban property with an unoccupied and dilapidated building on it. A competition was organized, prizes handed out, etc. Once that process was done, the first EUR 20,000 were spent. The remaining budget was EUR 180,000, which then served as the basis for calculating complementary funds that had to be paid from the HCU's budget and tuition fees. Upon closer examination, what had originally seemed to be the generosity of one of the partners, namely by advancing a budget out of their pocket, turned out to be an action based on the primary interest of initiating the project and committing the desired partner. Due to this approach, however, the project had EUR 40,000 less at its disposal. The base amount for the available budget was now EUR 540,000, a number that should have been doubled in the initial phase using the method mentioned at the start. You may ask why that is. Well, quite simply, because the rough calculation of funds needed for recommissioning and reconstructing the building was set at approximately 1,000 euros per square meter and, with the size of the existing building being around 500 square meters, this meant that the budget would have been used up by spending it on recommissioning and reconstruction alone.

Unfortunately, the application was unsuccessful. We were able to raise smaller amounts, for example, from the BBSR, for a research project called Jugendliche im Stadtquartier (Teenagers in an Urban Quarter), and from the Saga GWG and the redevelopment advisory council for the tree house workshops, as well as donations in kind, technical support and backing from our project sponsor Max Hofmann GmbH & Co. KG. Later, when the project had gained more visibility, Christian Roggenbuck at Max Hofmann established the connection to the Lawaetz Foundation. Consequently, the latter helped integration of the UoN within the Intereg 4B project SEEDS.

Thus, the application was well received and it was approved. We were able to use those financial means mainly for the final project stage, the hotel project in the IBA's presentation year, and for printing this book. That roughly sums up the project's financing as well as its institutional partners and supporters.

Stefanie Gernert: What made this project so complex were its many partners with their individual contracts. Each contract contained other options or a different guideline on how to spend the funds. They were not to be spent as we wished: the IBA's funds were to be spent only on building projects, the university's budget was not to be spent on individual salaries, etc. What might be of interest is the example of the contract and its interpretation: the financial administration of the city of Hamburg ceded the property to the university; the executive board drew up the contract and ordered the use of the property and the building, including all running charges, to be paid for from the project budget. Obviously, it was only a formulation in the contract for targets and services between the board and the project group that made the group aware of an issue. It was about snow removal, i.e. maintenance rights that the project group was now supposed to be responsible for. The consequences of this implementation quickly became clear, as well as the fact that using the budget to pay for the general overhead costs for five years wouldn't be possible. Then

there were minutes of a meeting stating that the university would pay these funds, because it is a university location, and that there would be a second budget dealing with the UoN's overhead, electricity, water, etc. There were continual meetings with internal and external partners.

Christopher Dell: You also had colleagues with whom you had curricular negotiations, for example. I remember how Ben Becker and I were at the introduction of the seminar on Intercultural Practice, a seminar that was attached to the Q-Studies–transdisciplinary studies. We had just transferred the Q-Studies format to the construction site. The reason for this format was to address all students, since building

internships interested only a few students, especially as most of them had already done that prior to studying.

How did those kinds of negotiations work? We had one problem, after all: we needed an "open" subject to implement in the curriculum, so that we could do hands-on work at the construction site. That sounds ironic, but the curricular structures were so rigid that we had a hard time implementing anything, really, that would make the site work continuously. We asked ourselves what we could do about it. At this point, we started looking at an important form of teaching that the HCU had taken up: the studium generale, here called Q-Studies. Their office in the former university building on Averhoffstrasse was in the same hallway as ours. It was only a stone's throw away, so we were on good terms. First, we noticed there was an open field (a curricular frame not yet fixed) that could possibly be used. Then we opted to propose a win-win strategy (while having coffee with the colleagues from the Q-Studies program) and said, "Here, we have something. We don't know what it will be yet, but it will be about concrete practical work, and we want to bring students from all degree programs together to practice on site what they are studying here." And then the

Q-Studies coordinator said, "Well, that's all fine and dandy, but what is there, apart from having a construction site, that would make students think outside the box or their discipline?" Our response was, "Well, then we'll do it like this. We'll call it 'Intercultural Practice.' I'll give my lectures on the site, and we will follow this procedure not only while building, but also while cooking." There is a photo of the moment when all events collided and even children showed up. We sat right at the center of the site, and I held a lecture on different questions about culture. This created the Lunch Lectures, where invited chefs cooked with students and gave lectures as well: the eating part had to be done anyway. We integrated all of this into the seminar and thus generated an overlap or hybridization of formats and contents, which at the same time made it possible to open up the process in the making.

Dominique Peck: This could lead to the question of how students actually earn their credits. Asked the other way around, what kind of students does the UoN project address?

Bernd Kniess: We're getting closer to the crucial point, regarding both content and organization: the structure and the relation it bears to the functional aspect of the project. There are always certain rules that are very apparent, as in whom to address, in which program, bachelor's, master's, on what level. On the other hand, the project's requirements have to be identified, and that's not always clear. When you bring both things together, you soon face challenges that generally come with inter- and transdisciplinarity. This may sound simple, but the more disciplines are involved, the more complicated it gets. This is already the case even with language barriers in the use of objects, their terms and meanings; a Tower of Babel all the way. One has no other possibility than to approach functional constellations through experimental setups. We pushed this all the way to a highly elaborate system that effectively represents a whole curriculum of its own, in which various offers of different levels, durations, and intervals are drawn up for various recipients. The crucial part was the project's diagrammatic reasoning, i.e. the careful designing of interfaces. One example that we'll discuss in more detail later is the Intercultural Practice (IKP) seminar series on tree houses. We offered IKPs for the master's programs in Architecture, Urban Design and Urban Planning, which is held once a week. Students prepare the whole project here. This overlaps with one IKP format from the Q-Studies for students from all bachelor's programs; they get together with master's students for the first time during project week to test prepared construction and material samples, to brainstorm on requirements for working with children, and to draft possible courses of action. After all, it's not just about planning and building; it's also about interacting with actors, in this case children. It's also about climbing, developing different constructions, acquiring material, playing, cooking, eating, etc. The master's students work on preparing a summer camp to be held in the week in which recess and summer holidays coincide. Here, students from the various IKP formats build tree houses with kids from neighboring schools and areas.

Christopher Dell: And there one sees, along with the organizational aspects, the nomenclature of what one signed up for, and with which this aspect creates an opening within the set of rules. Intercultural Practice offers a seminar that is formally more open-minded than the usual lecture. Ironically, this allows for many more specific tasks simultaneously. What helped us conceptually as well was the idea of material culture. While this idea had already been well formulated theoretically, we could now put it into use to frame a practice here. Because normally, you would never imagine that a seminar of intercultural practice would result in an actual built tree house project, conceived and realized in a university framing. This meant that there was this shift, which became possible through theoretical conception, and which we used extensively to then develop our plan more openly and consequently, and work more decidedly.

Bernd Kniess: Going back to the question regarding credit points (CP) once again, here we also find an economy where various forms of capital—I'm using this term in reference to Pierre Bourdieu's theory of capital—come into play. This play unfolds on the basis of credit points as a kind of time currency upon which all curricula and teaching formats are based. 1 CP equates to 30 hours; this exchange rate allows us to design the curriculum. We were able to decide how to plan and act with regard to certain circumstances: whether those hours were needed in total, regularly, each week, or at a stretch, and whether to require attendance or allow some degree of self-study.

Christopher Dell: There is something else to address about this kind of exchange, something Bernd mentioned earlier: common commissioning can't be done this way anymore. Now you no longer have a typical plan that you can use to set a certain process in motion and then to hire subcontractors. Everything is turned around. Now the strategy is to win over actors. In the case of credit points, this means that even though you have the credits, you have to get students to exchange them for something specific. That's why this book is called *Tom Paints the Fence*. It means that there is a constant win-win process in motion, which, however, requires the strategy to be open; in the end, you can't get someone to work with a closed strategy. In other words, social relations can only be established through a form of barter in which decisions can be made at the moment when things are being done.

Ben Becker: This exchange has expanded beyond the limits of assigning credits to students. After a certain point, we weren't building just with students, but also with teenagers from the area; not only because we needed helpers, but also because we wanted to include the urban district in the construction process. It was an educational initiative, Arbeit und Lernen Hamburg (ALH), that was supposed to further qualify young adults without an apprenticeship in the context of this measure. Due to this, we also tried to close this form of a deal with professional companies, whose expertise was essential for us. Our aim was to convince them to leave their journeymen at home and instead take young adults from the ALH to give them the opportunity to perhaps eventually find the "right" apprenticeship. So we tried to create an incentive and motivation, meaning it was more than just the credit points. You could say that this form of being able to prove yourself throughout the building process turned out to be a form of capital as well.

[see p. 402 – Materials]

Stefanie Gernert: Yes, the deal with Max Hoffmann was ultimately a special one. We couldn't offer a building internship, so they did it for us, and in turn we were able to offer that kind of placement at the UoN again.

Bernd Kniess: By taking over construction management, we were again Max Hoffmann's responsibility and had to make sure that the students took their internships seriously. It was, once again, Ben's challenge.

Christopher Dell: This relates to questions about the non-normative handling of normativity, which we discussed earlier in connection with structure. The fact that you continually face regulations, and then you try to figure out how they can be transformed into an enabling structure.

Dominique Peck: One last question about the first part. When looking at the website or the publishing information, next to Bernd Kniess and Christopher Dell, one also finds Michael Koch. How would you describe his role at the beginning of the project?

Christopher Dell: I would say this goes back to the thing about Max Hoffmann—if he puts a stamp on the building internship certificate, then he really gives you his trust. He trusts that everything is sound; he doesn't double-check. Technically, he's a mentor—he provides a certain kind of security. And Michael Koch played the same part, to a much greater extent. He was the protective hand that you need to even try to deal with regulations non-normatively.

Bernd Kniess: Michael was not just a mentor; he was with the project from day one. Surely he even cooked up the whole thing with Ulli Hellweg and perhaps even Jörn Walter. He essentially supported the competition and eventually made sure the project was handed to me once I started here. He trusted me to somehow manage it, in the same way that he trusted me on other levels, for instance in drafting the master's program. That was his idea, too. Of course, such trust doesn't come from nothing; several years ago we set up the master's program in Städtebau at the University of Wuppertal.

"In any case, practical men and women, in Keynes' view, have no choice but to rely on 'conventions, stories, rules of thumb, habits, traditions in forming our expectations and deciding how to act.'"[1]

1   John Maynard Keynes 1937, cited in Stephen Nelson and Peter Katzenstein, *Uncertainty and Risk and the Crisis of 2008* (San Diego: University of California-San Diego, 2010), 37f.

Dominique Peck: This is a thesis put forward by *International Organization* scholars Stephen Nelson and Peter Katzenstein, renewing the thinking of John Maynard Keynes, who in the mid-1930s was one of the first people to deal with the world's uncertain financial future. To edit this thesis, we chose the tree house workshops from the various projects at the UoN.

My question to Ben Becker: How do you build tree houses in the curricular context of a university?

[see p. 406 – Materials]

Ben Becker: While developing the project, you technically went ahead and proceeded by saying that a UFO didn't just land here and that instead, we were trying to connect existing questions, initiatives, and things, or to tackle whatever moved the citizens of that neighborhood. Around 2011, the focus was on reconstruction of the Rotenhäuser field, after the district said they wanted to redesign the park. They initiated a participatory process and commissioned a landscaping firm to take care of the planning. Another part of the proposed redesign was installing a climbing parkour at the Haus der Jugend. Of course, Sabine de Buhr from the IBA mentioned this and asked us whether we wanted to contribute to it. In the context of the IKP series, we (together with the students) agreed to take on the initiative, but we'd do it our way. In other words: we didn't commission some architecture firm or try to plan the parkour ourselves, but instead did it with the children there—the actual users. In a relatively liberal ad hoc planning process, we had to plan tree houses ourselves and actually build them afterwards. We wanted to use the opportunity to try out how participation can be practiced in a different way. So it wasn't about making something *for* the children; rather, we wanted to win them over as climbing experts for the planning process, work with them as equals, and learn from each other.

Dominique Peck: What were the challenges students had to face?

Ben Becker: The intention coming from the IKP series or the UoN's context in general really seemed to have been realized here— students having the opportunity to translate theoretical thoughts into concrete practice. To not just talk about it, but to really tackle the practical realization from the beginning, scour for potential, contact individual players such as the Haus der Jugend or the school at the Rotenhäuser Damm to get them on the project while convincing them of other approaches as well. To say we aren't building the sort of tree house that first comes to mind, made of wood, with a roof and a slide attached, but a completely different one. Perhaps one with fire hoses or materials that are reusable and recyclable. We also wanted to raise awareness about these topics throughout the district and, of course, challenge the children's imagination and detect creative potential. After all, that was the real challenge, because these were absolute no-budget projects. That means there was virtually no budget in the beginning. Students were not only asked to draft an organizational structure for the course of events; they also had to raise money, organize the material, implement it with the children and later convey it to the interested public and press as well. The practical aspect was the real challenge here. This wasn't something to be produced and then put in a drawer and forgotten. No. Sure, it's just a tree house, but it has to be functioning and in accordance with DIN, to perhaps one day turn into a TÜV-certified tree house. So it's about a real prototype, incorporating differentiated requirements, some of which may not make sense to classic architecture students at first—those who would rather design the next museum or a pianist's house overlooking a lake. Ultimately, generating something and believing in it in this specific situation with specific minimal parameters is, however, the bigger responsibility.

Christopher Dell: In terms of content, we related the IKP and the thesis stating that culture provides the framework for normative negotiations to Michel de Certeau: on the one hand, there are normativities in the form of legislative proposals that are determined and then applied. On the other hand, there is a field with negotiations open about what kind of law should be conceived and

passed in which context, and that is culture. That's how de Certeau defined it. We then said: okay, we'll now put this into practice. In this seminar. And then reflect on it in the field. That's why it's part of a student research project. And if Ben Becker says, yes, students have to learn how to realize minimal structures first, that's true. Then you would say: but that was what you do in the conventional planning process, too! Here, however, the whole thing is about doing something without knowing what it might become, and still designing organizational structures for it. In philosophy you'd say that's not a matter of reflexivity; you'd rather call it spontaneity, *adhocism*, or the like. And then you always end up back at planning vs. not planning. We found ourselves facing the very practical challenge to expand that thought, to overcome that dichotomy. We need to shape the openness, this acting in indeterminacy, in a reflective way.

Constanze Engelbrecht: You also created a multiplexity by putting students into special situations. The tree house projects in particular are good examples for demonstrating how students can suddenly become teachers. By working with the children, they stepped into a different role and entered a different mode of trying out and learning in a way that was only possible in the context of working with children. This low threshold enabled so much potential for easy development of the students' and children's creativity.

Philipp Löper: Of course, turning this construction site around like that is a great opportunity. Usually, products are defined in minute detail and then worked through, mostly on the other side and by people who have to do the job and then complain about this or that not being thought through. The Elbphilharmonie concert hall is a good example of a building process during which those in charge spent their time writing—instead of planning—because in this pre-planning phase, you just can't do everything right. If you leave the beaten path and say you'll take the profile of type A and not implement it the way the catalogue demands, you'll end up having discussions, worries and really only experience difficulties. This turning around of the planning process was such a great moment to give space to research and experimentation—to say you won't start with the finished product and somehow implement it, but rather develop the whole thing through the process. The children made it possible in these early phases—for instance, by trying out materials such as sails—to generate and take content from these attempts, which you could define with the children very well in a playful manner. That was the opportunity coming out of the process. That, and the motivation found in being in a situation where they could take matters into their own hands. It is also good fuel for the discussion of what the right or wrong decision is. This becomes redundant once you're responsible for the implementation with your colleagues, who give advice and their helping hands.

Christopher Dell: Yes, here one could also see the contrast to the pediatric apologists of the 1960s and the idealization of children's spontaneity, for example, with the Cobra artists' collective, with Asger Jorn and Constant, or the Smithsons with Nigel Henderson. The difference is that the Sixties tried to play off spontaneity against normativity. This isn't the same for the UoN; here, playing is part of the normative framework, which is itself basically being rewritten.

Ben Becker: Of course it's difficult that children arrive on site having a clear idea of what a tree house looks like. We always had them draw the tree house they wanted to have. Naturally, the wooden house with a roof and slide came up again and again; it's what they knew. That's the usual problem with traditional participation. Once the question of "What do you want?" is asked, you've already moved in the wrong direction, namely one of identitarian imaginations, fixed ideas. In other words: the result of this process is what you already know, and not what you don't yet know. The question is, how do you manage to involve children in a *structural* way and motivate them to feel free to make suggestions instead of delivering what they think is expected of them. To make suggestions that you can work with, without running the risk of ending up with the closed form. An open form doesn't mean it's without any form—the case is quite the opposite; you can't work without dealing with regulations according to building and planning laws, construction, etc. Basically, why does the house look the way it does, covered in securing straps and so on? In order not to spoil the children's fun by questioning their predetermined notion of a tree house, we tried to involve them in stories that we wanted to deduce new possibilities from. Thus, we tried to solve the issue on a didactic level. We said there are five characters who want to move to Wilhelmsburg and need tree houses. We only know their names and some of their preferences from their Facebook pages. We developed the individual characters with the children further in a kind of collage. Spider, for example, liked spiders, and when they mentioned spiderwebs, we knew the location's requirements. Next, the children took on the responsibility, as they had developed the building contractor's profile and his house themselves, something that worked well with the other materials and techniques. In the end, no child would have claimed that tree houses had to be this or that; instead, the fact that the tree house was a spiderweb, or a bird's nest, a lookout point, or something else, was as clear as day.

This brings me to another issue with this project: Of course, it's easy to say, "We're building with children," but children are different, for instance with regard to their attention span. They can't focus on anything for more than thirty minutes before needing a new challenge. Designing the work in a way that we could pause and then pick it up again at any time was something we experienced

in the beginning and learned to use in the subsequent phases. For instance, we tried to use only very simple techniques and set up special situations for them. The nest, for example, consisted of wooden triangles, which the children could screw together in the wood triangle workshop. Our aim was for them to learn how to do the work, while having the advantage that we could constantly alternate between teams; that way, we made sure there was always someone else in charge who held the children's attention. That's also how we split the stages of work into individual workshops. At the same time, we also played with them, cooked, ate, and experienced various other things, since it was also a summer camp—a place where you're supposed to have fun.

Christopher Dell: The story of the tree houses is a good example of how to describe the shift from form to structure. Typically, one only focused on the form: a tree house has to look like this or that. Children do this and adults, too. They set a form, which in turn should represent the content, and then this form is always reproduced, either exactly like the set form or with slight changes. But how can one let go of this teleological habit that always predicts the outcomes and therefore closes the process? How can one successfully switch to interpreting a project not as fixed form, but as a structural field that can be understood by perceiving it as elements with certain features, materiality, and qualities? These elements can then be reassembled in a new system and thus create a new form—in whatever way, but depending on the system it's always different.

Dominique Peck: How is that being translated into academic activities?

Bernd Kniess: I would say that starting with the form doesn't work that well anymore—with exceptions such as maybe in the Elbphilharmonie—even though the project, as Jacques Herzog admitted while talking to Olaf Scholz, has brought all participants to the verge of what's possible. That's something we've also seen with the Experiment auf der Insel; initiating the inevitably linear development doesn't work, because once all the funds have been spent, you'll end up asking yourself, "What are we going to do now?" Christopher just emphasized the form and contrasted it with structure. If it's not only about the form but about structure as well, then you have to design the process that can bring forth a form. That means the open form as the basis for the work process can naturally take on various forms: a building

or even a scientific paper. The requirement for both is having the relevant material available—or making it available—and the program that's being generated inspired by a motive and a question. Other kinds of evidence, for instance a list of indicators for assessing the level of quality in teaching and research, are not generated—there's just no time for that.

Of course you're constantly tensed up throughout a five-year process like this. It's not like we started something and then it continued by itself. We are right in the heart of it, and in small teams in particular, everyone in his or her respective role is invaluable. It's a game, and the invariable question is: What happens next? The process needs to be shaped, and shaping it is work. Course assessments can only be handled when they are absolutely necessary for maintaining operations, such as, for example, biannual statements of accounts to the UoN's advisory board ensure that needed funds are still available.

Thus, what we are doing in *Tom Paints the Fence* is to continue what has been characteristic of the whole project: not to talk about it, but to come together again according to its own logic, like we're doing now, to reorganize the material and give it its (book) form.

Christopher Dell:
That's basically what is being created beyond practice and what's supposed to become adaptable or pluggable. This isn't accessible through the concept of representation anymore, when a referent is displayed figuratively, but rather through the concept of a trace. Something is being traced here in order to be developed further, to be rewritten. Within the building, the trace for example could be the structure of the use for now: What is and was here? What is and was possible? A dormitory or public health office? What kind of building structure is there that you could continue using qualitatively? This questioning aims at revealing the trace's character. Plus, everything that emerges throughout the project as a representation is, after all, a trace, something that calls for being developed further, rather than being offered as closed form—the technical term for such a representation is called diagrammatic reasoning. This term was mentioned earlier in the context of the project's structure of action. The interpretation, the representation, and the action can be organized diagrammatically. Each category serves as its own respective forms and questions.

Dominique Peck:
Thank you, Christopher. Ben, what does such a procedure, such a practice, look like when dealing with extremely scant resources?

Ben Becker: Most people, when they hear the term "low budget," associate it with deficiency, for example, of money. But there is more to it. This deficiency also implies a potential, perhaps because it forces us to think differently and leads us to organize things differently. At Lacaton & Vassal that means: use standards, but don't think standard. And then, as soon as you've analyzed the possible materials available to work with, it's actually astounding—the tree house example shows this very well—to see how easily and fast you can get the materials. So, if I think about the sustainability of a project that will be demolished in five years, I really can't think about anything but low budget! What good does it do to spend 500,000 euros on a shack if I knock it down five years later?

Bernd Kniess: That's why that topic was embedded in the project, while we're developing different strategies and tactics for handling it constructively.

Christopher Dell: Yes, and by using these strategies and tactics, we understand the knowledge that's inside the building. This strategy is essential for our understanding of design. Take, for instance, the term "enabling architecture." I just want to give you a short definition: it's basically the second-order production of space. In other words, the production of space that enables the production of more space. What we realized throughout the work—and this also relates to us dealing with a university project here—is that the same applies to the production of knowledge. In other words: we need knowledge production that enables knowledge production, i.e. one that is of second order. However, this also means that this knowledge has to reveal itself in its making. This is what we, when starting the project, called "performative," and that's exactly what it was! Such a conceptual framing is also linked to science in the making as well as the Arts and Crafts movement, with workshops, learning by doing, and so on. After

all, historian of science Hans Jörg Rheinberger says, "We have to completely change the way we're looking at experiments. We can't continue the teleological story of 'problem identified, solution and experiment done'." We need to interpret all traces of experimental systems once again. All in all, this was part of the UoN from the beginning: interpreting your own traces differently, not by trying to reach the finished plan or by starting from there—you see, we didn't have one at all.

Dominique Peck: Stefanie, what did that mean for your responsibility in project management?

Stefanie Gernert: Principally, it was about making the site flexible, which meant we didn't reinvent the processes; we just restructured them. The screw, for example: when students wanted to buy something for the site, they

couldn't just take cash to the hardware store and shop there. You can't do that in public service. So we made a deal with the administration: there has to be an option for when we can't pay cash for something, to use something that works similar to cash. I won't describe the whole administrative process we had to go through to get a VOL voucher worth fifty or a hundred euros to make it possible to shop at the hardware store. This doesn't mean the difference would have been paid out, but the real invoice amount, which was below the voucher's face value, was deducted by administration as procurement … right?

[see p. 400 – Materials]

Bernd Kniess: What does VOL mean?

Ben Becker: *Vergabe- und Vertragsordnung für Leistungen* (Conditions Concerning Contracts for Supplies and Services). They regulate the tendering and placing of orders within the public sector.

Stefanie Gernert: The VOL voucher was our payment method in the hardware store, which was a contractual partner meeting the requirements of public procurement law.

I still had to go through the administration, but the result wasn't the screw itself, but the voucher for the screw. The consequence for Ben was namely that he didn't have to wait for the whole purchasing process to be over. The whole thing was actually checked again in a third step: Are the funds even there? Okay, they're there, now you can do this. That's when the VOL voucher was handed out and the order was placed, which didn't mean, however, that the screw was already on its way to the construction site. Ben and the students could use the VOL voucher to act directly. The whole procedure still existed, but it was separated from the actual process of buying.

Ben Becker: That's true, because the system that's really clear on this diagram wasn't there at the beginning of the project. When we started in 2008, there was nothing there; I couldn't abide by the rules that have been defined here. A conversation when shopping went something like this: "Yes, you can buy a screw, but only from one of our contractual partners." Then the question, "Where is the next contractual partner or hardware store in Hamburg?" "There is one in Altona." Which means I have a site in Wilhelmsburg and would like to buy an urgently needed screw, but I have to drive to Altona to buy the screw! It became clear that this wouldn't work. Completely hopeless; it drove you mad. Throughout this complicated situation, the administration slowly found an approach. There was someone who said, "Look, a VOL voucher, yes, but it's actually crazy: everything has to be accounted for. This means you're allowed to shop with the VOL voucher—screws, dowels, etc.—but you have to write down why you bought screws and dowels." Then Manuel sat down and listed a purchase of, let's say, two hundred euros, with—I don't know—85 items, and added a written explanation for each item.

We handed the list in, and of course, the whole thing exploded. This meant that it wasn't just us having to sit down and write explanations, but the administration had to read, evaluate, and check over the whole thing. Then they said, "Okay, this doesn't work." Only then did the whole situation calm down. I still remember them saying at first, "But this is totally illegal!"

Stefanie Gernert: Absolutely. But it should be heard. I can even remember appearing before the executive board to discuss this issue. It went all the way to the top.

Dominique Peck: This also illustrates very well how you have to change administrative processes in order to improvise on site. Unlike what's commonly believed, improvisation really has something to do with the administration; you just can't use the normative non-normatively. Is that something the administration can learn, too?

Constanze Engelbrecht: It definitely can. I'll go into some detail now. When you listen to the content of the last one and a half or two hours, you really have to ask yourself how management science got the idea to research projects separate from their context.

After all, new forms of organization were taken from their context at first, i.e. analyzed as isolated phenomena without any historical, social, or spatial dimension and independent of future perspectives. Only in the last ten or fifteen years has there been a growing number of scientists who include the context in their perspective and study organizational forms in light of this. One reason could be that there is an increased focus on temporary organizations that are in constant contact with their context. And that would be an example of needing this interface, in order to encourage creativity on site and to translate the content into an institutional structure. This may not necessarily create new structures, but it recombines certain paths to create shortcuts. The project's goal and framework should always be observed against this background. We have to include the future perspective, too. Many people take new routes, and as the temporary organizational form of a project always has its time limit, you constantly run the risk of losing knowledge that was acquired there. It's the sword of Damocles hanging over the people in charge who have to deal with it. You had to shape this situation constructively, too, just as we are doing sitting here today. The relevant aspect of projects like the UoN is the handling of the multiplexity—forms of relations within a network that are at the same time different from one another—of a project's organization. This can be examined with the concept of a project ecology: it's always denser and more extensive than it may seem in the beginning, especially due to the gathering of various organizational forms and partners. In your case it's children from the neighborhood or the EU funding program. Here, much bigger networks open up, which might not be chiefly spatial or don't even have any spatial focus. That's why I think, especially from a researcher's point of view, that it's an incredibly exciting example for urban forms of knowledge production.

Let me relate that to your tree house project again, the way it's hanging on the wall here. What seems to be characteristic of the UoN's project ecology is that it's technically open to welcoming new forms of knowledge, the possibility of incorporating new kinds of knowledge: children, restaurant proprietors, chefs—the initial roles are always temporary. Afterwards, of course, you also bring people into the project who are far removed from my field as a geographer or yours as architects on a disciplinary, cultural, and thus cognitive level. This means you took the chance that the innovation potential that comes into the project through new forms of knowledge would disappear because you could not find common ground.

Bernd Kniess: May I follow up on that? If you talk about uncertainties that we accepted with our eyes open, how do you evaluate the way this is being treated—by both us and by the students? Because technically, it's not like anybody really likes uncertainties?

Constanze Engelbrecht: Yes, sure!

Bernd Kniess: How does one navigate this? How did you perceive that?

Constanze Engelbrecht: On the one hand, I firmly believe that you really did have people on your team who managed to translate the requirements and balance risks in certain moments. That would be a very important aspect from my point of view. And then of course the question: How do you plan with uncertainties? You may be able to reflect on that in hindsight, but in the situation, however, many decisions are being made in the course of action—they *happen* in practice. And later on you realize, "Oh, we really just took the chance there. Can we still fix this somehow?" But yes, I believe you often don't even know that you're on shaky ground.

Bernd Kniess: In a way, you do try to work with safety nets. But you're not always sure if you have the correct mesh size.

Christopher Dell: Indeed, to consciously and critically be affirmative about indeterminacy was a conceptional program when we entered the project. It wasn't like we went along saying we had to improvise because everything went wrong once again. It was rather already a realization to say that indeterminacy needs a new connotation. When urban planning came into existence as a scientific discipline at the end of the 19th century, there was the general notion of wanting to eliminate indeterminacy. At the beginning of the twentieth century, the general idea behind this was to turn the city into a factory that functioned like a machine for living, working, and dwelling. Today one has to say: the industrial phase in its seemingly neat and homogenic order is over; we are in the middle of a new phase which Henri Lefebvre calls "urban."[2] And this phase involves a sort of clashing complexity. The plan comes too late in most cases.

However, this does not mean increasing the informal at all, like people did in the Sixties, when they considered *city* to be an adventure playground. Viewed historically, this only resulted in a backlash, namely the postmodern era's formalism. Thus, we asked how we could tackle indeterminacy differently, namely by analyzing urban situations in their components, the way they are, and according to their potentialities. Of course, this doesn't mean going after a form of traditionalism that claims everything is already there; nothing else would be transformed this way. Instead, we said we want to take what exists seriously as such and handle it very carefully—something that greatly slows down the planning process. The UoN is thus as slow as a snail, but it has to be that way in order to even notice the potential of existing structures. And so that's exactly what Bernd says: once we're done with the process, we really have something that we can build and act with, but there is no indeterminacy we have to deny. Because indeterminacy is what we see everywhere: migration, demographic change, economic shifts. The only way forward is to accept indeterminacy and try to turn it into a resource. I call this improvisation technology. Nevertheless, this is the opposite of a neoliberalism that sets subjects free while simultaneously reducing them to a closed-form commodity.

Bernd Kniess: So constructively handling indeterminacy is about a way in which material and structural elements are removed from situations and acquired so that they can be used for understanding new courses of action.

Getting back to the tree house: In the first year, we not only realized that there are building requirements we have to stick to, but also DIN standards. However, we were unable to tackle this new challenge while the summer camp was already running, so we had to save the issue for later. The following question became clear: What requirements are in place for a tree house that will be permanently installed in the public space? We explored them and their components to get an understanding of their possibilities with regard to the project ecology. Simultaneously, we tested prototypes on private properties to check whether or not they had acquired maturity for public use. That way, we often worked on various levels simultaneously, to analyze what we encountered in its components and causal networks, in order to bring it into a new form by pointedly influencing individual parameters.

2   Henri Lefebvre, *The Urban Revolution* (Minneapolis: University of Minnesota Press, 2003).

Christopher Dell: And that's how things like the voucher come into existence. It's not just a passive mediator between communication ideologies, but an effective mediator. You could call it an open actant that enables space for action. This actant has three potencies: first, it authorizes: I can go shopping. Second, it allows. Namely, it allows us to buy various things, but—and that's the third aspect—it also obligates. I can't mess with it. There is a benefit of the doubt that I have to honor, too.

Bernd Kniess: I agree, but let's get back to the project ecology again. You're saying that theory always lags behind. Yes, it has to; I've gained this knowledge from research. The object of research lies in the past.

Constanze Engelbrecht: Of course!

Bernd Kniess: The planner's designing process differs only because it tries to anticipate the future. The aim is to make the future as imaginable as possible. Keeping up the classical separation of research and planning doesn't make any sense from today's point of view. This separation wasn't originally considered as an opposite, but in terms of its complementarity. Why should planners refrain from available knowledge? Why should researchers refrain from options to cognitively anticipate possible developments? The experimental setup is the connection of both, as it brings together different bodies of knowledge and methods of disciplines dealing with *city*—on a researching and designing perspective and in a scientific manner. Of course, this is a challenge for both researching and designing disciplines, in

which such an undertaking can only be understood as contamination of their own approach at first; however, it's only an attempt to bring together the mind and the hand again, to make necessary synergies possible by reconnecting two potentialities.

Christopher Dell: This connection between nomothetic and idiographic theory assumes a new connection between text and image, similar to how it is arranged in the form of expression in diagrammatic reasoning. And there is another paradox. In architectural design, you tend to refrain from looking at the past, but at the same time, you cover up the future while progressing in your design. I dare to say that at the UoN, the terror of creativity has been shelved. The claim to innovation is virtually zero. Technically, the goal is to say that we'll work with what we have, with what has been developed and its set of conditions. All we do is read what is there, in its processual development, in order to understand and reassemble it with regard to inherent potentialities. This means adjusting the lens with which you look at things, to make it possible to interpret what has become or has been designed or, in Lefebvre's terms, to read it as something produced and connect it with its own vector. However, this vector—we also call it motive—may also emerge from dealing with what has become, while it can be enhanced and intensified. Again, we have the transition from form to structure: the motive serves as a structure that allows you to take a position, with which you can move within the open process. This means that creativity is a) not *ex nihilo*, and b) not a predetermined, fixed, or identitarian form that you project into the future and in so doing complete every process; instead it's formal and more functionally open as well as filled with structure.

Bernd Kniess: That's always the topic of discussion: Why are student projects, especially the urban design projects—if they're about research and design—so research-oriented? Why do they lack that little push to design, to draft something? It's obvious, because architectural or urbanist designs are usually conveyed by representing an object or structure that is an object in its composition as well. This generally happens with a three-dimensionally animated image, the rendering, and video as well lately. And if we are to say, "Okay, we'll transfer the object into the structure now, because it's what interests us"—then the result of this transfer can't be in the image again. Structure is revealed in catalogues, lists, diagrams, images, films, textual descriptions, etc., and also in its relational connection as diagrammatic reasoning. You can potentially derive explicit scenarios, forms, or options for action from newly gathered material. Still, it's clear that reading, identifying, and producing structures claims its own right; the same goes for the rights of form and function. And that's part of this developmental work that we've gotten ourselves into here.

Philipp Löper: That's a very slow process. Trying something out would have been unthinkable considering the pressure that people in charge of the project at the Elbphilharmonie were under. Improvisation was only possible once something went wrong.

Bernd Kniess: That's the rule, and that's why we need the experiment to test different approaches. Demonstrating the urban in its causal network is not just extremely difficult; it's also impossible. How do you even want to get your hands on it out there? Really, what do you want to get and how do you want to convey it? That's exactly the exercise that work in UD is based on and what we practice in our UoN lab. You can't catch hold of the urban totality; we can only describe what's given in terms of what's special about its phenomena and thus explore what has come into existence historically, in order to understand what it will become. And the task is to figure out and determine what's *right* about the whole thing. Well, yes, and that's why it takes us so incredibly long to practice that and to develop a certain precision while doing so.

Plus, once we have this underlying structure, catalogues, lists, the diagrammatic approach, it's easy to gather things and arrange them in a new way. It's not only this one form that emerges from the process anymore; it's countless forms that are part of this structural matrix. The diagram's structure is the result. And that isn't conveyed by an image.

Christopher Dell: The challenge now is to outline this. It is exactly with the shift towards the research on *city* that new representations and images emerge, attempting to prevent the representational from closing up. But we're all new to this. So what Bernd is saying is more of a task for the future.

To get back to the topic of creativity, especially when someone asked during the UD's interim presentation, "What about the design?"—the fact that students desperately wanted to design something new is what made them so nervous, even before the analysis was developed enough. That's why self-discipline is essential: having the discipline to allow an open analysis and to wait for things to appear.

Bernd Kniess: Yes, and maybe to check your own understanding of design as well. What results from these kinds of processes are not the images or plans anymore; instead, it's the books. The structure they are based on is designed; it proceeds from a methodology that is designed; the

motive is the result of a design process; and finally, the preparation of the results of the research, their process and synthesis, is designed. The book in its form is a result of design, and perhaps that's a new understanding of design; you can't interpret or recognize it as such while you're actively executing it.

Christopher Dell: I remember asking the students, "Where is all the scribbling, the notations, everything you've worked on during the whole process?" and they replied, "At some point we thought this was the best solution and then we focused on it, so we didn't pursue the other ideas." They really didn't document nor file the material. It was impossible to go back to a given point and pursue it. But that's exactly what matters: the research itself becomes the design in the way it is archived and diagrammatically made accessible for future work! To me, Cedric Price epitomizes that, to mention him again. He was the first to really sit through it. He spent ten years researching how to further develop the project in terms of archiving and notation.

Dominique Peck: Now for the third part of this Roundtable Redesign. I'll quickly read out the thesis, because the content is derived from the first two parts:

The coming society lies beyond the extended discussion of issues.

The term "issues" shows up in the context of Lucius Burckhardt, economist and creator of strollology, who promoted a new understanding of time, aesthetics, movement, and sociality throughout his lifetime. The term "issues" can also be found in Bruno Latour's *Parlament der Dinge* (translated into English as *Politics of Nature*). Both approaches have one thing in common, namely the search for an option to depict situations as problematic in a surprising and thus open form, in order to get other actors to take action. What depictions or forms of representation did you work with at the UoN?

Ben Pohl: Let's go back to the tree houses: sometimes, the children got to a point of frustration, because the result was not what they had expected. The question was how to use expectations differently, and just like that, the question was turned into play. We had briefly talked about what these books were during the first Roundtable, and a moment during Tabea's book presentation now comes to mind when Jan Wenzel called it an extroverted book that intentionally wanted to reach the outside world and wasn't only produced for the university alone. Who is the reader? Whom are you addressing? Maybe we'll determine this now with the tree house reports. Whom are they addressing?

Ben Becker: Throughout the tree house project it became clear how, for instance, the district office Hamburg-Mitte was changed by our approach and suddenly started attaching a different meaning to it. When we came upon this EN 1176 issue, we had a tough time with the people in charge, trying to prevent them from breaking up the whole summer camp. But then they saw how the children identified with what they had built themselves. That was a gradual process that eventually resulted in them calling us and asking, "Could you please come here? We have another meeting about the climbing parkour. Don't you want to continue your tree house project and get involved?" I believe, and I speak from own experiences, actors in politics or the administration would be possible readers. People who have responsibility and deal with the public space every day and perhaps do so way too schematically. They can use the documentation to realign their thinking and possibly even identify alternatives in it.

Bernd Kniess: Sure, in the case of Tabea Michalis' book[3] or the book series *Everyday Urban Design*, a certain boundary is crossed. University projects find broader interest among the public. In most cases, however, what remains is still the inward process. Only universities offer protected space to make projects like this. Further, it's also about making the process reflexive, which means envisioning project development in the group and understanding it once again. That's why these documentations are necessary for the time being.

Ben Becker: Absolutely! Because those moments when you experience a strong urge for action severely define the process, which is an important task to find modes in which actors become aware of the way they are making something while they're making it.

3   Tabea Michaelis, *Showtime Wilhelmsburg: A Randonnée of Possibilities* (Leipzig: Spector Books, 2015).

Bernd Kniess: And that's the structure that practice is based on.

Christopher Dell: Yes, and that's exactly why the concept of project development is rewritten here, and development is not considered something teleological. Usually, a project means having a goal as form and then implementing that form; a very good project developer then shows up and does the job. At the UoN, however, we're dealing with meta-goals: the goal is created within a target range while products are created out of the making. This making comprises knowledge that would normally remain enclosed, because you don't deem it relevant, just because it wasn't based on any plan. In other words: the process can't become part of knowledge without a predetermined *telos*. Here, however, it's the other way round, and the supposed lack of a plan is reinterpreted as a resource. Action then has to be documented in an epistemological sense, and those documentations then become part of the knowledge archive of the project again.

Ben Pohl: The books that we made throughout the UD studies, especially in the first two semesters, were absolutely essential to always understanding that as a basis for our own actions. We used them again and again; we took them out to look at our own stuff. What did we do there again? What were we thinking and writing? And most notably, how did we do it? Go back to that point and ask, "Is this still valid, or do you have to turn it around?" Or, "How can we pursue this thread further?" Nobody ever said, "Okay, now it's done and we're going to do something completely different. I'll deal with that." It was always about questions that arose on one level and using them again on the next. Whether with completely different levels of measurement or with another focus, it was really always about a concatenation or movement.

Christopher Dell: Yes, in this respect, the meaning of a book or a theory changes in its mediating function: from form to structure. It is not a completed report, no complete theory that explains this fixed problem. Instead, it's understood as a structural field that allows me to go along with a range of actions and to approach it differently again by gathering these structures, by intervening and representing.

Constanze Engelbrecht: Technically, that's similar to the workings of the Chicago School in the 1930s, whether you compare it consciously or subconsciously. You have been researching on site for a while and have thus created an insanely broad spectrum of student work. Even though people was probably often thought, "Oh, Wilhelmsburg! I would like to take up a different topic!" That already creates a depth that you would normally not achieve in five or six months at all, let alone get access to a field. And even though I wasn't able to witness all of the tree house project, I can relate to the context very well: you are in a place and you see that the children visiting the site are not those of rich parents on vacation. You cooperate with schools and are in direct contact with the parents, who enjoy letting their children participate in this project because they can't take them on vacation. Acquiring the depth of this topic is perhaps what accounts for the Takes' form of teaching.

Christopher Dell: Absolutely. You're not the researcher anymore, who's researching his topics the way the Chicago School discovered a new continent, namely the city. They entered it as inconspicuously as possible—observing the city's natives through a hole in their newspaper—which was very important. But at the UoN, everything was very relaxed: you are the subject matter yourself. We're neither community center nor an ethnological endeavor but a university. We arrived like a UFO and have to wrap our heads around what's here. That's why it's a form of teaching, because I have to justify what I am doing here, why I'm doing it and how. This reflexive factor was very crucial for letting go of the field ideology.

Ben Pohl: Besides, it resolves this dichotomy of research and design, namely because in this situation you're naturally designing while researching already. Even if you say, "I'm doing a little bit of research," I design the situation in a way that allows me to communicate with people to show them that this is the direction I want to go in.

Christopher Dell: The intervention here always comes from a desire to also produce representations. And vice versa: ensuring that representations allow for new interventions. The artistic intervention is replaced by the scientific one, while the pedagogical aspect is moved to the background.

Bernd Kniess: But that's nothing new, of course. There are approaches in terms of designing and researching, and that's what cognitive processes are based on.

Christopher Dell: True, but let's get back to the concept of design. Because a lot of what is going on at Research by Design is research for or on design. It has nothing to do with what Ben described. Thus, design is being turned into a different way of making, one that is at times not even recognizable as design.

Dominique Peck: What do you mean by saying the pedagogical aspect was moved to the background?

Christopher Dell: What I mean is that this endless "reaching people where they happen to be" only ever results in people always staying where they are. There is none of that here. It's just an open field, and you can participate if you follow your own interests or motives. After all, that's what *Tom Paints the Fence* is about. You give yourself up to it, or you simply don't. One might say it's like a form of potlatch. And then you wait and see what happens, what forces of attraction are at work.

For instance, the kitchen. Aside from the kitchen block itself, nothing was there in the beginning. Not only was a pot missing; everything was missing. We could have organized a competition in the neighborhood and people could have wished for certain Ikea products to be put in the kitchen. That would be "reaching people," not where they happen to be, but where you think they happen to be—and where they shop. But what Ton Matton contributed was a completely different approach. You contributed yourself. When you had tomato seedlings, you just offered them, looked around the neighborhood and swapped them for remaining dishes and cutlery. And that right there is a complete turnaround.

Bernd Kniess: If it's about which actors deal with indeterminacy throughout a process, then we're also talking about the question that Philipp experienced in the Elbphilharmonie megaproject as well. We know from the media that there had been countless conflicts. How can actors in complex situations learn from processes and restructure them accordingly?

Philipp Löper: Those are gridlocked situations. Someone makes an accusation, which the other party then has to debunk legally without allowing any additional accusations. In doing so, you always proceed by thinking of compromises as defeat, because it's not about the actual matter anymore. It's incredibly hard to begin to understand these processes.

Christopher Dell: Compared to that, the UoN is of course on a small scale. But when thinking about the curriculum, the embedded architects and urban planners can practice learning about processes, in order to scale up the method afterwards. And that should happen at the same time: the disciplinary part as well as learning how to read processes.

Stefanie Gernert: Perhaps another aspect from project coordination: at the very beginning, we often sat together and determined a lot of things in advance, because there wasn't too much on site and not much that could happen as yet. Gradually, this support for project coordination should be passed on to someone else, through processes happening on site, which then—more or less—would take over these matters automatically. However, because you lived there and took on tasks, those of mine should be eliminated, reduced or at least decreased or transferred, so that there can be more free space for other processes. Project coordination probably has to surrender more to the process than actually happens in the project itself. But still, there have always been meetings where we said, "Now things are getting a little out of hand." That means you had to step in, intervene, and see that there was a need for more coordination. Maybe there is some aspect of that that you can be mindful of.

Christopher Dell: But there is no fixed target. Instead, there's a target range through which you move, and that opens up like a diagrammatic field. Without a strategy, this field overwhelms you, because you get too many options. And then you need people who are able to read that and make connections.

Ben Pohl: Nevertheless, the danger remains that in such processes, because it's incredibly strenuous to work like that, people try to shorten or fixate the range, keeping it small, since they just doesn't have the energy anymore.

Bernd Kniess: This cross-connection, however, always creates interest at a higher level to which you then readjust.

Christopher Dell: At this point, two levels merge. For one thing, you eventually run out of energy, so you have others in your collective who can step in as a corrective. But for another, you're not really able to justify the money's origins, why you're doing what you're doing, and why it's important to practice improvisation as technology and so on. That way, you end up realizing in hindsight that you have and have had way too few resources, because the work is not being appreciated enough. But that's of course a political battle, happening everywhere. Legitimizing the pay: research as a product and as part of this teaching.

Round Table
Redesign:
What is Urban Design
to Do in an Age
on Uncertainty?

MATERIALS

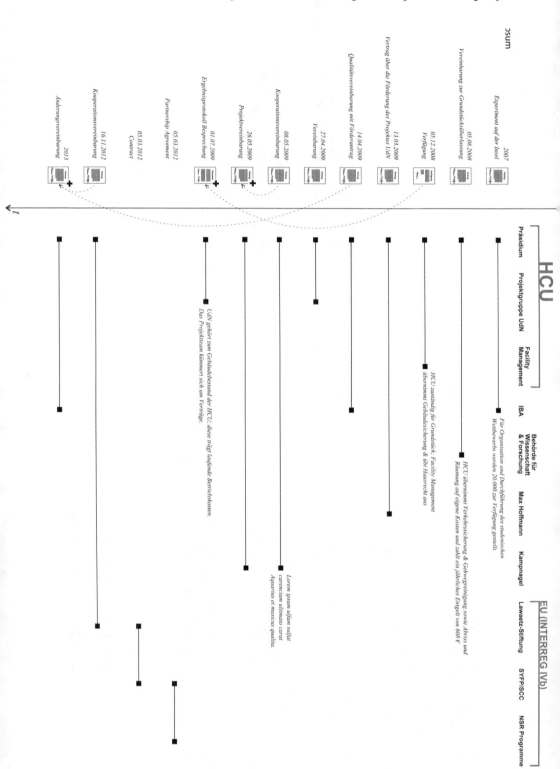

Diagrams by Jakob Kempe and Yannik Hake

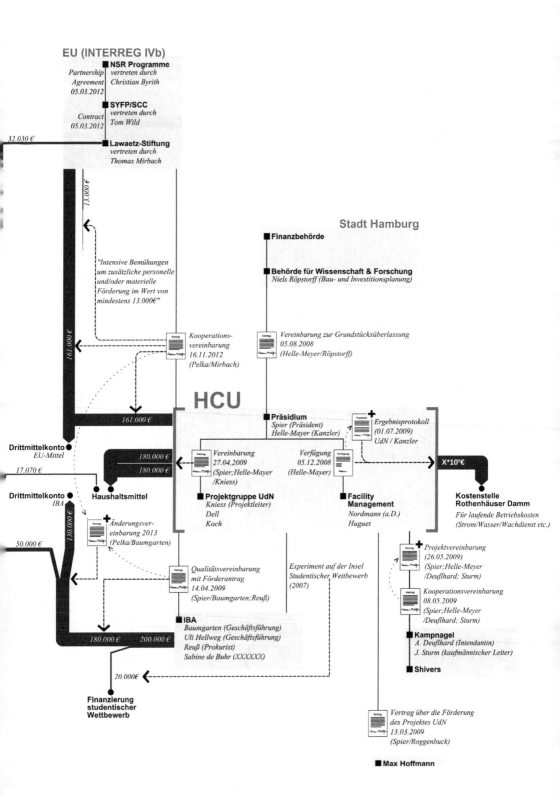

EU (INTERREG IVb)

■ **NSR Programme**
vertreten durch
Christian Byrith

Partnership Agreement 05.03.2012

■ **SYFP/SCC**
vertreten durch
Tom Wild

Contract 05.03.2012

32.030 €

■ **Lawaetz-Stiftung**
vertreten durch
Thomas Mirbach

13.000 €

"Intensive Bemühungen um zusätzliche personelle und/oder materielle Förderung im Wert von mindestens 13.000€"

161.000 €

Stadt Hamburg

■ **Finanzbehörde**

■ **Behörde für Wissenschaft & Forschung**
Niels Röpstorff (Bau- und Investitionsplanung)

Kooperations-vereinbarung 16.11.2012 (Pelka/Mirbach)

Vereinbarung zur Grundstücksüberlassung 05.08.2008 (Helle-Meyer/Röpstorff)

HCU

161.000 €

■ **Präsidium**
Spier (Präsident)
Helle-Mayer (Kanzler)

+ *Ergebnisprotokoll (01.07.2009) UdN / Kanzler*

Drittmittelkonto ●
EU-Mittel

17.070 €

180.000 €
180.000 €

Vereinbarung 27.04.2009 (Spier;Helle-Mayer /Kniess)

Verfügung 05.12.2008 (Helle-Mayer)

*X*10⁵€*

Drittmittelkonto ●
IBA

Haushaltsmittel

■ **Projektgruppe UdN**
Kniess (Projektleiter)
Dell
Koch

■ **Facility Management**
Nordmann (a.D.)
Huguet

Kostenstelle Rothenhäuser Damm
Für laufende Betriebskosten (Strom/Wasser/Wachdienst etc.)

50.000 €

130.000 €

+ *Änderungsver-einbarung 2013 (Pelka/Baumgarten)*

Qualitätsvereinbarung mit Förderantrag 14.04.2009 (Spier/Baumgarten;Reuß)

Experiment auf der Insel Studentischer Wettbewerb (2007)

+ *Projektvereinbarung (26.05.2009) (Spier;Helle-Meyer /Deuflhard; Sturm)*

Kooperationsvereinbarung 08.05.2009 (Spier;Helle-Meyer /Deuflhard; Sturm)

■ **IBA**
Baumgarten (Geschäftsführung)
Uli Hellweg (Geschäftsführung)
Reuß (Prokurist)
Sabine de Buhr (XXXXXX)

■ **Kampnagel**
A. Deuflhard (Intendantin)
J. Sturm (kaufmännischer Leiter)

■ **Shivers**

180.000 €   *200.000 €*

20.000€

Finanzierung studentischer Wettbewerb

Vertrag über die Förderung des Projektes UdN 13.03.2009 (Spier/Roggenbuck)

■ **Max Hoffmann**

Der Weg bis zur Schraube

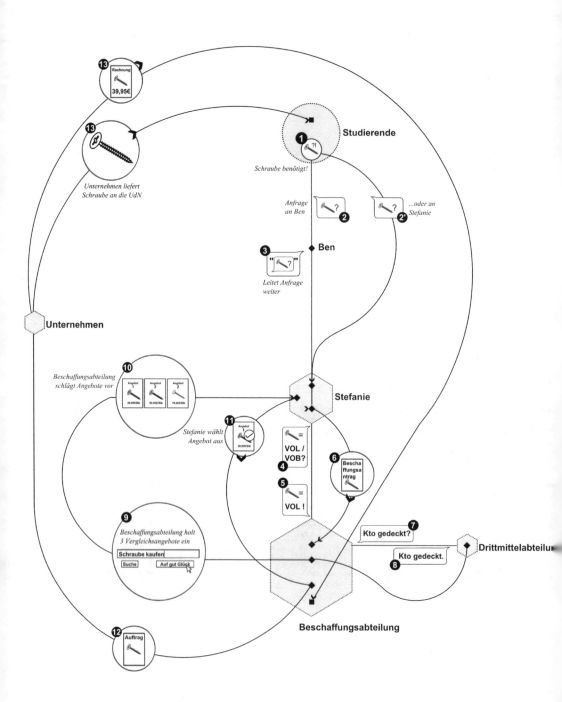

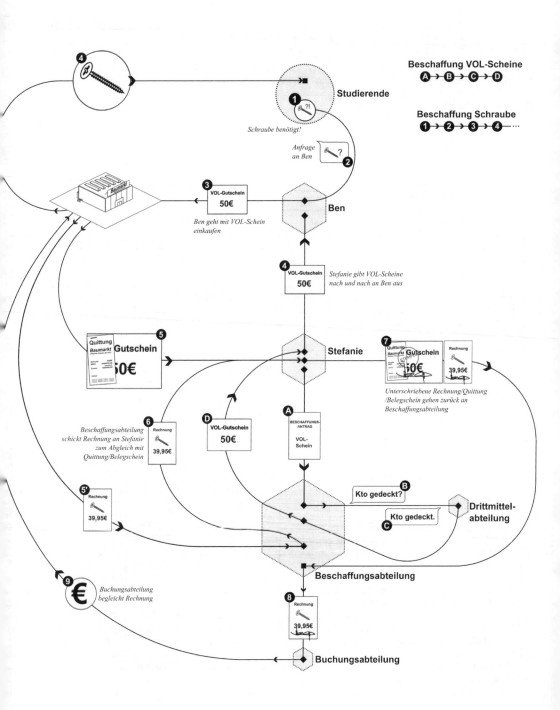

Die Abkürzung zur Schraube

Beschaffung VOL-Scheine
Ⓐ ➤ Ⓑ ➤ Ⓒ ➤ Ⓓ

Beschaffung Schraube
❶ ➤ ❷ ➤ ❸ ➤ ❹ ⋯

Studierende

Schraube benötigt!

Anfrage an Ben

Ben

VOL-Gutschein
50€

Ben geht mit VOL-Schein einkaufen

VOL-Gutschein
50€

Stefanie gibt VOL-Scheine nach und nach an Ben aus

Quittung
Baumarkt **Gutschein**
50€

Stefanie

Quittung
Baumarkt **Gutschein**
50€

Rechnung
39,95€

Unterschriebene Rechnung/Quittung /Belegschein gehen zurück an Beschaffungsabteilung

Beschaffungsabteilung schickt Rechnung an Stefanie zum Abgleich mit Quittung/Belegschein

Rechnung
39,95€

VOL-Gutschein
50€

BESCHAFFUNGS-ANTRAG
VOL-Schein

Rechnung
39,95€

Kto gedeckt? Ⓑ

Kto gedeckt. Ⓒ

Drittmittel-abteilung

Beschaffungsabteilung

Rechnung
39,95€

Buchungsabteilung begleicht Rechnung

Buchungsabteilung

Terminplan UdN Sommersemester 2010 Planstand: 27.04.10 Erstellt: I.Mihm		TERMINPLAN / PERSONALVERTEILU					
Nr.:	**Arbeitspaket**	**Geschoss**	**Start**	**Ende**	**Dauer [Tagen]**	**Besonderheiten**	**2**
4	Bestandfußboden vorbereiten (Ausgleichsschicht usw.)	EG			12	Material	4
5	Fußboden Turnhalle (Abbau)	TH/EG			12	Schlüssel Turnhalle	5
6	Schlot verfüllen, Abbruch Foyer, Mauern DG (Eingang)	DG			8	Oldenburg? Mterial?	6
7	Giebelvormauerwand, mauern	DG + EG			4	Oldenburg? Mterial?	7
8	Verputzen Foyer	DG + EG			8	Oldenburg? Mterial?	8
9	Dacharbeiten	DG			8		9
10	Heizung demontieren	EG			2	Schrotti	10
11	Treppen u. Podeste zum Heizungsraum	EG			4		11
12	Wohnung: Terasse, Tür, Türen/Fenster lackieren	EG			4		12
13	Tür in Giebelwand einbauen, Sanitärobjekte installieren	EG			4		13
14	Wohnung streichen	DG + EG			12		14
15	Lichtplanung, E-Planung	DG + EG			4	Elektriker	15
16	Wohnung: Küche bauen	EG			8		16
17	Wohnung: Fußboden	EG			4		17
19	Einbruchsicheren Conti erstellen	EG			8	Kontainer	19
20	Wohnung verputzen	EG			4	Material	20
21	Tor Rodeca - Fensterläden	EG			8	Rupp u. Hellmold	
		Planung		**mogl. Ausführung**		**Ausführung**	

Nr	Studierende	Projektwoche	Grund	CP-Anzahl	Tel:	Einsatzbereiche:
1	Vatin Sophie- ok	?	?	2,3,5	015784535530	1,2,3,6,11,13
2	Putos Eloise- ok	?	?	?	015783598828	1,2,3,4,6,10,11,12,13
3	Nicolas Wolter- ok	ja	-	5	017678255970	4,5,----7,10,8,11,12,13
4	Steffen Plath- ok	ja	-	3	015776812429	5,2
5	Hanna Noller	ja	-	2-3	017622086213	-
6	Hanna Vers ---am 27.04.10 nicht anwesendt---	ja	-	3	01735802191	9,5,7,3
7	Michael Gätjens – ok	ja	-	5	01736123300	2,4,10,11,12,13
8	Malte Bösche- ok	ja	-	3	01732444847	9,5,7
9	Meret Boss ---am 27.04.10 nicht anwesendt---	ja	-	2-3	01723873157	
10	Natalie Krützmann- ok	ja	-	2-3	01703284367	
11	Kathrin Rupp- ok	ja	-	4 (2x2) = 5?	017622062767	1,2,7,8
12	Anne-Kathrin Hellmold -ok	ja	-	2-3	017622280612	1,2,7,8,
13	Ole Brügmann- ok	ja	-	3-5	01734111170	7, 9, 16, 19
14	Kathrin Burwitz ---am 27.04.10 nicht anwesendt---	ja	-	2	-	12, 9, 7, 15
15	Kim Lauterbach – ok	ja	-	2	015152550198	12, 15, 9
16	Jana Müller ---am 27.04.10 nicht anwesendt---	ja	-	2-3	01747024700	12, 15
17	Sarah Güth - ok	Ja	-	2	015775735956	12, 15
18	Elin Kuttimalai ---am 27.04.10 nicht anwesendt---	ja	-	2-5	017621101850	
19	Ole Schott – ok	ja	-	3	017620672272	7, 16, 9, 19
20	Rico Wittke- ok	ja	-	3	015119672086	7,9,16,19
21	Fabian Reier -ok	ja	-	3	01724044566	9, 16, 19, 7
22	Kristina Lorenz ---am 27.04.10 nicht anwesendt---	ja	-	3	01739140983	9, 5, 7, 3
23	Romano Hirsch ---am 27.04.10 nicht anwesendt---					
24	Jörn Führmann ---am 27.04.10 nicht anwesendt---					
24	Silvan Idler -ok	Ja	-	3	01626552865	9, 16, 19
25	Matihas Schröder					Tribüne
26	Ruven Wagner					Tribüne
27	Ole Harder					Tribüne
29	Kathrin Köppe- ok	Ja		3	01782145854	
30	Matino Hutz- ok	Ja	-	2		

Stand: 27.04.10

		KW 17						KW 18			
.04.2010	28.04.2010	29.04.2010	30.04.2010	01.05.2010	02.05.2010	03.05.2010	04.05.2010	05.05.2010	06.05.2010	07.05.2010	08.05
Di	Mi	Do	Fr	Sa	So	Mo	Di	Mi	Do	Fr	Sa
						4					
						5					
			Schlot verfüllen, Abbruch Foyer, Mauern DG (Eingang)							Schlot verfüllen, Abbruc	
						Giebelvormauerwand, mauern					
						8					
						9					
						10					
						11					
						12					
						13					
						14					
						15					
						16					
						17					
						19					
						20					
			Gerüst =>			17.00 Planung					
						Maurer ?					
			Abbruch Foyer, Mauern DG (Eingang)			Giebelvormauerwand, mauern					Schlot v
			Abbruch Foyer, Mauern DG (Eingang)			Giebelvormauerwand, mauern				Schlot verfüllen, Abbruc	
										Schlot verfüllen, Abbruc	
						Giebelvormauerwand, mauern				Schlot verfüllen, Abbruc	
			Abbruch Foyer, Mauern DG (Eingang)			Giebelvormauerwand, mauern					
						Giebelvormauerwand, mauern					
										Schlot verfüllen, Abbruc	
						Giebelvormauerwand, mauern				Schlot verfüllen, Abbruc	
						Giebelvormauerwand, mauern					
						Giebelvormauerwand, mauern					

9.2010	14.05.2010	15.05.2010	16.05.2010	17.05.2010	18.05.2010	19.05.2010	KW 20 20.05.2010	21.05.2010	22.05.2010	23.05.2010	24.05.2010
	Fr	Sa	So	Mo	Di	Mi	Do	Fr	Sa	So	MO
				4							4
			Fußboden Turnhalle (Abbau)					Fußboden Turnhalle (Abbau)			5
				6							6
				7							7
				8							8
				9							9
				10							10
				11							11
				12							12
				13					Tür in Giebelwand einbauen, Sanitärobjekte		
				14							14
				15							15
				16							16
				17							17
				19							19
				20							Wohnung ve
									Tor Rodeca - Fensterläden		
ntel?						? Turnhalle ?					
			Fußboden Turnhalle (Abbau)					Fußboden Turnhalle (Abbau)			Wohnung ve
			Fußboden Turnhalle (Abbau)					Fußboden Turnhalle (Abbau)			Wohnung ve
			Fußboden Turnhalle (Abbau)						Tür in Giebelwand einbauen, Sanitärobjekte		
			Fußboden Turnhalle (Abbau)							Fußboden Turnhalle (Abbau	
									Tor Rodeca - Fensterläden		
				Fußboden Turnhalle (Abbau)					Fußboden Turnhalle (Abbau)	Wohnung ve	
			Fußboden Turnhalle (Abbau)						Tür in Giebelwand einbauen, Sanitärobjekte		
									Fußboden Turnhalle (Abbau)	Wohnung ve	
				Fußboden Turnhalle (Abbau)							
				Fußboden Turnhalle (Abbau)					Tor Rodeca - Fensterläden		
									Tor Rodeca - Fensterläden		
									Tor Rodeca - Fensterläden		
											Wohnung v
											Wohnung v
									Tor Rodeca - Fensterläden		

	KW 21					KW 22					
	26.05.2010	27.05.2010	28.05.2010	29.05.2010	30.05.2010	31.05.2010					
	Mi	Do	Fr	Sa	So	Mo					
	Projektwoche										
er											
sse, Tür, Türen/Fenster Lackieren											
				Wohnung streichen							
Wohnung: Küche bauen											
				Nachbarschaftsfest							
Wohnung: Küche bauen			Wohnung streichen		Gesperrt Entwurfswoche	3 CP (oD)					
Wohnung: Küche bauen			Wohnung streichen		Gesperrt Entwurfswoche	3 CP (oD)					
r						3,2 (Bh+IKP+D) =>16 Tage Baustelle = 4CP + Doku = 5CP					
r	Nachbarschaftsfest					3 CP (8Tage + Doku)					
						3 CP (9Tage + Doku)					
						3,2 (Bh+IKP+D) =>16 Tage Baustelle = 4CP + Doku = 5CP					
sse, Tür, Türen/Fenster lackieren						3 CP (9Tage + Doku)					
Wohnung: Küche bauen			Wohnung streichen			3,2 (Bh+IKP+D) =>16 Tage Baustelle = 4CP + Doku = 5CP					
						3 CP (9Tage + Doku)					
						2,2 CP (12 Tage Baustelle Unb.m16)					
nsterläden						3 CP (8 Tage Baustelle Doku)					
						2 CP (4 Tage Baustelle + Planung))-> Dach					
sse, Tür, Türen/Fenster lackieren						2 CP (4 Tage Baustelle + Planung))-> Treppen und Podeste					
						2 CP (4 Tage Baustelle + Planung)->Rodeca Tor					
sse, Tür, Türen/Fenster lackieren						2 CP (4 Tage Baustelle + Planung)-> Lichtplanung					
r	Nachbarschaftsfest					2 CP (4 Tage Baustelle + Planung)-> Lichtplanung					
						3 CP (9 Tage Baustelle + Lichtplanung)					
se, Tür, Türen/Fenster lackieren						2 CP (4 Tage Baustelle + Planung))-> Treppen und Podeste					
						2 CP (4 Tage Baustelle + Planung)-> Rodeca Tor					
						2 CP (4 Tage Baustelle + Planung)->Dach					
						3 CP (8Tage Baustelle + Doku)					
						Q-Studi nachtrag					
Vohnung: Küche bauen						2 CP (5 Tage Baustelle + Planung Rotenbaumchaussee)					
						3 CP (8 Tage Baustelle + Doku)					
						IKP					
						IKP					
						IKP					
						3 CP (8 Tage + Doku					
	Nachbarschaftsfest					2 CP (4 Tage Baustelle + Planung))-> Treppen und Podeste					

2011/12

2011

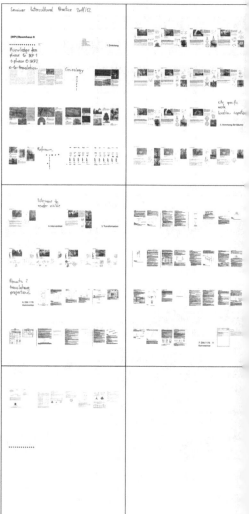

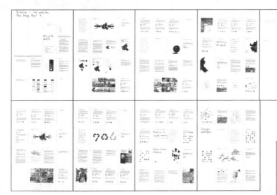

2012

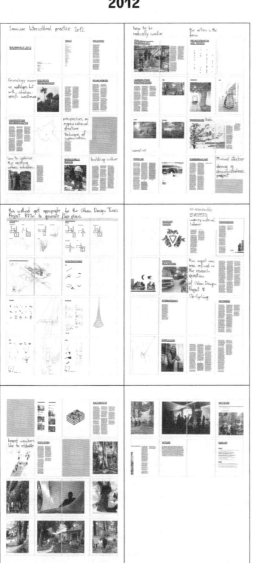

2013

the

AUSGANGS SITUATION

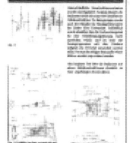

O HOAI

ot, collabo-

KONZEPTIONSPHASE

AKTEURE

NGS-

s 1

FINANZIERUNG

Budgeting

FERIENPROGRAMM

this method got appropriate
Project RD3o to generate

Three Questions to the Contributors

Arne "Tingel," Wagma Abdul, Mario Abel, Björn Akelbein, Francesca Albera,
Feltin Aleksandrs, Arik Alev, Anais Alfieri, Mohammed Alfiky, Kilian
Allmann, Jörg Amelung, Abdel Andeus, Shahira Andeus, Sarah Andreae,
Giacomo Angeletti, Alev Arik, Hatice Arli, Markus Aslan, Sarah Assel,
Ingrid Bach, Markus Bader, Björn Bahnsen, Rozeen Balay, Michael Baltzer,
Peter Bando, Constanze Barbuceanu, Coralie Bariou, Mustafa Batman,
Julian Bauer, Brigitte Bauer, Ise Baumgart, Ruedi Baur, Janusz Beck,
Ben Becker

How did you get to the University of Neighborhoods?

As an architect with work experience in architectural offices in
Germany and the Netherlands, in the building administration and
within the framework of German development cooperation in Mali,
West Africa (GIZ), I was a research assistant in the UoN project
from 2008.

What did you do at the University of Neighborhoods?

From 2008 to 2014 I was responsible for construction, teaching
and project development. That means I was accompanying the
planning and coordination of all (self-)construction measures,
the development of the project content, as well as supervising
and managing of courses and participation projects.

What are you doing now with what you took from the
University of Neighborhoods?

Supervision of individual building projects and topics of superordinate urban planning at the Department of Urban and Landscape
Planning Altona. Cooperation between the department in Altona
and the study course UD on topics of superordinate planning
(e.g. Magistralen).

Andrea Behnke, Dennis Behrendt, Lene Benz, Carsten Bergner, Matthias
Bernd, Elke Beyer, Paula Bialski, Maik Binner, Laura Birina, Kristina
Bischoff, Regina Bittner, Sabine Bittner, Ute Bittner, Kate Bitz, Richard
Blöcher, Dirk Blum, Elisabeth Blum, Lisa Blümel, Steven Boato, Jan
Hendrik Bock, Katharina Böttger

How did you get to the University of Neighborhoods?

As an Urban Design Student in Hamburg

What did you do at the University of Neighborhoods?

Study, divers Seminars.
Being part of the Organisationteam of the Neighborhoodworkshops
"Veddel-Cairo."
Tutor at the Seminar "Hotel Wilhelmsburg"

What are you doing now with what you took from the
University of Neighborhoods?

Curating Exhibitions and researching the City for the CityLab
(Historical Museum Frankfurt). Working participative with
People from Frankfurt and developing Exhibitions together.
Using tools from UoN for reasearch and design.

Hasan Bogatekin, Jasin Bogatekin, Aron Bohmann, Christoph Bohnenkamp,
Katrin Borchers, Oliver Bormann, Sihuar Borstelmann, Mark Botko, Marcus
Braeger, Katrin Brandt, Sven Braun, Ingrid Breckner

How did you get to the University of Neighborhoods?

As professor at HafenCity University I was engaged in several
activities at the University of Neighborhoods and followed its
development as well as external and internal reactions with
sociological interest.

What did you do at the University of Neighborhoods?
> I taught different lectures in the Urban Planning and Urban
> Design program and participated in several public activities.

What are you doing now with what you took from the
University of Neighborhoods?
> I remember the project as a courageous and innovative incentive
> for academic education under difficult conditions and hope that
> academics engaged in urban issues use this experience for new
> ways of research and teaching in contact with urban realities.

Heike Breitenfeld, Eva Brinkmann, Ulrich Brudereck, Ole Brügmann, Lisa
Brunnert, Florian Bruns, Sebastian Bührig

How did you get to the University of Neighborhoods?
> I learned about the University of Neighborhoods through my study
> friends. One night, shortly before the beginning of the workshop
> "Made In," remained in my memory: Ben and I spontaneously stayed
> overnight to supervise delivered technology.

What did you do at the University of Neighborhoods?
> The "Wilhelmsburg Orchestra" — an improvisational orchestra —
> in which I worked for a few semesters, has a very special meaning
> for me.

What are you doing now with what you took from the
University of Neighborhoods?
> The University of Neighbourhoods was not only a reconstruction
> of an old building, it was also an essential part of the joint
> construction of possibilities for cooperation and the explora-
> tion of necessary restrictions. Thinking about this influences my
> work in many areas.

Arne Bunk, Matthias Burke, Barbara Burkel, Maria Burkhardt, Amrita
Burmeister, Ole Burmester, Kathrin Burwitz, Annette Buschermöhle, Julian
Bustamante, Andreas Campagno, Doro Carl, Boris Čeko

How did you get to the University of Neighborhoods?
> Kampnagel in Hamburg asked us whether we could imagine devel-
> oping and realising a project in Wilhelmsburg, in an abandoned
> health centre, in cooperation with the University of Neighbor-
> hoods.

What did you do at the University of Neighborhoods?
> In the course of this cooperation with the University of Neigh-
> borhoods, God's Entertainment has realized the project
> "Shivers," which uses the entire building over several days,
> in which the various ideas were artistically realized on site
> together with Wilhelmsburg citizens

What are you doing now with what you took from the
University of Neighborhoods?
> God's Entertainment continue to practice the processes that we
> did then. With diverse and mostly discriminating social groups
> in the city, we continue to try to draw attention to socio-polit-
> ical and socio-cultural problems or make them visible.

Nihan Cengiz, AnaRosa Chagas Cavalcanti, Hardy Cheer, Lena Christoffers,
Simon Clasen, Selim Coban, Muhammed Conga, Suzana Cosic, Alison Courtot,
Sabine de Buhr, Jürgen Dege-Rüger, Olaf Dehalde, Christopher Dell

How did you get to the University of Neighborhoods?

> I got to UoN by conceptionalizing its open form together with Bernd Kniess and Katja Heinecke during a weekend workshop after Bernd had asked me kindly to take over the chair for theory at the newly formed Department of Urban Design.

What did you do at the University of Neighborhoods?

> Besides teaching, organizing and conceptualizing on the fly, I tried to find out, what teaching organizing and conceptualizing is.

What are you doing now with what you took from the University of Neighborhoods?

> At the moment I teach urban design and urban renewal at the Department of Architecture and Urban Design at Berlin University of the Arts (UdK) and still try to find out, what teaching is.

Fa. Delmes Heitmann, Cem Dennis Özhan, Heike Derwanz, Laurenz deSilva, Amelie Deuflhard, Wolfgang Dickhaut, Kai-Michael Dietrich

How did you get to the University of Neighborhoods?

> Asking someone if I could stay a while. Taking some stuff on the bike.

What did you do at the University of Neighborhoods?

> Working on the Urban Design Project III - Up-Cycling in local production. The city as a resource. Defending my master thesis Urban Re-Generation in China; Creative Gateway Shenzhen; Organization, Communication, Decisionmaking. Building a bookshelf Celebrating my 30th. Birthday

What are you doing now with what you took from the University of Neighborhoods?

> The bookshelf became a shoe shelf. The UDP III Project and the thesis went to another shelf. My office manufacturing cities is operating in the fields I was working on in the UoN, working with people I met there and using methods we practiced there.

Karin Dietz, Carsten Dittus, Jamil Djamtorki, Tore Dobberstein, Alice Dörscher, Klaus Drewer, Kathrin Dröppelmann, Andreas Dwenger, Christine Ebeling, Fa. Ehlert & Söhne, Gottfried Eich, Maximilian Eichhoff, Wesam ElBardisy, Koral Elci, Oskar Ellwanger, Frank Elster, Constanze Engelbrecht, Judy Engelhard, Ugur Erden, Tessa Ermer, Cordula Ernsing, Bianca Eschrich, Orhan Esen, Juan Esteban Vallejo, Lotta Ewert, Nora Fanderl, Xiaoshi Fang, Alexa Färber

How did you get to the University of Neighborhoods?

> As a professor in cultural studies. The first and for the next 5 years the only time I came by car was a few weeks before I started working at HCU. René Tribble gave me a ride in a VW bus (?). I was supposed to give a lecture at a summer school in the early evening: hookah cafés and urban diversity - didn't get much response.

What did you do at the University of Neighborhoods?

> In the following years I have taught different formats in the UD or KM curriculum, or I have done research events there, like a workshop with my French colleagues from "Penser l'urban par l'image" or an international young scholars workshop within the research project "Low-budget-urbanity."

What are you doing now with what you took from the
University of Neighborhoods?
> From the UoN I have learned how important extraordinary spatial
> arrangements are for opening up learning and research for new
> things. But also how much these spaces multiply time: working
> time, leisure time, waiting time and more.

Peter Fattinger
How did you get to the University of Neighborhoods?
> I was invited by Bernd Kniess to hold a workshop to design and
> build a part of "Hotel Wilhelmsburg" as an extension of UoN
> together with students of HCU in Spring 2013.

What did you do at the University of Neighborhoods?
> As the last sequence of a workshop-series, we continued to
> design & build the hotel-structure, which Ton Matton

How did you get to the University of Neighborhoods?
> I came early morning of the very first day from an event in
> Rotterdam with a lot of tomato-plants in my car. I asked students
> to trade these for cookery in the neighborhood for the not-yet-
> existing kitchen. And it worked, we cooked a nice meal the first
> evening!

Veronique Faucheur, Ernst Fehling, Maria Ferrer, Jesko Fezer
How did you get to the University of Neighborhoods?
> I was invited by Bernd to join a student project presentation.
> This was a great chance for me to finally visit the project I
> heard already so much about. Even better than expected I could
> join a dinner afterwards and a beautiful evening on the terrace.

What did you do at the University of Neighborhoods?
> After listening, watching and commenting for quite a while I was
> mainly hanging out there. Enjoying the environment and what was
> happening all around, the leftovers and records of former activ-
> ities and the collective spirit of this neighborhood-related
> academic space.

What are you doing now with what you took from the
University of Neighborhoods?
> The University of Neighborhoods reminded me of the necessity to
> work locally connected, of the social generosity of collective
> work, of the energy of experimental research, the potential of
> critical pedagogy and that a nice and decent place can allow
> active appropriation.

Gunnar Fiebelkorn, Ellen Fiedelmeier
How did you get to the University of Neighborhoods?
> I was looking for a new challenge to test how strong positive
> changes, which are not based on an economical or municipal
> development, could be for a district. Which role would the
> project play in it to encourage initiatives coming out of the
> neighborhood?

What did you do at the University of Neighborhoods?
> Keep balls in the air: To work at the interface between the HCU,
> IBA and economic partners meant to juggle different rules, esti-
> mations and time ideas to open up a building which slept over
> 13 years a dreamless sleep.

What are you doing now with what you took from the
University of Neighborhoods?

> In my hometown Rostock we try to recreate a vacant former Kauf-
> halle into something new with untypical partners, utilizations
> and processes. Our experiences so far: We are new neighbors.
> It is like it is - deal with it. Outside the comfort zone.

Julia Fiege, Florian Finke, Bettina Fitz, Bianca Flamming, Nicki
Fleischmann, Benjamin Foerster-Baldenius, Christine Franz, Holm Friebe,
Eva Maria Friedel, Sebastian Fritzsche, Hannes Frömel, Edda G.E.
Frühling, Jörn-Frederik Fuhrmann, Paolo Fusi, Anna Fuy, Mattia
Gammarotta, Mareike Gärtner, Michael Gätjens, Rüdiger Gebert, Anja
Gehrcke, Marie Gely, Yvonne Gerhardt, Stefanie Gernert

How did you get to the University of Neighborhoods?

> During my studies in Münster and my scientific occupation as a
> researcher at the university of Wuppertal I was always very much
> interested and attracted to new ideas of building construction
> and urban design. The vibrant scene of young scientists, archi-
> tects, and city planners in NRW, as well as in Hamburg or Berlin,
> discussing new ways of living and city planning, brought my
> attention to the University of Neighborhoods. As soon as I saw
> the job announcement I enthusiastically applied and was lucky
> enough to be accepted.

What did you do at the University of Neighborhoods?

> I was the project manager of the UoN. I mediated between the
> project, the funding body (EU), and administration, was respon-
> sible for controlling and budget planning, delayed contracts,
> coordinated and planned events, and was responsible for public
> affairs. My research during the project was on the theory of
> counter spaces. I coordinated the student experiments of the
> project. Some called me the ‚mother of the UoN'.

What are you doing now with what you took from the
University of Neighborhoods?

> In my recent job as a portfolio analysist in the administration
> for real-estate management and immovable properties of the city
> of Hamburg (Landesbetrieb Immobilienmanagement und Grundver-
> mögen (LIG) Hamburg) T apply the ideas, concepts, and methods of
> the UoN to Hamburg city planning. Some of my recent expertise
> include Green City planning, urban district management, or sus-
> tainable urban development, addressing problems like affordable
> housing, climate change, or mobility. Additionally, I teach at
> the university of applied science (HAW) and am engaged in envi-
> ronmental noise control.

Leyla Gersbach, Daniel Geyer, Jana Gienke, Thomas Giese, Ana Tereza
Gironi Da Costa, Monia Gläske, Fritz Goldschläger, Ulrich Gomolzig,
Matthias Görlich, André Görtz, Gernot Grabher, Isabelle Grabo, Lucia
Graf, Pascale Grange, Stefanie Graze, Lukas Grellmann

How did you get to the University of Neighborhoods?

> Seminars of UD master program

What did you do at the University of Neighborhoods?

> International workshops, workshops with students of nearby
> schools, neighborhood-events, cultural events.

What are you doing now with what you took from the
University of Neighborhoods?
    Dreams can become true, just do it!

Nina Gribat, Jonathan Gröne, Iris Groscurth, Kira Groth, Sören Groth,
Hande Gür, Sarah Güth, Anke Haarmann, Klaus Habermann-Nieße, Anita
Habisch, Dana-Janina Hachmann, Anke Hagemann
    How did you get to the University of Neighborhoods?
        Starting from Averhoffstraße, I took the U3 from Mundsburg,
        changed to S-Bahn at Hauptbahnhof, took the number 13 bus from
        Veddel to Vogelhüttendeich, and walked the remaining 600m.
    What did you do at the University of Neighborhoods?
        In particular, I remember the celebrations and events at the
        UoN: bustling neighborhood festivals, Christmas parties with
        hearty kale, master theses presentations, lively talks and
        discussions, as well as farewell drinks when I left the HCU.
    What are you doing now with what you took from the
    University of Neighborhoods?
        I took the awareness that university must not be limited to the
        campus and the virtual sphere:
        'operating in the real world' triggers students' enthusiasm and
        engagement while unfolding momentum in the interaction with
        urban everyday life.

Johannes Hahn, Viktoria Hahn, Metin Hakverdi, Alice Hansen, Tim Hansen,
Ohle Harder, Lutz Hartmann, Brigitte Hartwig, Liina Haug, Ute Haverkamp,
Florian Haydn, Matthias Hederer, Katja Heinecke, Christoph Heinemann,
Yasmin Heinemann, Fa. Heinrich Buhk, Esther Heißenbüttel, Mandy Held,
Katharina Held, Niels Helle-Meyer, Angela Hellenbach, Uli Hellweg
    How did you get to the University of Neighborhoods?
        The idea of the "University of Neighborhoods" (UoN) emerged from
        a student competition that IBA Hamburg held with HafenCity Uni-
        versity in 2007. Starting in 2008, the project was realized by
        IBA, HafenCity University and Kulturfabrik Kampnagel as a space
        for experimentation, learning and living.
    What did you do at the University of Neighborhoods?
        As Managing Director of IBA Hamburg, I was one of the original
        initiators and supporters of the project.
    What are you doing now with what you took from the
    University of Neighborhoods?
        For me, the processual study character of the project was always
        in the foreground. I am sure that today we need more of such
        spaces of experience at our universities and that we should have
        more such intermediate uses in the cities.

Hildebrandt Henatsch, Frieder Hepting, Johannes Herberger, Rahel
Hermann, Johannes Herrberger, Martina Hessler, Juliane Hildebrandt,
Bernd Hilgenbrink, Moritz Hinck, Leif Hinrichs, Theresa Hochhaus,
Volkmar Hoffmann, Andrea Hofmann, Mareike Holfeld, Christiane Hollander,
Dirk Holm, Jan Holtmann, Beke-Marie Hörmann, Katrin Hovy, Patrick Huguet,
Olga Hungar, Iulia Hurducas, Jean-Pierre Hürsch, Isabelle Ihle,
AnnaDuelo Isern, Anna Duelo Isern, Serdar Iskender, Ove Jacobsen, Sören
Jansen, Irina Janssen, Joachim Januschek, Frederick Jensch, Nadine
Jessen, Maren Jonseck-Ohrt, Steffen Jörg, Adrian Judt, Ralf Junker,
Ole Junker, Anna Jurck, Jörg Kallmeyer, Martin Kaltwasser, Hila Karansai,

Anita Kaspar, Anja Kazocins, Janne Kempe, Nora Kern, Anne Kersting,
Ali Khadija, Bettina Kiehn, Astrid Kirk, Juliana Kleba, Magdalena
Klingemann, Rosemarie Klingemann, Katrin Klitzke, Ragnhild Klußmann,
Heidi Knaut, Darinka Kniesberg, Bernd Kniess

How did you get to the University of Neighborhoods?

I got to UoN by conceptionalizing its open form together with
Christopher Dell and Katja Heinecke during a weekend workshop
after my dear friend Michael Koch asked me kindly to take over
the Island Experiment.

What did you do at the University of Neighborhoods?

Trying to keep the balls in the air we all were playing with
standing with one foot on the tightrope while knitting the net
underneath to avoid falling to hard.

What are you doing now with what you took from the
University of Neighborhoods?

Going on juggling the balls and rehearsing the improvisation of
space to make it accessible to architectural and urban practice.

Andrea Knobloch, Matthias Knobloch, Tim Koblun, Michael Koch

How did you get to the University of Neighborhoods?

With my professorship (on district development and urban
planning) at HCU and as Dean of the urban planning study-program
I was involved in the urban design curriculum and the beginning
of the University of Neighborhoods.

What did you do at the University of Neighborhoods?

Co-Teaching from time to time in different formats.

What are you doing now with what you took from the
University of Neighborhoods?

Talking about lessons learned: The University of Neighborhoods
as a way of researching and teaching approaches to a practice of
an adequate urban development through the coproduction of space
and usages by different actors.

Dennis Köhler, Anna Kokalonova, Jonas Kolenc, Ayca Konal, Timo Kontarski,
Burkar Konur, Cathrin Köppe, Kira Korneeva, Melih Kös, Florian Kossak,
Monika Kotlarz, Carl-Walter Kottnik, Jana Kowitzki, Manuel Krahwinkel,
Elke Krasny, Karolina Krause, Hille Krause, Carolin Krieg, Claus Kriegs,
Bernd Kritzmann, Nicolai Krolzik, Natalie Krützmann, Andreas Kuerschner,
Vanessa Kügler, Edmund Kuhlmann, Sabine Kühnast, Marco Kuhnke, Stefan
Kunert, Elin Kuttimalai, Ayse Kuzer, Joanna Kwiatkowska, Charlotte
Laatsch, Leo Lagos, Uta Lambertz, Bettina Lamm

How did you get to the University of Neighborhoods?

We visited UoN as part of the EU project SEEDS where both, UoN
and University of Copenhagen (KU), were partners. SEEDS explored
reuse of derelict sites and buildings and we studied UoN as an
innovative approach to transforming a building, a neighborhood
as well as university didactics.

What did you do at the University of Neighborhoods?

We joined a SEEDS seminar hosted by UoN and later revisited UoN
independently.
We invited UoN to speak at the Copenhagen conference: ThinkSpace
2012.
Students from Urban Intervention Studio, KU joined UoN in 2013
for a weeklong design-build exploration. We published a booklet
on the 20 European SEEDS cases including UoN.

What are you doing now with what you took from the
University of Neighborhoods?

UoN has been a great source of inspiration for our own enquiries
into the relation between production of places through small-
scale spatial interventions and cultivation of community (See
current research project ign.ku.dk/english/move-the-neighbour-
hood/). UoN has influenced how we create learning environments at
the Urban Intervention Studio. Here students are immersed into
spaces and communities interacting and producing interventions
and where socializing, dining and living becomes an integrated
part of the didactics. See the forthcoming book (Teaching Landscape Architecture — the Studio Experience.

Marek Lamprecht, Bastian Lange, Elena Langer, Stephan Lanz, Dieter
Läpple, Sandra Latussek, Kim Lauterbach, Jörg Leeser, Sandra Lehmann,
Harald Lemke, Ruth Lenz, Julia Lerch Zajączkowska

How did you get to the University of Neighborhoods?

I tried to spent as much time as possible there while completing
the master's program Urban Design. I was a student at and within
the UoN.

What did you do at the University of Neighborhoods?

'One night in the »second skin« of the Hotel' was a task given by
the artist Jan Holtmann when we started the 'Hotel?' project in
2012. The task required us to spend one night outside in late
October along with 15 fellow students, no roof, no electricity.
It was the starting point of many projects, exhibitions and
encounters. In the summer of 2013, I moved into the UoN until the
building was torn down in 2014.

What are you doing now with what you took from the
University of Neighborhoods?

Today I work in curatorial projects and exhibitions. Besides all
the great people I met here I learned what quality of space can
mean and that reducing or removing certain architectural elements and adding programs is a key element in respect of the aes-
thetical and social power of spaces, especially when it comes to
dealing with the existing.
I miss this place.

Peter Lewin, Lidia Liachowitsch, Palina Liachowitsch, Sebastian Lietz,
Marina Lindemann, Sabrina Lindemann, Mathias Lintl, Christian Lips,
Catharina Loesche, Philip Löper

How did you get to the University of Neighborhoods?

Some friends were involved in different projects in the UoN. So I
was invited to some events and was asked to give a workshop for
building treehouses in the summer school.

What did you do at the University of Neighborhoods?

I was lecturer in the summer semester 2012 and 2013. The project
was part of the MA Urban Design-seminar to develop and execute a
two weeks summer camp. The topic was building treehouses with
international students and children from the neighborhood at the
age of 8-11.

What are you doing now with what you took from the
University of Neighborhoods?

The UoN was an inspiring place which showed a successful strategy
how teaching can combine social and intercultural exchange with
experimental constructions. I believe that these concepts could
be transferred in many different disciplines.

Kristina Lorenzen, Sandra Lösel, Uwe Lübbermann

How did you get to the University of Neighborhoods?

I was invited to give a talk about "radical" forms of cooperation, to a brainstorming about our experience with different
kinds of businesses, to an additional round table, to be inter-
viewed for a master thesis, and last but not least to give a
workshop about consensus democracy.

What did you do at the University of Neighborhoods?

I did all of the above, feedback was good, however I'm unsure if
I contributed well to UoN. was it successful? how is "success"
defined and measured for such a project? maybe the book will provide answers.

What are you doing now with what you took from the
University of Neighborhoods?

I guess I have a better understanding now about how living in
cities can be developed on a cultural level. also, I'm connected
to the Zunderbüchse / Mobile Machenschaften collective, helped
them a little with group processes, and am working to become a
skipper to support the local multi-purpose cultural platform
Schaluppe (which is a boat, but much more than that).

Sylvia Luesmann, Chibugo Luke, Chichi Luke, Chinemerem Luke, Kathrin
Lüngen, Margarete Lupin, Sebastian Maaß, Solveis Maaß, Jan Maaßen, Ian
Mac Donald, Elisa Machirus, Mohamed Mahrous

How did you get to the University of Neighborhoods?

I got to know UoN through the International Design+Build Workshop of the Hotel Wilhelmsburg, March 2013, which was recommended by one of my professors during my master's degree study in
Stuttgart University (IUSD).

What did you do at the University of Neighborhoods?

I participated in the construction of the Hotel Wilhelmsburg
along with other talented participants. For three weeks, I took
part in realizing two rooms using the different available materials, which was very enlightening for myself in dealing with a
live project as it was a continuous and very dynamic learning
process.

What are you doing now with what you took from the
University of Neighborhoods?

Being inspired by what I experienced in UoN, I took that inspiration back to Egypt. Recently, I have initiated a cultural center
in Aswan, Egypt, together with the local community in one of the
Nile Islands. The design development and construction works were
done through an international Design+Build workshop, which
gathered volunteers and international students from eight different nationalities. Currently, I'm working towards the activation of the center in participation with the local community.

Magdalena Maierhofer

How did you get to the University of Neighborhoods?

I just had arrived in Hamburg. Even before the semester started, I walked around Wilhelmsburg. I took the line 13, crossed the Reiherstiegviertel and suddenly I found myself having a coffee in the kitchen of the UoN.

What did you do at the University of Neighborhoods?

I spent more than a year with the UoN. I was all a student, research assistant, tutor and resident at the same time. I used to cook, I built a hotel, examined social interactions and learned a lot about urban design, production and neighbourhoods.

What are you doing now with what you took from the University of Neighborhoods?

Back at the Vienna UT my research focuses on the urban planning dimension of healthcare and hospitals. In that, I'm still an urban designer. Frankly it makes no difference to me whether I'm working on regions, cities, a breakfast room or even a hospital.

Juliana Mainka, Alessandra Manzini, Marco Antonio Reyes Loredo, Ton Matton, Phillip Maus, Sebastiano Mazzola, Meghan McAllister, Melis Mecit, Daniela Mehlich, Franziska Meichelböck, Janina Meiners, Sebastian Menzel, Yuca Meubrink, Valeria Micara, Tabea Michaelis

How did you get to the University of Neighborhoods?

As a Master student at Urban Design from 2009 to 2012.

What did you do at the University of Neighborhoods?

On the one hand for the conception and organization of the one-week international Spring School and Symposium "Made in - local practices of urban production" 2013 together with Ben Pohl in cooperation with Civic City Zurich, Switzerland. On the other hand, to explore the Elbe islands from the perspective of the 'Program of Opportunities' 2012 as part of the master thesis, which was published by spectorbooks with the title "Showtime Wilhelmsburg - A Randonnée of Possibilities"in 2015. During my research, the UoN served as a local research station - and a temporary home. In addition, I was tutor for the seminar Urban Territories from 2011 to 2012, which took place in the UoN.

What are you doing now with what you took from the University of Neighborhoods?

I brought with me valuable experience for my current job at Denkstatt sàrl, which performative formats and interventions for activating and programming the UoN worked and which did not: which methods and approaches use to build trust in the different actors and to integrate the various resources and talents/skills; which complexity an open-ended process contains and which vectors shape it.

In the changing roles and the associated perspectives as a 'Participating Observer,' researcher and resident, the UoN was a unique 'Möglichkeitsraum' to explore and test the urban with professors, lecturer, students, guests, residents and neighbors.

Karol Michalik, Agata Mielczarek, Immanuel Mihm, Maja Mijatovic, Valentina Milan, Thomas Mirbach, Ponya Mirzaei, Philipp Misselwitz, David Möller, Maja Momic

How did you get to the University of Neighborhoods?

Through a colleague from the HCU whom I've met at an international workshop in Ferrara. Some months after the workshop I decided to do an internship abroad, so I asked her if she could recommend an interesting project in Hamburg. She put me in contact with the UoN team.

What did you do at the University of Neighborhoods?

Building, co-planning the hotel Wilhelmsburg, helping with the workshops organization, working on the application for the building permit, guided tours, Sunday's Café, living, master thesis research,… before I arrived I had no idea what to expect, even after a week or so it was unclear, but the philosophy that tasks find people turned out to be true.

What are you doing now with what you took from the University of Neighborhoods?

It helped me to work with open processes, think in terms of open structures and deal with uncertainties- especially in collaborative projects with many diverse actors (with different interests). #life/work lessons.

For other projects/collectives with a shared space I've been active in since: collective care of the place; Paten-/host-system for external events; every new person needs to find their own role in the project based on their motivation …

Azadeh Montazer Haghighi, Stella Moysidou, Maximilian Müller, Nora Müller, Jana Müller, Frank Muschke, Enis Musliji, Martin Muth, Martin Nachbar, Berit Nagel, Sara Nalaskowska, Matteusch Nansinski, Reza Narzarian, Ramezani Nasim, Aya Nassar, Julie Natasada, Kim(berly) Natasada, Aruna Natascha, Sanne Neumuth, Heiner Nickels, Martina Nitzl, Hanna Noller

How did you get to the University of Neighborhoods?

During my second semester of studying Architecture at HCU UoN was part of a course I took. I was a mandatory course and I don't know if I had chosen it if it wasn't for that.

What did you do at the University of Neighborhoods?

It was a two-week work session at the construction site. We repaired doors, parts of the kitchen and the garden and we opened the roof with a big concrete saw for the skylight.

What are you doing now with what you took from the University of Neighborhoods?

I work at the professorship of Urban Planning and Design, University of Stuttgart. I coordinate the research project Future City Lab — Reallabor für nachhaltige Mobilitätskultur and I am co-founder of the collective Stadtlücken e.V.

Being part of the UoN and experiencing first-hand how community-based planning and learning is done was crucial for me as a student and still is for my work.

Kerrin Nommensen, Edgar Nordmann, Frauke Nordmann, Katharina Oberlik
>   How did you get to the University of Neighborhoods?
>> I heard about it from Nadine Jessen from Kampnagel, when I was looking for a Spielstättenbescheinigung (venue certificate) for a theatre production
>   What did you do at the University of Neighborhoods?
>> I founded the 'ghettoakademie' where I worked with youngsters from the neighborhood in theatre, performance and video. Also we created a summer workshop called 'in my room'.
>   What are you doing now with what you took from the University of Neighborhoods?
>> I continued to work with the youngsters to establish an inter-cultural young performance ensemble which is called Inner Rise. I kept on producing plays and performances with them for 9 years now. www.ghettoakademie.de

Jenny Ohlenschlager
>   How did you get to the University of Neighborhoods?
>> took the "wild 13".
>   What did you do at the University of Neighborhoods?
>> Everything but living.
>> Search, inquire, wander, listen, observe, improvise, partici-pate, discover, follow, perceive, collect, discard, formulate, find, document.
>> Assemble, negotiate, communicate, contextualize, participate, enable, moderate, sort, theorize, code, categorize, research, understand, link, visualize, present.
>> Produce, sketch, visionize, try out, reject, define, calculate, clarify, detail, materialize, formulate, set, visualize, dis-cuss, convince, accompany.
>   What are you doing now with what you took from the University of Neighborhoods?
>> Academic staff member TH OWL + office parntership Brunnert u. Ohlenschlager Landschaften + freelancer for JAS e.V. To be able to work in the evening hours Kim, a former participant of the treehouse workshop (now 21), is taking care of my son. With Oskar i often watch the current construction site. Still living close to the former UoN site i often get in (private) touch with former stakeholders …

Laura Ohnesorge, Fin Oldach, Wojcieck Olkusnik, Nihmet Orhan, Florence Orrilard, Eva Osinski, Philipp Oswalt, Birke Otto, Klaus Overmeyer, Rüya Özdemir, Carlos Padilla Mora, Jürgen Pahl, Janette Paltian, Merle Pannecke, Ligia Papoi, Dharmik Parikh, Seungwon Park, Sara Parrat-Halbert, Iulia Patru, David Patzelt, Pierre Payot, Dominique Peck
>   How did you get to the University of Neighborhoods?
>> A presentation of the work of b&k+ in Vienna. Christopher Dell's Replay City and a former fellow student from Vienna who studied Urban Design and suggested I should do the same. One evening during my first week in Hamburg he took me to the UoN.
>   What did you do at the University of Neighborhoods?
>> We produced the Hotel?Wilhelmsburg.

What are you doing now with what you took from the
University of Neighborhoods?

> The perspectives, skills, theories and methods used there enable
> me to bring research, teaching and practice into play.

Walter Pelka, Ulrike Pelz, Bianca Penzlien, Akos Pesci, Jan Petersen,
Jens-Phillip Petersen, Martje Petersen, Weronika Philipp,
Christopher Phiphak

How did you get to the University of Neighborhoods?

> I got to the University of Neighborhoods and precisely in the
> "Hotel?Wilhelmsburg" project, through my Erasmus year in Urban
> Design at the HCU.

What did you do at the University of Neighborhoods?

> I was part of the Architecture Team that designed the guiding
> idea for the "Hotel?Wilhelmsburg" project. I was as well part of
> the documenting Team of the Project and part of organisational
> team for the hotel's restaurant night.

What are you doing now with what you took from the
University of Neighborhoods?

> Well as an architect-designer, I mostly use what I took from
> the UoN in design, in resources search and/or when to look for
> potential local collaborators.

Lukasz Pienczykowski, Malte Pill, Olaf Pindzig, Claudia Pittelkow,
Steffen Plath, Kerstin Pöhls

How did you get to the University of Neighborhoods?

> I got to UoN through Alexa Färbers advice to come to Hamburg and
> look for material effects of Europeanization in an urban setting
> — for example in the port of Hamburg and its museums.

What did you do at the University of Neighborhoods?

> After having agreed to come to UoN and to stay in its studio
> in 2012, I accepted a post as junior professor at Hamburg Univer-
> sity. I explored Freihafen by bike, held a workshop with new
> colleagues at UoN, talked to Hans and had inspiring encounters
> in the kitchen.

What are you doing now with what you took from the
University of Neighborhoods?

> My explorations of flows of goods through the port is now an
> ethnography of sugar as global commodity in a post-colonial
> world. I am fascinated by this substance stored not far from the
> former UoN at Hamburg Sugar Terminal and how it is connected to
> moralities. UoN strengthened my understanding of research as
> a collective endeavor — with colleagues you like to share a meal
> or two with: www.cityindustries.org

Ben Pohl

How did you get to the University of Neighborhoods?

> My first impression is from early 2010 when the "in my house"
> group had a video screening. Katja Heinecke asked me to come and
> take some pictures. I had recently started to study UD and moved
> from St.Georg to an affordable room in Wilhelmsburg.

What did you do at the University of Neighborhoods?

> I have been student, lecturer, researcher, host and guest of UoN
> in oscillating rolls. Being one of the first and last full-time

inhabitants, I spend my time sleeping, cooking, toothbrushing, reading, writing and relating with the neighborhood.

What are you doing now with what you took from the University of Neighborhoods?

I took with me a practical experience of dense relational space and what is structurally needed to frame socio-material spaces that enable activities and uses to emerge. This diagrammatic knowledge is enacted and updated on a daily basis at our practice of denkstatt sàrl in Basel.

André Poirtiers, Giovanni Pontis, Marc Postrach, Marc Pouzel, Jacopo Puccio, Eloise Pujos, German Pump, Cornelius Puschke, Leonhard Rabensteiner, Laura Raber, Nicole Raddatz, Christiane Radtke, Nihal Ragab, Tim Ranisch, Michael Rath, Paul Raupach, René Reckschwardt, Fabian Reier, Stephan Reifenrath, Inga Reimers

How did you get to the University of Neighborhoods?

As a researcher at the HafenCity University I joined a lot of events and presentations at the University of Neighborhoods and what's more, the UoN was part of my neighborhood in Hamburg-Wilhelmsburg.

What did you do at the University of Neighborhoods?

Convinced of the openness of this place, I decided to hold my research dinner entitled "Taktsinn. Ein experimenteller Abend zum Nicht-Visuellen" at the UoN. It was the kickoff of my PhD research on collective eating and cooking settings.

What are you doing now with what you took from the University of Neighborhoods?

The findings of this event and my observations made at the Hotel Wilhelmsburg events became part of my research material. Here, the UoN serves as an example e.g. for open, temporary spaces where encounter is created through collective eating/cooking.

Freya Reimers, Anton Reinig, Michelle Renz

How did you get to the University of Neighborhoods?

Through my UD-Master. The project was exciting because of the new context, the geographical space, the spatial setting and the topic - especially the interface between research and practice in the model of acting and designing oneself appealed to me.

What did you do at the University of Neighborhoods?

Generate/pass on knowledge, try out new practice, experience/ design a different setting, move chairs, eat, drink, get to know people, discuss, give/listen to presentations, experiment, cook, build, work together interdisciplinary and international

What are you doing now with what you took from the University of Neighborhoods?

Personal and professional: Adaptation and adaptability, identifying needs, analysing situations and places, interdisciplinary view, open-minded approach … help me to advise the public sector on digitization.

Jan Rettig, Alexander Reznik, Anna Richter

How did you get to the University of Neighborhoods?

I came to UoN when I joined the academic team of UD staff in October 2013 and was lucky enough to be able to live in the studio apartment from October to December 2013.

What did you do at the University of Neighborhoods?

Sleep, cook, eat, talk, read, discuss, clean, drink into the small hours… We also partied, hosted presentations, invited neighbors, organized official programs and events, watched movies, and worked together.

What are you doing now with what you took from the University of Neighborhoods?

I experienced a good share of what it means to share a space for recreation, work and leisure with students, colleagues and neighbors and above all the mind-set of the crazy house.

Joana Richter, Marianne Riecke, Elke Rieger, Martin Rieger, Tim Rieniets, Larissa Riepl, Daniel Ringeisen, Claas Rodeike, Alexander Roemer, Christian Roggenbuck

How did you get to the University of Neighborhoods?

I got into the project right in the beginning. Steven Spier and Bernd Kniess were looking for collaborators on the project. I really liked the idea of the UoN and joined the team. To me it was very important working on a project with an intellectual and physical basis.

What did you do at the University of Neighborhoods?

I supported the students by building their designs, teaching them to organize the construction site and finding ways to collect building materials.

What are you doing now with what you took from the University of Neighborhoods?

To me the project proofed it's best to work in teams. You don't need lots of money to realize a good project, it's the core, the concept and the idea that matters. The best ideas arrive in a diverse team, where each participant approaches the project from his individual point of view.

Jochen Roller, Matthias Römer, Mariana Rösel, Mariana Rösel de Laurenca, Sarah Rosenau, Holger Rosenburg, Michael Rostalski, Jasmin Rother, Gabriele Roy, Rüdis Rubenis, Claudia Rudolph, Grit Ruhland, Kathrin Rupp, Vivian Rutkowski, Sebastian Saatweber, Hikoyat Salimova, Hanna Santoro, Christoph Schäfer, Luisa Schäfer, Axel Scharper, Katja Scheer, Marion Scheffler, Viktoria Scheifers, Christian Scheler, Ulrich Schenck

How did you get to the University of Neighborhoods?

The Lawaetz Foundation was coordinating the EU-project SEEDS at Hamburg — with the University of Neighbourhoods as one of three local pilot-projects.

What did you do at the University of Neighborhoods?

The different European partners (Cities, Universities, NGO) tried to develop, test and disseminate innovative approaches and models of temporary use.

What are you doing now with what you took from the University of Neighborhoods?

The spirit is still influencing our work, we are looking for new opportunities to implement innovative ways of urban planning, living and housing.

Stefan Scheuermann, Susanne Schindler, Dieter Schirr, Ann-Kristin
Schlapkohl, Ines Schlesinger, Rosa Schlindwein, Jana Schmelin, Anne
Schmetterfeder, Alessandra Schmid, Christian Schmid, Christoph Schmidt,
Tobias Schmidt

How did you get to the University of Neighborhoods?

I applied and was invited as a researcher in residence during
fall 2013. I lived on the ground in an apartment made of upcycled
materials. It was pretty cold, I remember, but it was fun anyway!
Thank You!

What did you do at the University of Neighborhoods?

As a sociologist, I was gathering data for my PhD-Thesis on power
and conflict in participatory governance and urban planning.
Talking and eating with Ben, Hans, Vedran and many others was
very inspiring. I enjoyed a very inviting atmosphere and
inspiring projects throughout my stay.

What are you doing now with what you took from the
University of Neighborhoods?

At the moment I am initiating and coordinating service-learning
projects at the University of Applied Sciences in Augsburg. The
University of Neighborhoods gave me a good portion of hands-on
philosophy when doing projects and I both shared and increased
my knowledge on locally engaged actors and projects in Hamburg-
Wilhelmsburg. I got deep insights in theory and practice of
urban planning and participation which I took with me. As I
am going to teach some lessons for Social Work in the next semesters, I will apply my experiences in my service learning-semi-
nars, as I am going to do some neighborhood research with my
students in Augsburg next time.

Volker Schmidt, Angélique Schmitt, Tatjana Schneider

How did you get to the University of Neighbourhoods?

Curiosity. Coupled with an Erasmus grant—which took me from
Sheffield to Hamburg where I took the S-Bahn from Hauptbahnhof
across the river Elbe to Wilhelmsburg. From there I walked,
traversing, in just over 15 minutes, multiple cosmoses before
arriving at the site.

What did you do at the University of Neighbourhoods?

I talked with people, helped prepare and cook food, had lunch and
dinner, talked some more afterwards; I listened to stories, sat
in hammocks and other fantastical contraptions high above the
ground and let the world go by.

What are you doing now with what you took from the
University of Neighbourhoods?

I took thoughts and observations—which influenced, merged with
and into other thoughts: on the role and possibilities of universities, the nature and potential of different educational
settings, contexts and situations of learning.

Thomas Schnell, Matthias Schnell, Frauke Schreck, Matthias Schröder,
Friederike Schröder, Julian Schühlke, Tim Schulenburg, Julian Schülke,
Joachim Schultz, Marie-Alice Schultz, Thomas Schulze, Heiko Schulze,
Silke Schumacher, Hans-Reimer Schumacher, Nicola Schwalbe, Jörg Seifert,
Linda Shoruppa, Lars Siebels, Arno Siebert, Andras Siebold, Jorg Sieweke,
Vedran Skansi, Linda Skoruppa, Mohammed Soffar, Witali Späth, Christine

Sperling, Torben Spieker, Tereza Spindlerova, Michael Spolnik, Michael Staffa, Ricarda Steffen, Anja Steglich, Tina Steiger

How did you get to the University of Neighborhoods?

> Physically, with the Bus 13, in the summers by bicycle through the Elbtunnel. My interest was sparked when I saw a presentation about the UoN at a conference in Copenhagen, and subsequently became involved through the Department of Urban Design at the HCU.

What did you do at the University of Neighborhoods?

> The spectrum of what I did at the UoN spanned as broadly as its name; as diffuse as its definition and as wide as it's aims. Cooking and being cooked for, hosting and being hosted, teaching and being taught, giving and receiving, building and tearing down, dirtying and cleaning, keeping out and inviting in - it was about discovering what it meant to claim privacy while opening it all. All the while trying to document and depict ourselves, as the objects of study. It was a research experiment of collective living - in an urban setting, somewhere in northern Europe.

What are you doing now with what you took from the University of Neighborhoods?

> I work for an architecture exhibition space in Berlin. Conceptually, it is very similar — opening a space to the public, aiming to capture the human experience in the built environment. What I took, I can't say - but the UoN changed me forever.

Simon Steinhauser, Mareike Stillwachs, Sabine Stövesand, Felix Striegler, Julia Strohwald, Janine Stüber, Anke Stübner, Jörn Sturm, Robert Stürzl, Vanessa Subke, Dirk Südekum, Hacer Süleyman, Jessica Tag, Florian Tampe, Marion Tants, Fu Taotao, Angela Tautrims, Ana Tereza Gironi da Costa, Mark Terkessidis, Ulla Thamm, Gerti Theis, Arne Theophil, Daniel Thiel, Joachim Thiel, Korinna Thielen, Michaela Thoms, Stefanie Thoms, Sara Timm, Sarah Timmermann, Sven Timmermann, Janine Tramp, HongPhucLinda Tran, Nicole Trennert-Wellhausen, Renée Tribble, Joana Tril, Andrea Ubben, Oguzhan Uenal, Kilian Ulsamer, Christian Urner, Fuat Uzunpinar, Juan Esteban Vallejo, Anja van Eijden, Jeanne van Heeswijk, Francois Vangoyean, Jean-Philippe Vassal

How did you get to the University of Neighborhoods?

> I had been invited by the University of Neighborhood in August 2009 to a small forest inside Wilhemsburg, where a small group of students and teachers had gathered in a derelict wooden hut for discussions on the subject of architecture and urbanism.

What did you do at the University of Neighborhoods?

> It was very nice to stay for about 2 days in this hut in the urban forest, to talk with the students and my colleagues, then to do a little lecture, and to experiment all together the practice of the neighborhood.

What are you doing now with what you took from the University of Neighborhoods?

> There are more approaches to architecture and urbanism based on kindness and politeness. The question of the neighborhood which expresses the quality of the relations between the inhabitants, is the essential element for the development of this urbanism.

Hanna Vers, Joachim Versemann, Jana Vichorcová, Rocio Villar, Anne Vogelpohl, Jönna Voll, Hans Vollmer

How did you get to the University of Neighborhoods?

By bike. By interest. By Urban Design Programme.

What did you do at the University of Neighborhoods?

Building. Writing Master Thesis. Dwelling. Writing a Book about UpCycling. Cooking. Investigating. Making Jam. Hosting and being guest. Research. Everything.

What are you doing now with what you took from the University of Neighborhoods?

The UoN experience gives me the confidence and competence to take part in theoretical discourse and practical intervention in the professional field of landscape architecture and urban design.

Ute Vorkoeper, Max Voß, Andreas Wachsmuth, Anne Wagner

How did you get to the University of Neighborhoods?

We visited UoN as part of the EU project SEEDS where both, UoN and University of Copenhagen (KU), were partners. SEEDS explored reuse of derelict sites and buildings and we studied UoN as an innovative approach to transforming a building, a neighborhood as well as university didactics.

What did you do at the University of Neighborhoods?

We joined a SEEDS seminar hosted by UoN and later revisited UoN independently.
We invited UoN to speak at the Copenhagen conference: ThinkSpace 2012
Students from Urban Intervention Studio, KU joined UoN in 2013 for a weeklong design-build exploration. We published a booklet on the 20 European SEEDS cases including UoN.

What are you doing now with what you took from the University of Neighborhoods?

UoN has been a great source of inspiration for our own enquiries into the relation between production of places through small-scale spatial interventions and cultivation of community (See current research project ign.ku.dk/english/move-the-neighbour-hood/). UoN has influenced how we create learning environments at the Urban Intervention Studio. Here students are immersed into spaces and communities interacting and producing interventions and where socializing, dining and living becomes an integrated part of the didactics. See the forthcoming book (Teaching Landscape Architecture – the Studio Experience.

Rouven Wagner, Cynthia Wagner, Sofie Wagner, Rouven Wagner, Garrit Walther, Grzegorz Wasik, Helmut Weber, Markus Weck, Carmen Wegner, Mark Wehrmann, Jelena Weigel, Ralf Weißleder, Kirk Weisgerber, Inga Wellmann, Anne Wendt, Jan Wenzel, Alexander Wenzel, Philipp Wetzel, Janna R. Wieland

How did you get to the University of Neighborhoods?

During my BA in Metropolitan Culture I occasionally visited the UoN and was already involved in the project 'Urban Soccer' and the performance group 'Inner Rise' with Katharina Oberlik, where we worked together with young people from Wilhelmsburg at the intersection of dance, performance, film, biographical and educational aspects.

What did you do at the University of Neighborhoods?

> A variety of activities that went far beyond the university con-
> text of 'credit point collecting,' but can rather be compared to
> collaborative and at the same time self-study. The project and
> its dynamics beyond the university apparatus enabled learning
> and further education on different levels, in which conflicts were
> also fought out and at the same time joint successes were cele-
> brated and in a certain way also framed performatively and aes-
> thetically.

What are you doing now with what you took from the
University of Neighborhoods?

> Now I am doing my PhD at the Art Academy Düsseldorf in the field
> of cultural education research. Explorative formats, aesthetic
> working methods, and approaches as 'as found' have proven to
> be very productive in current research as well.

Petra Wiesbrock, Wnuk Wiktor, Katrin Wildner, Neil Winstanley, Dorothea
Wirwall, Jakub Witecki, Rico Wittke, Cordula Wolf, Wolfgang Wölffel, Nico
Wolter, Arne Wortmann, Tobias Wulff, Erol Yildiz, Mustafa Yilmaz, Buket
Yucer, Jana Zdenkova, Ulrich Zeiger, Torsten Zeitler, Gesa Ziemer

How did you get to the University of Neighborhoods?

> As a Professor for Cultural Theory and Cultural Practice in the
> Metropolitan Cultures study programme at the HCU I was involved
> in a lot of activities regarding the UoN. And I remember that
> it was sometimes tricky to travel to and from the UoN.

What did you do at the University of Neighborhoods?

> I attended numerous presentations and parties at the UoN and,
> nevertheless, I gave a seminar on knowledge and knowledge pro-
> duction in urban spaces at the UoN.

What are you doing now with what you took from the
University of Neighborhoods?

> I kept the UoN in mind as a place and example of open, temporal
> spaces in academic research and learning. It was an important
> place for experimentation for the Urban Design programme and,
> not least, for the HCU in the implementation process.

Michael Zinganel, Georg Zoche, Gregor Zock, Aneta Zvakova

A

Natascha Adamowsky, "Spiel und Wissenschaftskultur," in idem, ed., *Die Vernunft ist mir noch nicht begegnet* (Bielefeld: Transcript, 2005).

Leon Battista Alberti, *Zehn Bücher uber die Baukunst*, vol. 1 and 2 (Darmstadt: Wissenschaftliche Buchgesellschaft, 2005).

Leon Battista Alberti, *Das Standbild – Die Malkunst – Grundlagen der Malerei / De Statua – De Pictura – Elementa Picturae* (Darmstadt: Wissenschaftliche Buchgesellschaft, 2012).

Christopher Alexander, *Notes on the Synthesis of Form* (Cambridge, MA: Harvard University Press, 1964).

Hannah Arendt, *Was ist Politik?* (Munich: Piper Taschenbuch, 2005).

Aristoteles (Aristotle), *Über die Seele*, Book II, 4 (Berlin: Akademie-Verlag, 1959).

Atelier Bow-Wow, Made in Tokyo: Guide Book (Tokyo: Kajima Institute Publishing, 2001).

Pier Vittorio Aureli and Stanley Mathews, *Potteries Thinkbelt & Fun Palace: Deux théories de levolution selon Cedric Price* (Paris: Edition B2, 2016).

B

Roland Barthes, *Wie zusammen leben: Simulationen einiger alltäglicher Räume im Roman. Vorlesung am Collége de France 1976–1977* (Frankfurt am Main: Suhrkamp, 2007).

Eva Barlösius, *Soziologie des Essens. Eine sozial- und kulturwissenschaftliche Einführung in die Ernährungsforschung* (Weinheim: Beltz Juventa, [1999] 2016).

Jean Baudrillard, *The System of Objects*, trans. James Benedict (London and New York: Verso, 1996).

August Bebel, *Unsere Ziele. Eine Streitschrift gegen die "Demokratische Korrespondenz"* (Berlin: Expedition der Buchhandlung Vorwärts (Th. Glocke), [1869] 1903).

Thomas Bedorf and Kurt Röttgers, ed., *Das Politische und die Politik* (Frankfurt am Main: Suhrkamp, 2010).

Walter Benjamin, *The Arcades Project*, trans. Howard Eiland and Kevin McLaughlin (Cambridge, MA, and London: Belknap Press of Harvard University Press, 1999).

Andreas Blank, *Prinzipien des lexikalischen Bedeutungswandels am Beispiel der romanischen Sprachen* (Berlin: de Gruyter, 1997).

Hans Heinrich Blotevogel, "Rationality and Discourse in (Post) Modern Spatial Planning," in *The Revival of Strategic Spatial Planning*, ed. William Salet and Andreas Faludi (Amsterdam: Royal Netherlands Academy of Arts and Sciences, 2000).

Hartmut Böhme, *Fetischismus und Kultur* (Hamburg: Rowohlt Taschenbuch, 2007).

Lucius Burckhardt, *Bauen ein Prozess* (Teufen: Verlag Arthur Niggli, 1972).

Lily Braun, *Die Frauenfrage* (1901); *Frauenarbeit und Hauswirtschaft* (1901/02); *Was wir wollen* (1902).

Neil Brenner, David J. Madden, and David Wachsmuth, "Assemblage urbanism and the challenges of critical urban theory," *City* vol. 15 no. 2 (2011).

Jean Anthelme Brillat-Savarin, *Physiologie du goût, ou méditations de gastronomie transcendante* (Paris: A. Sautelet, 1826).

Victor Buchli, *An Anthropology of Architecture* (London and New York: Bloomsbury Academic, 2013).

Frank Bunker Gilbreth, *Motion Study: A Method for Increasing the Efficiency of the Workman*, with an introduction by Robert Thurston Kent (Michigan: D. Van Nostrand Company, 1911).

C

Roger Caillois, *Man, Play, and Games*, trans. Meyer Barash (Chicago: University of Illinois Press, 2001).

Chan-Fai Cheung, "Separation and Connection: Phenomenology of Door and Window," in Space, Time, and Culture, ed. D. Carr and Chan-Fai Cheung, *Contributions to Phenomenology vol. 51* (Dordrecht: Springer, 2004), 253–62, link.springer.com/chapter/10.1007/978-1-4020-2824-3_17, doi:10.1007/978-1-4020-2824-3_17.

Constant, "Manifest van de experimentele groep," *Reflex: Orgaan van de experimentele groep in Holland 1* (1948), 2–11.

Le Corbusier, *Kommende Baukunst*, ed. Hans Hildebrandt (Stuttgart/Berlin/Leipzig: Deutsche Verlags-Anstalt, 1926).

Le Corbusier, "A Contemporary City" (1929), cited in: Gary Bridge and Sophie Watson, eds., *The Blackwell City Reader* (Blackwell Publishers, 2000).

Albrecht Cordes, *Stuben und Stubengesellschaften* (Stuttgart: Fischer, 1993).

Colin Crouch, *Postdemokratie* (Frankfurt am Main: Suhrkamp, 2008).

Kimberlé Crenshaw, *On Intersectionality: Essential Writings* (New York: New Press, 2018).

Beatriz Colomina, "The Century of the Bed," in *The Century of the Bed*, ed. ARGE curated by_vienna (Vienna: Verlag für moderne Kunst, 2014), work-body-leisure.hetnieuweinstituut.nl/247-bed.

Georges Cuvier, *Vorlesung über vergleichende Anatomie*, vol. 1 (Leipzig: Paul Gotthelf Kummer, 1809–1810).

D

Pierre Dardot and Christian Laval, *Commun. Essai sur la révolution au XXIe siécle* (Paris: La Découverte, 2014).

G.-E. Debord, *Situationistische Internationale Nr. 2*, 1958.

Gilles Deleuze, "Ecrivain non: un nouveau cartographe," *Critique 343* (1975)

Christopher Dell, *The Improvisation of Space* (Berlin: Jovis, 2019).

Christopher Dell, *Epistemologie der Stadt* (Bielefeld: Transcript, 2016).

Christopher Dell, *Die Stadt als offene Partitur. Diagramm, Plan, Notation, Prozess, Improvisation, Repräsentation, Citoyenneté, Performanz in Musik, Kunst, Design, Stadtentwicklung* (Zurich: Lars Müller Publishers, 2016).

Christopher Dell, *Die improvisierende Organisation* (Bielefeld: Transcript, 2012).

Christopher Dell, "Reverse Functionalism," in Tomás Valena, Tom Avermaete, and Georg Vrachliotis, eds., *Structuralism Reloaded* (Stuttgart: Axel Menges, 2011).

Christopher Dell, "Subjekte der Wiederverwertung (Remix)," in Hans-Friedrich Bormann, Gabriele Brandstetter, and Annemarie Matzke, *Improvisieren. Paradoxien des Unvorhersehbaren: Kunst – Medien – Praxis* (Bielefeld: Transcript, 2010), 220.

Christopher Dell, "Performanz des Raumes," Arch+ 183 (2007): 134.

Christopher Dell, Bernd Kniess, Dominique Peck, Anna Richter., "The Assembly of the University of the Neighbourhoods (UoN): A Documentation of Making New Forms of Agencies Available," in *Housing – A Critical Perspective*, ed. Graham Cairns (Liverpool: Architecture_Media_Politics_Society, 2016).

René Descartes, *Von der Methode* (Hamburg: Meiner, [1637] 1960).

Emile Durkheim, *Regeln der soziologischen Methode* (Neuwied and Berlin: Suhrkamp Taschenbuch Wissenschaft, 1961).

Frédéric Druot, Anne Lacaton, and Jean-Philippe Vassal, *Plus: Large-Scale Housing Development* (Barcelona: Editorial Gustavo Gilli, 2007).

E

Keller Easterling, *Extrastatecraft: The Power of Infrastructure Space* (London: Verso, 2014).

Keller Easterling, "Management," in *OfficeUS Agenda*, ed. Eva Franch i Gilabert, Ana Milijački, Ashley Schafer, Michael Kubo, and Amanda Reeser Lawrence (Zurich: Lars Müller Publishers, 2014).

Friedrich Engels and Karl Marx, *Werke*, vol. 19, 4th ed. of the unrevised reprint of the 1st ed. 1962 (Berlin (GDR): (Karl) Dietz Verlag, 1973), 177–228.

F

Alfred Faber, *1000 Jahre Werdegang von Herd und Ofen. Ausgewählte Kapitel aus ihrer technischen Entwicklung bis zu Beginn des 19. Jahrhunderts* (Munich, Oldenburg, and Düsseldorf: Deutscher Ingenieur-Verlag, 1950).

Alexa Färber, "Greifbarkeit der Stadt. Überlegungen zu einer stadt- und wissensanthropologischen Erforschung stadträumlicher Aneignungspraktiken," *dérive. Zeitschrift für Stadtforschung* 40 (2010) 100–5.

Erika Fischer-Lichte, *The Transformative Power of Performance: A New Aesthetics*, trans. Saskya Iris Jain (Oxfordshire: Routledge, 2008).

Vilém Flusser, *The Shape of Things: A Philosophy of Design* (London: Reaktion, 1999), 82–83.

Forensic Architecture, *Forensis: The Architecture of Public Truth* (Berlin: Sternberg Press, 2014).

Kurt W. Forster und Hubert Locher, *Theorie der Praxis. Leon Battista Alberti als Humanist und Theoretiker der bildenden Künste* (Berlin: De Gruyter, 1999), 97.

Michel Foucault, *Discipline and Punish: The Birth of the Prison*, trans. from the French by Alan Sheridan (New York: Vintage Books, 1995).

Michel Foucault, "The Subject and Power," *Critical Inquiry 8*, no. 4 (Summer 1982), 777–95.

Michel Foucault, "The Confession of the Flesh," in Colin Gordon, *Power/Knowledge: Selected Interviews & Other Writings 1972–1977* (New York: Pantheon Books, 1980).

Michel Foucault, *Discipline and Punish: The Birth of the Prison* (New York: Pantheon Books, 1977).

Michel Foucault, *The Order of Things: An Archaeology of the Human Sciences* (London: Routledge, [1966] 2006).

Charles Fourier, "1846: 132–133," in Martin Burghardt, Charles Fourier. *Der Philosoph der Kleinanzeige* (Berlin: Semele Verlag, 2006).

G

Clifford Geertz, *Deep Play: Notes on the Balinese Cockfight* (Münster: Daedalus, 2005).

Paul Gilroy, *After Empire: Melancholia or Convivial Culture?* (London: Routledge, 2004).

Erving Goffman, *Wir alle spielen Theater. Die Selbstdarstellung im Alltag* (Munich: Piper, 1983).

Rüdiger Görner, *Grenzen, Schwellen, Übergänge. Zur Poetik des Transitorischen* (Göttingen: Vandenhoeck & Ruprecht, 2001).

Isabelle Graw, "Gruppenspiele," in *Die Vernunft ist mir noch nicht begegnet*, ed. Natascha Adamowsky.

Gernot Grabher, "Temporary Architectures of Learning: Knowledge Governance in Project Ecologies," *Organization Studies 25*, no. 9 (2004), 1491–1514.

Gernot Grabher and Joachim Thiel, *Self-Induced Shocks: Mega-Projects and Urban Development* (Berlin: Jovis Verlag, 2015).

Claude Grignon, "Commensality and Social Morphology: An Essay of Typology," in *Food, Drink and Identity: Cooking, Eating and Drinking in Europe Since the Middle Ages*, ed. Peter Scholliers (Oxford: Oxford University Press, 2001).

Jacob und Wilhelm Grimm, "Stube," in Deutsches Wörterbuch, vol. 20, 157; Grimm, "Wirtsstube," in *Deutsches Wörterbuch, vol. 30*, 704.

H
Ian Hacking, *Representing and Intervening* (Cambridge: Cambridge University Press, 1983).

Thomas Hafner, *Kollektive Wohnreformen im Deutschen Kaiserreich (1871–1918) – Anspruch und Wirklichkeit* (Stuttgart: Universität Stuttgart, 1992).

Anne Harris and Stacy Holman Jones, "Genderfication," in Nelson Rodriguez, Wayne Martino, Jennifer Ingrey, and Edward Brockenbrough, eds., *Critical Concepts in Queer Studies and Education: An International Guide for the Twenty-First Century* (New York: Palgrave Macmillan, 2016).

Ulf Hestermann, Dietrich Neumann, and Ulrich Weinbrenner, Frick/Knöll *Baukonstruktionslehre* (Wiesbaden: Springer Vieweg, 2006).

Nadine Holdsworth, *Joan Littlewood's Theatre* (Cambridge: Cambridge University Press, 2011).

Edmund Husserl, *Ideen zu einer reinen Phänomenologie und phänomenologischen Philosophie* (Den Haag: Martinus Nijhoff, 1950), 30–31, pp. 62–69.

I
Ivan Illich, *Tools of Conviviality* (Glasgow: Fontana, 1975).

J
Charles Jencks, *The Iconic Building: The Power of Enigma* (London: Francis Lincoln, 2005).

K
Immanuel Kant, Paul Guyer, Allen W. Wood, and Immanuel Kant, *Critique of Pure Reason* (Cambridge and New York: Cambridge University Press, 1998).

Immanuel Kant, *Kritik der Urteilskraft*, in idem, *Werkausgabe*, ed. Wilhelm Weischedel, vol. X, 9.

Habbo Knoch, *Grandhotels* (Göttingen: Wallstein Verlag, 2016).

Rem Koolhaas, *Elements of Architecture: Central Pavilion* (2014).

Rem Koolhaas and Bruce Mau, "The Generic City," in idem, S M L XL, 2nd ed. (New York: Monacelli Press, 1997), 1239–64.

Rem Koolhaas, *Delirious New York* (New York: Moncalli Press, 1994 [1978]), 157.

Wajiro Kon, *Retrospective* (Kyoto: Seigensha Art Publishing, 2011).

Jens Kuhlenkampf, Immanuel Kant: *Köche ohne Zunge* (Göttingen: Steidl, 1997).

L
Royston Landau, "A Philosophy of Enabling: The Work of Cedric Price," *AA Files 8* (January 1985): 3–7, www.jstor.org/stable/29543432 (last accessed October 31, 2019).

Bruno Latour, *Reassembling the Social: An Introduction to Actor-Network-Theory* (Oxford: Oxford University Press, 2005).

Bruno Latour, "Why Has Critique Run Out of Steam? From Matters of Fact to Matters of Concern," *Critical Inquiry: Special Issue on the Future of Critique*, vol. 30, no. 2 (Winter 2004): 25–248. Republished in *Harper's Magazine*, April 2004, 15–20. Republication reprinted in Bill Brown, ed., Things (Chicago: The University of Chicago Press, 2003), 151–74.

John Law, "Pinboards and Books: Juxtaposing, Learning and Materiality," version of 28 April 2006, 18. Available at: www.heterogeneities.net/publications/Law2006PinboardsAndBooks.pdf

Henri Lefebvre, *The Urban Revolution* (Minneapolis: University of Minnesota Press, 2003).

Henri Lefebvre, *The Production of Space* (Oxford and Cambridge: Blackwell [1974], 1991).

Henri Lefebvre, *Metaphilosophie* (Frankfurt am Main: Suhrkamp, 1975 (1965)).

Rolf Lindner, "Die Angst des Forschers vor dem Feld," *Zeitschrift für Volkskunde 77* (1981): 51–66.

Adolf Loos, *On Architecture*, selected and introduced by Adolf and Daniel Opel, trans. Michael Mitchel (Riverside, CA: Ariadne Press, 2002).

Claude Lefort, "Permanence du theologico-politique?," in idem, *Essais sur le politique* (Paris: Seuil, 1986).

Cordula Loidl-Reisch, "Im Freien. Von Spielorten, Spielplätzen und der bespielbaren Stadt," in Felderer et al., *Spiele der Stadt*, 202.

M
David H. Maister, "Balancing the Professional Services Firm," *Sloan Management Review* (Fall 1982): 15–29.

Marcel Mauss, "Die Gabe. Form und Funktion des Austauschs in archaischen Gesellschaften," in *Soziologie und Anthropologie*, vol. 1 (Munich: Ullstein, [1924] 1978).

Karl Marx and Martin Nicolaus, *Grundrisse: Foundations of the Critique of Political Economy* (Rough Draft) (London: Penguin Books, 1993).

Karl Marx and Martin Milligan, *Economic and Philosophic Manuscripts of 1844* (Amherst, NY: Prometheus Books, 1988).

Ernst May, ed., *Das neue Frankfurt: Internationale Monatsschrift für die Probleme kultureller Neugestaltung 1* (Frankfurt am Main: Verlag Englert und Schlosser, 1926/1927).

Tabea Michaelis, *Showtime Wilhelmsburg: A Randonnée of Possibilities* (Leipzig: Spector Books, 2015).

Christoph Menke, *Die Kraft der Kunst,* (Frankfurt am Main: Suhrkamp, 2013).

Thomas Möbius, *Russische Sozialutopien von Peter I. bis Stalin* (Berlin: Lit Verlag, 2012).

N
Alexander Neupert-Doppler, *Utopie. Vom Roman zur Denkfigur* (Stuttgart: Schmetterling Verlag, 2015).

Kathrin Heinz and Irene Nierhaus, ed., *Matratze/Matrize* (Bielefeld: Transcript, 2016).

Stephen Nelson and Peter Katzenstein, *Uncertainty and Risk and the Crisis of 2008* (San Diego: University of California-San Diego, 2010).

O

Rolf Oerter, "Zur Psychologie des Spiels," *Psychologie und Gesellschaftskritik 31*, no. 4 (2007): 7–32, nbn-resolving.de/urn:nbn:-de:0168-ssoar-292301.

Kay Owens, "Visuospatial Reasoning in Twentieth-Century Psychology-Based Studies," in *Visuospatial Reasoning*, Mathematics Education Library 111 (2015).

P

Susan M. Pearce, *Museums, Objects, and Collections* (Washington, DC: Smithsonian Books, 1993).

Plato, "Nomoi 804b3," in idem, *The Laws*, transl. Tom Griffith (Cambridge: Cambridge University Press, 2016).

Ute Poerschke, *Funktionen und Formen. Architekturtheorie der Moderne* (Bielefeld: Transcript, 2014).

Emily Post, *Etiquette in Society, in Business, in Politics, and at Home* (New York: Cosimobooks New York, [1922] 2007).

R

Hans J. Rheinberger, *Experiment, Differenz, Schrift. Zur Geschichte epistemischer Dinge* (Marburg an der Lahn: Basilisken-Presse im Verlag Natur & Text, 1992).

Hans-Jörg Rheinberger, *Experimentalsysteme und epistemische Dinge. Eine Geschichte der Proteinsynthese im Reagenzglas* (Göttingen: Wallstein Verlag, 2002).

Irma Rybnikova, "Management as 'Purity Apostle': A Cultural-Anthropological Approach," *in ReThinking Management: Perspectives and Impacts of Cultural Turns and Beyond*, ed. Wendelin Küpers, Stephan Sonnenburg, and Martin Zierold (Wiesbaden: Springer VS, 2017), 59–77, doi: 10.1007/978-3-658-16983-1_3.

S

Ulrich Schädler, "Vertreibung aus dem Paradies, über das Tempelhupfen," in Brigitte Felderer, Ernst Strouhal, and Friedrich Schiller, "Über die ästhetische Erziehung des Menschen [2. Teil; 10. bis 16. Brief.]," in idem, ed., *Die Horen, 2. Stück* (Tübingen: J. G. Cottaische Buchhandlung, 1795).

Uwe Schröder, "Die Wand. Grenze der Architektur – Architektur der Grenze," *Der Architekt 4* (2016).

Gottfried Semper, *Die vier Elemente der Baukunst* (Braunschweig: Vieweg, 1851). Semper.

Michel Serres, *The Parasite*, trans. Lawrence R. Schehr (Baltimore: Johns Hopkins University Press, 1982).

Walter Siebel, *Die Kultur der Stadt* (Berlin: Suhrkamp, 2015).

Georg Simmel, "Die Großstadt. Vorträge und Aufsätze zur Städteausstellung," in *Jahrbuch der Gehe-Stiftung Dresden*, ed. Th. Petermann (Dresden, 1903), 185–206.

Georg Simmel, *Brücke und Tür* (Stuttgart: F. H. Koehler, 1957), 3–4.

Gertrude Stein, "Plays," in Gertrude Stein, *Last Operas and Plays* (Baltimore and London: Johns Hopkins University Press, 1995), xxix–lii.

T

Bruno Taut, *Die neue Wohnung. Die Frau als Schöpferin* (Leipzig: Klinkhardt & Biermann, 1925).

Georges Teyssot, *A Topology of Everyday Constellations* (Cambridge, MA: MIT Press, 2013).

Victor Turner, *The Ritual Process: Structure and Anti-Structure* (Ithaca: Cornell University Press, 1966).

Mark Twain, *The Adventures of Tom Sawyer* (1876), excerpt reprinted in "Whitewashing the Fence," Lapham's Quarterly 8, no. 2 (Spring 2015), accessed April 10, 2019, www.laphamsquarterly.org/swindle-fraud/whitewashing-fence.

V

Robert Venturi, *Complexity and Contradiction in Architecture* (New York: Museum of Modern Art, 1977).

Robert Venturi, Denise Scott Brown, and Steven Izenour, *Learning from Las Vegas, Revised Edition: The Forgotten Symbolism of Architectural Form* (Cambridge, MA: MIT Press, 1977).

Vitruvius, *Ten Books on Architecture*, trans. Morris Hicky Morgan (Cambridge, MA: Harvard University Press, 1914).

Vitruv (Vitruvius), *Zehn Bücher über Architektur, translated and with comments by Curt Fensterbusch* (Darmstadt: Wissenschaftliche Buchgesellschaft, [1964] 2013).

W

Torsten Wiechmann, *Planung und Adaption* (Dortmund: Rohn Verlag, 2008).

Lambert Wiesing, *Sehen lassen. Die Praxis des Zeigens* (Frankfurt am Main: Suhrkamp Taschenbuch Wissenschaft, 2013).

Frederick Winslow Taylor, "Shop Management," *Transactions of the American Society of Mechanical Engineers 28* (1903): 1337–1480.

Ludwig Wittgenstein, *Tractatus logico-philosophicus: Logisch-philosophische Abhandlung*, ed. Kevin C. Klement, Side-by-Side by-Side Edition, Version 0.58 (May 24, 2020), accessed June 21, 2020, people.umass.edu/klement/tlp/, p. 16, para. 2.151.

Max Weber, *Grundriß der Sozialökonomik III. Abteilung Wirtschaft und Gesellschaft* (Tübingen: Mohr, 1922).

Z

Clara Zetkin, *Die Arbeiterinnen- und Frauenfrage der Gegenwart* (Berlin: Verlag der Berliner Volks-Tribüne, 1889).

Sharon Zukin, *Landscapes of Power: From Detroit to Disney World* (Berkeley: University of California Press, 1993).

Manfred Zollinger, eds., *Spiele der Stadt. Glück, Gewinn und Zeitvertreib* (Vienna and New York: Springer, 2012).

p. 177
– Hang on! Tree houses, UoN Project Archive / Ben Becker, 2013
– Gehry Residence, Frank Gehry, 1978
– Judy Chicago addresses a gathering of volunteers in the Dinner Party Studio, Amy Meadow/NMWA, 1978

p. 178
– Wilhelmsburg Orchestra, UoN Project Archive, 2011
– Jérôme Bel's The Show Must Go On, Yi-Chun Wu, 2016
– Hang on! Tree houses, UoN Project Archive / Ben Becker, 2013
– Artists in the Big Top: Perplexed (Die Artisten in der Zirkuskuppel: Ratlos), Alexander Kluge mit Hannelore Hoger, Sigi Graue, Alfred Edel, 1968
– Wilhelmsburg Orchestra, 48h Wilhelmsburg, UoN Project Archive, 2012
– Theaster Gates, 12 Ballads for Huguenot House, dOCUMENTA (13), Kassel, Germany, 2012

p. 180
– Hang on! Tree houses, UoN Project Archive / Ben Becker, 2013
– Hang on! Tree houses, UoN Project Archive / Ben Becker, 2013
– Wilhelmsburg Orchestra, UoN Project Archive, 2010
– Hotel?Wilhelmsburg, UoN Project Archive, 2012
– The Pepsi Pavilion in Osaka Spherical Mirror Upside Down, Fujiko Nakaya, 1970
– Hotel?Wilhelmsburg, Building and inhabiting a common low-budget luxury shelter, with Alexander Römer, UoN Project Archive / Martin Rieger, 2013

p. 182
– The Hostage in Stratford, Theatre Royal Stratford East, Joan Littlewood, © J.B. Hanley / Paul Popper / Popperfoto / Getty Images, 1959
– First transformation phase, construction site internship, UoN Project Archive / Ben Becker, 2010
– Intercultural Soccer Tournament, Wilhelmsburg Art and Sports Club, UoN Project Archive, 2010
– Inner Rise, Ghetto Academy – In my Room, UoN Project Archive / Alexandra Heneka, 2010
– Teaching, Research, Projects, UoN Project Archive / Bernd Kniess, 2009
– Bar for nice people (Bar für nette Leute), Culture Kitchen / Shivers / Ton Matton, UoN Project Archive, 2009

p. 184
– Hotel?Wilhelmsburg at "Soul Kitchen" warehouse, UoN Project Archive / Vedran Skanski, 2013
– Wilhelmsburg Orchestra, UoN Project Archive, 2011
– Windows, UoN Project Archive / Maja Momic and Adrian Judt, 2013
– Seminar, UoN Project Archive, 2012
– Window detail, UoN Project Archive / Ben Becker, 2010
– Inside France's "Modernity, Promise or Menace?" Prouvé Exhibition – Bernd Kniess, 2014

p. 186
– Made in … Local practices of urban production, Workshop, UoN Project Archive / Michele Sbrissa, 2011
– Concept for securing and sealing the windows, UoN Project Archive, 2009
– Christopher Walking, UoN Project Archive / Ben Becker, 2009
– First transformation phase, construction site internship, UoN Project Archive / Ben Becker, 2009
– Hotel?Wilhelmsburg, UoN Project Archive, 2013
– Household of a newly-married couple, Entrance and home office, Modernologio, Kon Wajiro, 1925

p. 188
– Minutes of the meeting UoN, UoN Project Archive / Ellen Fiedelmeier, 2009
– Made in … Local practices of urban production, Workshop, UoN Project Archive / Michele Sbrissa, 2011
– Site visit, UoN Project Archive / Christopher Dell, 2009
– Site visit, UoN Project Archive / Ellen Fiedelmeyer, 2009
– Rotenhäuser nurseries – Garden laboratory, UoN Project Archive, 2011
– Hospital Hall in the Cistercian Monastery in Kloster Eberbach in the Rheingau region, 13th century

p. 190
– Cellule No.3 (Prototype), Absalon, Installation view KW Institute for Contemporary Art, 2010
– Farewell party, UoN Project Archive / Katrin Borchers, 2014

– Hang on! Tree houses, UoN Project Archive / Martin Rieger, 2013
– Hotel?Wilhelmsburg, Building and inhabiting a common low-budget luxury shelter, International Building Workshops, UoN Project Archive / Ben Becker, 2013
– Hotel?Wilhelmsburg, Building and inhabiting a common low-budget luxury shelter International Building Workshops, UoN Project Archive / Katrin Borchers, 2013
– Capsule Hotel Tokyo, allabout-japan.com, 2016

p. 192
– Stacking daybed (*Stapelliege*), Building workshops, UoN Project Archive / Ben Becker, 2012
– Studio appartment UoN, Building workshops, UoN Project Archive, 2012
– Stacking daybed (*Stapelliege*), Rolf Heide, 1966
– Hang on! Tree houses, UoN Project Archive / Martin Rieger, 2013
– Hang on! Tree houses, UoN Project Archive / Ben Becker, 2013
– Student life and work at the UoN International Summer School 2011, UoN Project Archive / Michele Sbrissa, 2009

p. 194
– Living as practice – Hotel Hamburg | [k]-stage | UoN Pension Wilhelmsburg, UoN Project Archive / Bernd Kniess, 2012
– Farewell party, UoN Project Archive / Katrin Borchers, 2014
– Live, Haus-Rucker-Co, 1971

– Hotel?Wilhelmsburg International Building Workshop, UoN Project Archive / Ben Becker, 2013
– Cobrafestival. Cobra II. How To Live Together, UoN Project Archive / Katrin Borchers, Tina Steiger, Julia Lerch Zajączkowska, 2013
– Hotel?Wilhelmsburg International Building Workshop, UoN Project Archive / Ben Becker, 2013

p. 196
– Cobrafestival. Cobra II. How To Live Together, UoN Project Archive / Katrin Borchers, Tina Steiger, Julia Lerch Zajączkowska, 2013
– Lecture Alexander Römer – EXYZT, Hotel?Wilhelmsburg, Building and inhabiting a common low-budget luxury shelter, International Building Workshops, UoN Project Archive, Martin Rieger, 2013
– Building Workshops, UoN Project Archive / Ben Becker, 2012
– Building Workshops, UoN Project Archive / Ben Becker, 2012
– Tanikawa House, Kazuo Shinohara, 1974
– Tanikawa House, Kazuo Shinohara, 1974

p. 198
– Martin Kaltwasser, Hotel?Wilhelmsburg International Building Workshop, UoN Project Archive, 2013
– Student life and work at the UoN International Summer School 2009, UoN Project Archive / Michele Sbrissa, 2011
– Flying City, Georgii Krutikov, 1928

– Student life and work at the UoN International Summer School 2009, UoN Project Archive / Michele Sbrissa, 2011
– Engraving depicting daily life at the Hôtel-Dieu in the 16th century Exhibition at the Musée de l'Assistance publique de Paris, Author unknown, about 1500
– Hotel?Wilhelmsburg, UoN Project Archive / Ben Becker, 2013

p. 200
– Hotel?Wilhelmsburg International Building Workshop, UoN Project Archive / Bojan Nisevic, 2013
– Living as practice – Hotel Hamburg | [k]-stage | UoN Pension Wilhelmsburg, UoN Project Archive / Bernd Kniess, 2012
– Comics & Capsule Hotel Comicap KYOTO
– Made in … Local practices of urban production, Workshop, UoN Project Archive / Ben Pohl, 2011
– Carte de Paris avant, Guy Debord, 1957
– Hotel?Wilhelmsburg International Building Workshop, UoN Project Archive, 2013

p. 202
– Housewives' Kitchen Apron, Birgit Jürgenssen, 1975
– First transformation phase, Construction site internship, UoN Project Archive / Ben Becker, 2010
– Semiotics of the Kitchen, Martha Rosler, 1975
– Restaurant evening, Hotel?Wilhelmsburg International Building Workshop, UoN Project Archive / Vedran Skansi, 2013

– Just what is it that makes today's homes so different, so appealing? Richard Hamilton, 1956
– Hans presents the lamb, Hang on! Tree houses, UoN Project Archive, 2013

p. 204
– Guest at the Conspiratorial cuisine concerts *(Konspirative Küchenkonzerte)*, UoN Project Archive, 2009
– "FOOD," Gordon Matta-Clark, 1970s
– Guest at the Conspiratorial cuisine concerts *(Konspirative Küchenkonzerte)*, UoN Project Archive, 2009
– Hang on! Tree houses, UoN Project Archive / Martin Rieger, 2013
– Cobrafestival. Cobra II. How To Live Together, UoN Project Archive / Martin Rieger, 2013
– Neighbourhood Festival, Experts of everyday life and God's Entertainment, UoN Project Archive / Ben Becker, 2009

p. 206
– Waffle iron, UoN Project Archive, 2013
– Hotel?Wilhelmsburg, Building and inhabiting a common low-budget luxury shelter International, UoN Project Archive, 2013
– Neighborhood Workshops
– Learning from each other in Hamburg and Cairo, HafenCity Universität Hamburg: Research and Teaching Programme Urban Design; Cairo University: Center for civilization studies and dialogue of cultures, UoN Project Archive / Mathias Schnell, 2012

– Bye Bye UoN, UoN Project Archive / Vedran Skansi, 2014
– Neighborhood Workshops
– Learning from each other in Hamburg and Cairo, HafenCity Universität Hamburg: Teaching and Research Program Urban Design; Cairo University: Center for civilization studies and dialogue of cultures, UoN Project Archive / Mathias Schnell, 2012
– The new flat. The woman as creator *(Die neue Wohnung. Die Frau als Schöpferin)*, Bruno Taut, 1924

p. 208
– Untitled (Woman at the Stove) [ohne Titel (Frau am Herd)], Rosemarie Trockel, 1994
– Untitled Film Still #84, Cindy Sherman, 1980
– UoN at Westwerk Gallery, UoN Project Archive / Ben Becker, 2013

p. 249
– Hotel?Wilhelmsburg, UoN Project Archive / Ben Becker, 2013
– Hotel?Wilhelmsburg, UoN Project Archive / Ben Becker, 2013
– Capsule Hotel Asahi Plaza Shinsaibashi, 1979

p. 250
– UoN at Westwerk Gallery, UoN Project Archive / Ben Becker, 2013
– Tower Shaped Community, Kiyonori Kikutake, 1958
– Precarious Tasks #0 Communal Tea Drinking, Koki Tanaka, 2012
– Cobrafestival. Cobra II. How To Live Together, UoN

Project Archive / Martin Rieger, 2013
– William Forsythe. The Fact of Matter, Dominik Mentzo, 2015
– "Cörper Cabel Construktionen" UoN Studio contribution, UoN Project Archive / Marie-Alice Schulz, 2012

p. 252
– Artists in the Big Top: Perplexed *(Die Artisten in der Zirkuskuppel: Ratlos)* Alexander Kluge mit Hannelore Hoger, Sigi Graue, Alfred Edel, 1968
– Intercultural practice, summer camp, tree houses, UoN Project Archive / Ben Becker, 2012
– Festive unveiling of the IBA stela, UoN Project Archive / Ben Becker, 2010
– Theaster Gates, House of Huguenots, Boris Roessler, 2012
– Administrative structure within the thematic fields, UoN Project Archive / Christopher Dell and Bernd Kniess, 2018
– Administrative structure within the thematic fields, translated for layout in the book, UoN Project Archive / Dominique Peck, 2018

p. 254
– *Baukonstruktionslehre, Dachtragwerke als Zimmermannskonstruktion* (Roof supporting structures as carpenter's construction), Frick / Knöll, 1996
– Drawings and calculations, UoN builder's hut, UoN Project Archive / Jonathan Gröne, 2009/10
– Drawings and calculations, UoN builder's hut, UoN

Project Archive / Jonathan Gröne, 2009/10
– Tanikawa House, Kazuo Shinohara, 1974
– Metavilla, French pavilion – 10th Venice Architecture Biennale – EXYZT Küche, 2006
– Kitchen, UoN Project Archive, 2010

p. 256
– Student life and work at the UoN, UoN Project Archive / Adrian Judt, 2013
– UoN Summerfest, UoN Project Archive / Ben Pohl, 2011
– Tanikawa House, Kazuo Shinohara, 1974
– Gramsci Bar at the art pavillon "Gramsci Monument" Dia Art Foundation, Thomas Hirschhorn, 2013
– Neighborhood Workshops – Learning from each other in Hamburg and Cairo, HafenCity Universität Hamburg: Teaching and Research Program Urban Design; Cairo University: Center for civilization studies and dialogue of cultures, UoN Project Archive / Mathias Schnell, 2012
– Neighborhood Workshops – Learning from each other in Hamburg and Cairo, HafenCity Universität Hamburg: Teaching and Research Program Urban Design; Cairo University: Center for civilization studies and dialogue of cultures, UoN Project Archive / Mathias Schnell, 2012

p. 258
– Hotel?Wilhelmsburg, Building and inhabiting a common low-budget luxury shelter International Building Workshops, UoN Project Archive, 2013
– First transformation phase, UoN builder's hut, Construction site internship, UoN Project Archive / Ben Becker, 2010
– Marcus Steinweg, daily lectures @ Thomas Hirschhorn, Gramsci Monument, New York, 2013
– Pots, pans and other cookware and equipment in the kitchen of the UoN, UoN Project Archive
– Housing Is a Human Right, Martha Rosler, 1989
– A photography class in a cabbage patch at Black Mountain College, Barbara Morgan, 2019

p. 260
– Hotel?Wilhelmsburg, Building and inhabiting a common low-budget luxury shelter International Building Workshops, UoN Project Archive / Ben Becker, 2013
– Construction site internship, UoN Project Archive / Ben Becker, 2010
– Demolition of the UoN, UoN Project Archive / Maja Momic / Kai Michael Dietrich, 2014
– DIE 120 TAGE VON BOTTROP, Christoph Schlingensief, 1997
– Announcement for Shivers, UoN Project Archive, 2009
– Student life and work at the UoN, UoN Project Archive, 2013

p. 262
– Relationship diagram of a head office with 800 persons (Beziehungsschema einer Hauptverwaltung mit 800 Personen). / from: Ottomar Gottschalk Flexible administrative buildings (Flexible Verwaltungsbauten), Verlag Schnelle, Quickborn – Karin Eckl, 1968
– UoN Matrix, UoN Project Archive / Christopher Dell, 2009
– Conceptual Drawing of Fun Palace, Cedric Price, 1964
– Fun Palace, Cedric Price, 1964
– Intercultural practice, summer camp, tree houses, UoN Project Archive / Ben Becker, 2012
– Hotel?, UoN Project Archive / Mattia Gammarotta, 2013

p. 264
– Forming UoN places. The story of three young people. (UdN-Orte prägen. Die Geschichte dreier Jugendlicher.), UoN Project Archive, 2008
– Stefanie Gernert (Project development, project management), UoN Project Archive, 2010
– Still image of Tina Girouard from Food, Gordon Matta-Clark, 1972
– Ten hours of UoN Neighbourhood Festival, Experts of everyday life and God's Entertainment, UoN Project Archive, 2009
– Neighborhood Workshops – Learning from each other in Hamburg and Cairo, HafenCity Universität Hamburg: Teaching and Research Program Urban Design; Cairo University: Center for civilization studies and dialogue of cultures, UoN

Project Archive / Mathias Schnell, 2012
– The Kitchen Monument in front of the Berlinische Galerie, Discursive Dinner, raumlabor berlin, 2014

p. 266
– Kitchen, UoN Project Archive, 2011
– Bye Bye UoN, UoN Project Archive / Vedran Skansi, 2014
– The Great Kitchen, John Nash, 1826
– Hotel?Wilhelmsburg International Building Workshop, UoN Project Archive / Vedran Skansi, 2013
– Views and material list for the extension of the main room and the kitchen as a terrace, UoN Project Archive / Maja Momic, 2013
– Restaurant evening, Hotel?Wilhelmsburg International Building Workshop, UoN Project Archive, 2013

p. 268
– Hotel?Wilhelmsburg International Building Workshop, UoN Project Archive, 2013
– UoN – Enabling architecture for the learning city. Research and design project 2008/09. Rural/urban Hybrids, UoN Project Archive / Kilian Allmann, Sven Braun, Kathrin Rupp, Linda Skoruppa, Sarah Timmermann, 2008/09
– UoN – Enabling architecture for the learning city. Research and design project 2008/09. Exterior research and design, UoN Project Archive / Kilian Allmann, Sven Braun, Kerrin Nommensen, 2008/09
– Tableau Phase 1, Starting

the UoN curriculum – Culture Kitchen / Shivers / Ton Matton, UoN Project Archive / Research and Teaching Programme Urban Design, 2009
– Bilderatlas Mnemosyne, Aby Warburg, 1920s
– Hotel?Wilhelmsburg International Building Workshop, UoN Project Archive, 2013

p. 270
– Contribution to the annual exhibition of HafenCity University Hamburg, UoN Project Archive / Research and Teaching Programme Urban Design, 2009
– First transformation phase, UoN builder's hut, Construction site internship, UoN Project Archive / Ben Becker, 2010
– Modells from the planning competition Experiment on the island, UoN Project Archive / Martina Nitzl, 2008
– Bruno Taut, The new flat. The woman as creator (Die neue Wohnung. Die Frau als Schöpferin), Christine Frederick, 1912
– Hotel?Wilhelmsburg, UoN Project Archive / Bernd Kniess, 2013
– The first living creature in space, Sputnik II, 1957

p. 272
– Nurturant Kitchen, Robin Weltsch, 1972
– Studio Kitchen, Construction site internship, UoN Project Archive / Ben Becker, 2011
– Küchenmonument, A raumlaborberlin and Plastique Fantastique project coproduction with the Duisburger Akzenten and

Ringlokschuppen, Mülheim, 2006
– Neighborhood Workshops
– Learning from each other in Hamburg and Cairo, HafenCity Universität Hamburg: Teaching and Research Program Urban Design; Cairo University: Center for civilization studies and dialogue of cultures, UoN Project Archive / Mathias Schnell, 2012
– Ant Farm, The World's largest Snake, James Burns, 1971
– UoN Open Air, UoN Project Archive / Martin Rieger, 2013

p. 274
– Historical photograph of the unmarried home, women at table, 1950s
– Culture Kitchen / Workshop Ton Matton, UoN Project Archive / Christopher Dell, 2009
– Trailmaster GTO + 2 with beefed rear axle and drivetrain Transcontinental "Instant Split-Level" trailer home, François Dallegret, 1965
– Hotel?Wilhelmsburg International Building Workshop, UoN Project Archive, 2013
– Intercultural practice, summer camp, tree houses, UoN Project Archive / Martin Rieger, 2012
– The American Woman's Home. fig. kitchen and stove room, Harriet Beecher Stowe, Catharine Beecher, 1869

p. 276
– Ten hours of UoN Neighbourhood Festival, Experts of everyday life and God's

Entertainment, UoN Project Archive / Ben Becker, 2009
– Intercultural Soccer Tournament, Wilhelmsburg Art and Sports Club, UoN Project Archive, 2010
– Orphanage Amsterdam, Aldo van Eyck, 1960
– Kaiser dishwasher and Instant Disposal Unit, Advertisement for "merit specified," published in Arts and Architecture, May 1948
– Cobrafestival. Cobra II. How To Live Together, UoN Project Archive, 2013
– "Steril-dry" brochure cover, 1944

p. 278
– Lillian Gilbreth: A Pardoe kitchen, inspired by Gilbreth's Kitchen Practical design, by the Kitchen Equipment Co., Theodor Horydczak – Nurturant Kitchen, Robin Weltsch, 1972
– Cobrafestival. Cobra II. How To Live Together, UoN Project Archive / Katrin Borchers, Tina Steiger, Julia Lerch Zajączkowska, 2013
– Construction trailer on the UoN property, UoN Project Archive / Felix Anselm, 2011
– Historical photograph of the Ledigenheim, personal items on a shelf above the bed, 1950s.
– Made in … Local practices of urban production, Workshop, UoN Project Archive, 2011

p. 280
– The Private Chef of Pope Pius V (large kitchen), Bartolomeo Scappi, 1570
– Student life and work at the UoN, UoN Project Archive, 2013

– Culture Kitchen / Workshop Ton Matton, UoN Project Archive, 2009

p. 313
– Hotel?Wilhelmsburg International Building Workshop, UoN Project Archive / Ben Pohl, 2013
– Hotel?Wilhelmsburg International Building Workshop, UoN Project Archive / Vedran Skansi, 2013
– View of Patio and Pavilion by Nigel Henderson, Eduardo Paolozzi and Alison and Peter Smithson, 1956

p. 314
– First transformation phase, Construction site internship, UoN Project Archive / Ben Becker, 2010
– First transformation phase, Construction site internship, UoN Project Archive / Ben Becker, 2010
– Splitting, Gordon Matta-Clark, Electronic Arts Intermix, New York, 1974
– First transformation phase, UoN builder's hut, Construction site internship, UoN Project Archive / Ben Becker, 2010
– Hotel?Wilhelmsburg International Building Workshop, UoN Project Archive, 2012
– Gramsci Bar at the art pavillon "Gramsci Monument" Dia Art Foundation, Thomas Hirschhorn, 2013

p. 316
– Neighborhood Workshops – Learning from each other in Hamburg and Cairo, HafenCity Universität Hamburg: Teaching and Research Program Urban Design; Cairo University: Center for

civilization studies and dialogue of cultures, UoN Project Archive / Mathias Schnell, 2012
– Neighborhood Workshops – Learning from each other in Hamburg and Cairo, HafenCity Universität Hamburg: Teaching and Research Program Urban Design; Cairo University: Center for civilization studies and dialogue of cultures, UoN Project Archive, 2012
– UoN at Westwerk Gallery, UoN Project Archive / Ben Becker, 2013
– Lecture Christopher Dell, UoN Project Archive, – Hanna Noller, 2011
– Neighborhood Workshops – Learning from each other in Hamburg and Cairo, HafenCity Universität Hamburg: Teaching and Research Program Urban Design; Cairo University: Center for civilization studies and dialogue of cultures, UoN Project Archive / Mathias Schnell, 2012
– Spring Fest, UoN Project Archive / Ben Pohl, 2011

p. 318
– Liquid sealing, Construction site internship, UoN Project Archive / Ben Becker, 2013
– First summer school, UoN Project Archive, 2010
– Hang on! Tree houses, UoN Project Archive / Ben Becker, 2013
– Ten hours of UoN Neighbourhood Festival, Experts of everyday life and God's Entertainment, UoN Project Archive, 2009
– Ten hours of UoN Neighbourhood Festival, Experts

of everyday life and God's Entertainment, UoN Project Archive, 2009
– Neighborhood Workshops
– Learning from each other in Hamburg and Cairo, HafenCity Universität Hamburg: Teaching and Research Program Urban Design; Cairo University: Center for civilization studies and dialogue of cultures, UoN Project Archive / Mathias Schnell, 2012

p. 320
– Ten hours of UoN Neighbourhood Festival, Experts of everyday life and God's Entertainment, UoN Project Archive, 2009
– UoN at Westwerk Gallery, UoN Project Archive / Ben Becker, 2014
– Couvent Sainte-Marie-de-la-Tourette, Le Corbusier, 1953
– Lecture Alexander Römer
– EXYZT, Hotel?Wilhelmsburg International Building Workshop, UoN Project Archive, Martin Rieger, 2013
– Site visit, Construction site internship, UoN Project Archive, June 2009
– Hotel?Wilhelmsburg International Building Workshop, UoN Project Archive / Martin Kess, 2013

p. 322
– First transformation phase, UoN builder's hut, Construction site internship, UoN Project Archive / Ben Becker, 2009
– First transformation phase, UoN builder's hut, Construction site internship, UoN Project Archive / Ben Becker, 2009

– Hotel?Wilhelmsburg International Building Workshop, UoN Project Archive / Vedran Skansi, 2013
– Crate Chair, Building Workshop, UoN Project Archive / Imanuel Mihm, 2012
– Crate Chair, Building Workshop, UoN Project Archive / Imanuel Mihm, 2012
– Crate-Chair, Gerrit Rietveld, 1934, 2012

p. 324
– First summer school, UoN Project Archive, 2010
– Mémoires, Guy Debord & Asger Jorn, 1958
– Tree houses, summer camp, UoN Project Archive / Ben Becker, 2011
– Wall scribbling, UoN Project Archive
– Reader: Urban Territories 2 summer term 2011. Dipl. Ing. Katja Heinecke / Katrin Klitzke, M.A. / Prof Bernd Kniess (Hrsg.). Master program Urban Design / HafenCity Universität Hamburg.
– Award Ceremony for Outstanding Places in the Land of Ideas, Michael Koch, UoN Project Archive, 2014

p. 326
– Franz Erhard Walther "1. Werksatz," Timm Rautert, 1970
– Intercultural practice, summer camp, tree houses, UoN Project Archive / Ben Becker, 2012
– Hang on! Tree houses, UoN Project Archive / Ben Becker, 2013
– Experiments in Environment, Group games for exploring the human-environment relationships, James Burns, 1971

– Summer camp, tree houses, UoN Project Archive / Ben Becker, 2011
– Provisional Studies: Workshop #7 How to Live Together and Sharing the Unknown, Koki Tanaka, 2017

p. 328
– Intercultural Soccer Tournament, Wilhelmsburg Art and Sports Club, 48h Wilhelmsburg, UoN Project Archive, 2010
– Theaster Gates, 12 Ballads for Huguenot House, 2012. Deconstructed timbers and other construction materials from 6901 South Dorchester, Chicago. Commissioned by dOCUMENTA (13) in collaboration with the Museum of Contemporary Art, Chicago with support from Phillip Keir and Sarah Benjamin, London; Kavi Gupta, Chicago. – Bernd Kniess, 2012.
– Actors, formats, agreements, activities in the superposition, UoN Project Archive, 2010
– Georgii Krutikov's Flying City (1928) tableaus, Anna Bokov, 2020
– untitled event, John Cage, 1952
– Space matrices, UoN Project Archive / Christopher Dell, 2009

p. 330
– Marquise de Rambouillet's Chambre Bleue, Abraham Bosse, 17th century (?)
– Housing misery in Germany around 1919. 11 people lived in this flat, which consisted of a parlour and kitchen. Federal Archive, Image 183-1983-0225-309

– Second Skin, Hotel?Wilhelmsburg, UoN Project Archive / Dominique Peck, 2013
– Inner Rise, Ghetto Academy – In my Room, UoN Project Archive / Alexandra Heneka, 2010
– Hotel Hamburg, UoN Project Archive, 2012
– Hotel?Wilhelmsburg, Building and inhabiting a common low-budget luxury shelter International Building Workshops, UoN Project Archive / Ben Becker, 2013

p. 332
– A Private Residence, Milan Triennale: "The Greater Number," Archigram, 1967
– Yellow Heart (Gelbes Herz), Vienna, Haus-Rucker-Co, 1968
– Cobrafestival. Cobra II. How To Live Together, UoN Project Archive / Katrin Borchers, Tina Steiger, Julia Lerch Zajączkowska, 2013
– Haus Rucker
– Cobrafestival. Cobra II. How To Live Together, UoN Project Archive / Katrin Borchers, Tina Steiger, Julia Lerch Zajączkowska, 2013
– Phalanstère, Charles Fourier, 1832

p. 334
– Hotel?Wilhelmsburg, Building and inhabiting a common low-budget luxury shelter International Building Workshops, UoN Project Archive, 2013
– Construction phase plan (Baustufenplan Wilhelmsburg), UoN Project Archive / District building office Harburg, 1955
– Made in … Local practices of urban production,

Workshop, UoN Project Archive / Ben Pohl, 2009
– UoN Project Archive, 2013
– Rotenhäuser nurseries – Garden laboratory, UoN Project Archive, 2011
– Hotel?Wilhelmsburg, Building and inhabiting a common low-budget luxury shelter International Building Workshops, UoN Project Archive / Katrin Borchers, 2013

p. 336
– Dismantling and removal of the gym floor of a nearby school, UoN Project Archive / Ben Becker, 2010
– Site visit, UoN Project Archive / Ben Becker, 2009
– Existing situation and current planning considerations, UoN Project Archive / Bezirksamt Hamburg Mitte, 2009
– Insurance policy, building fire insurance, UoN Project Archive / Hamburger Feuerkasse, 2009
– View of the Vienna General Hospital, Coloured engraving, 1784
– Elevation, Amendment to the building application: Student project of HCU Hamburg, University of the Neighbourhoods (UoN) Rothenhäuserdamm 30, UoN Project Archive / Architect: Prof. Bernd Kniess, 2010

p. 338
– (Part of) urban re-identification grid, Alison and Peter Smithson, 1953
– Urban Design Thesis Project, Final exam, UoN Project Archive, 2012
– Das Kapital Raum 1970-1977, Joseph Beuys,

Hamburger Bahnhof, 1980
– Contribution to the annual exhibition of HafenCity University Hamburg, UoN Project Archive / Ben Becker, 2009
– Mémoires, Guy Debord & Asger Jorn, 1958
– Hotel?Wilhelmsburg, International Building Workshop with Peter Fattinger, UoN Project Archive / UoN Architecture office, 2013

p. 340
– Elevation Villa Savoye a Poissy, Le susier and Pierre Jeanneret, 1929-31
– Section UoN Hotel?Wilhelmsburg extension, Student project of HCU Hamburg, University of the Neighbourhoods (UoN) Rothenhäuserdamm 30, UoN Project Archive / Architect: Prof. Bernd Kniess, 2013
– UoN Project Archive, 2009
– UoN Project Archive, 2011
– Transformation diagram, UoN Hotel?Wilhelmsburg extension, Student project of HCU Hamburg, University of the Neighbourhoods (UoN) Rothenhäuserdamm 30, UoN Project Archive / Architect: Prof. Bernd Kniess, 2013
– Summer School, UoN Project Archive, 2009

p. 342
– UoN – Enabling architecture for the learning city. Foyer – the germ cell of the UoN-transformation. Research and design project 2008/09, UoN Project Archive.
– Elevation, UoN

Hotel?Wilhelmsburg exten-
sion, Student project of HCU
Hamburg, University of the
Neighbourhoods (UoN)
Rothenhäuserdamm 30,
UoN Project Archive / Archi-
tect: Prof. Bernd Kniess,
2013
– Floor plan (extract): New,
Demolition, Existing, Stu-
dent project of HCU Ham-
burg, University of the
Neighbourhoods (UoN)
Rothenhäuserdamm 30,
UoN Project Archive / Archi-
tect: Prof. Bernd Kniess,
2010
– Demolition permit plan,
UoN Rothenhäuserdamm
30, UoN Project Archive /
Architect: Prof. Bernd
Kniess, 2014
– Hotel?Wilhelmsburg,
International Building Work-
shop with Benjamin Förster-
Baldenius, UoN Project
Archive / UoN Architecture
office, 2013
– The Imaginary Museum,
André Malraux, Maurice
Jarnoux / Paris Match via
Getty Images, 1954

p. 344
– Simplified isometry, UoN
Hotel?Wilhelmsburg exten-
sion, Student project of HCU
Hamburg, University of the
Neighbourhoods (UoN)
Rothenhäuserdamm 30,
UoN Project Archive / Archi-
tect: Prof. Bernd Kniess,
2013
– Retrospective, Wajiro Kon,
Seigensha Art Publishing
2011
– First transformation phase,
construction site internship,
UoN Project Archive / Ben
Becker, 2010

BERND KNIESS is an architect and urban planner. In 2008, when he was appointed to the professorship of Urban Design at the HafenCity University Hamburg, he founded the M.Sc. program of the same name. Shortly after, together with a team of colleagues, he began to take on the project University of Neighborhoods.

He is interested in understanding the contemporary city as a produced assemblage, its agencies in different modes of having become-ness and becoming, its translation into forms of diagrammatic representation and its transfer into procedures of relational practice. A particular focus of Bernd Kniess is the conception, design and realization of Living Lab projects such as the University of Neighborhoods (2008–14), Building a Proposition for Future Activities (2015–18) and *Zukunftsstadt Friedrichstadt* (2016–22). Bernd Kniess teaches in the formats Urban Design Project: Research and Design, Theoretical-Conceptual Foundations, Methodology, Intercultural Practice, Diagrammatics and the Hamburg Open Online University teaching and learning platforms Translating Dwelling Knowledge (*WohnWissen Übersetzen*) and Urban Types – of Houses and People (*Von Häusern und Menschen*).

As a member of the research initiative Low Budget Urbanity, he initiated the project Building Supply Store 2.0 – Practices and Materialities of Urban Self Building and Frugality.

In 2019–20 he held the Graham Willis Professorship at Sheffield School of Architecture. He has been a member of the North Rhine-Westphalian Academy of Sciences, Humanities and the Arts since 2009.

CHRISTOPHER DELL works as a theoretician in urban design and architecture, as a musician, composer, and as an artist. He is the head of ifit, Institute for Improvisation Technology, Berlin. In 2008 he was asked by Bernd Kniess to join the team at the HafenCity University Hamburg as a professor for Urban Design Theory to contribute to the establishment of the newly founded M.Sc. program Urban Design. Shortly thereafter, he was involved in the team that conceptualized and launched the University of Neighborhoods. Christopher Dell also held a professorship for Urban Design Theory at the Technical University Munich and at the University of Fine Arts, Berlin.

Holding a PhD in Organization Psychology and a habilitation in Cultural Science, Christopher Dell has published numerous books and articles, mainly on the subject of urban studies. In 2017 Dell has been appointed as a Member of the North Rhine-Westphalian Academy of Sciences, Humanities and the Arts. Since 2021 he is an associated member of integral designers, Paris. In 2021 he collaborated with Christophe Hutin Architectes at the French Pavilion at the Architecture Biennale Venice. In 2022 he will be a fellow for architecture and urban design at the Cité Internationale des Paris. His monographies include a.o.: The Commodity of Living (*Ware: Wohnen!*), Berlin 2013 and The Urban (*Das Urbane*), Berlin 2014, Epistemology of the City (*Epistemologie der Stadt*) Bielefeld 2016, The City as an Open Score (*Stadt als offene Partitur*), Zürich 2016, The Improvisation of Space Berlin 2019, *The Working Concert*, Leipzig 2020.

DOMINIQUE PECK is an academic assistant at the Urban Design teaching
and research program at the Hafen-
City University Hamburg. He participated as a student in teaching formats
around the Hotel?Wilhelmsburg project
and supported the University of Neighborhoods' staff, first and foremost
Stefanie Gernert and Ben Becker, as a
student assistant in the last months of
the project. After some gigs in urban
and transport planning offices, he
moved to HCU to coordinate the publication *Tom Paints the Fence*.
Together with UoN alumni Renée Tribble and Marieke Behne, Marius Töpfer
and Lisa Marie Zander, Dominique
Peck forms projektbüro – an urban design office in Hamburg whose working
methods bring into play UoN-tested
approaches such as the interweaving
of research, teaching and practice, the
perspective on agency and participation among children and young people
and the problematization of the urban
as open form.
Dominique Peck recently published in
collaboration with Anna Richter, Christopher Dell and Bernd Kniess on issues of organizing work in Living Lab
Projects. At the M.Sc. program Urban
Design, he supervised thesis projects
on the topic of cooperative housing,
infrastructure and life projects and is
co-responsible for the book series
Everyday Urban Design and the Urban
Design Reader platform. For the Hamburg Open Online University, he developed the teaching formats Project
Management in Urban Design and
The Knowledge of Design – The Design
of Knowledge (*Das Wissen der Gestaltung – Die Gestaltung des Wissens*)
together with Christopher Dell, Bernd
Kniess, Marko Mijatovic and other
contributors.

Tom Paints the Fence
Editors: Bernd Kniess, Christopher
Dell and Dominique Peck, Teaching
and Research Program Urban Design,
HafenCity University Hamburg

Editorial Coordination:
Dominique Peck, Robert Stürzl
Graphic Design: Helmut Völter
Translation: Sara Hoss
Text Editor: Mike Pilewski

Published by
Spector Books
Harkortstraße 10
04107 Leipzig
www.spectorbooks.com

Distribution
Germany, Austria: GVA, Gemeinsame
Verlagsauslieferung Göttingen
GmbH&Co. KG, www.gva-verlage.de
Switzerland: AVA Verlagsauslieferung
AG, www.ava.ch
France, Belgium: Interart Paris,
www.interart.fr
UK: Central Books Ltd.,
www.centralbooks.com

USA, Canada, Central and South
America, Africa: ARTBOOK/D. A. P.,
www.artbook.com
South Korea: The Book Society,
www.thebooksociety.org
Japan: twelvebooks,
www.twelve-books.com
Australia, New Zealand:
Perimeter Distribution,
www.perimeterdistribution.com

First Edition printed in Germany
ISBN 978–3–95905–061–6

© 2022 The editors, the contributors
and Spector Books, Leipzig

Urban Design

Made possible by
the Teaching and Research Program
Urban Design, HafenCity University
Hamburg,
www.ud.hcu-hamburg.de
www.udn.hcu-hamburg.de
www.urban-design-reader.de

[Q] Studies
www.hcu-hamburg.de/en/bachelor/fa-
chuebergreifende-studienangebote/
study-programme/

HafenCity University Hamburg,
Henning-Voscherau-Platz 1, 20457
Hamburg
www.hcu-hamburg.de

International Building Exhibition
IBA Hamburg 2006–2013
www.internationale-bauausstellung-
hamburg.de/en/story/iba-hamburg.
html

Kampnagel
www.kampnagel.de

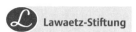

Max Hoffmann
www.max-hoffmann.de

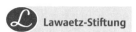

Johann Daniel Lawaetz-Foundation
www.lawaetz.de

The Interreg IVB North Sea Region
Programme
www.northsearegion.eu

SEEDS (Stimulating Enterprising
Environments for Development and
Sustainability)
www.ec.europa.eu/regional_policy/
en/projects/belgium/seeds-promotes-
temporary-use-and-reuse-of-
abandoned-buildings-and-spaces

Deutschland – Land of Ideas
www.land-der-ideen.de